As a Reincarnated ARISTOCRAT, I'll Use My Appraisal Skill to Rise in the World

[Story] Miraijin A
[Art] Natsumi Inoue
[Character Design] jimmy

CONTENTS

Chapter 27: A Warrior's Eyes

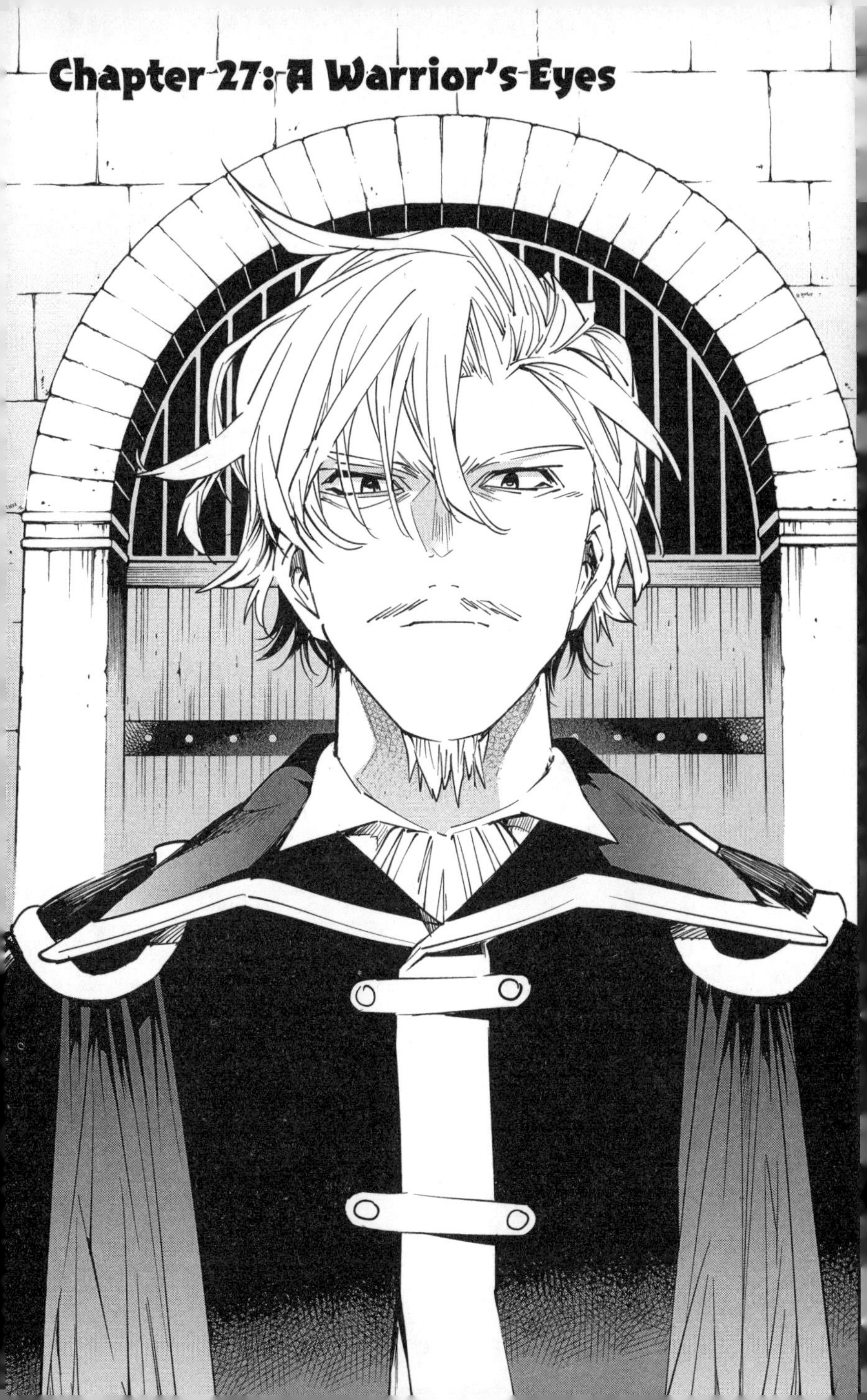

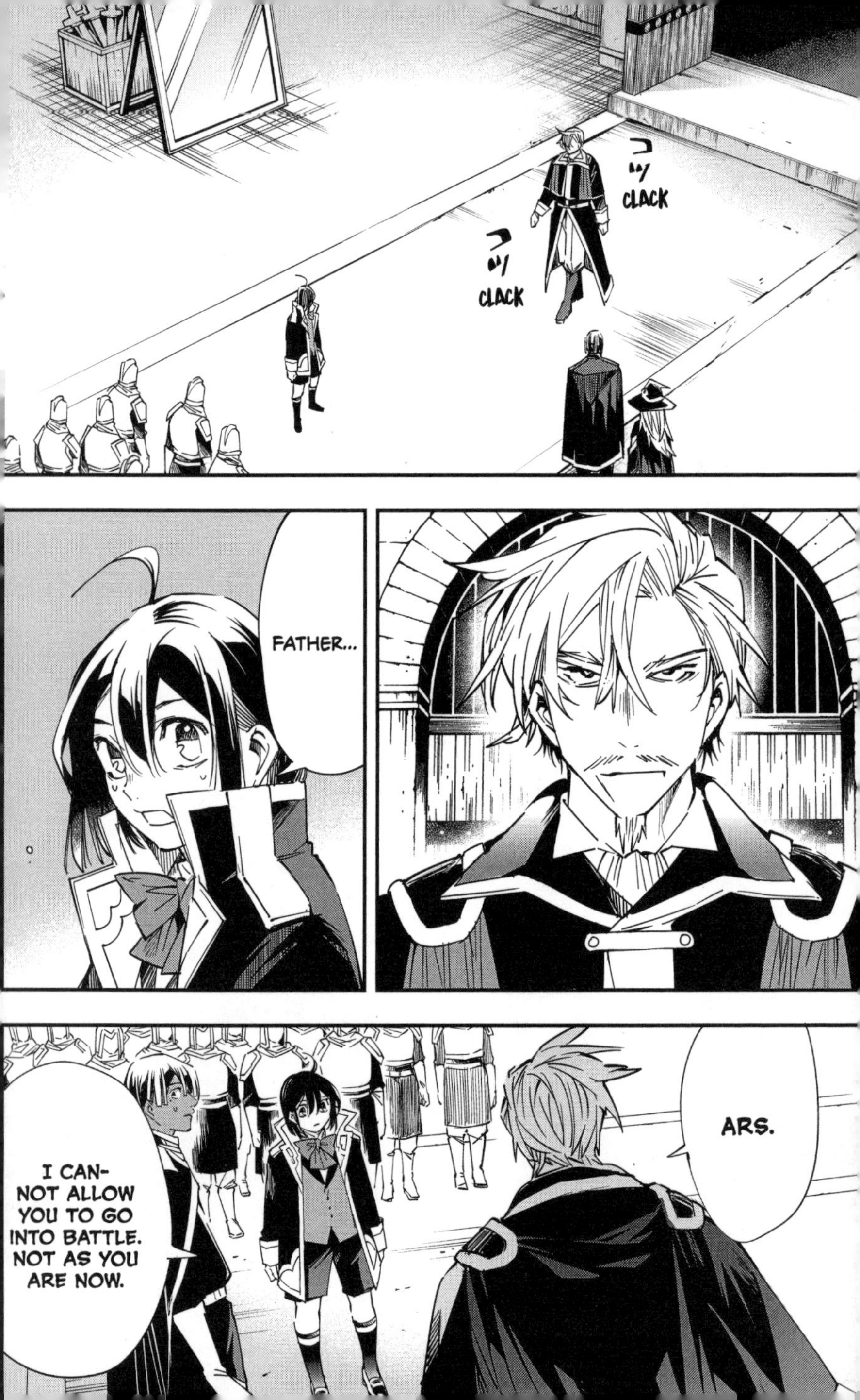
コッ
CLACK
コッ
CLACK
FATHER...
ARS.
I CAN-NOT ALLOW YOU TO GO INTO BATTLE. NOT AS YOU ARE NOW.

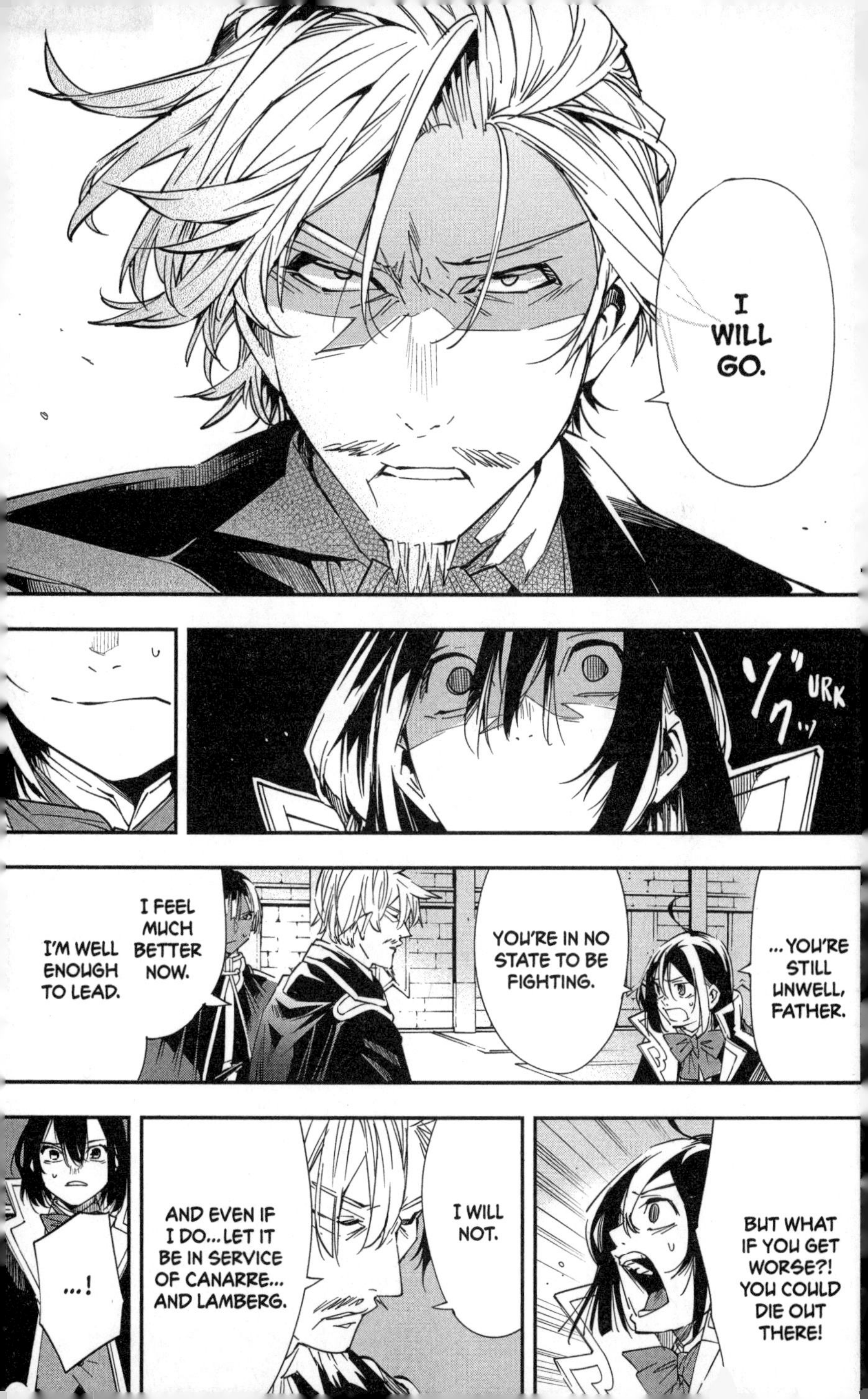
I WILL GO.
ゾクッ
URK
...YOU'RE STILL UNWELL, FATHER.
YOU'RE IN NO STATE TO BE FIGHTING.
I FEEL MUCH BETTER NOW.
I'M WELL ENOUGH TO LEAD.
BUT WHAT IF YOU GET WORSE?! YOU COULD DIE OUT THERE!
I WILL NOT.
AND EVEN IF I DO... LET IT BE IN SERVICE OF CANARRE... AND LAMBERG.
...!

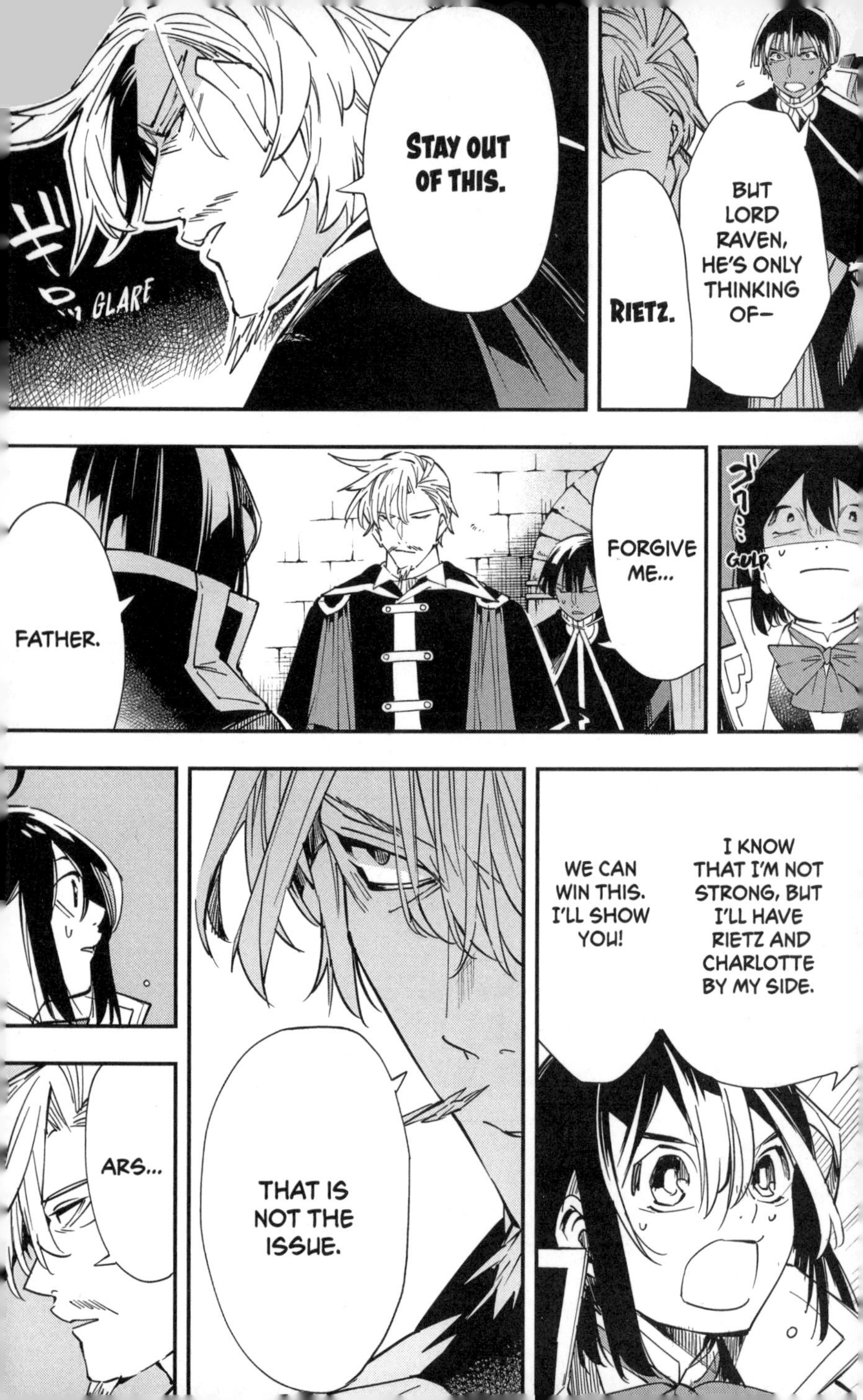
BUT LORD RAVEN, HE'S ONLY THINKING OF–
RIETZ.
STAY OUT OF THIS.
GLARE
GULP
FORGIVE ME...
FATHER.
I KNOW THAT I'M NOT STRONG, BUT I'LL HAVE RIETZ AND CHARLOTTE BY MY SIDE.
WE CAN WIN THIS. I'LL SHOW YOU!
THAT IS NOT THE ISSUE.
ARS...

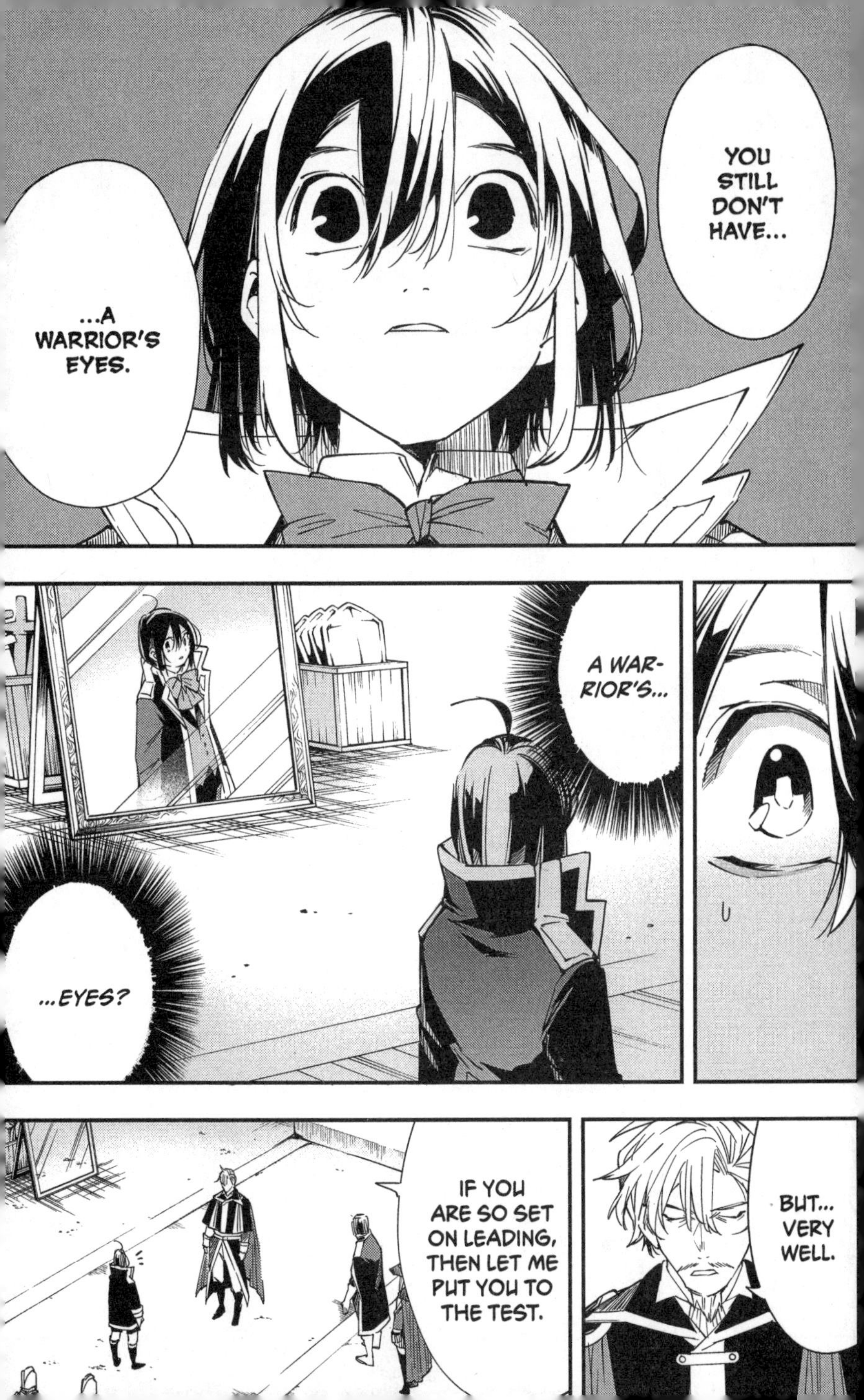
YOU STILL DON'T HAVE...
...A WARRIOR'S EYES.
A WAR-RIOR'S...
...EYES?
BUT... VERY WELL.
IF YOU ARE SO SET ON LEADING, THEN LET ME PUT YOU TO THE TEST.

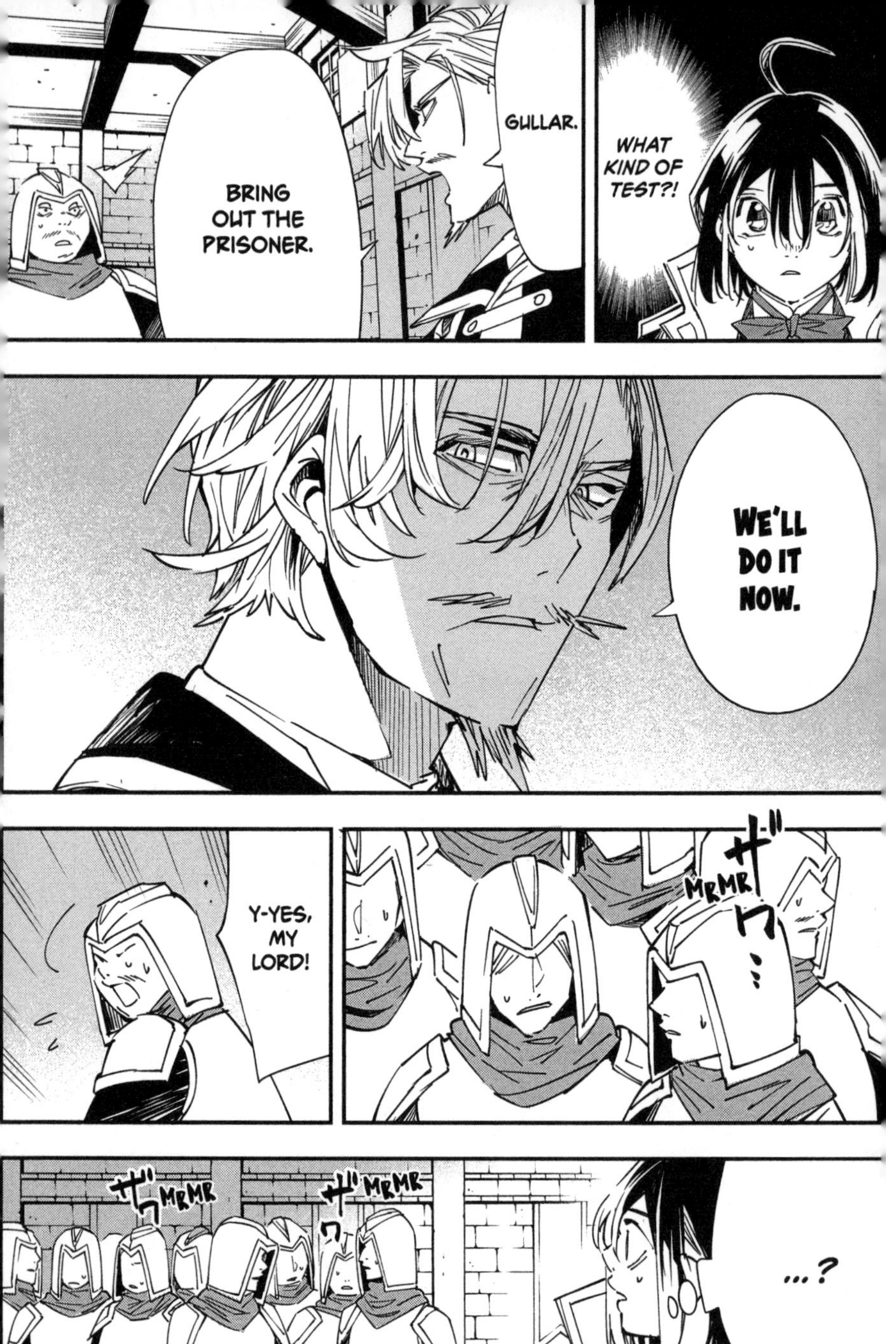
WHAT KIND OF TEST?!
GULLAR.
BRING OUT THE PRISONER.
WE'LL DO IT NOW.
ザワ…
MRMR
Y-YES, MY LORD!
…?
ザワ
MRMR
ザワ
MRMR

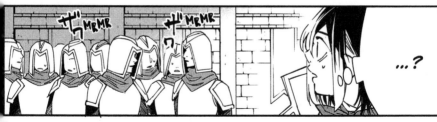

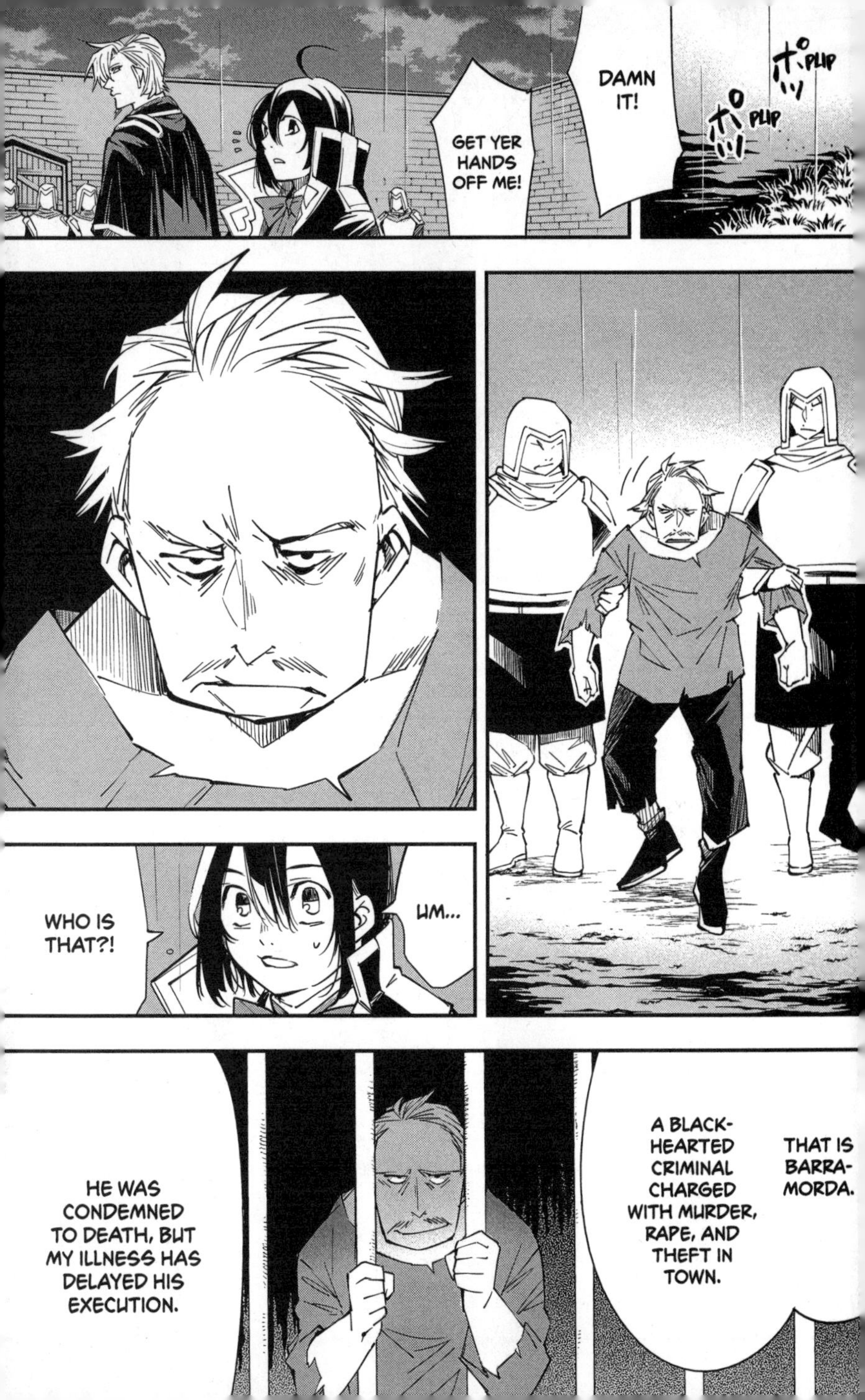
PLIP
PLIP
DAMN IT!
GET YER HANDS OFF ME!
UM...
WHO IS THAT?!
THAT IS BARRAMORDA.
A BLACK-HEARTED CRIMINAL CHARGED WITH MURDER, RAPE, AND THEFT IN TOWN.
HE WAS CONDEMNED TO DEATH, BUT MY ILLNESS HAS DELAYED HIS EXECUTION.

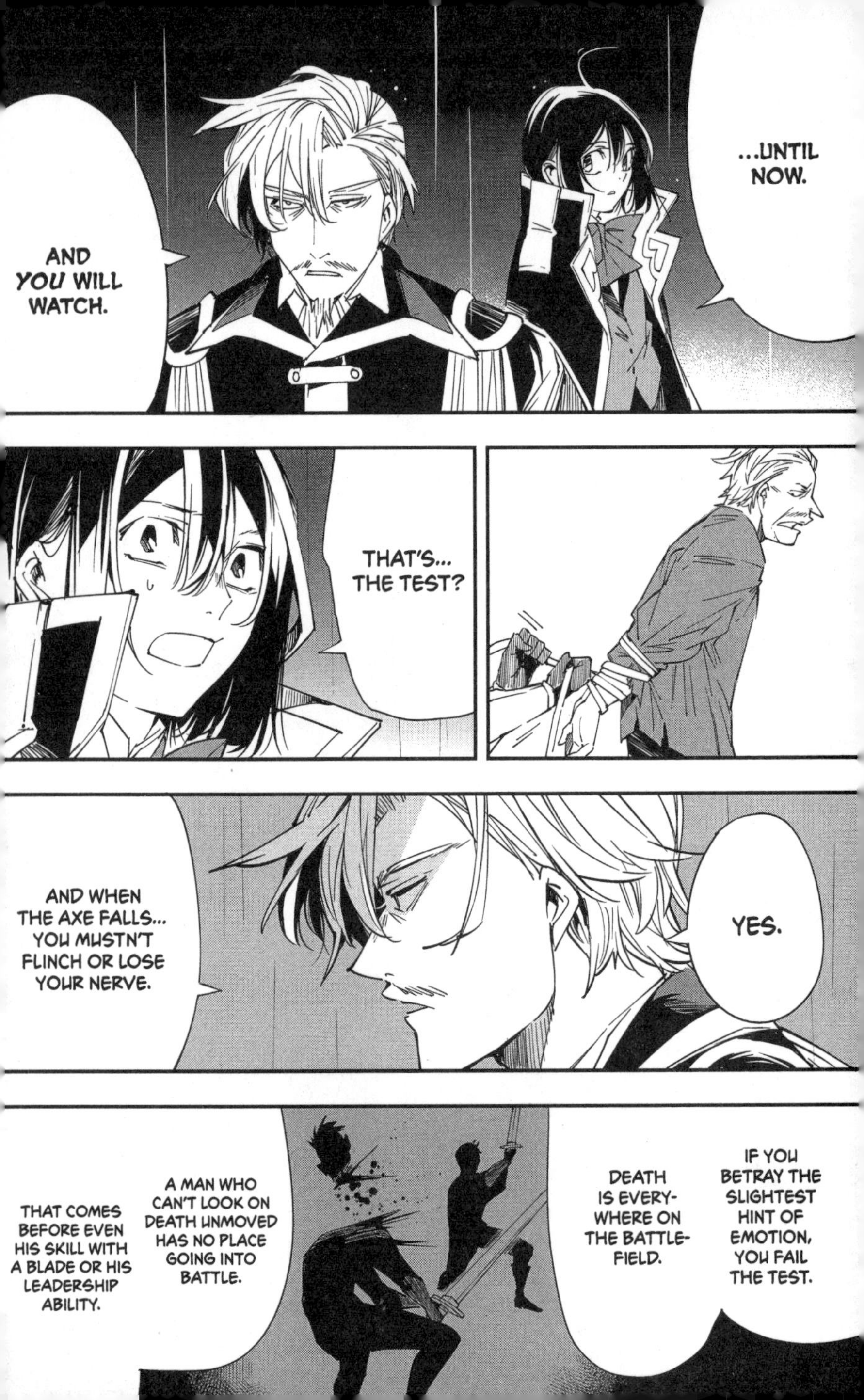
...UNTIL NOW.
AND *YOU* WILL WATCH.
THAT'S... THE TEST?
YES.
AND WHEN THE AXE FALLS... YOU MUSTN'T FLINCH OR LOSE YOUR NERVE.
IF YOU BETRAY THE SLIGHTEST HINT OF EMOTION, YOU FAIL THE TEST.
DEATH IS EVERY-WHERE ON THE BATTLE-FIELD.
A MAN WHO CAN'T LOOK ON DEATH UNMOVED HAS NO PLACE GOING INTO BATTLE.
THAT COMES BEFORE EVEN HIS SKILL WITH A BLADE OR HIS LEADERSHIP ABILITY.

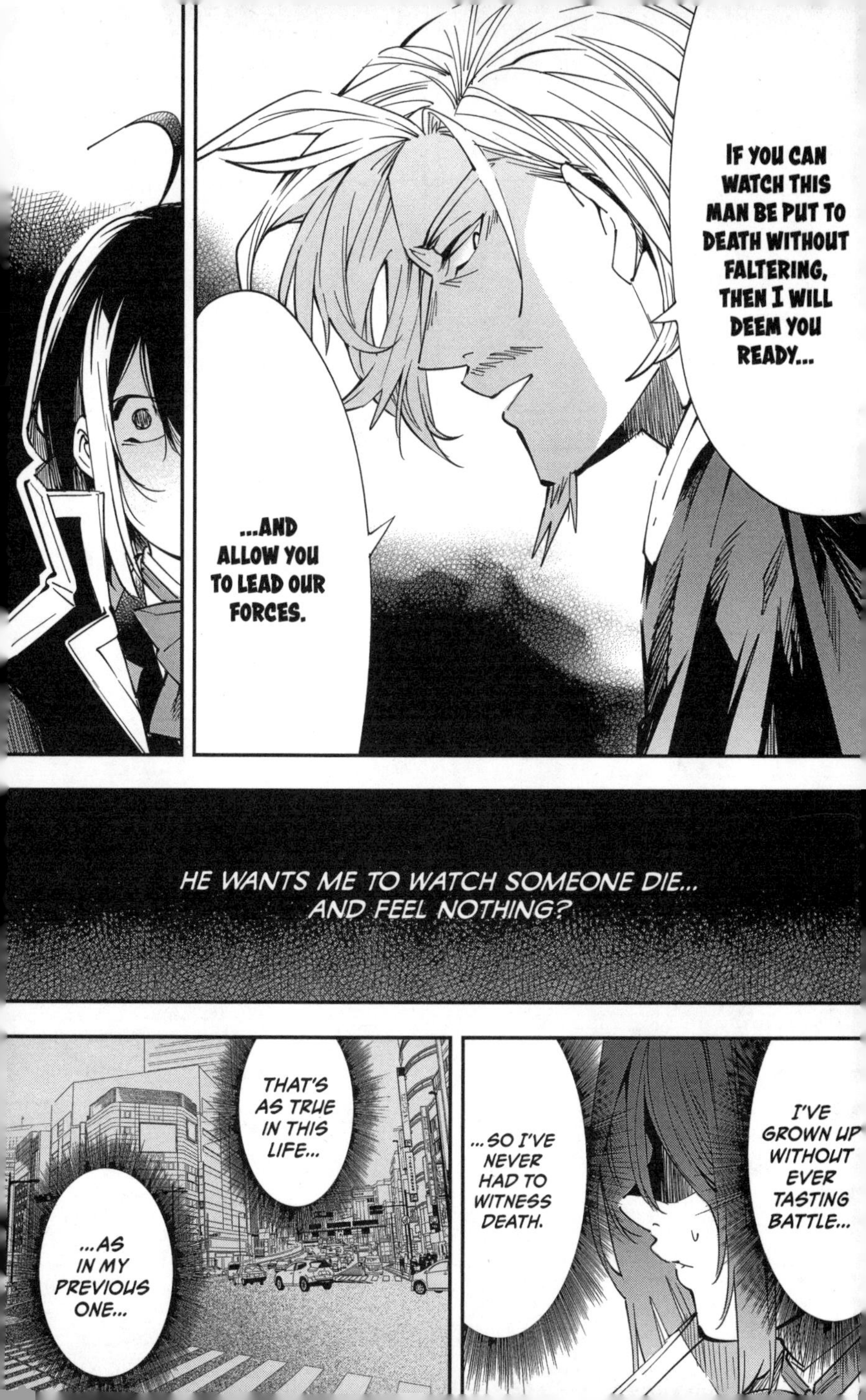
IF YOU CAN WATCH THIS MAN BE PUT TO DEATH WITHOUT FALTERING, THEN I WILL DEEM YOU READY...
...AND ALLOW YOU TO LEAD OUR FORCES.
HE WANTS ME TO WATCH SOMEONE DIE... AND FEEL NOTHING?
I'VE GROWN UP WITHOUT EVER TASTING BATTLE...
...SO I'VE NEVER HAD TO WITNESS DEATH.
THAT'S AS TRUE IN THIS LIFE...
...AS IN MY PREVIOUS ONE...

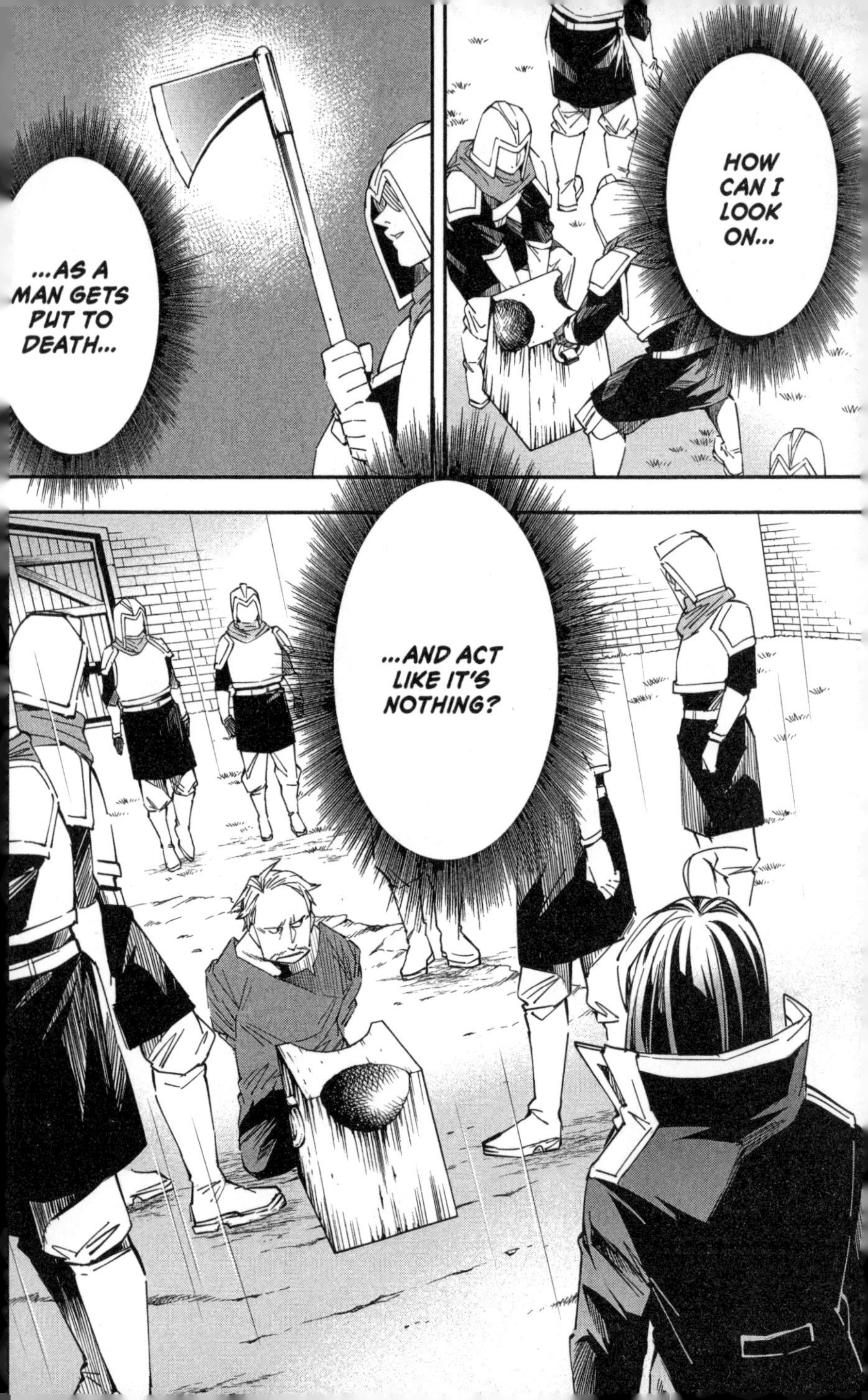
HOW CAN I LOOK ON...
...AS A MAN GETS PUT TO DEATH...
...AND ACT LIKE IT'S NOTHING?

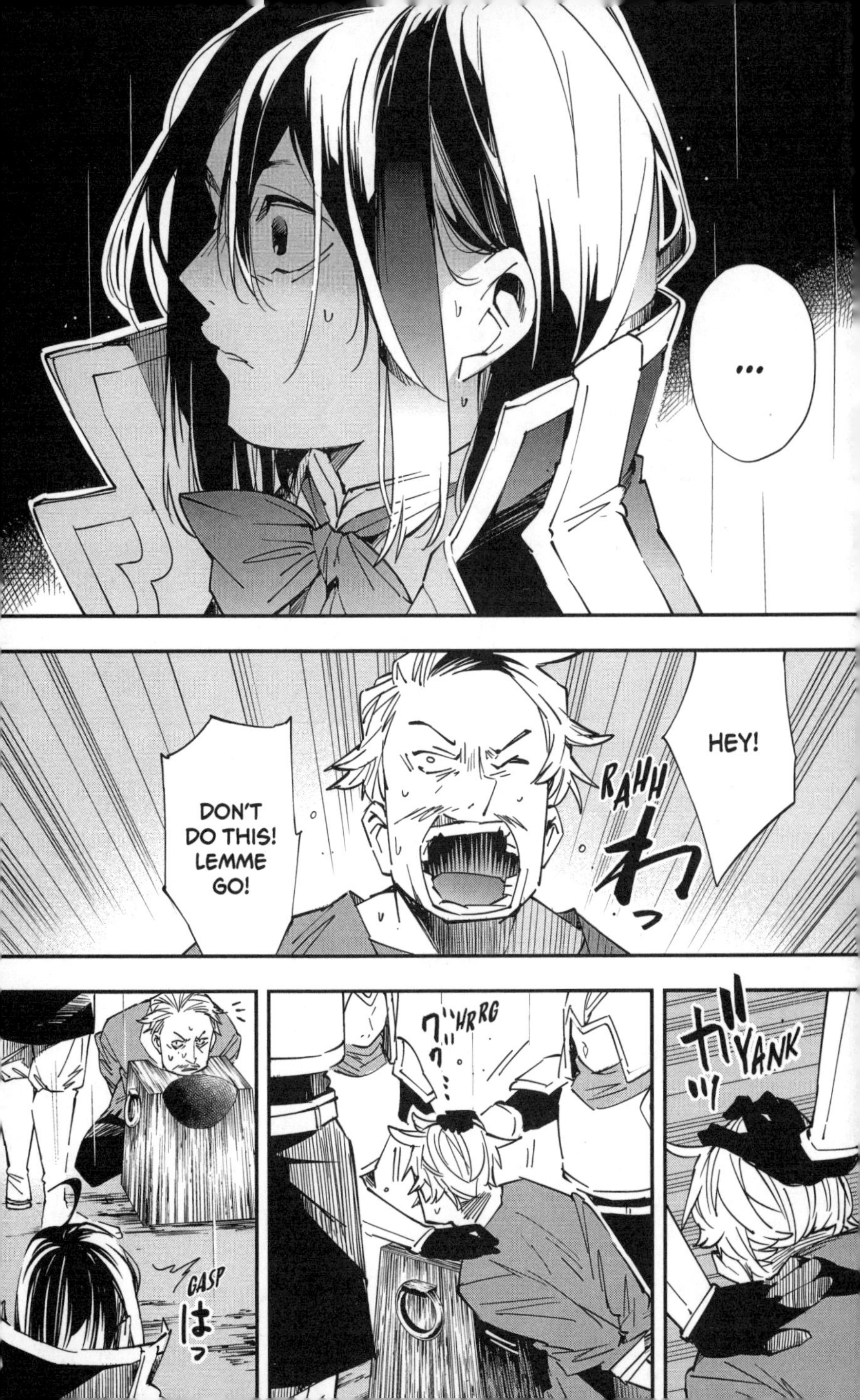
...
HEY!
RAHH
わっ
DON'T DO THIS! LEMME GO!
ガッ
YANK
HRRG
GASP
はっ

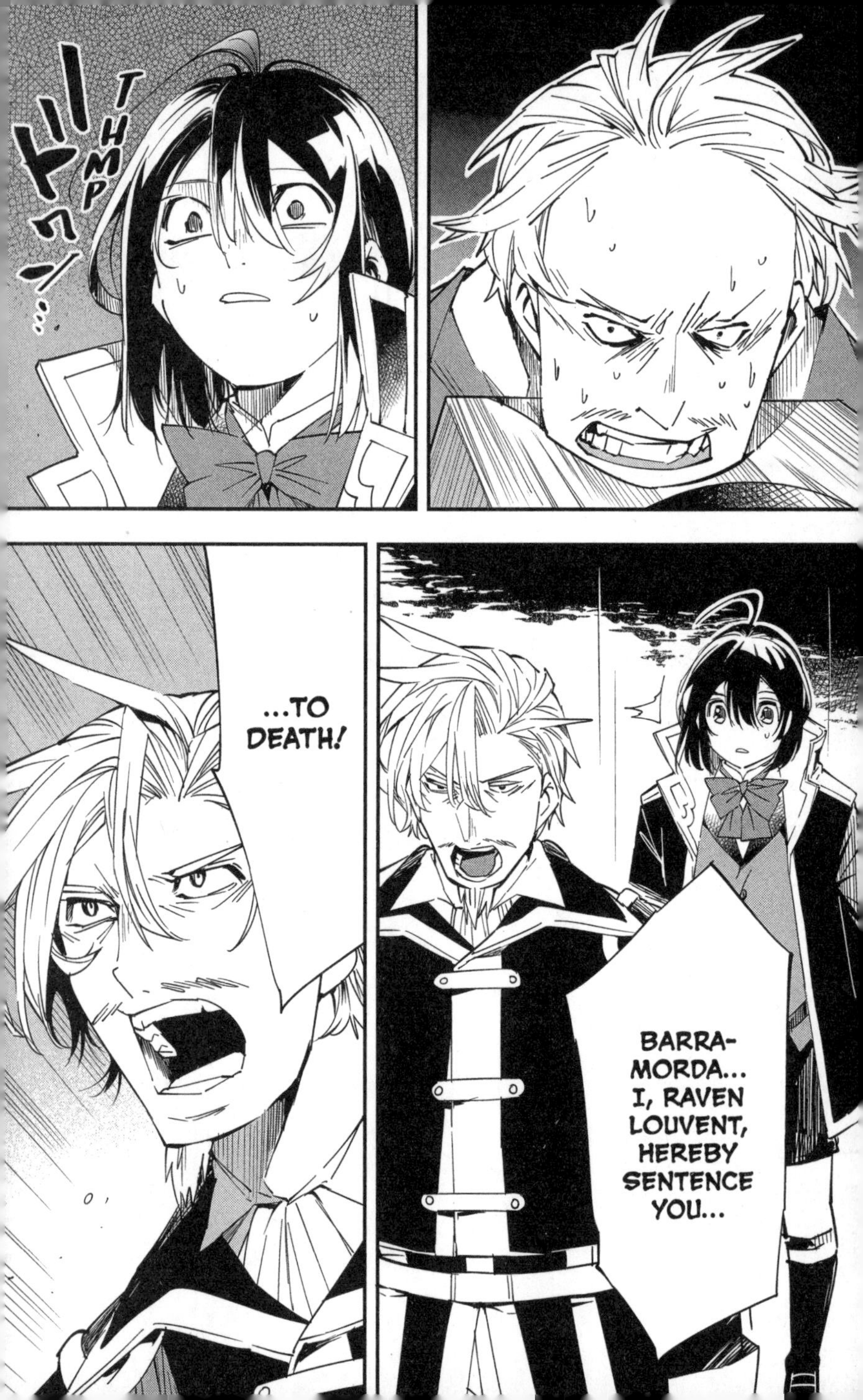
THUMP
BARRA-MORDA... I, RAVEN LOUVENT, HEREBY SENTENCE YOU...
...TO DEATH!

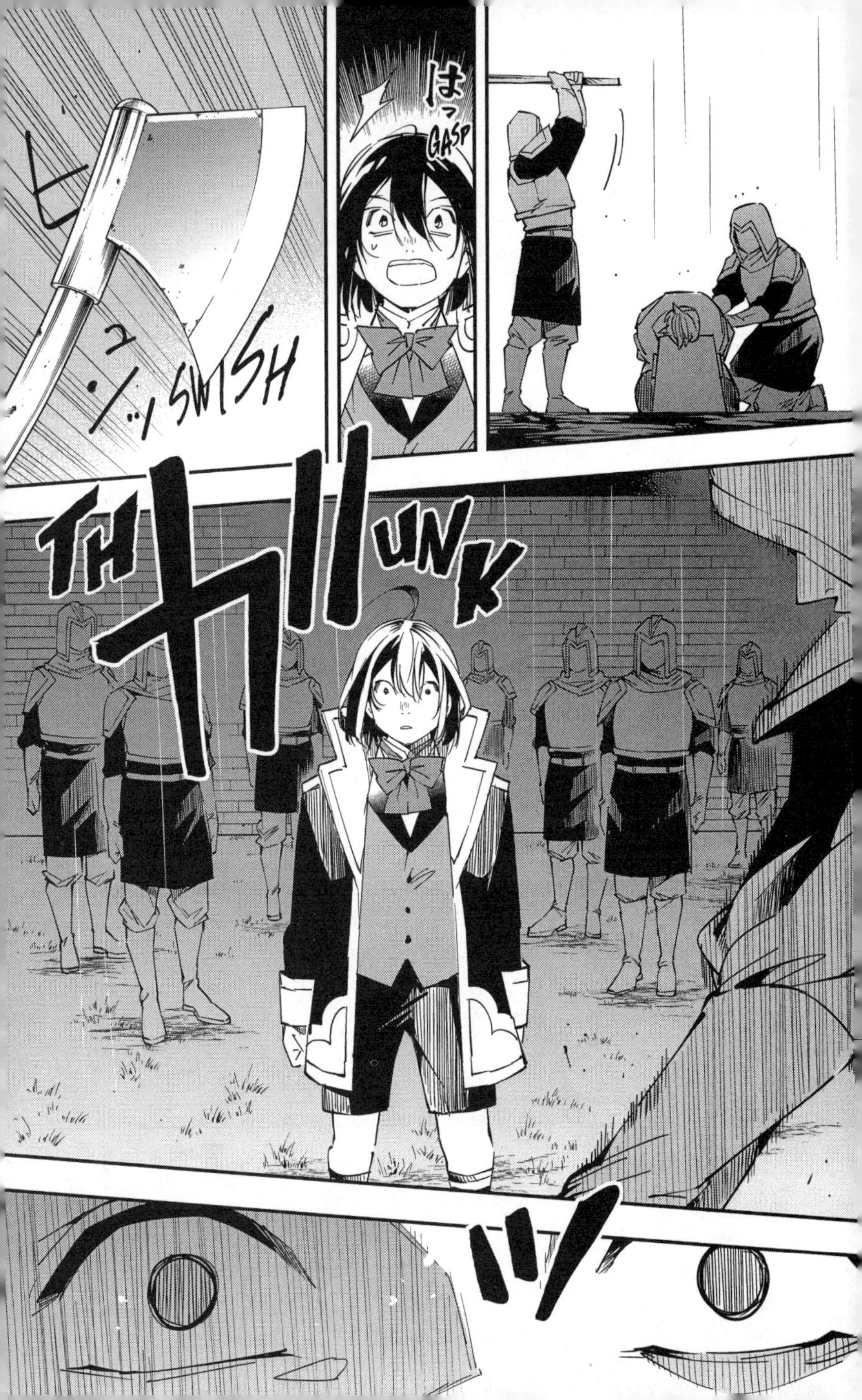
はっ
GASP
SWISH
THUNK

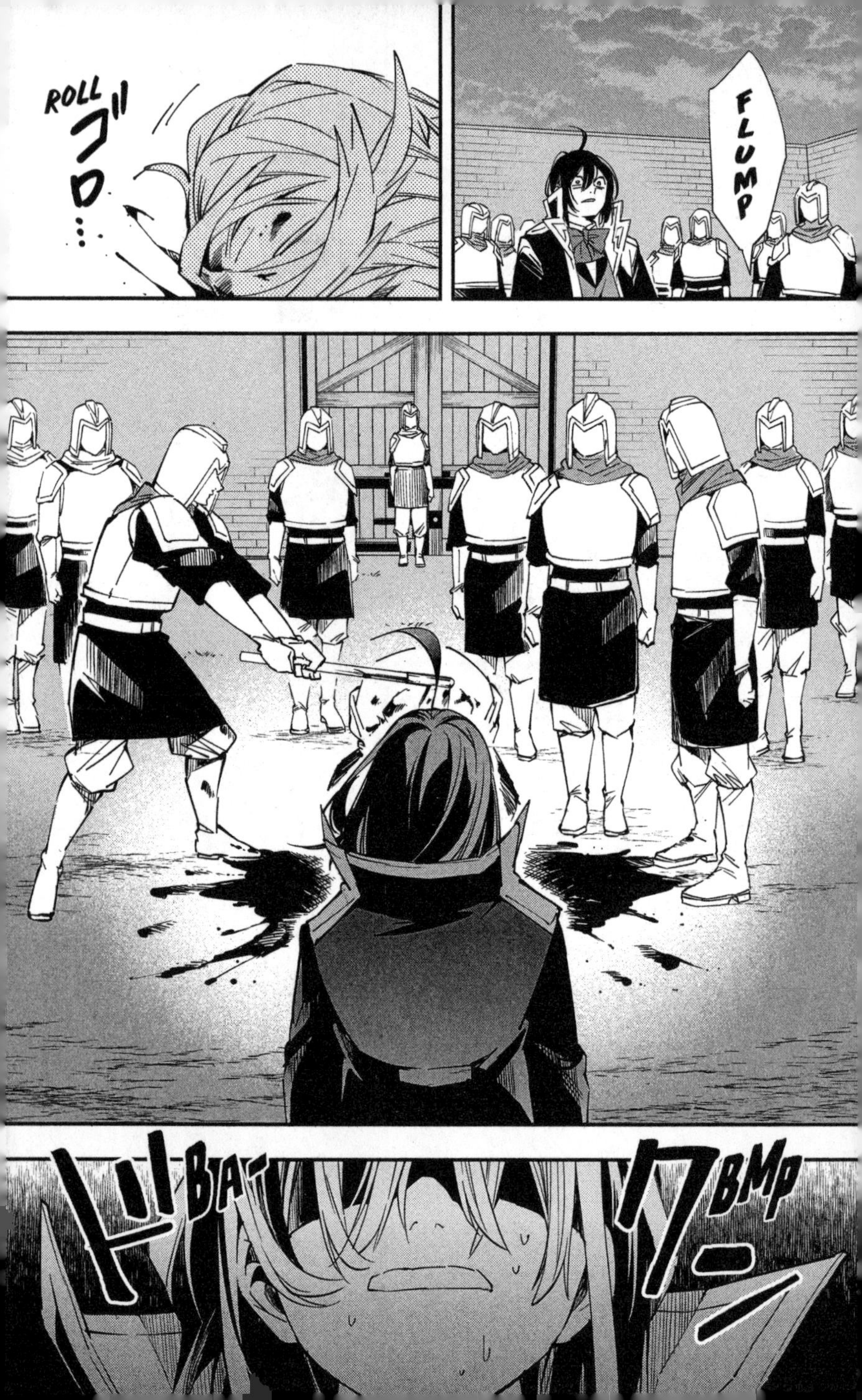
FLUMP
ROLL
ゴロ…
BMP
BAT

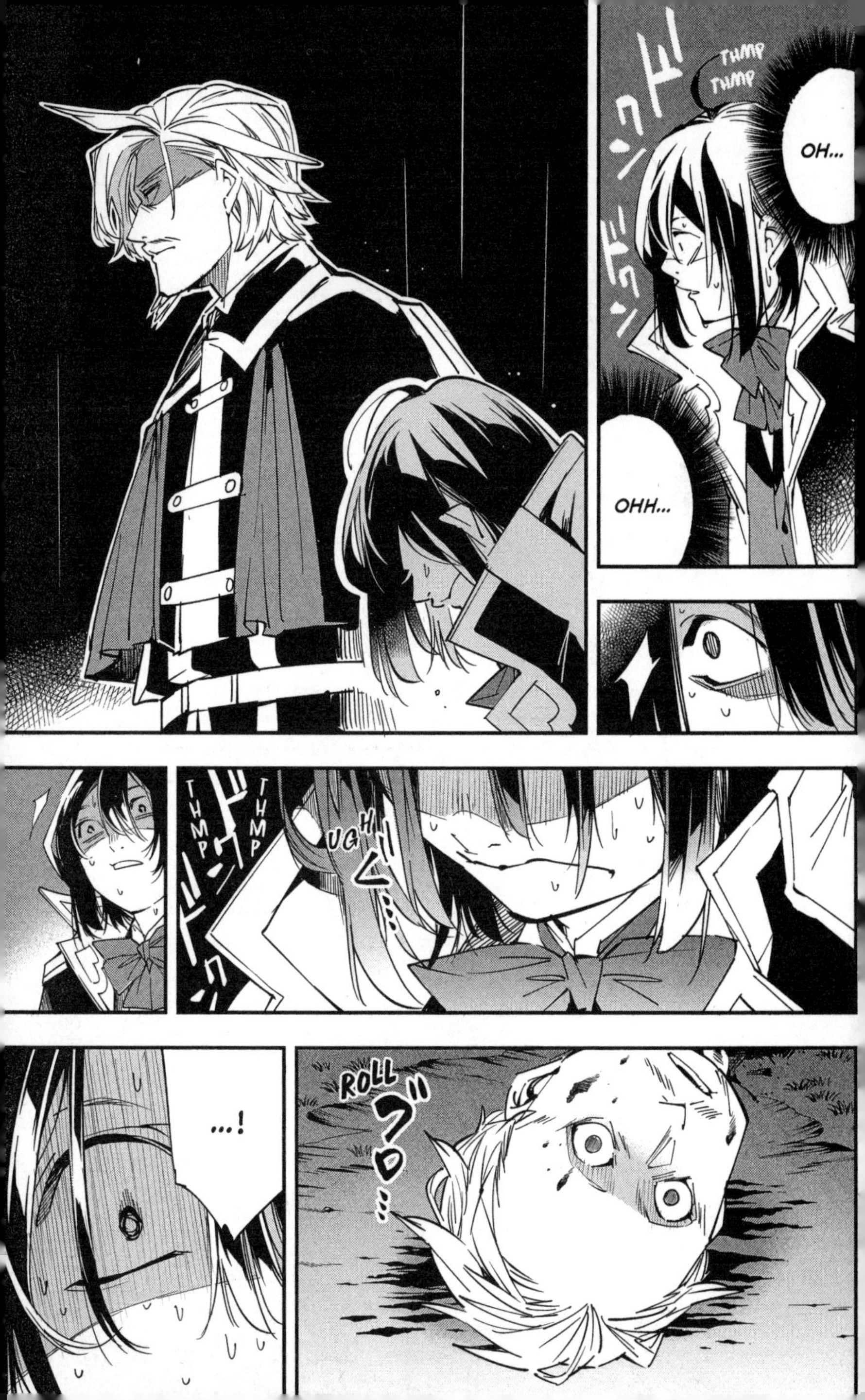
THMP THMP
OH...
OHH...
THMP THMP
UGH
...!
ROLL

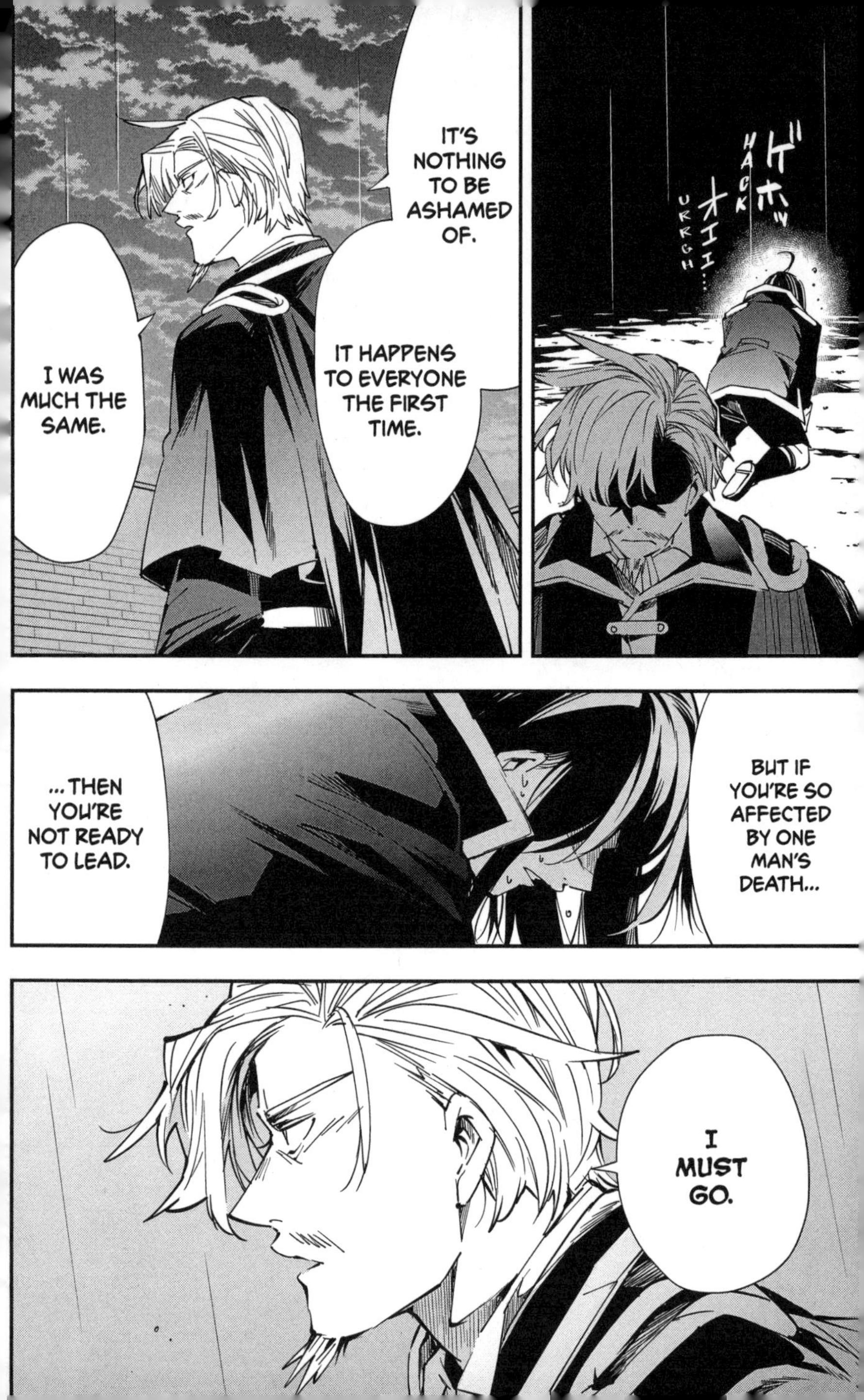
HACK
URRGH
IT'S NOTHING TO BE ASHAMED OF.
IT HAPPENS TO EVERYONE THE FIRST TIME.
I WAS MUCH THE SAME.
BUT IF YOU'RE SO AFFECTED BY ONE MAN'S DEATH...
...THEN YOU'RE NOT READY TO LEAD.
I MUST GO.

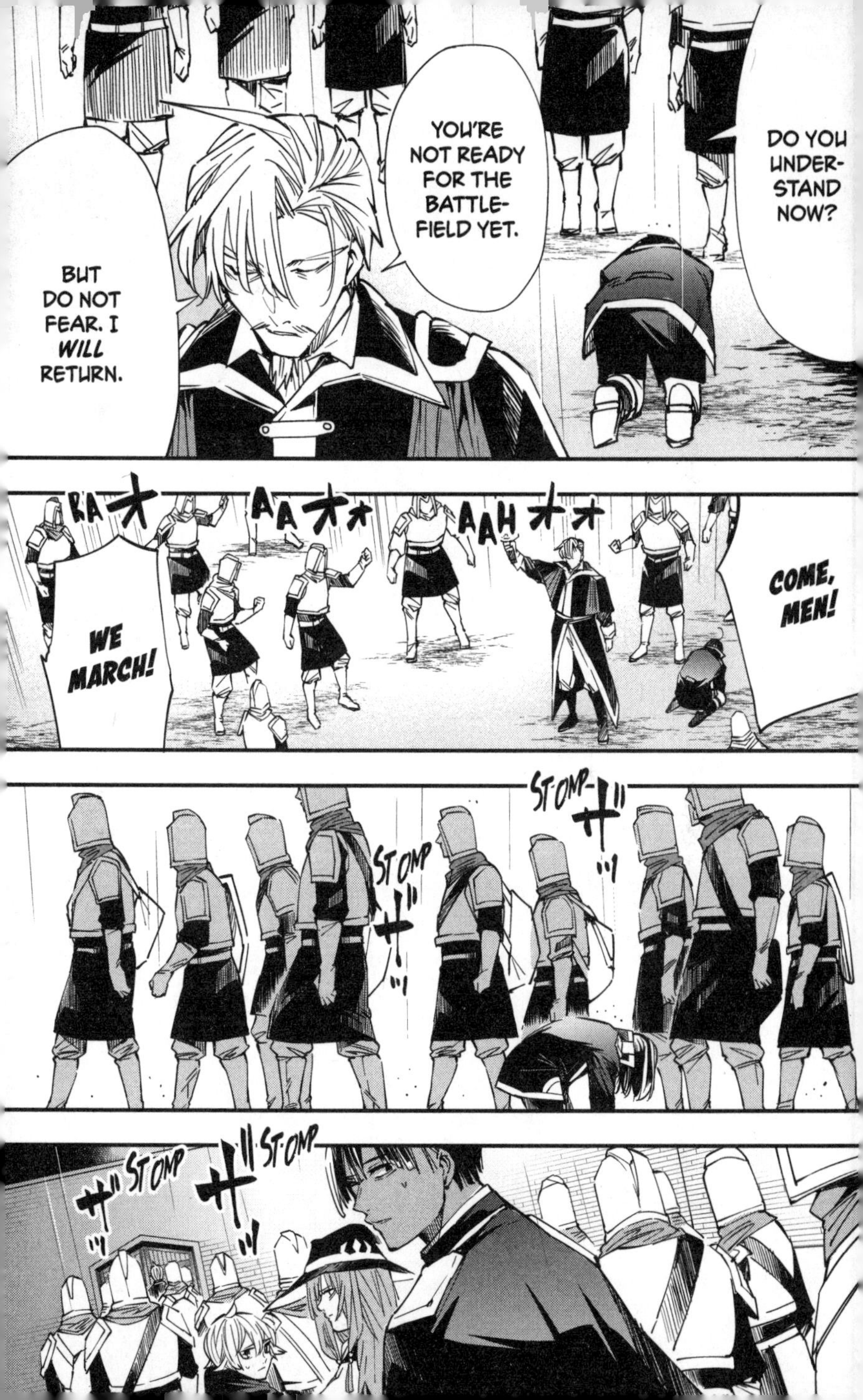
DO YOU UNDERSTAND NOW?
YOU'RE NOT READY FOR THE BATTLEFIELD YET.
BUT DO NOT FEAR. I *WILL* RETURN.
COME, MEN!
RA AA AAH
WE MARCH!
ST·OMP
STOMP
ST·OMP
STOMP

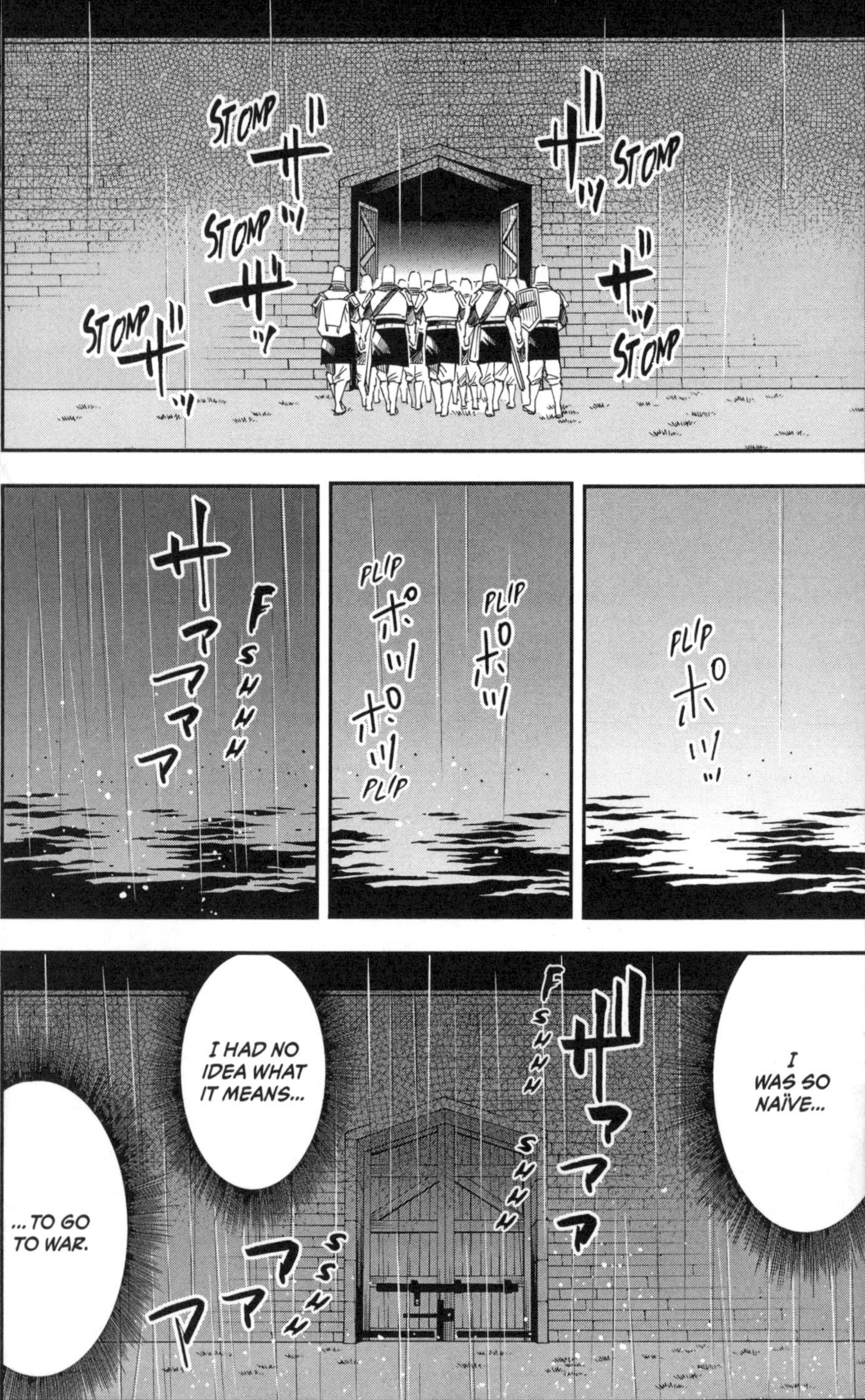
STOMP
STOMP
STOMP
STOMP
STOMP
PLIP
PLIP
PLIP
PLIP
FSHHH
I WAS SO NAÏVE...
I HAD NO IDEA WHAT IT MEANS...
...TO GO TO WAR.
FSHHH
SSHHH

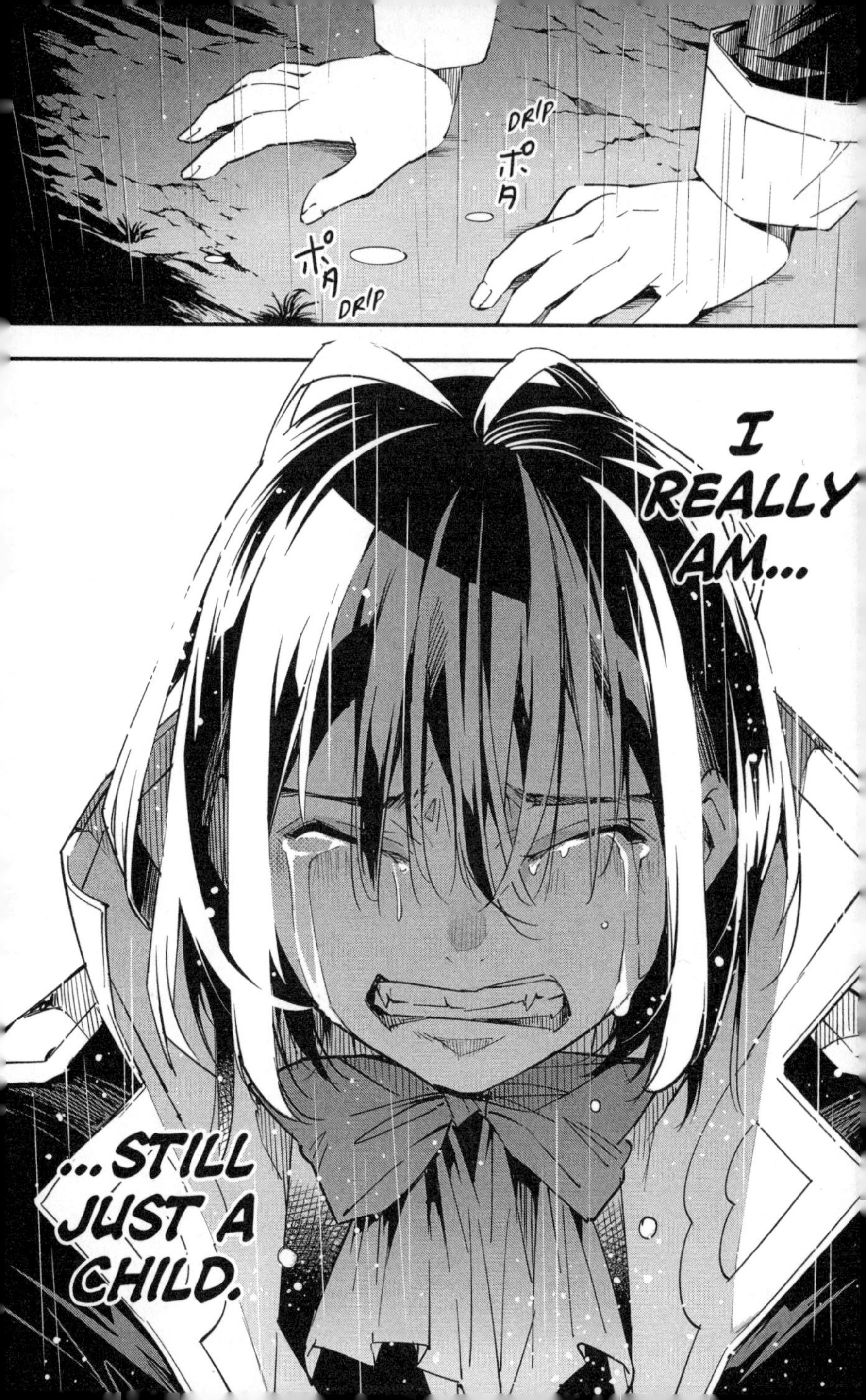
DRIP ポタ
ポタ DRIP
I REALLY AM...
...STILL JUST A CHILD.

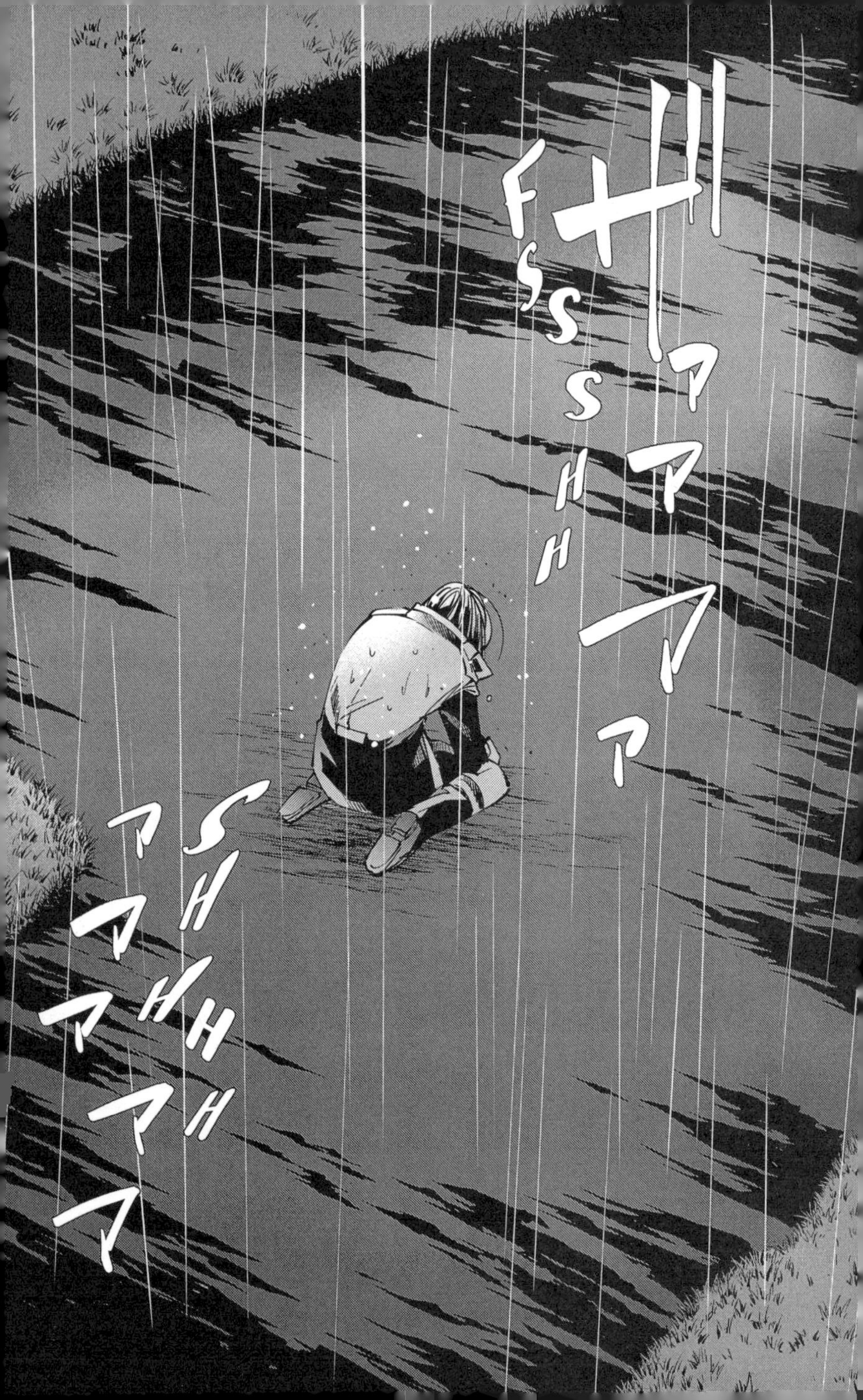
FSSSHHH
SHHHH

As a Reincarnated
ARISTOCRAT,
I'll Use My Appraisal Skill to
Rise in the World

As a Reincarnated
ARISTOCRAT,
I'll Use My Appraisal Skill to
Rise in the World

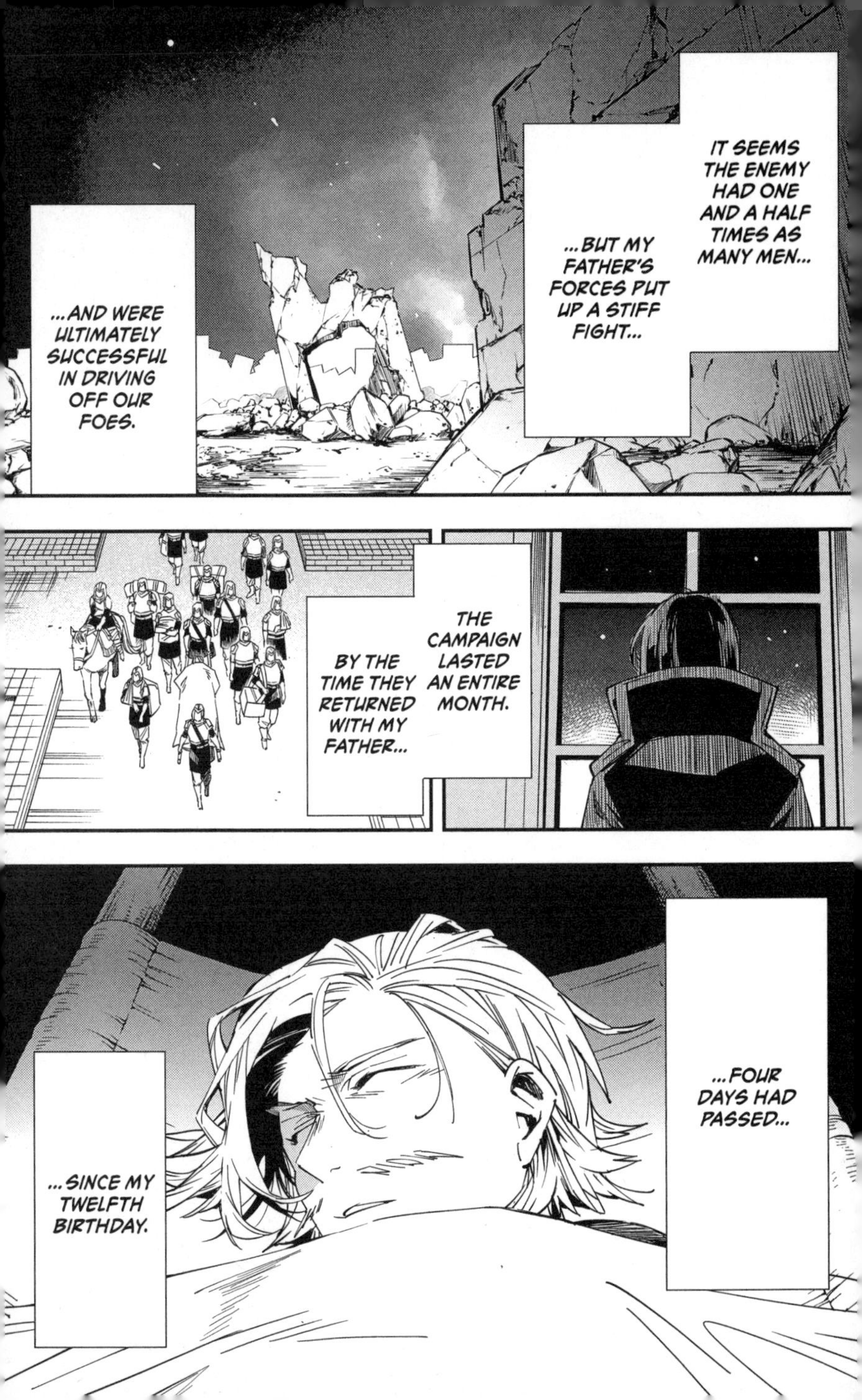
IT SEEMS THE ENEMY HAD ONE AND A HALF TIMES AS MANY MEN...
...BUT MY FATHER'S FORCES PUT UP A STIFF FIGHT...
...AND WERE ULTIMATELY SUCCESSFUL IN DRIVING OFF OUR FOES.
THE CAMPAIGN LASTED AN ENTIRE MONTH.
BY THE TIME THEY RETURNED WITH MY FATHER...
...FOUR DAYS HAD PASSED...
...SINCE MY TWELFTH BIRTHDAY.

Chapter 28: The Strength to Protect

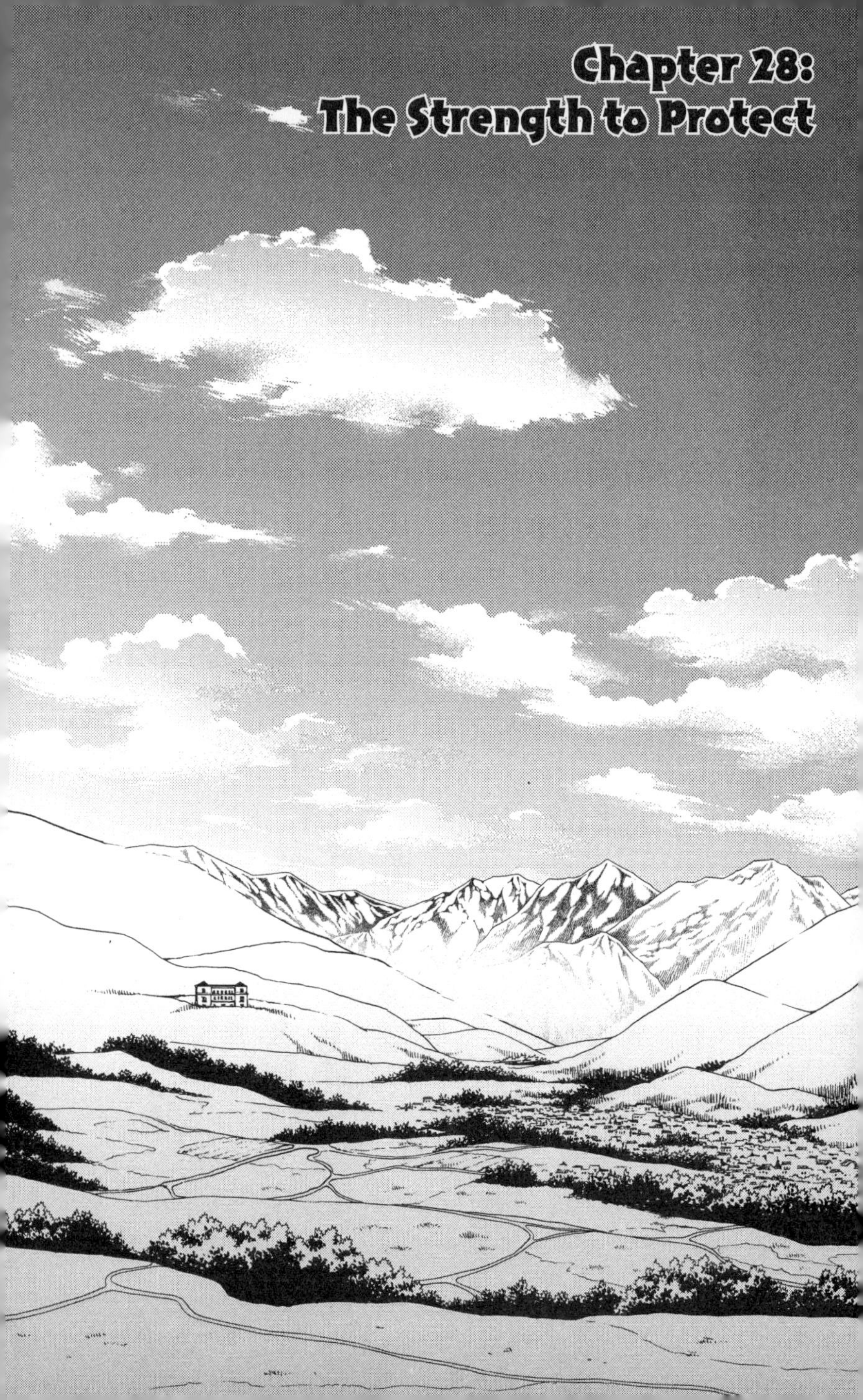

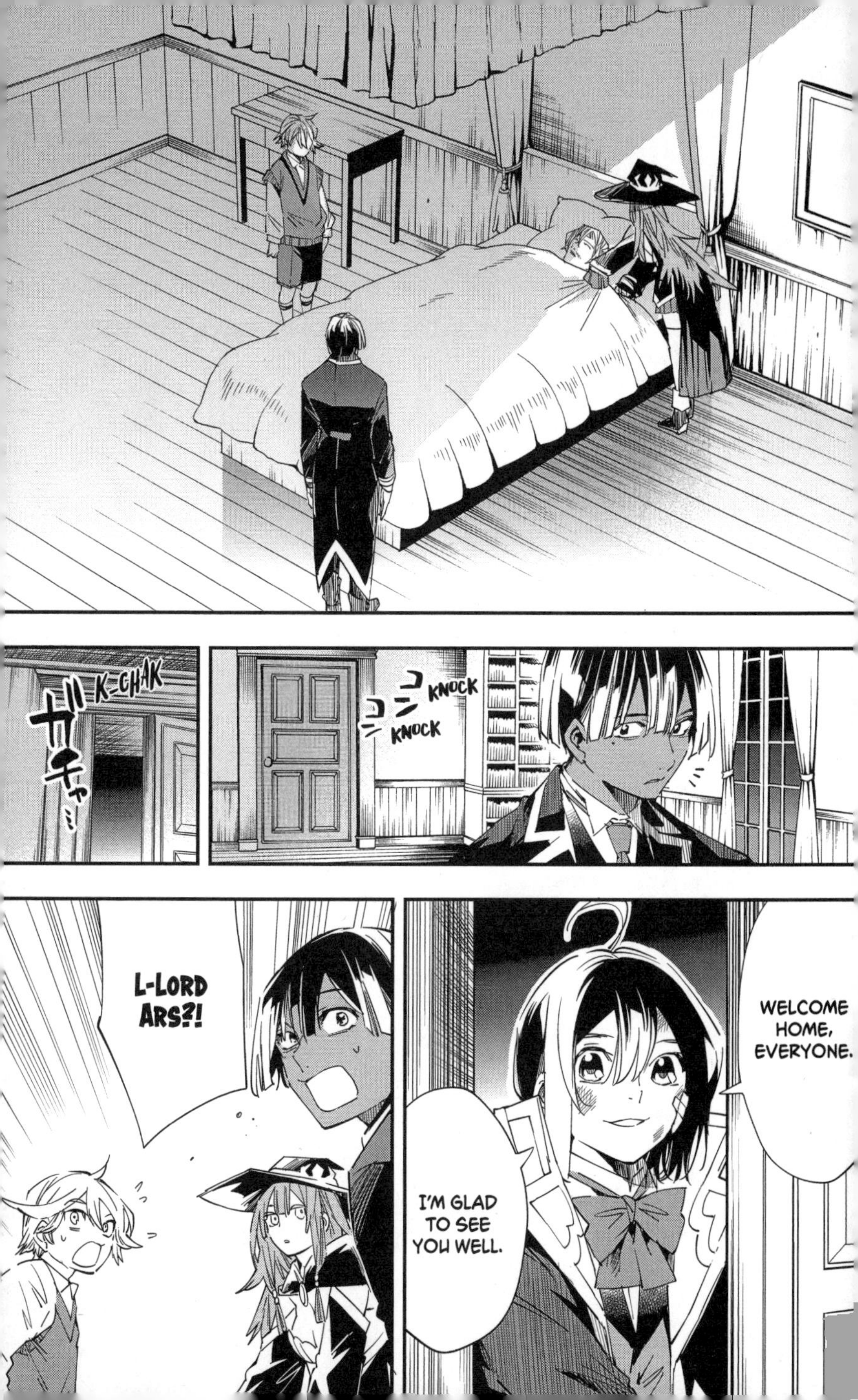
コンコン
KNOCK KNOCK
ガチャ
K-CHAK
WELCOME HOME, EVERYONE.
I'M GLAD TO SEE YOU WELL.
L-LORD ARS?!

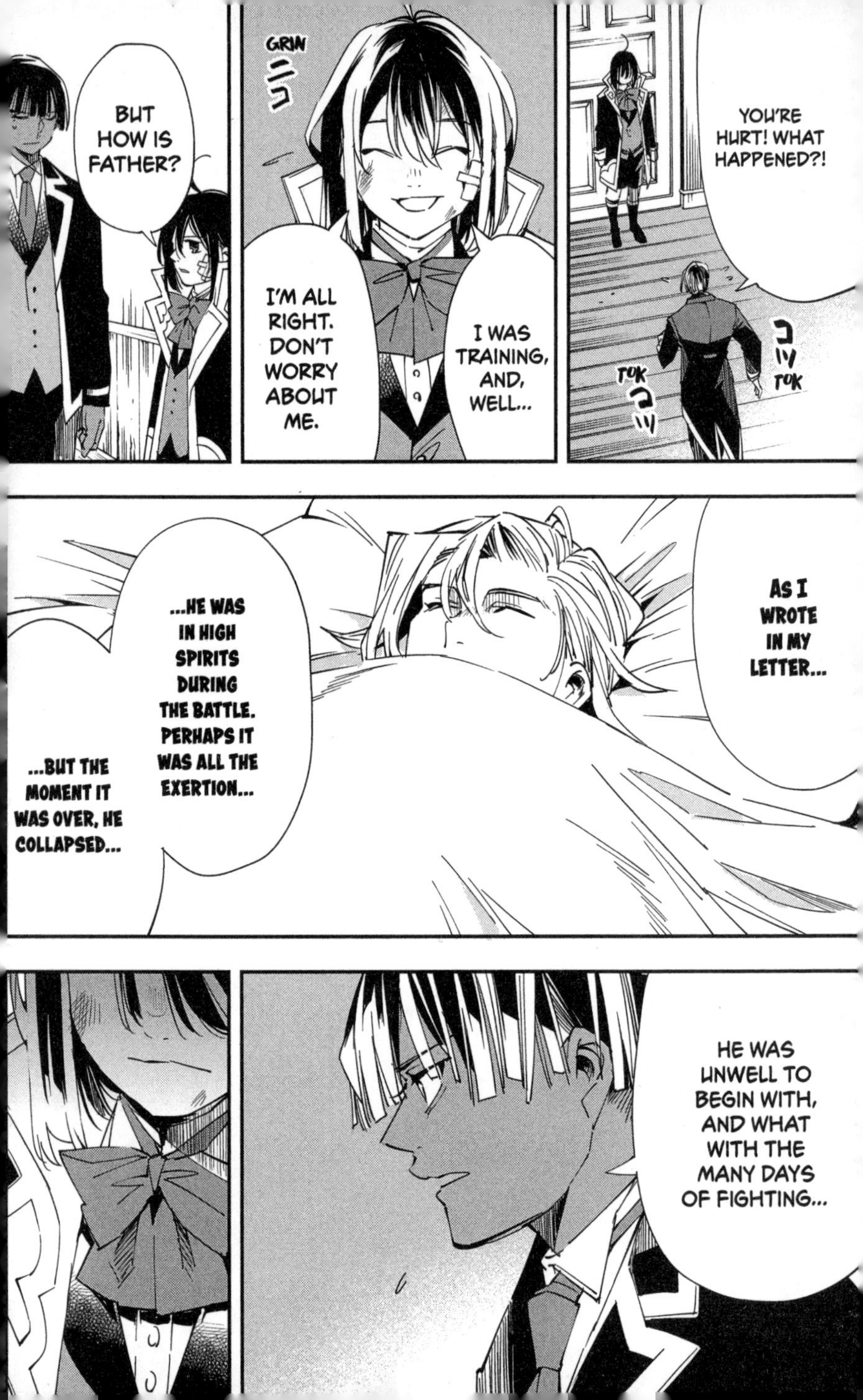
YOU'RE HURT! WHAT HAPPENED?!
コツ TOK
コツ TOK
ニコ GRIN
I WAS TRAINING, AND, WELL...
I'M ALL RIGHT. DON'T WORRY ABOUT ME.
BUT HOW IS FATHER?
AS I WROTE IN MY LETTER...
...HE WAS IN HIGH SPIRITS DURING THE BATTLE. PERHAPS IT WAS ALL THE EXERTION...
...BUT THE MOMENT IT WAS OVER, HE COLLAPSED...
HE WAS UNWELL TO BEGIN WITH, AND WHAT WITH THE MANY DAYS OF FIGHTING...

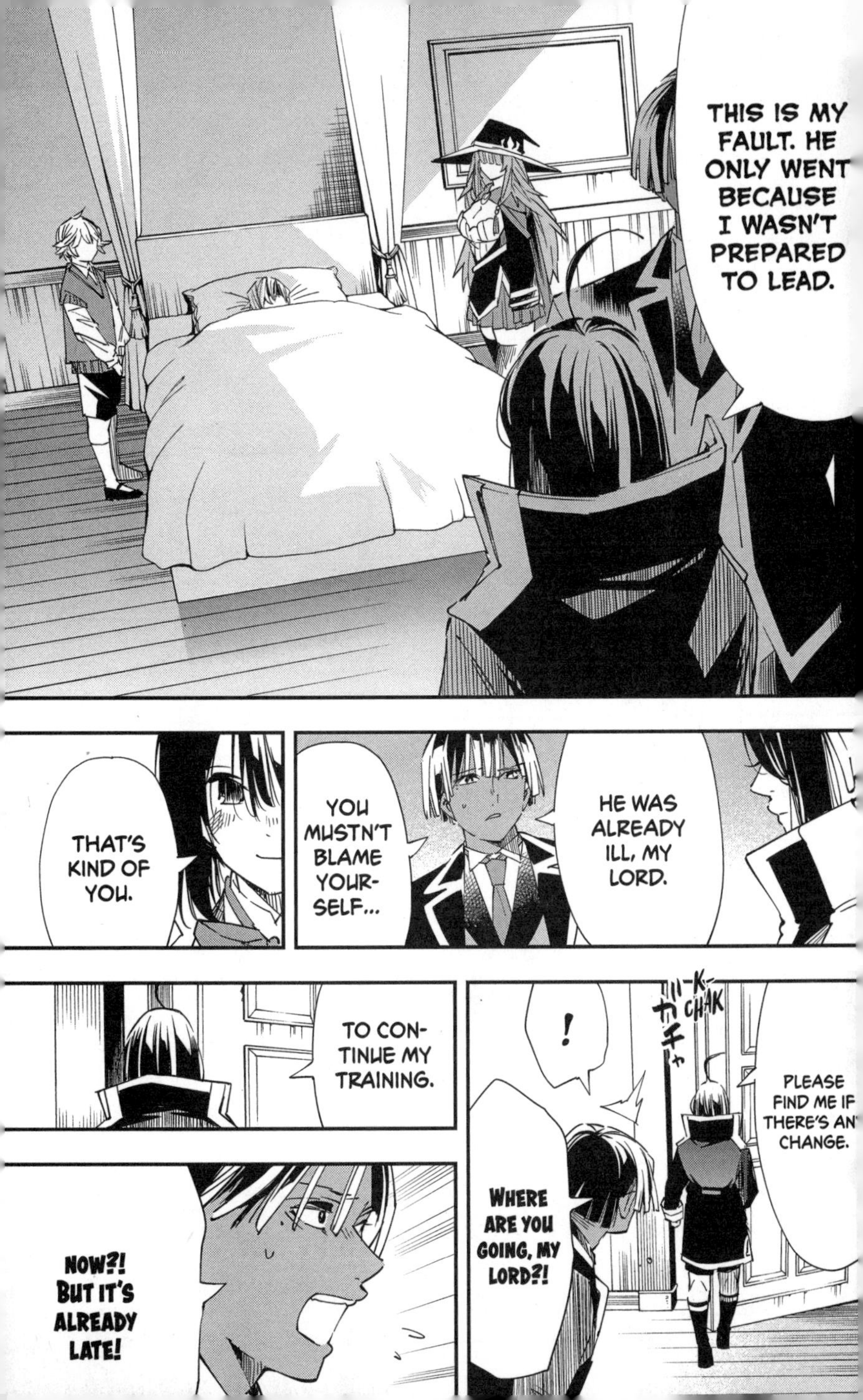
THIS IS MY FAULT. HE ONLY WENT BECAUSE I WASN'T PREPARED TO LEAD.
HE WAS ALREADY ILL, MY LORD.
YOU MUSTN'T BLAME YOUR-SELF...
THAT'S KIND OF YOU.
K-CHAK
カチャ
PLEASE FIND ME IF THERE'S AN CHANGE.
!
WHERE ARE YOU GOING, MY LORD?!
TO CON-TINUE MY TRAINING.
NOW?! BUT IT'S ALREADY LATE!

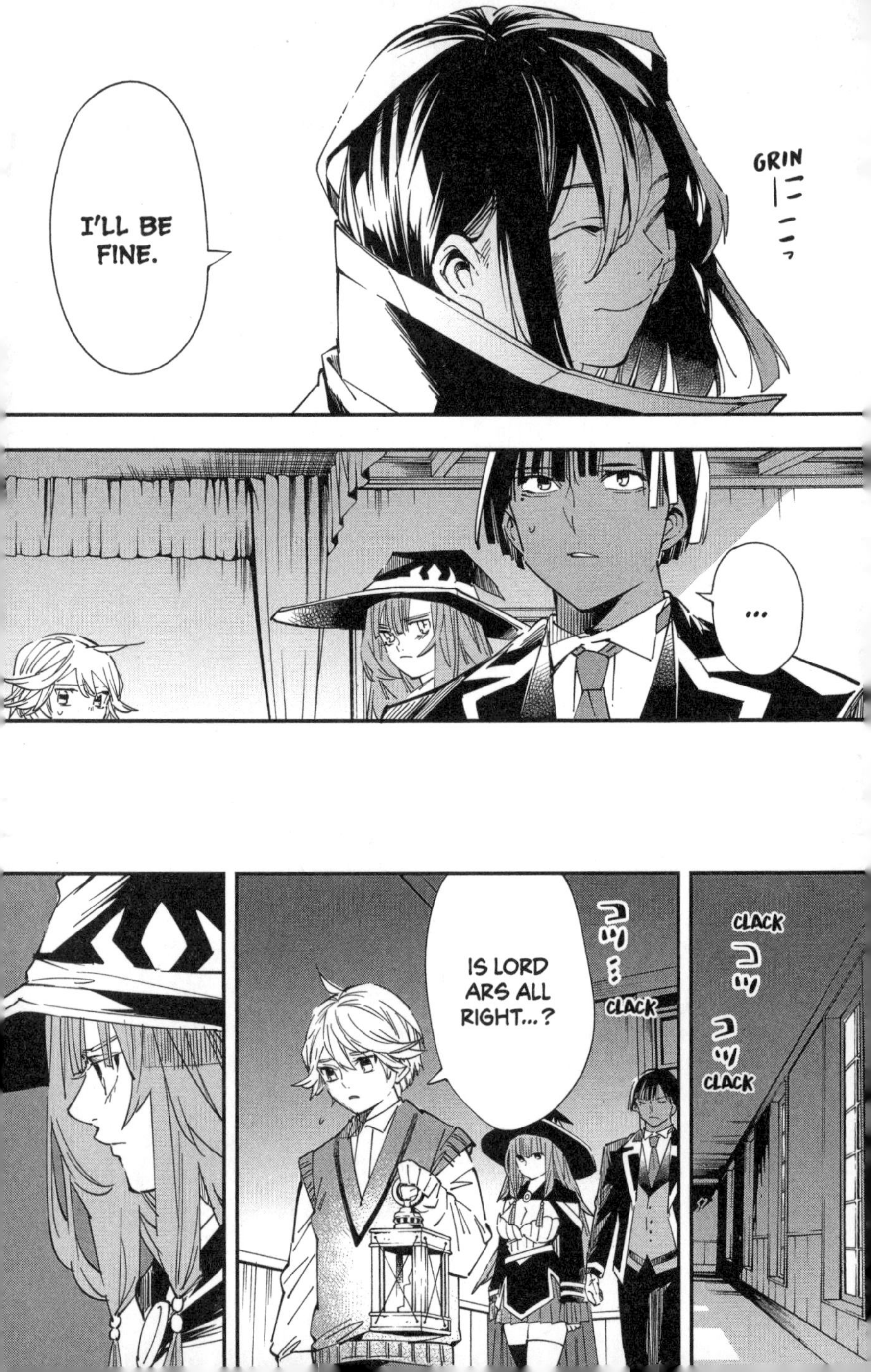
GRIN
I'LL BE FINE.
...
CLACK
CLACK
IS LORD ARS ALL RIGHT...?
CLACK

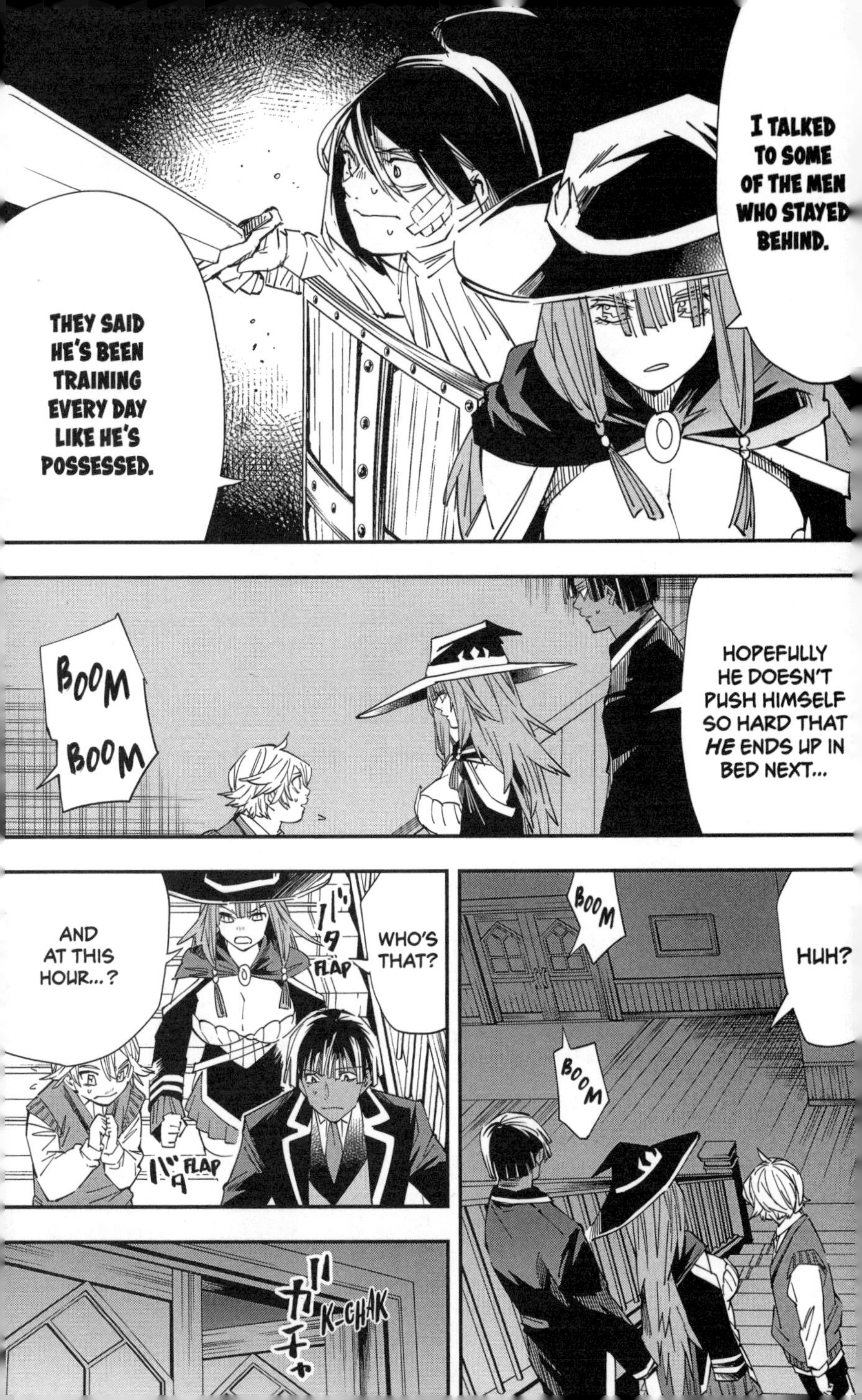

I TALKED TO SOME OF THE MEN WHO STAYED BEHIND.
THEY SAID HE'S BEEN TRAINING EVERY DAY LIKE HE'S POSSESSED.
HOPEFULLY HE DOESN'T PUSH HIMSELF SO HARD THAT *HE* ENDS UP IN BED NEXT...
BOOM
BOOM
HUH?
BOOM
BOOM
WHO'S THAT?
FLAP
AND AT THIS HOUR...?
FLAP
K-CHAK

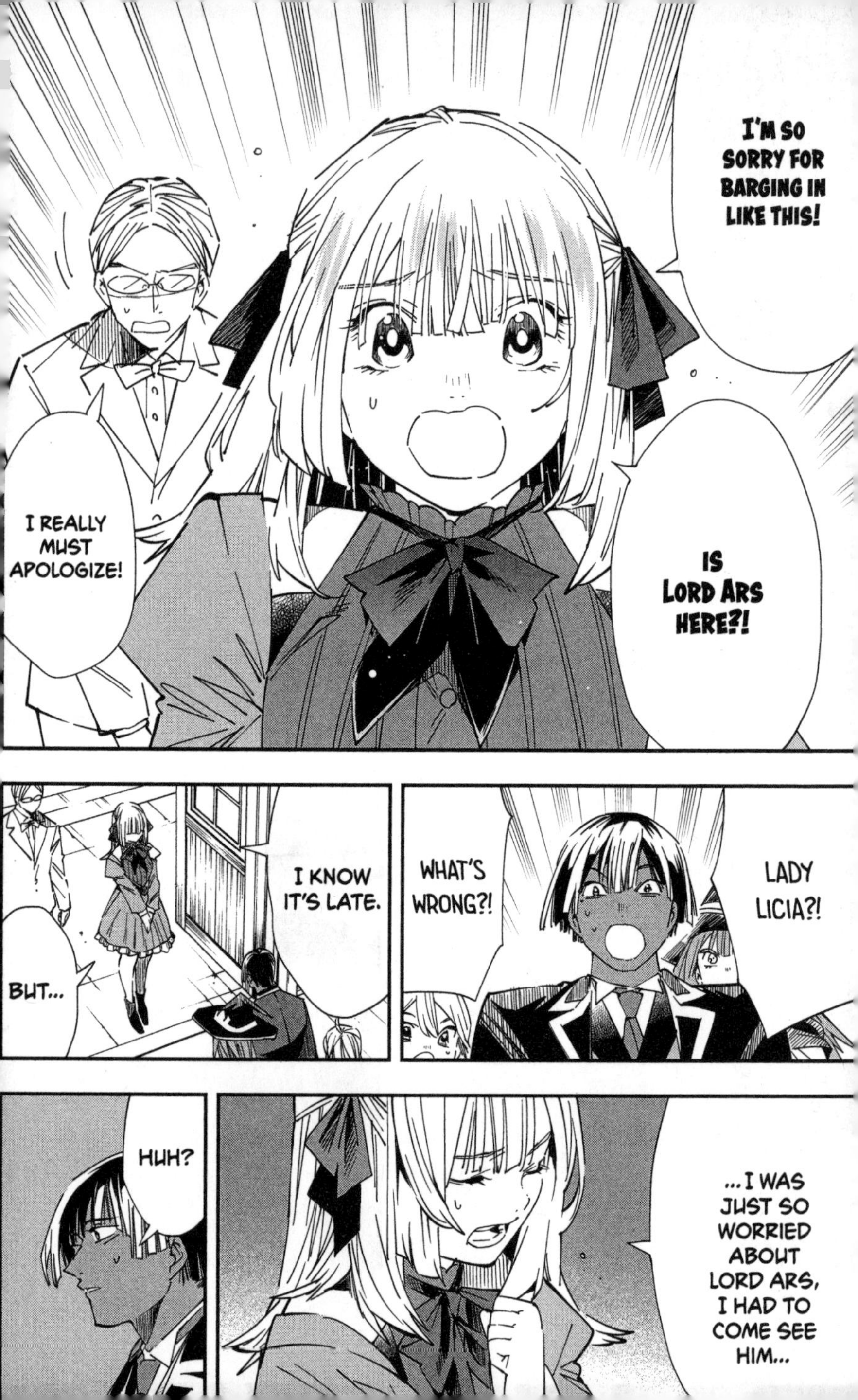
I'M SO SORRY FOR BARGING IN LIKE THIS!
IS LORD ARS HERE?!
I REALLY MUST APOLOGIZE!
LADY LICIA?!
WHAT'S WRONG?!
I KNOW IT'S LATE.
BUT...
...I WAS JUST SO WORRIED ABOUT LORD ARS, I HAD TO COME SEE HIM...
HUH?

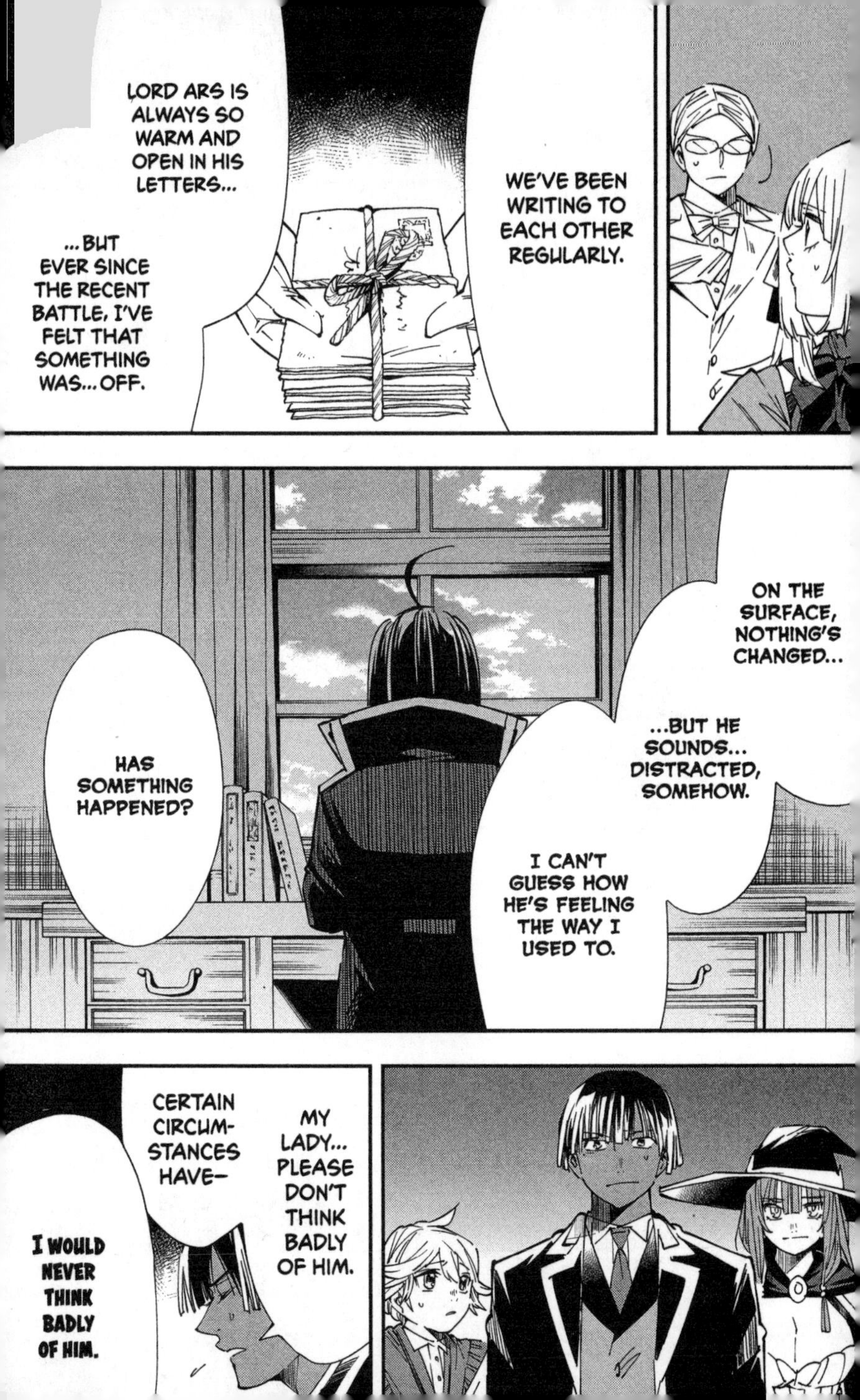
WE'VE BEEN WRITING TO EACH OTHER REGULARLY.
LORD ARS IS ALWAYS SO WARM AND OPEN IN HIS LETTERS...
...BUT EVER SINCE THE RECENT BATTLE, I'VE FELT THAT SOMETHING WAS...OFF.
ON THE SURFACE, NOTHING'S CHANGED...
...BUT HE SOUNDS... DISTRACTED, SOMEHOW.
I CAN'T GUESS HOW HE'S FEELING THE WAY I USED TO.
HAS SOMETHING HAPPENED?
MY LADY... PLEASE DON'T THINK BADLY OF HIM.
CERTAIN CIRCUM-STANCES HAVE–
I WOULD NEVER THINK BADLY OF HIM.

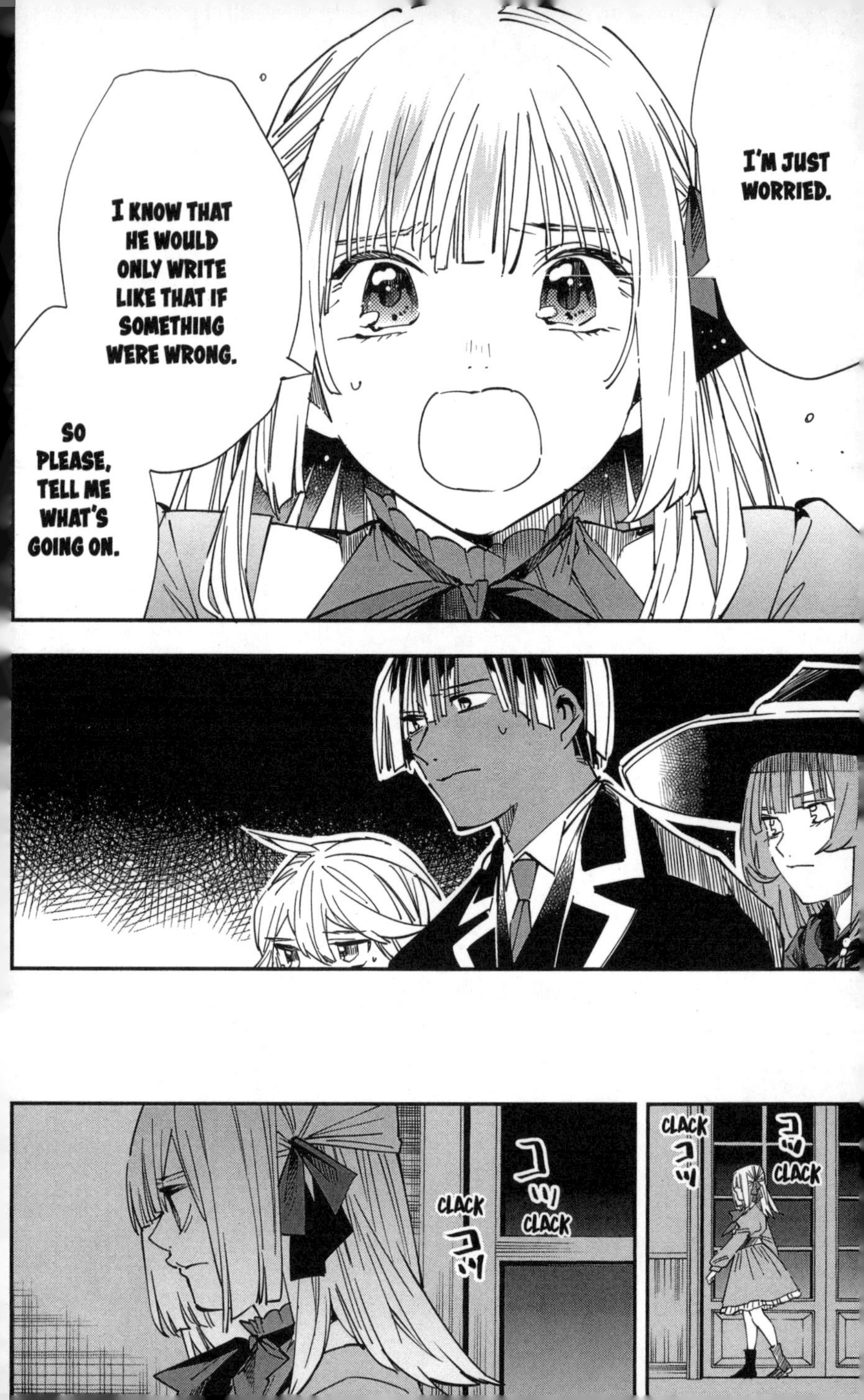
I'M JUST WORRIED.
I KNOW THAT HE WOULD ONLY WRITE LIKE THAT IF SOMETHING WERE WRONG.
SO PLEASE, TELL ME WHAT'S GOING ON.
コッ CLACK
CLACK コッ
コッ CLACK
CLACK コッ

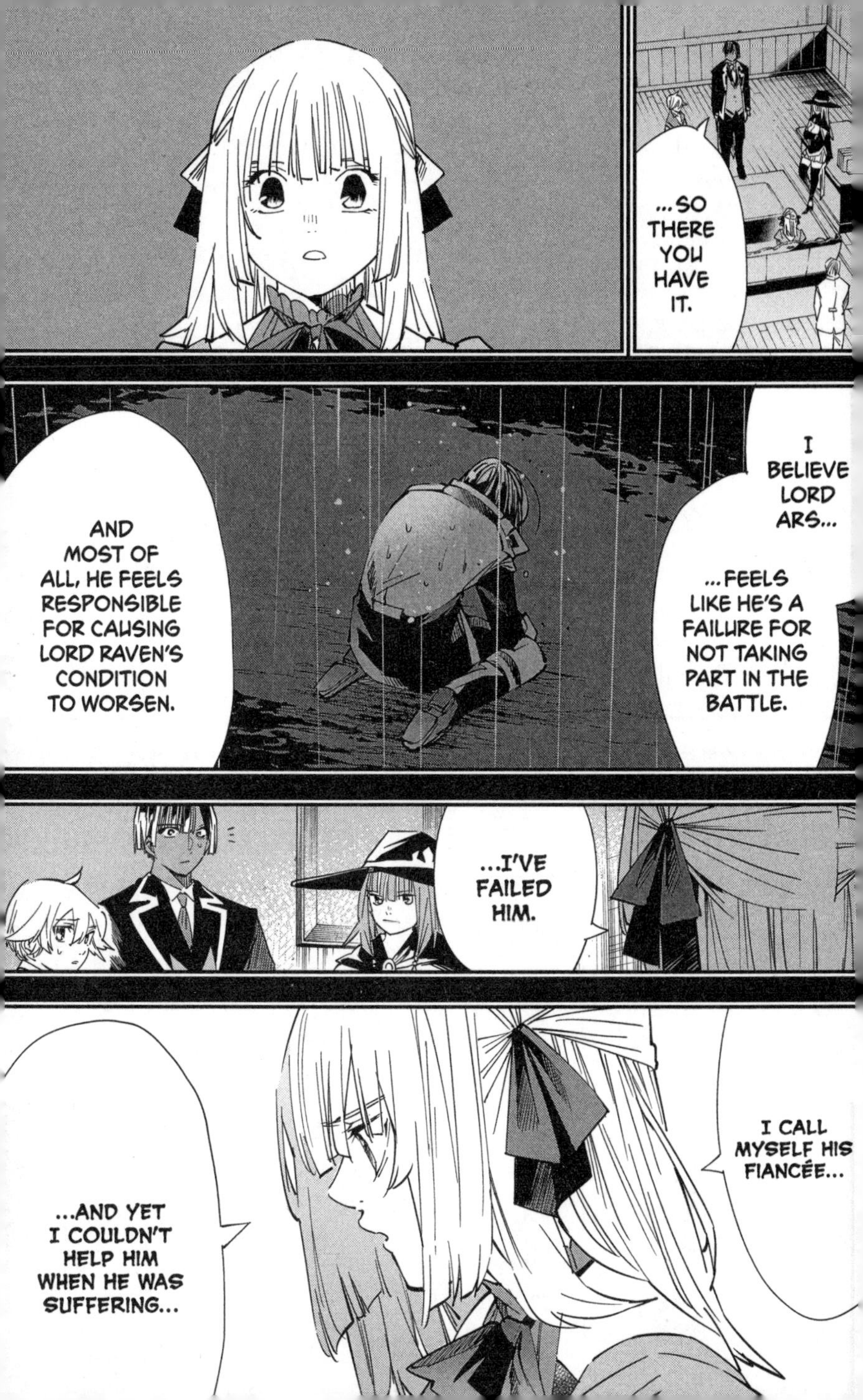
...SO THERE YOU HAVE IT.
I BELIEVE LORD ARS...
...FEELS LIKE HE'S A FAILURE FOR NOT TAKING PART IN THE BATTLE.
AND MOST OF ALL, HE FEELS RESPONSIBLE FOR CAUSING LORD RAVEN'S CONDITION TO WORSEN.
...I'VE FAILED HIM.
I CALL MYSELF HIS FIANCÉE...
...AND YET I COULDN'T HELP HIM WHEN HE WAS SUFFERING...

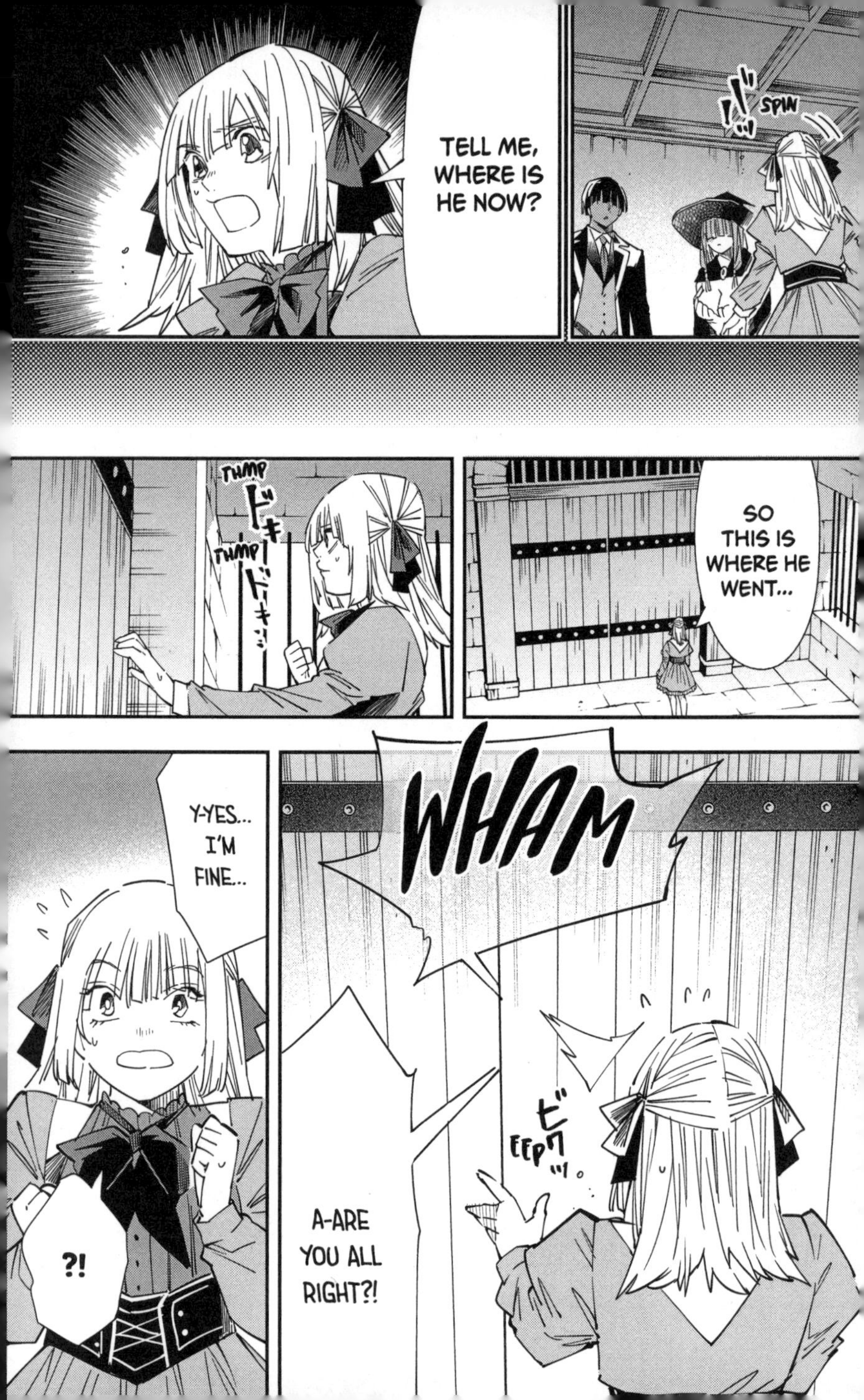
SPIN
TELL ME, WHERE IS HE NOW?
SO THIS IS WHERE HE WENT...
THMP ドキ
THMP ドキドキ
WHAM
EEP ビクッ
A-ARE YOU ALL RIGHT?!
Y-YES... I'M FINE...
?!

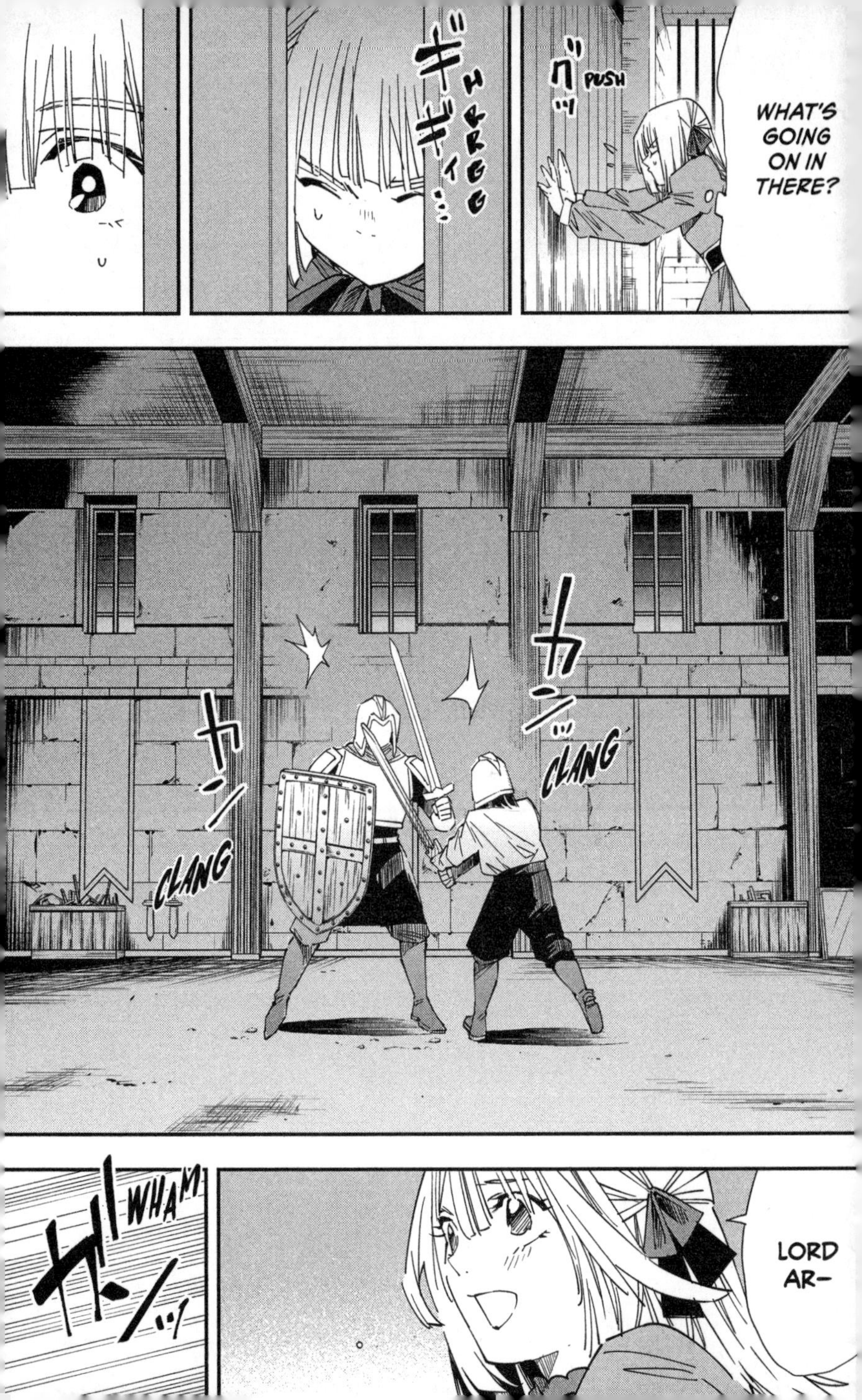
WHAT'S GOING ON IN THERE?
グッ
PUSH
ギギイ…
HRRGG
カーン
CLANG
カーン
CLANG
LORD AR-
バン
WHAM

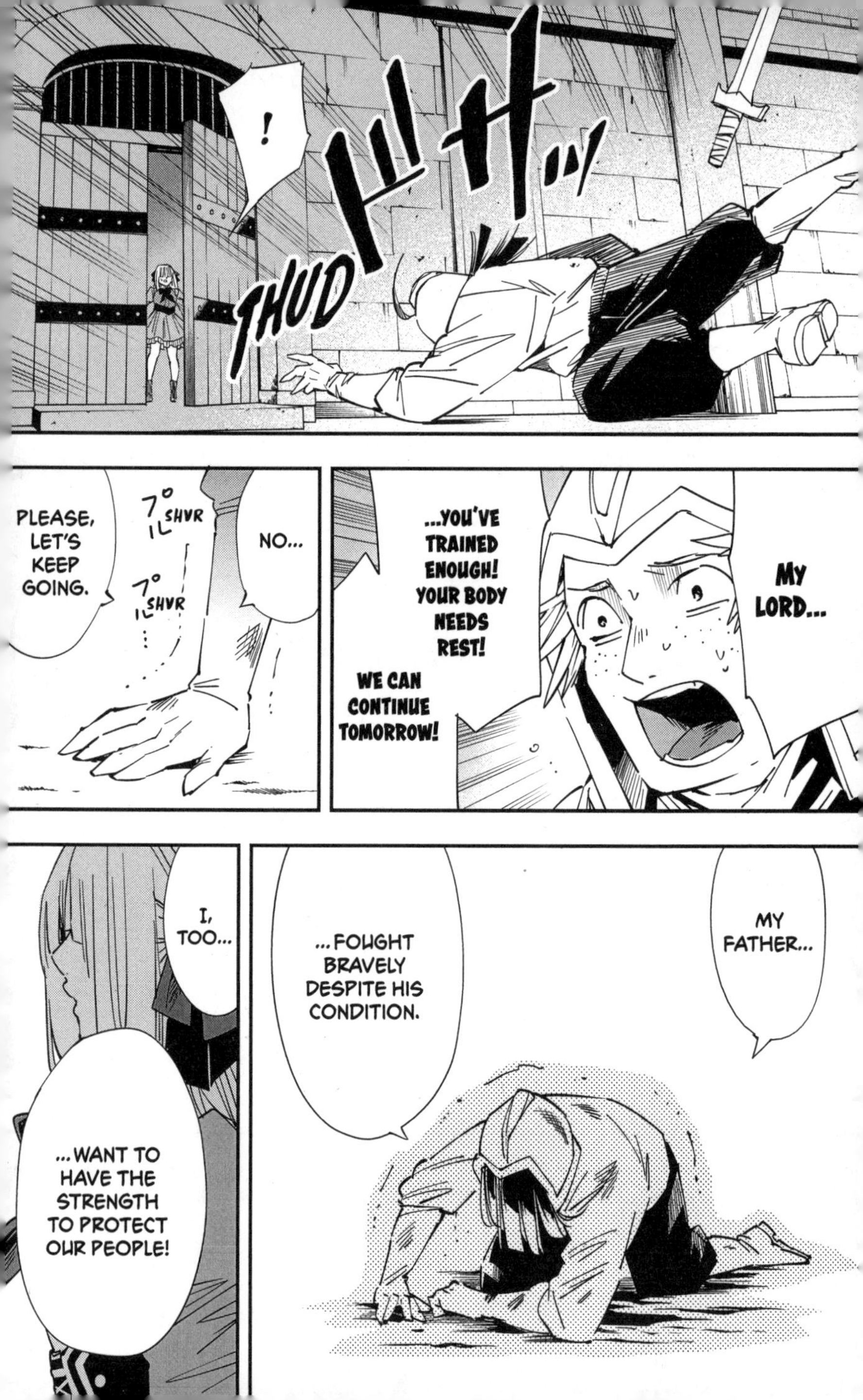
!
ドサッ
THUD
MY LORD...
...YOU'VE TRAINED ENOUGH! YOUR BODY NEEDS REST!
WE CAN CONTINUE TOMORROW!
NO...
プル SHVR
プル SHVR
PLEASE, LET'S KEEP GOING.
MY FATHER...
...FOUGHT BRAVELY DESPITE HIS CONDITION.
I, TOO...
...WANT TO HAVE THE STRENGTH TO PROTECT OUR PEOPLE!

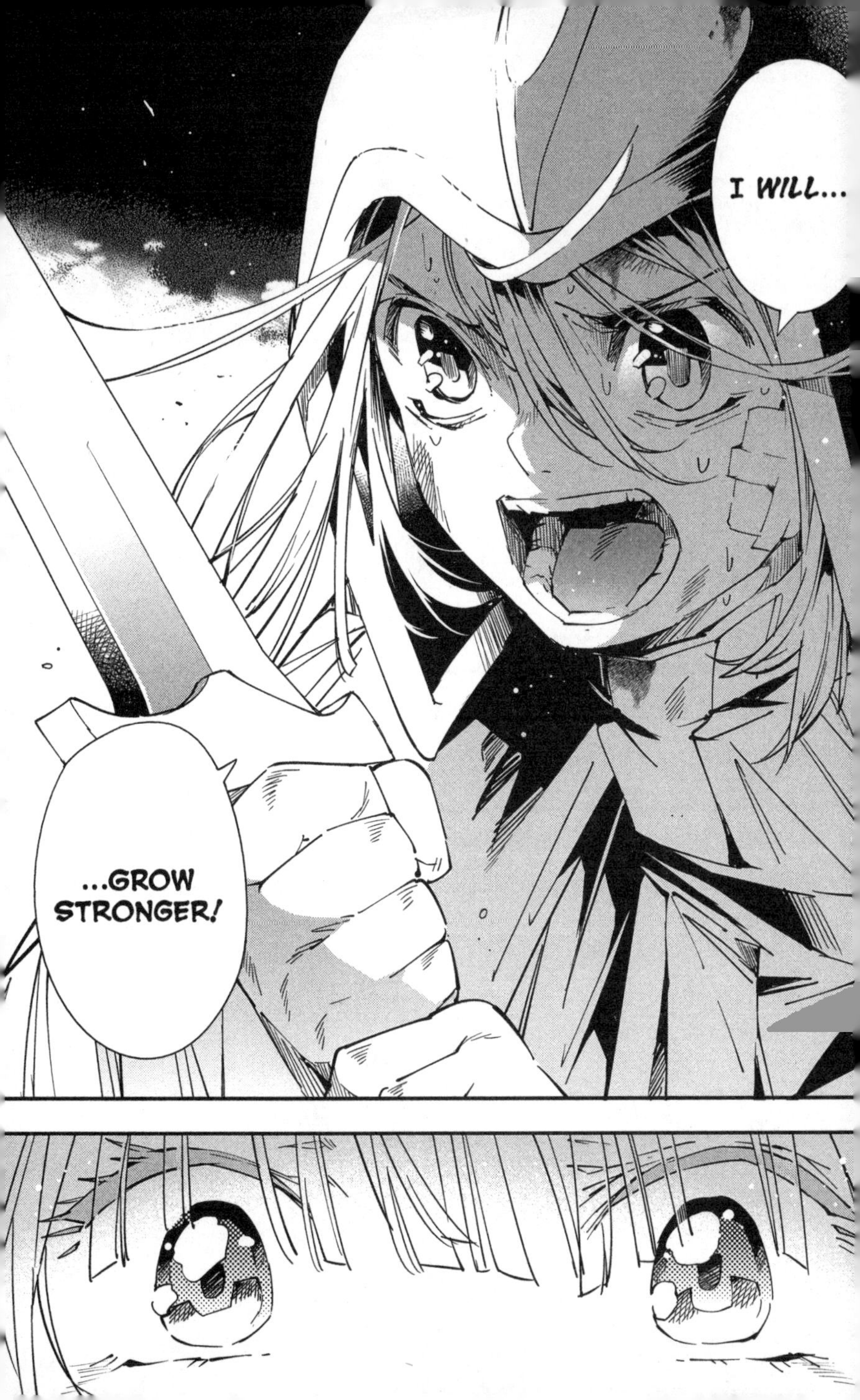
I WILL...
...GROW STRONGER!

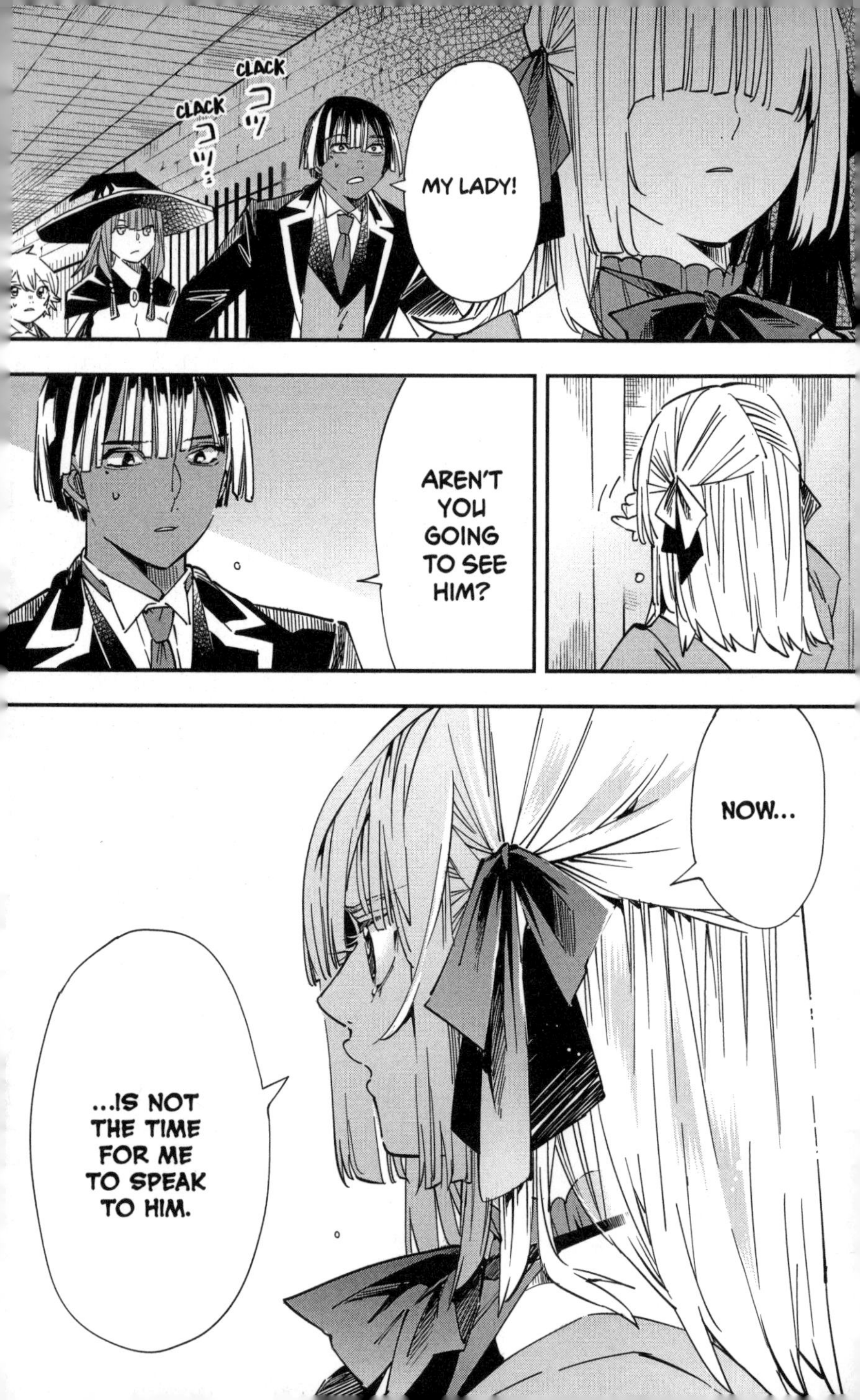
CLACK
コッ
CLACK
コッ
MY LADY!
AREN'T YOU GOING TO SEE HIM?
NOW...
...IS NOT THE TIME FOR ME TO SPEAK TO HIM.

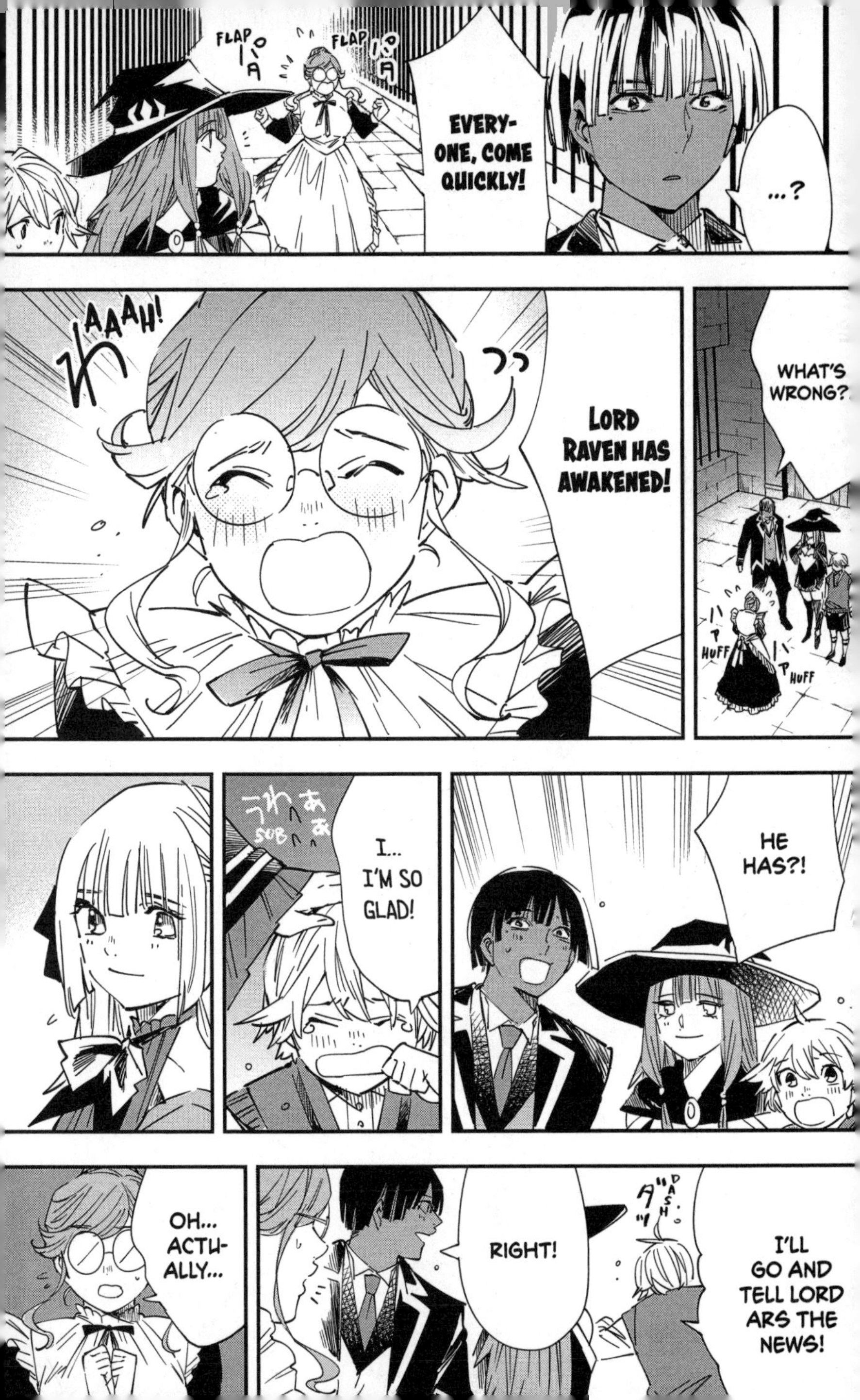
...?
FLAP FLAP
EVERY-ONE, COME QUICKLY!
WHAT'S WRONG?
HUFF HUFF
LORD RAVEN HAS AWAKENED!
AAAH!
HE HAS?!
I... I'M SO GLAD!
SUB
I'LL GO AND TELL LORD ARS THE NEWS!
DASH
RIGHT!
OH... ACTU-ALLY...

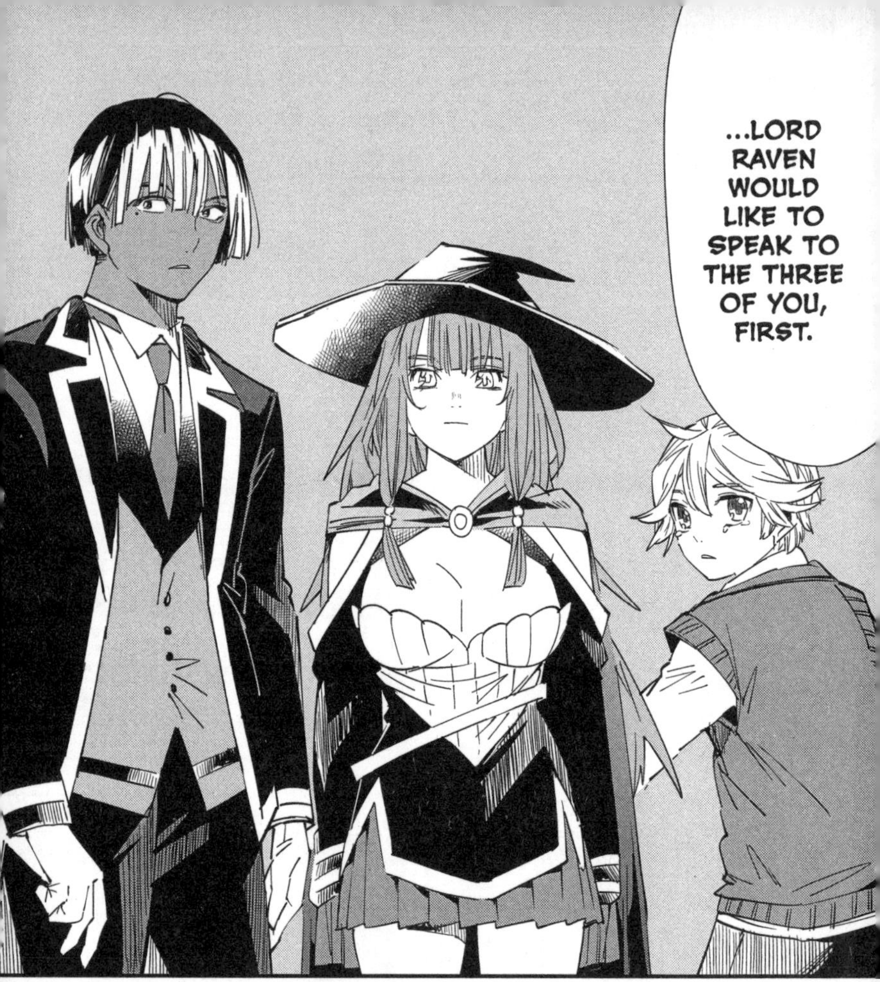
...LORD RAVEN WOULD LIKE TO SPEAK TO THE THREE OF YOU, FIRST.
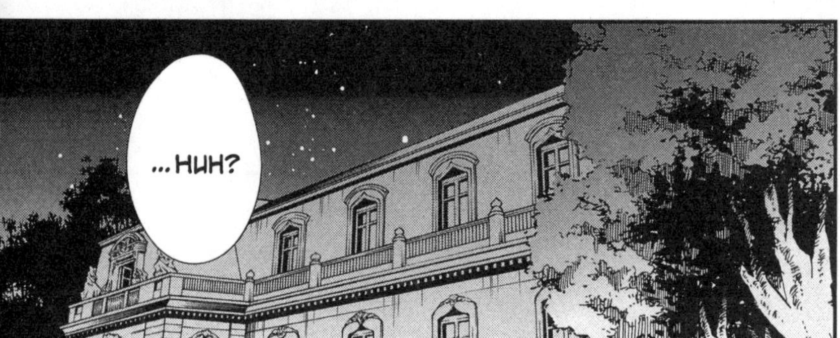
...HUH?

As a Reincarnated
ARISTOCRAT,
I'll Use My Appraisal Skill to
Rise in the World

As a Reincarnated ARISTOCRAT, I'll Use My Appraisal Skill to Rise in the World

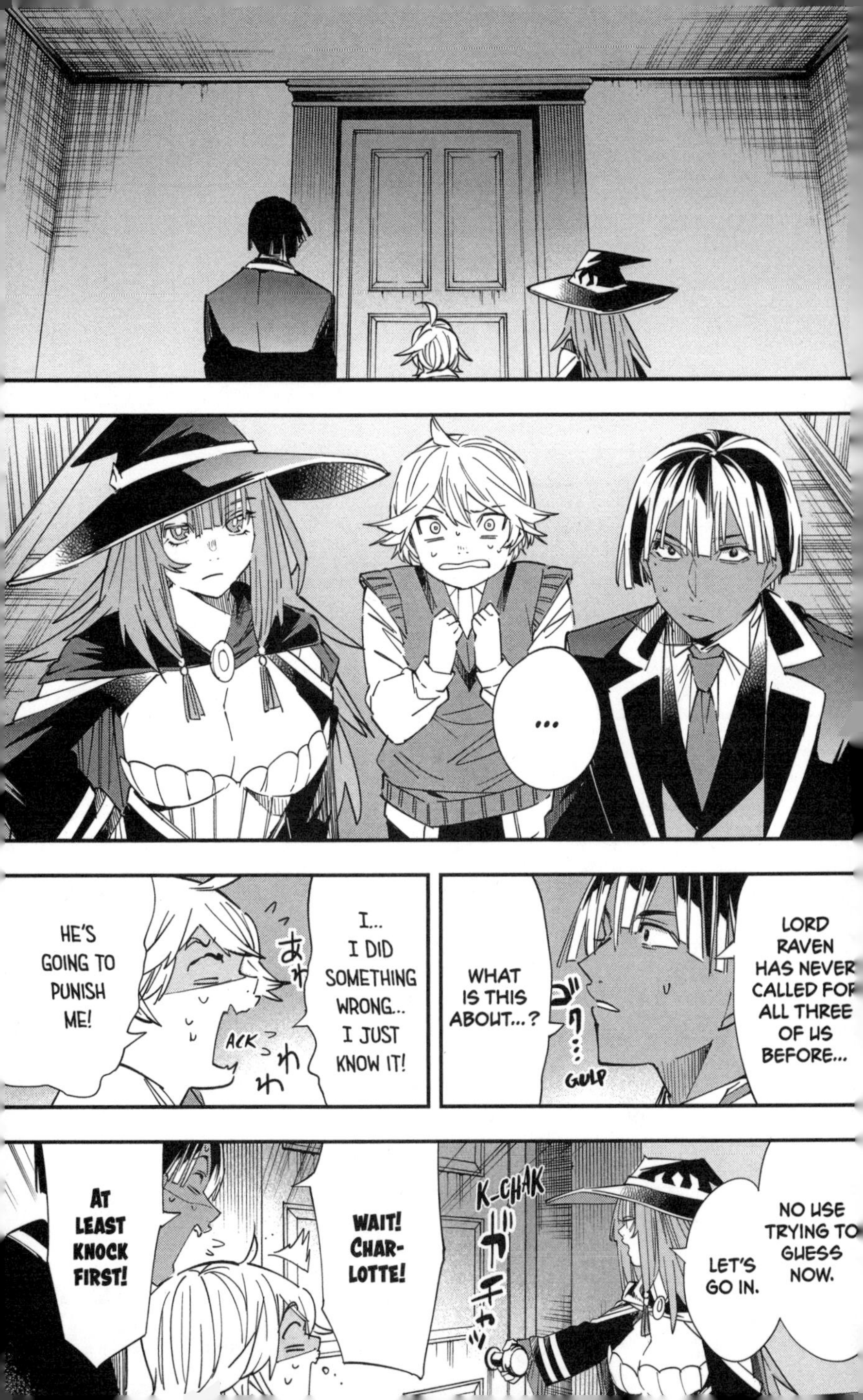
...
LORD RAVEN HAS NEVER CALLED FOR ALL THREE OF US BEFORE...
WHAT IS THIS ABOUT...?
GULP
I... I DID SOMETHING WRONG... I JUST KNOW IT!
ACK
HE'S GOING TO PUNISH ME!
NO USE TRYING TO GUESS NOW.
LET'S GO IN.
K-CHAK
WAIT! CHARLOTTE!
AT LEAST KNOCK FIRST!

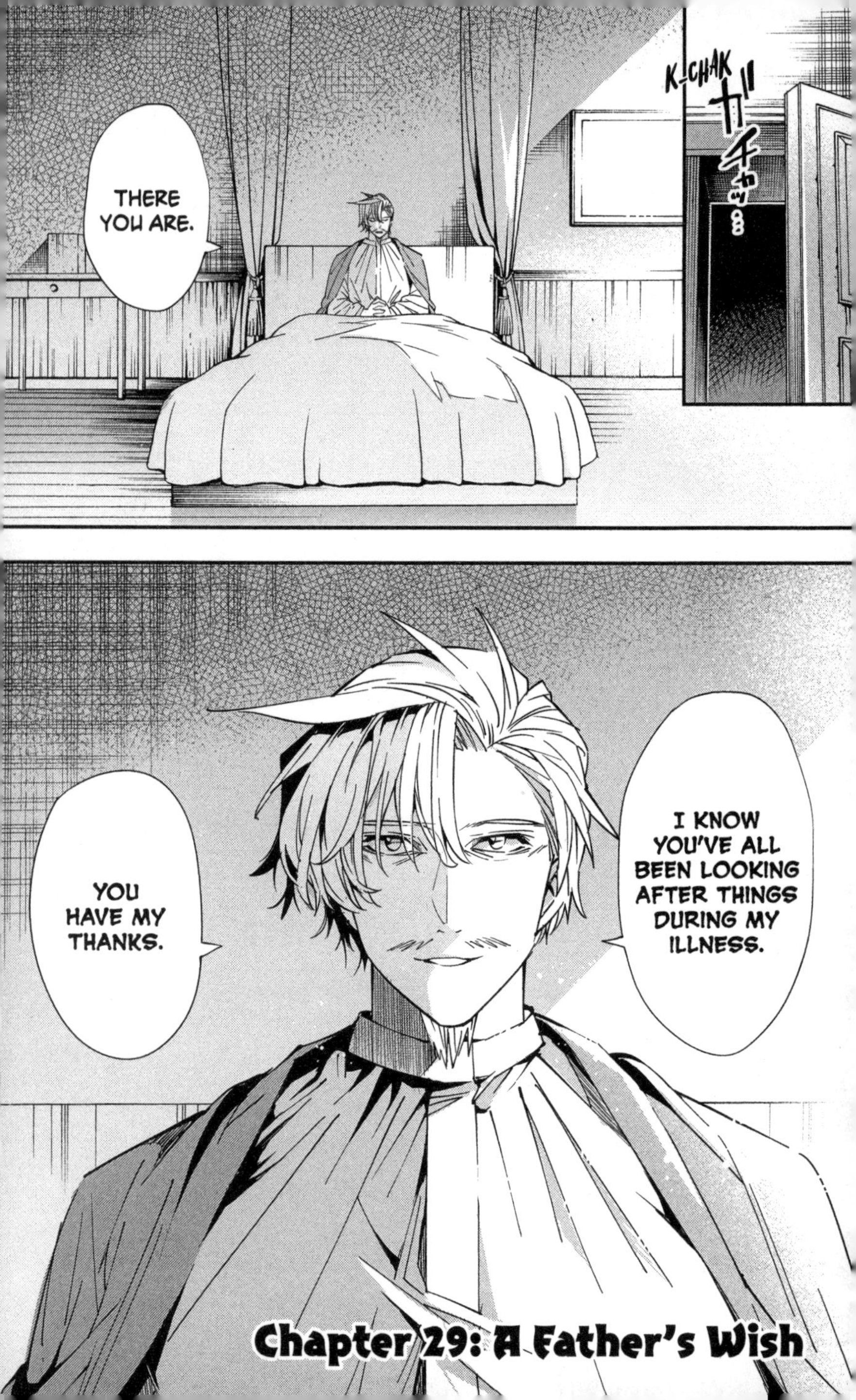
K-CHAK
ガチャッ…
THERE YOU ARE.
I KNOW YOU'VE ALL BEEN LOOKING AFTER THINGS DURING MY ILLNESS.
YOU HAVE MY THANKS.

Chapter 29: A Father's Wish

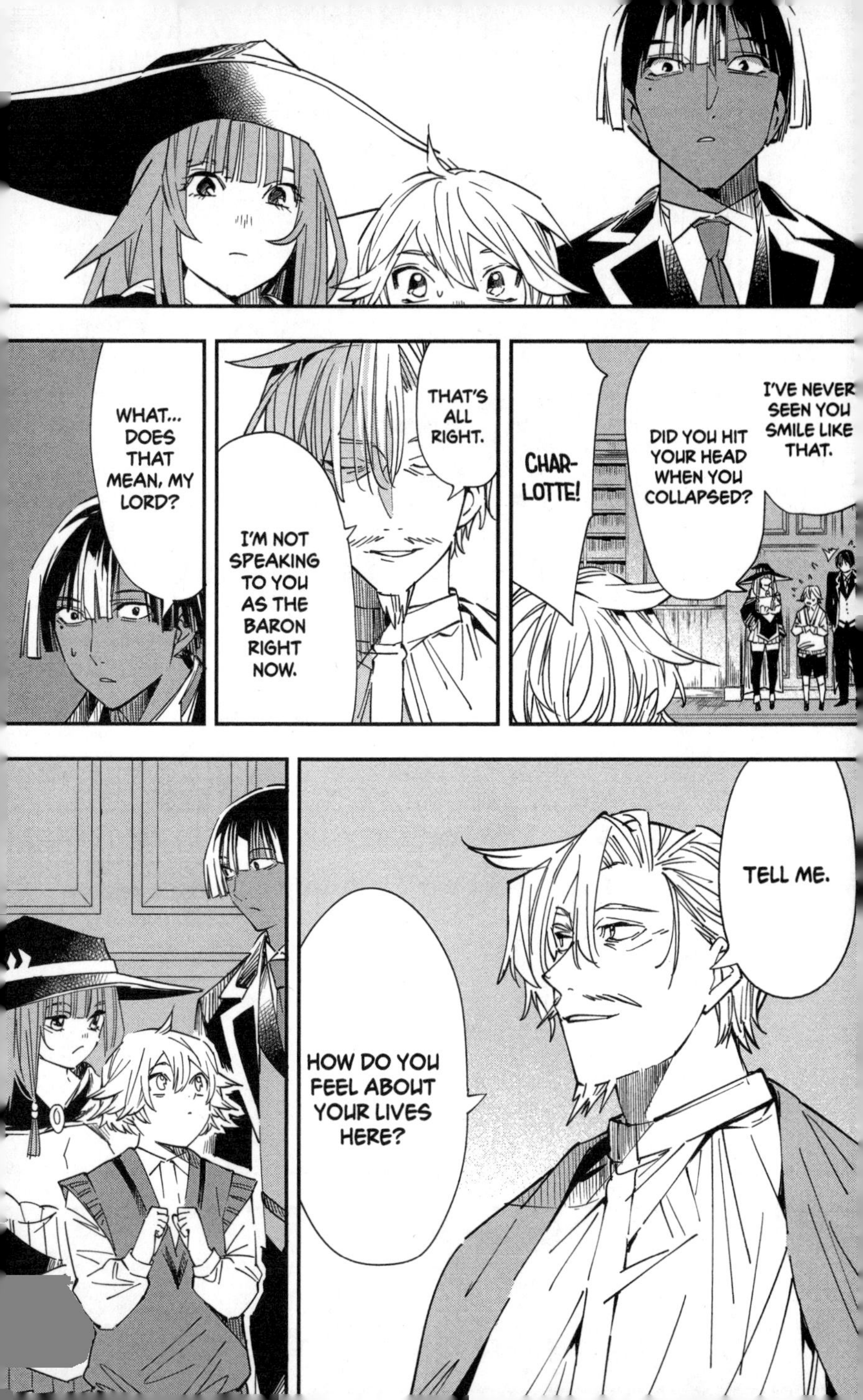
I'VE NEVER SEEN YOU SMILE LIKE THAT.
DID YOU HIT YOUR HEAD WHEN YOU COLLAPSED?
CHAR-LOTTE!
THAT'S ALL RIGHT.
I'M NOT SPEAKING TO YOU AS THE BARON RIGHT NOW.
WHAT... DOES THAT MEAN, MY LORD?
TELL ME.
HOW DO YOU FEEL ABOUT YOUR LIVES HERE?

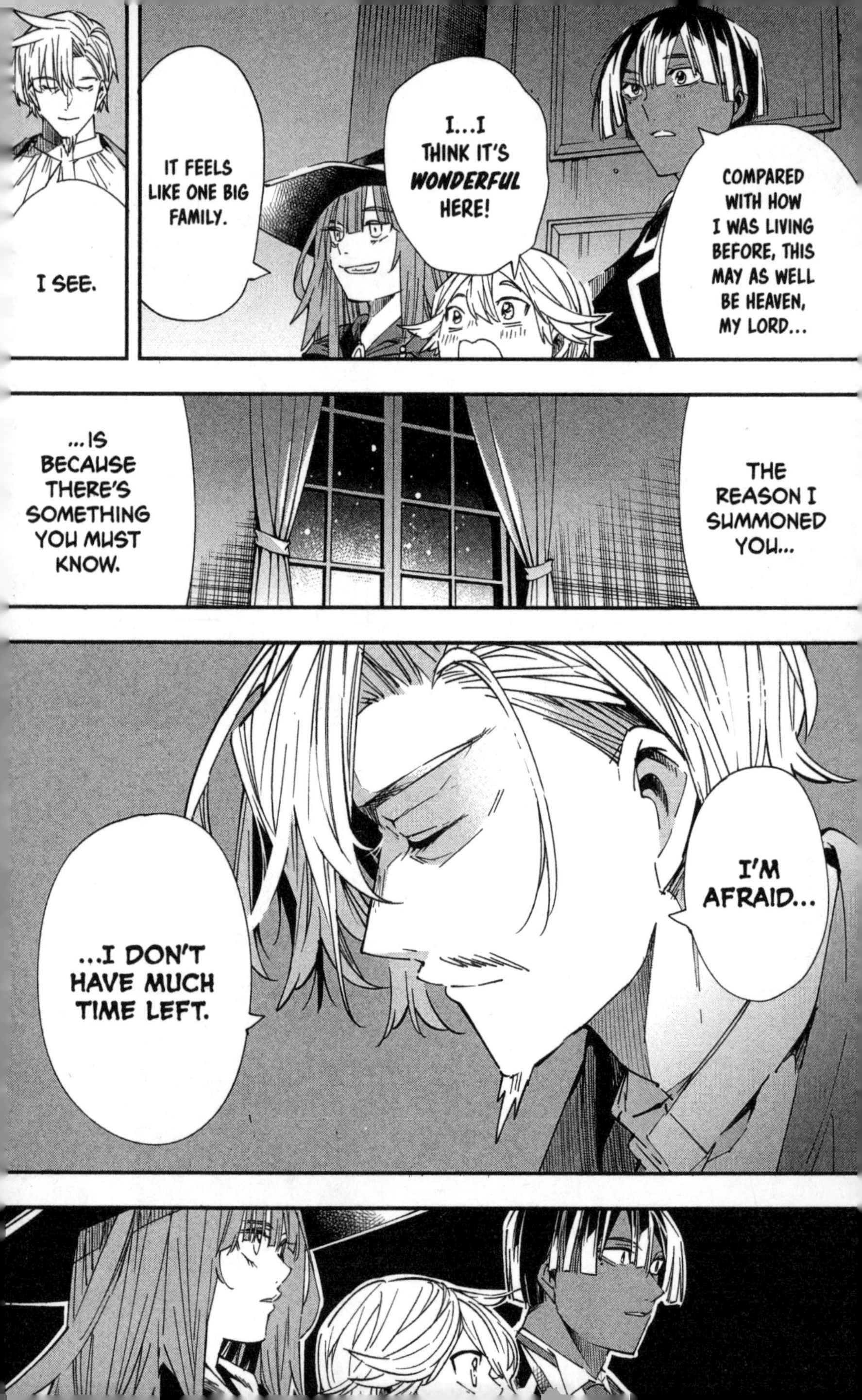
COMPARED WITH HOW I WAS LIVING BEFORE, THIS MAY AS WELL BE HEAVEN, MY LORD...
I...I THINK IT'S *WONDERFUL* HERE!
IT FEELS LIKE ONE BIG FAMILY.
I SEE.
THE REASON I SUMMONED YOU...
...IS BECAUSE THERE'S SOMETHING YOU MUST KNOW.
I'M AFRAID...
...I DON'T HAVE MUCH TIME LEFT.

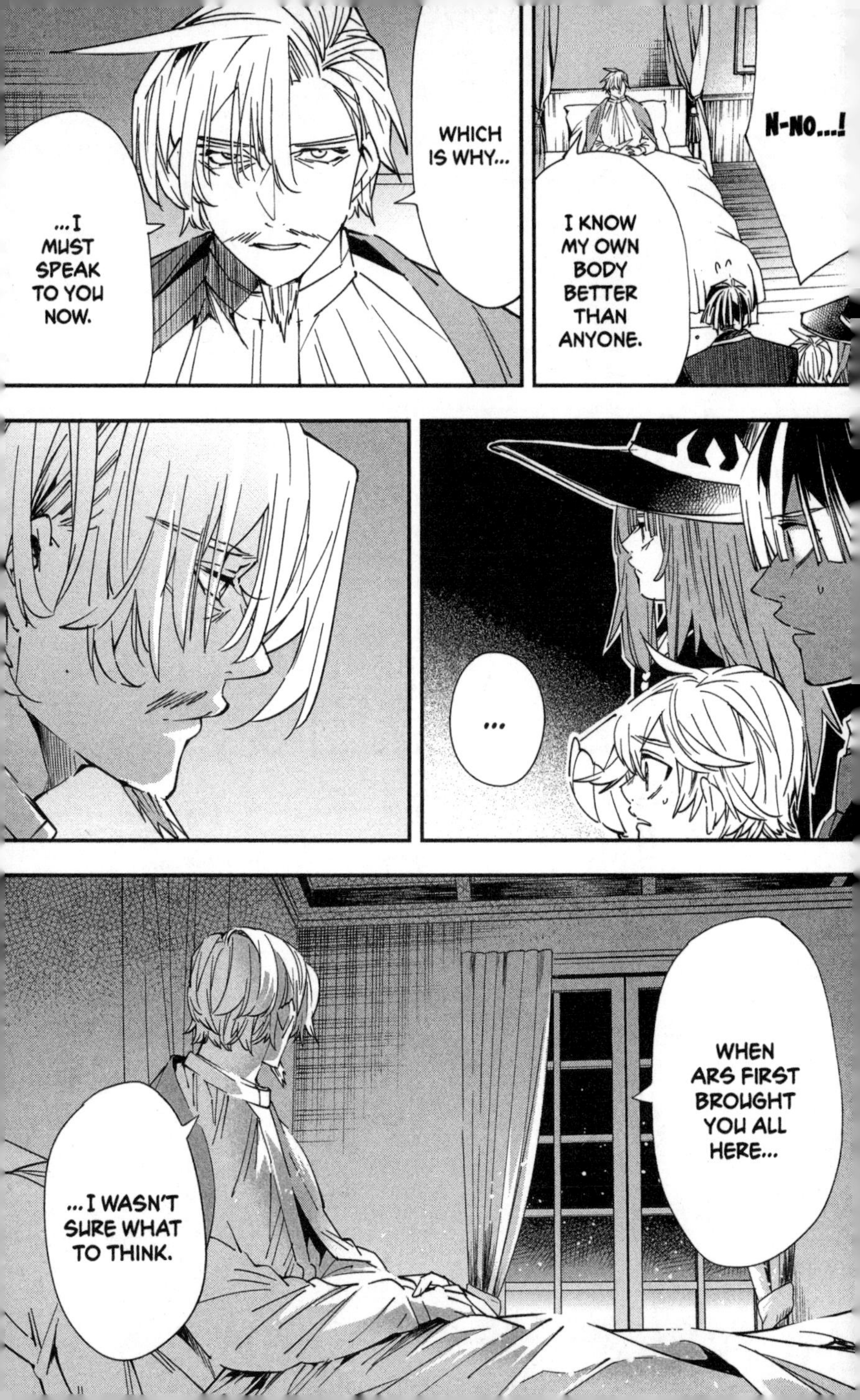
N-NO...!
I KNOW MY OWN BODY BETTER THAN ANYONE.
WHICH IS WHY...
...I MUST SPEAK TO YOU NOW.
...
WHEN ARS FIRST BROUGHT YOU ALL HERE...
...I WASN'T SURE WHAT TO THINK.

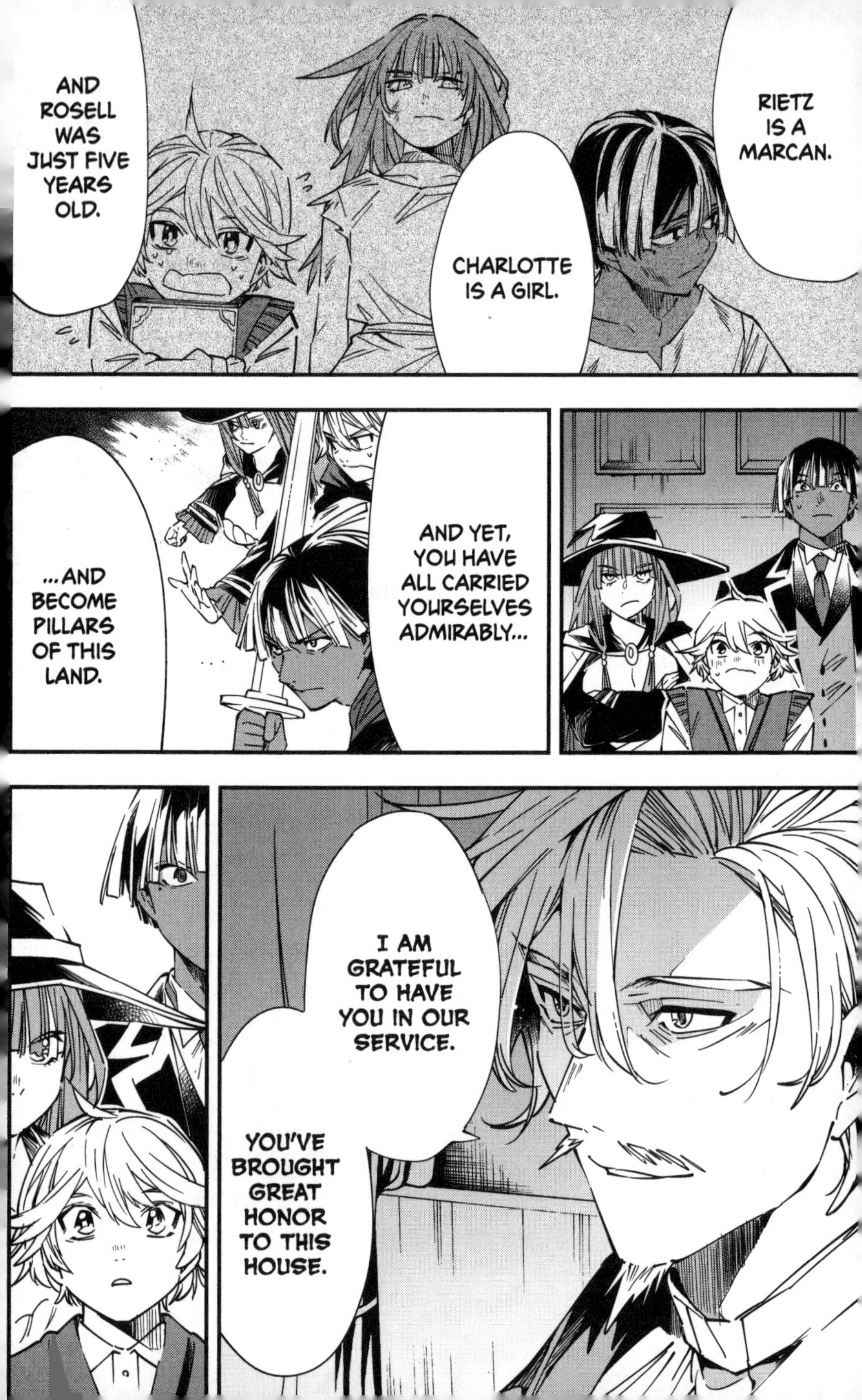
RIETZ IS A MARCAN.
CHARLOTTE IS A GIRL.
AND ROSELL WAS JUST FIVE YEARS OLD.
AND YET, YOU HAVE ALL CARRIED YOURSELVES ADMIRABLY...
...AND BECOME PILLARS OF THIS LAND.
I AM GRATEFUL TO HAVE YOU IN OUR SERVICE.
YOU'VE BROUGHT GREAT HONOR TO THIS HOUSE.

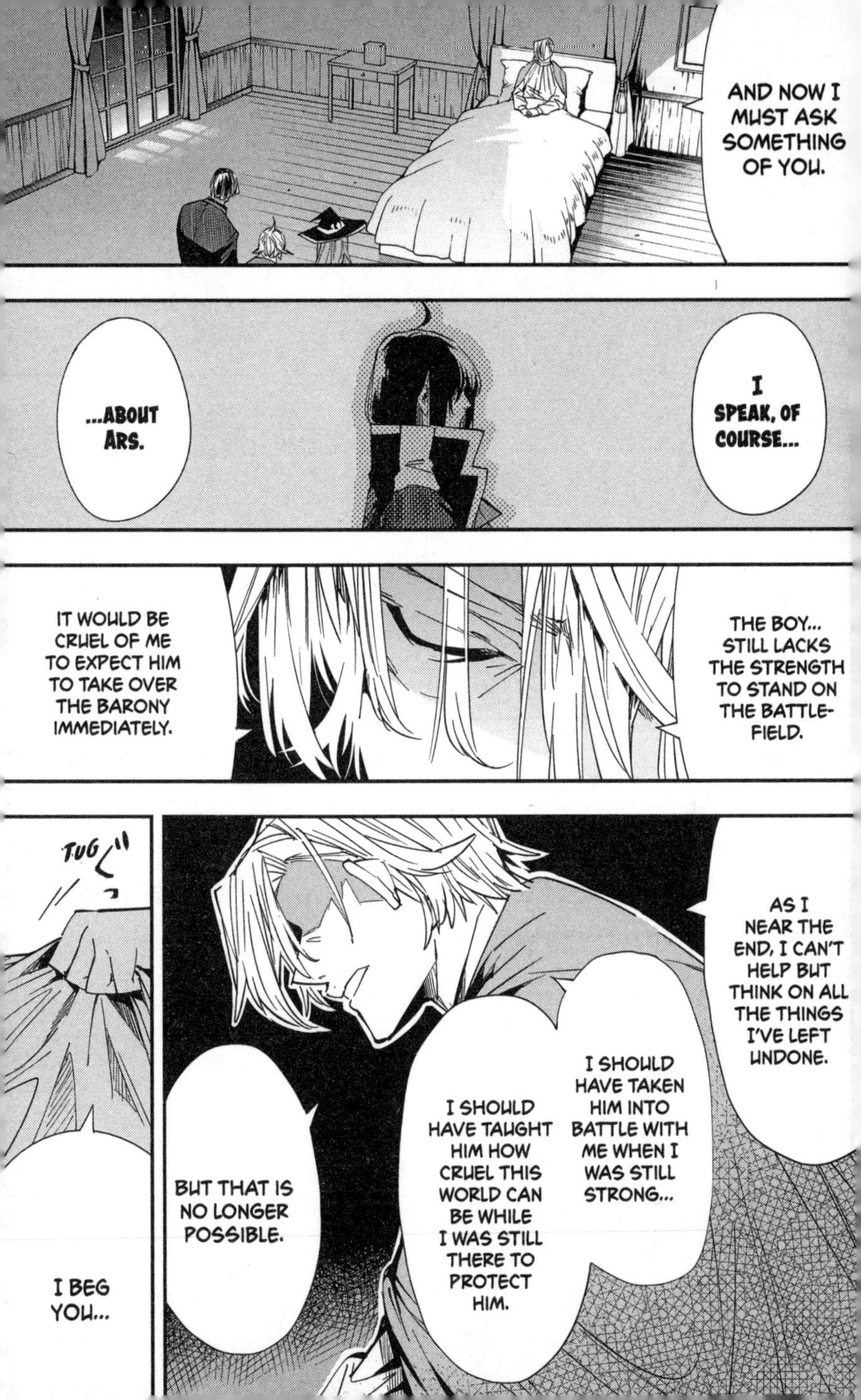
AND NOW I MUST ASK SOMETHING OF YOU.
I SPEAK, OF COURSE...
...ABOUT ARS.
THE BOY... STILL LACKS THE STRENGTH TO STAND ON THE BATTLE-FIELD.
IT WOULD BE CRUEL OF ME TO EXPECT HIM TO TAKE OVER THE BARONY IMMEDIATELY.
AS I NEAR THE END, I CAN'T HELP BUT THINK ON ALL THE THINGS I'VE LEFT UNDONE.
I SHOULD HAVE TAKEN HIM INTO BATTLE WITH ME WHEN I WAS STILL STRONG...
I SHOULD HAVE TAUGHT HIM HOW CRUEL THIS WORLD CAN BE WHILE I WAS STILL THERE TO PROTECT HIM.
BUT THAT IS NO LONGER POSSIBLE.
TUG
I BEG YOU...

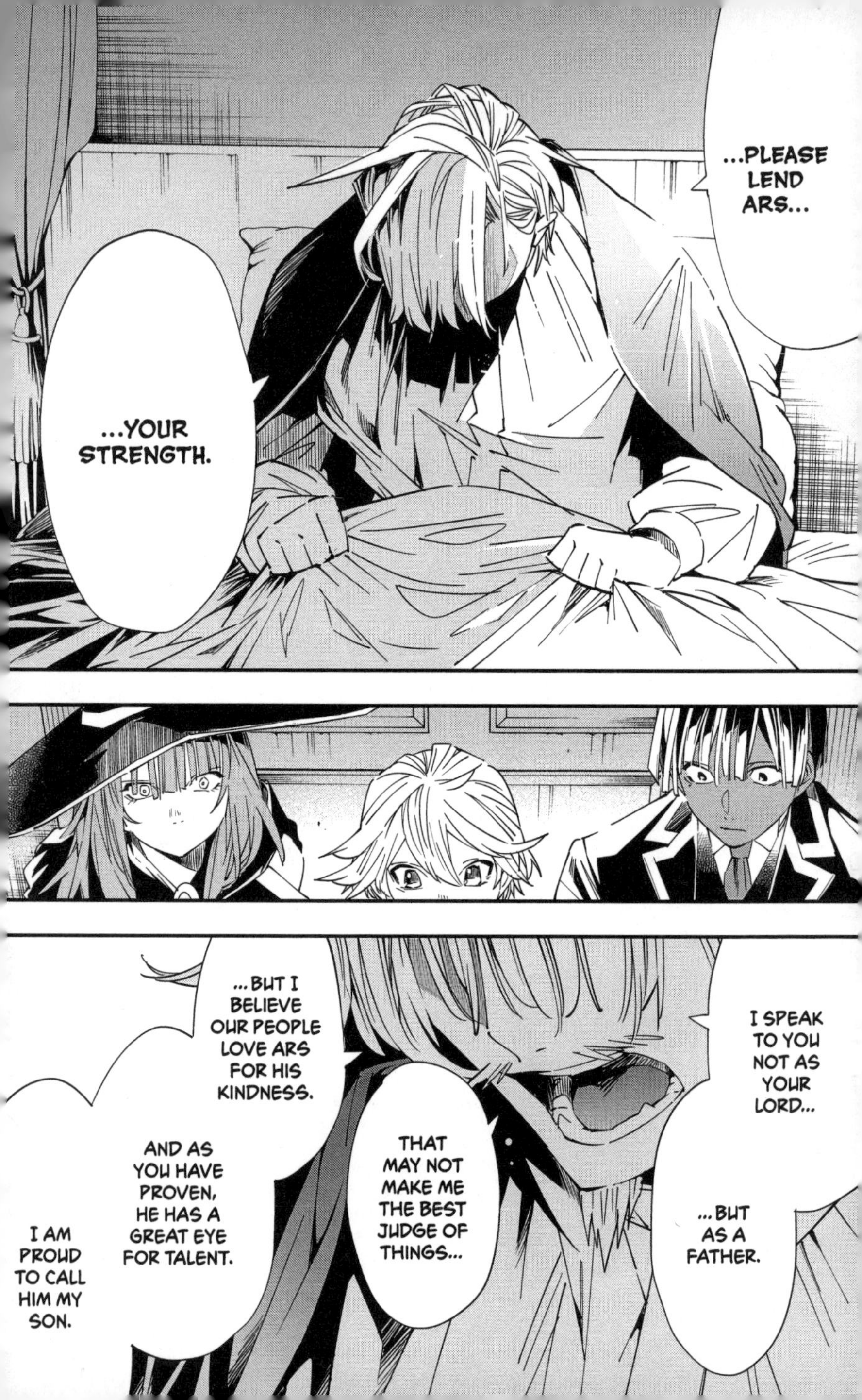
...PLEASE LEND ARS...
...YOUR STRENGTH.
I SPEAK TO YOU NOT AS YOUR LORD...
...BUT AS A FATHER.
THAT MAY NOT MAKE ME THE BEST JUDGE OF THINGS...
...BUT I BELIEVE OUR PEOPLE LOVE ARS FOR HIS KINDNESS.
AND AS YOU HAVE PROVEN, HE HAS A GREAT EYE FOR TALENT.
I AM PROUD TO CALL HIM MY SON.

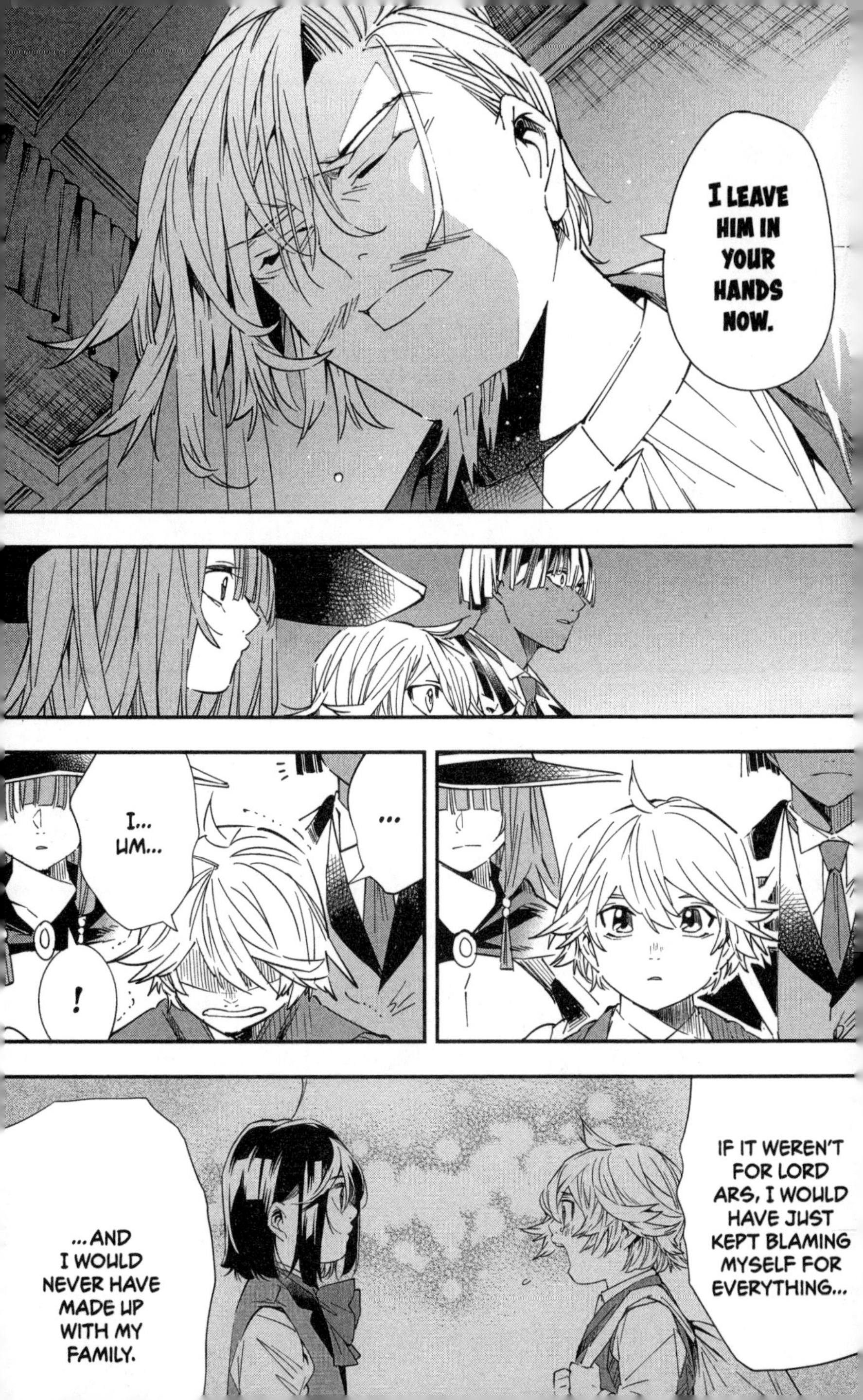
I LEAVE HIM IN YOUR HANDS NOW.
...
I... UM...
!
IF IT WEREN'T FOR LORD ARS, I WOULD HAVE JUST KEPT BLAMING MYSELF FOR EVERYTHING...
...AND I WOULD NEVER HAVE MADE UP WITH MY FAMILY.

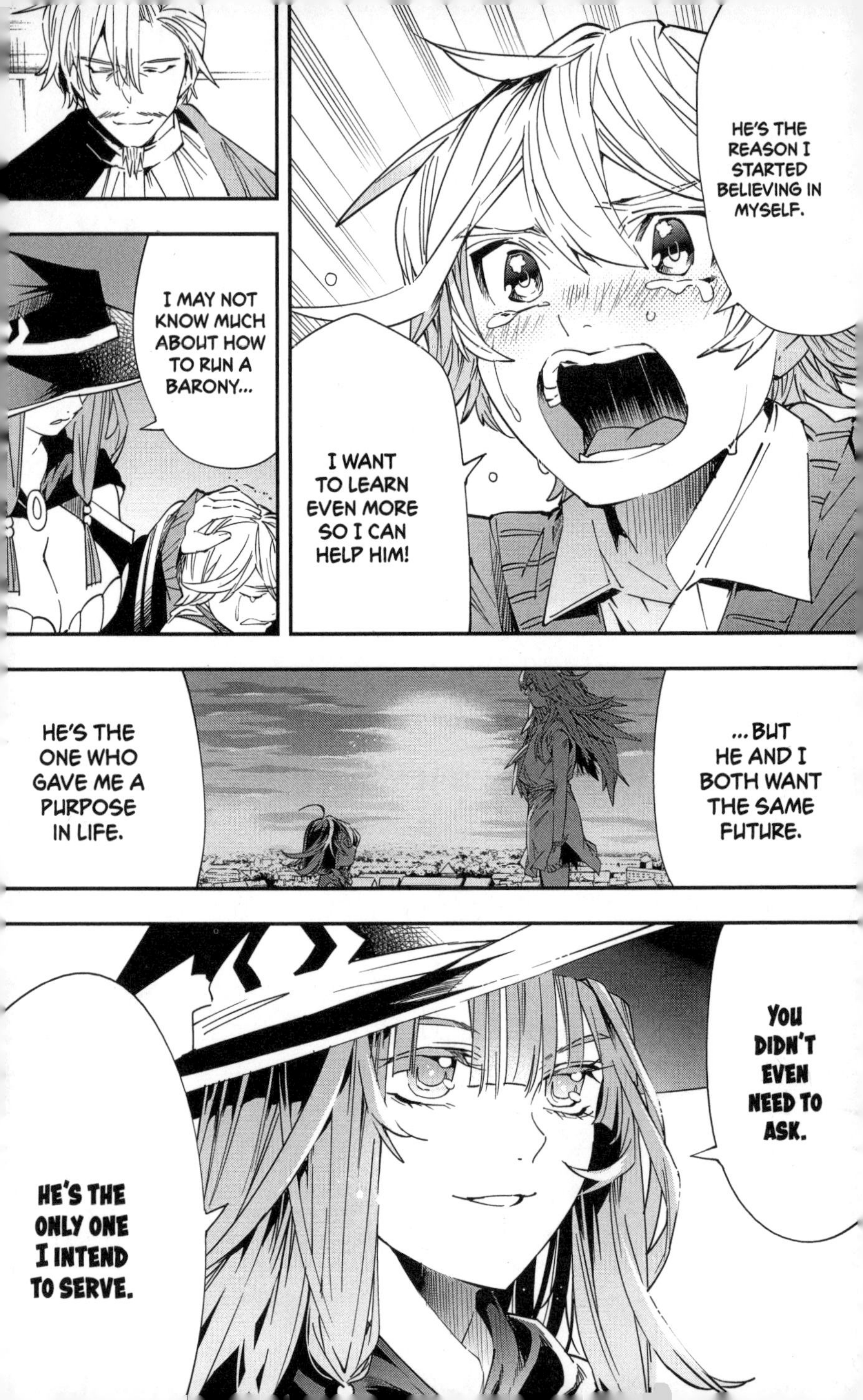
HE'S THE REASON I STARTED BELIEVING IN MYSELF.
I WANT TO LEARN EVEN MORE SO I CAN HELP HIM!
I MAY NOT KNOW MUCH ABOUT HOW TO RUN A BARONY...
...BUT HE AND I BOTH WANT THE SAME FUTURE.
HE'S THE ONE WHO GAVE ME A PURPOSE IN LIFE.
YOU DIDN'T EVEN NEED TO ASK.
HE'S THE ONLY ONE I INTEND TO SERVE.

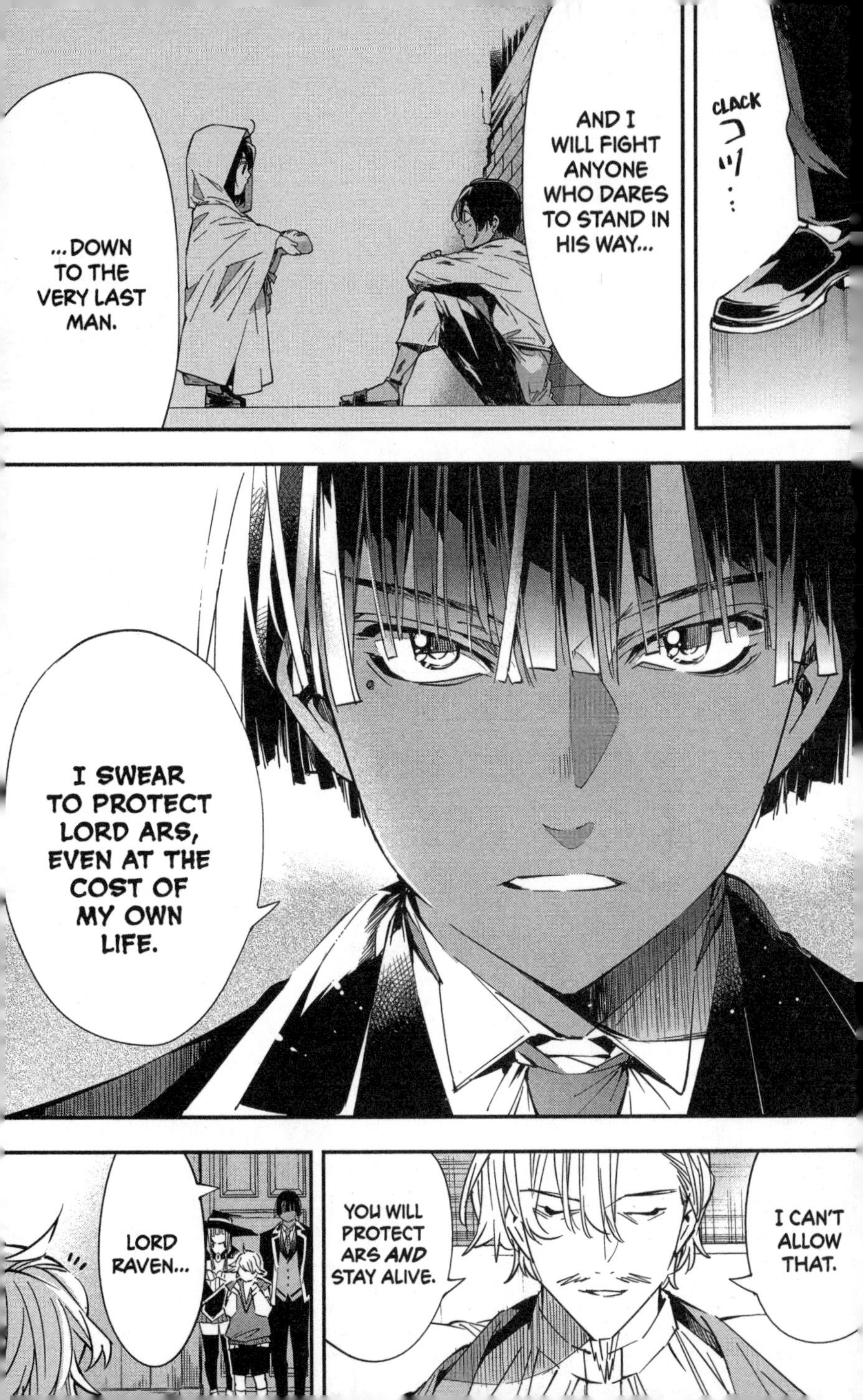
CLACK
コツ…
AND I WILL FIGHT ANYONE WHO DARES TO STAND IN HIS WAY...
...DOWN TO THE VERY LAST MAN.
I SWEAR TO PROTECT LORD ARS, EVEN AT THE COST OF MY OWN LIFE.
I CAN'T ALLOW THAT.
YOU WILL PROTECT ARS *AND* STAY ALIVE.
LORD RAVEN...

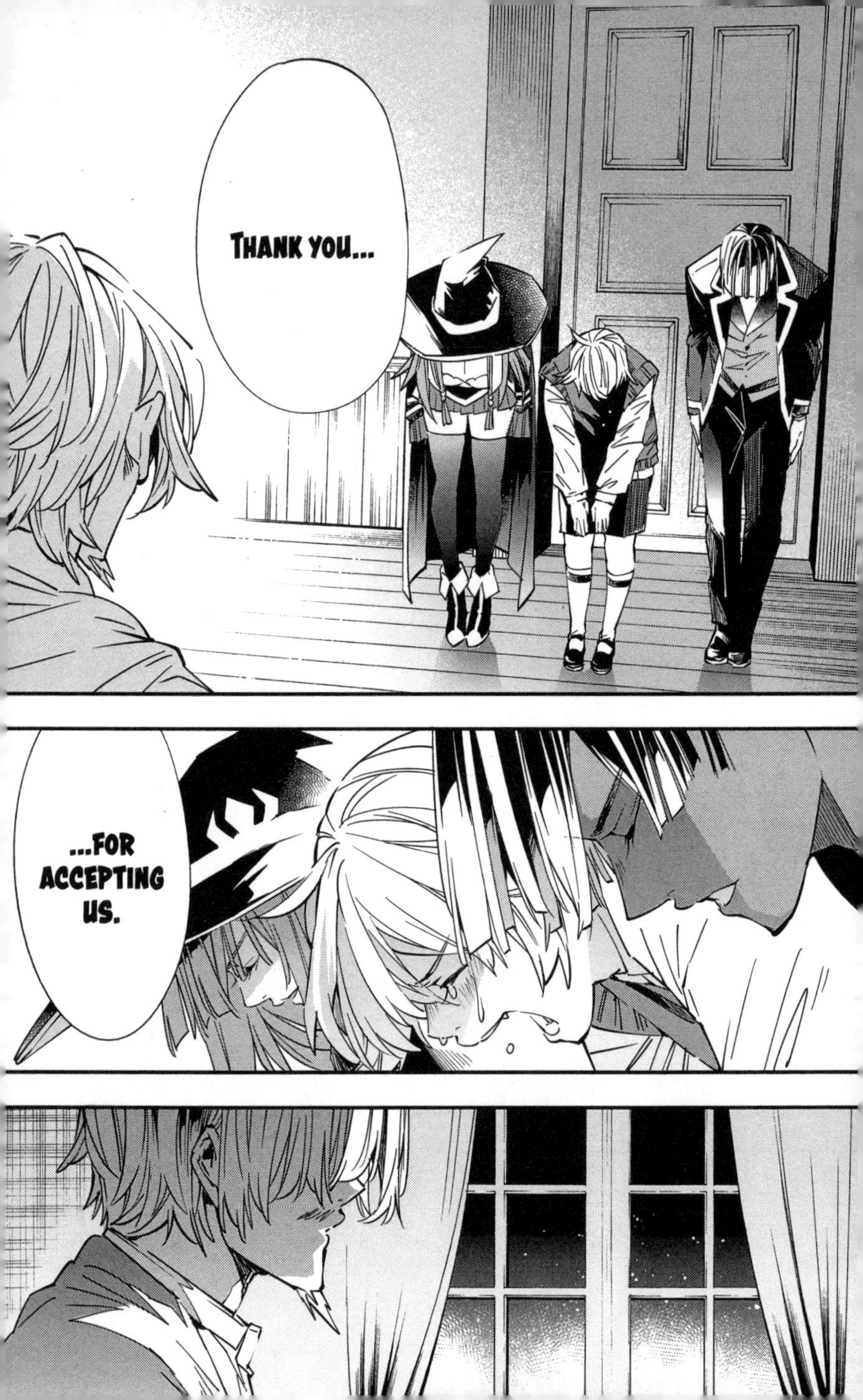
THANK YOU...
...FOR ACCEPTING US.

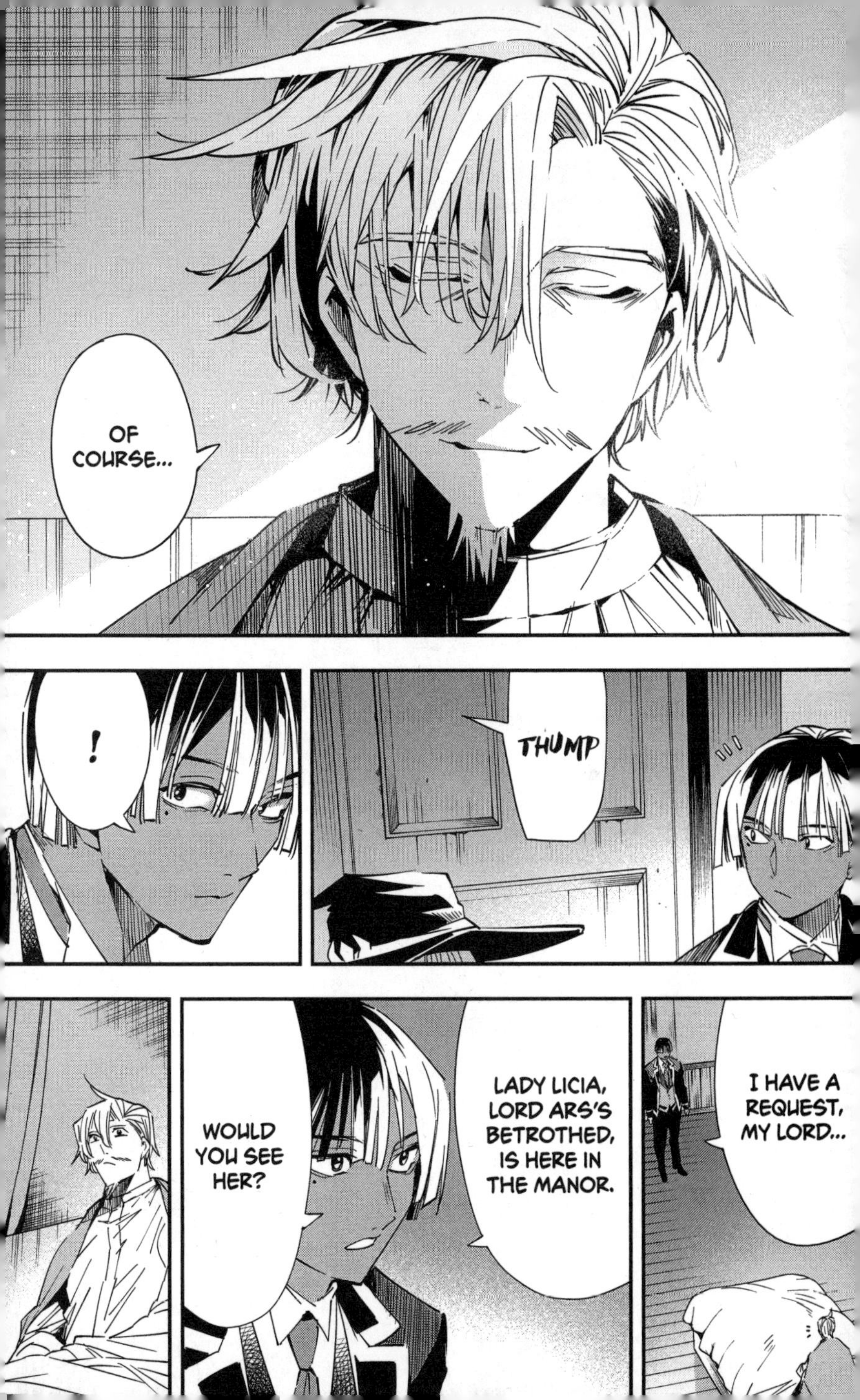
OF COURSE...
THUMP
!
I HAVE A REQUEST, MY LORD...
LADY LICIA, LORD ARS'S BETROTHED, IS HERE IN THE MANOR.
WOULD YOU SEE HER?

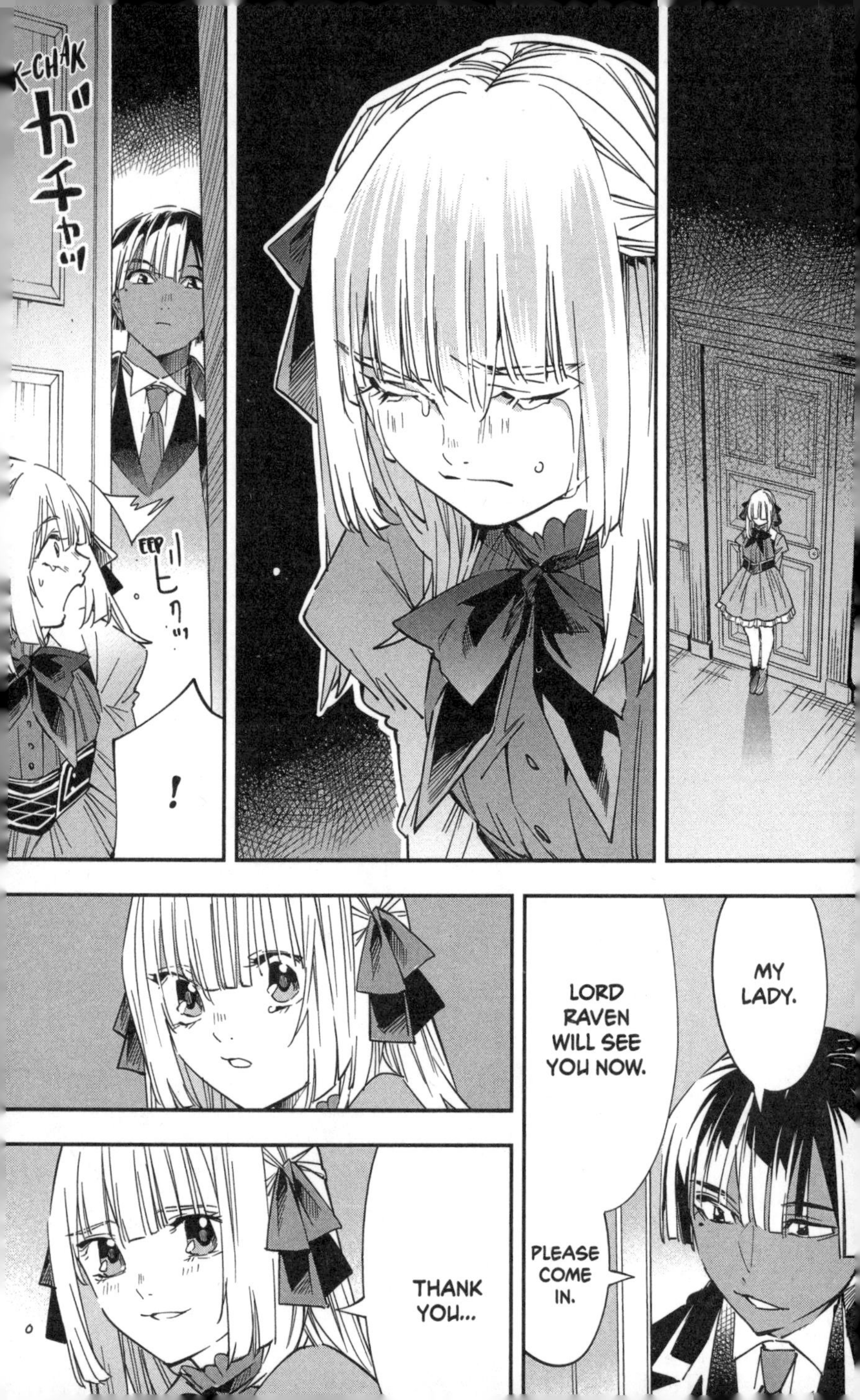
K-CHAK
ガチャッ
EEP
ビクッ
!
MY LADY.
LORD RAVEN WILL SEE YOU NOW.
PLEASE COME IN.
THANK YOU...

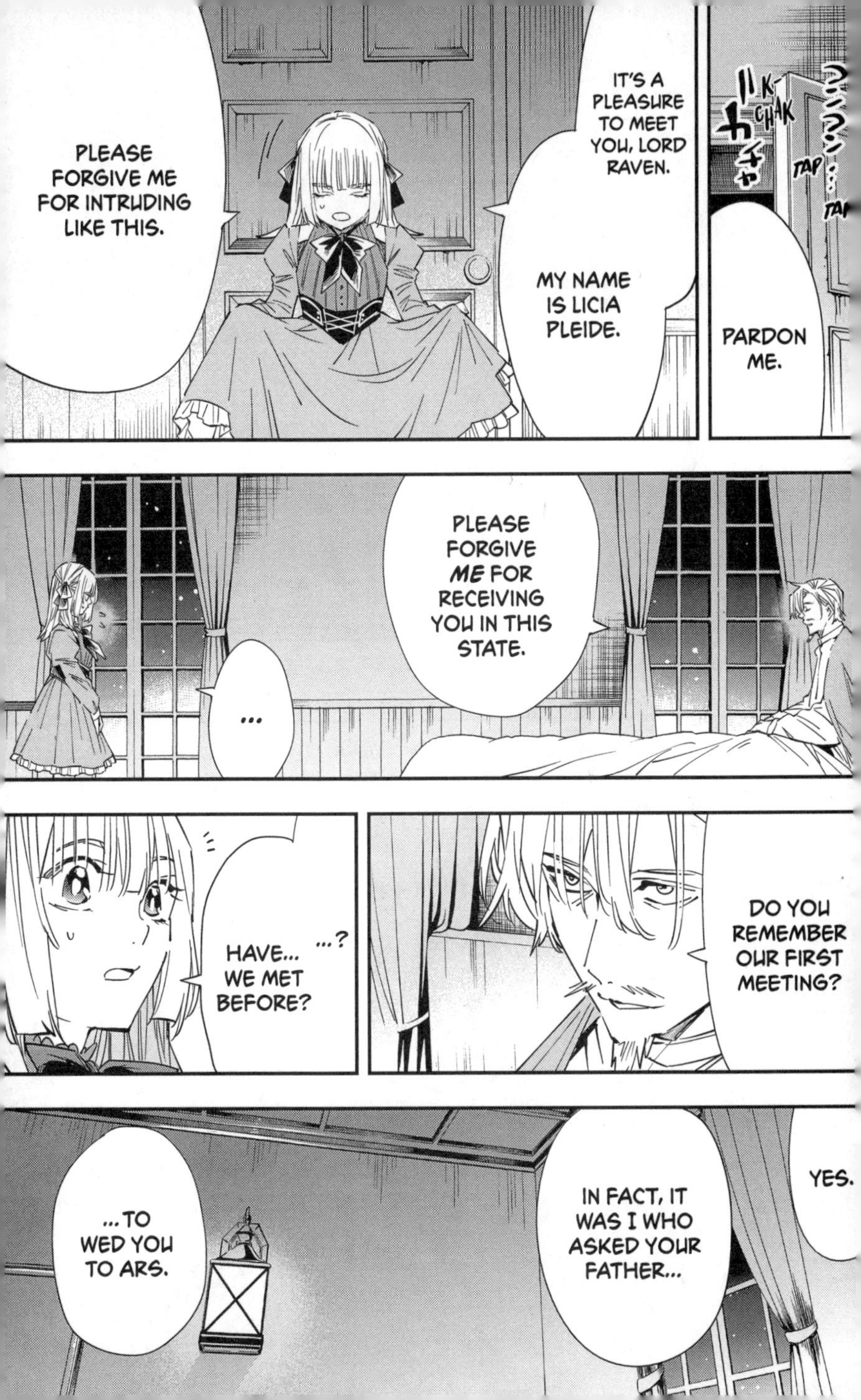
K-CHAK
TAP
PARDON ME.
IT'S A PLEASURE TO MEET YOU, LORD RAVEN.
MY NAME IS LICIA PLEIDE.
PLEASE FORGIVE ME FOR INTRUDING LIKE THIS.
PLEASE FORGIVE *ME* FOR RECEIVING YOU IN THIS STATE.
...
DO YOU REMEMBER OUR FIRST MEETING?
...?
HAVE... WE MET BEFORE?
YES.
IN FACT, IT WAS I WHO ASKED YOUR FATHER...
...TO WED YOU TO ARS.

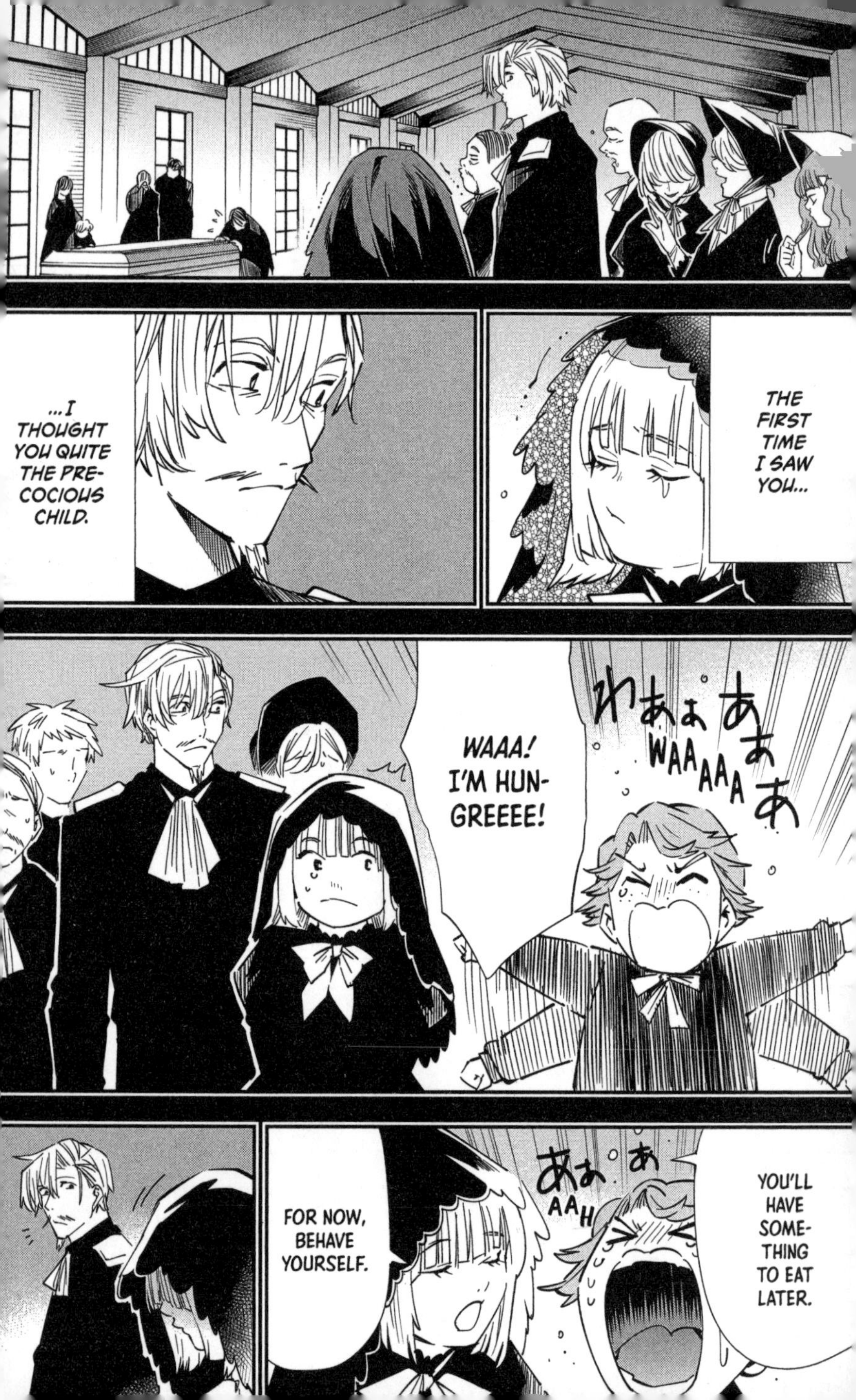
THE FIRST TIME I SAW YOU...
...I THOUGHT YOU QUITE THE PRE-COCIOUS CHILD.
わあぁあぁあ
WAAAAAA
WAAA! I'M HUN-GREEEE!
YOU'LL HAVE SOME-THING TO EAT LATER.
あぁあ
AAH
FOR NOW, BEHAVE YOURSELF.

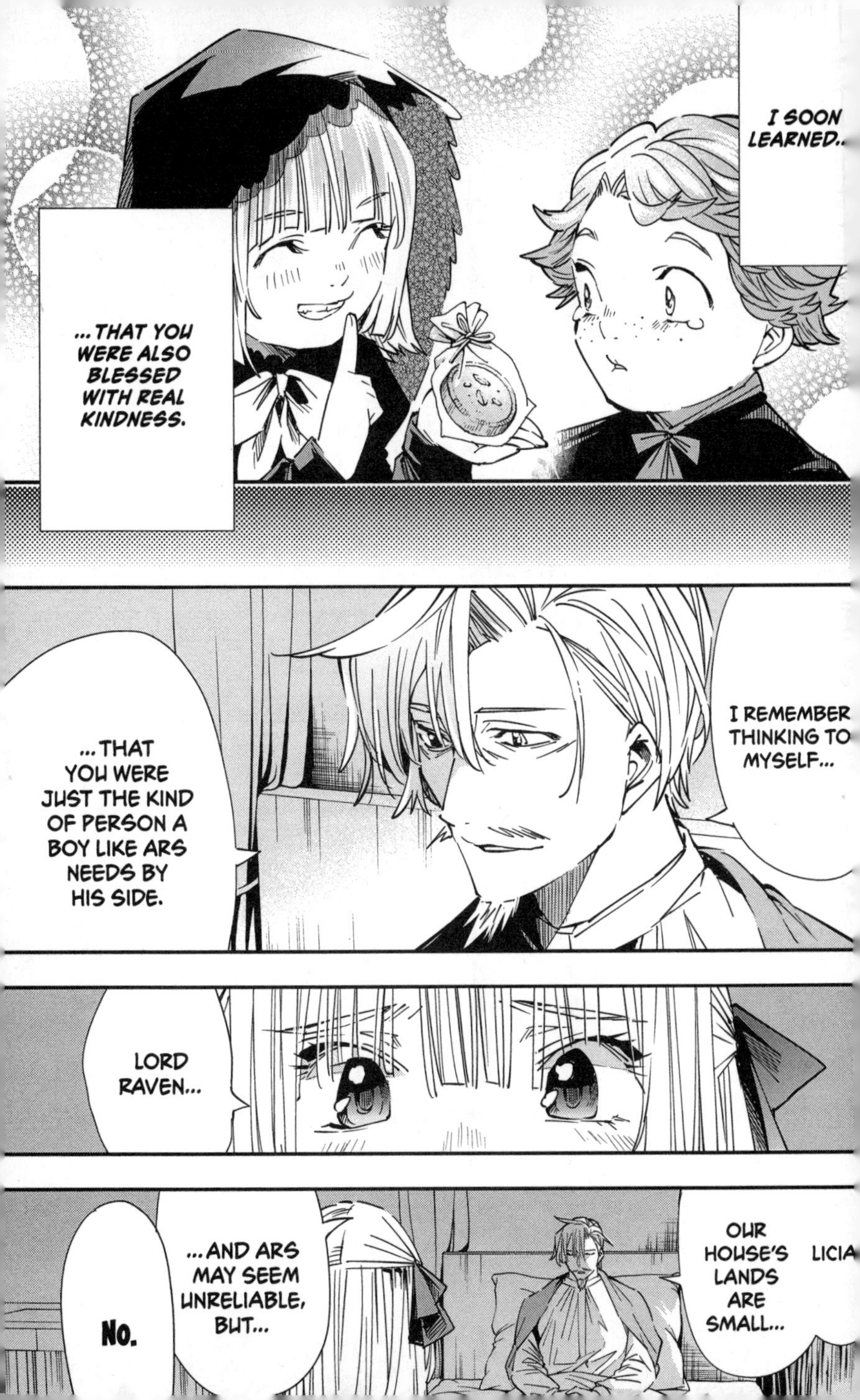
I SOON LEARNED...
...THAT YOU WERE ALSO BLESSED WITH REAL KINDNESS.
I REMEMBER THINKING TO MYSELF...
...THAT YOU WERE JUST THE KIND OF PERSON A BOY LIKE ARS NEEDS BY HIS SIDE.
LORD RAVEN...
LICIA
OUR HOUSE'S LANDS ARE SMALL...
...AND ARS MAY SEEM UNRELIABLE, BUT...
No.

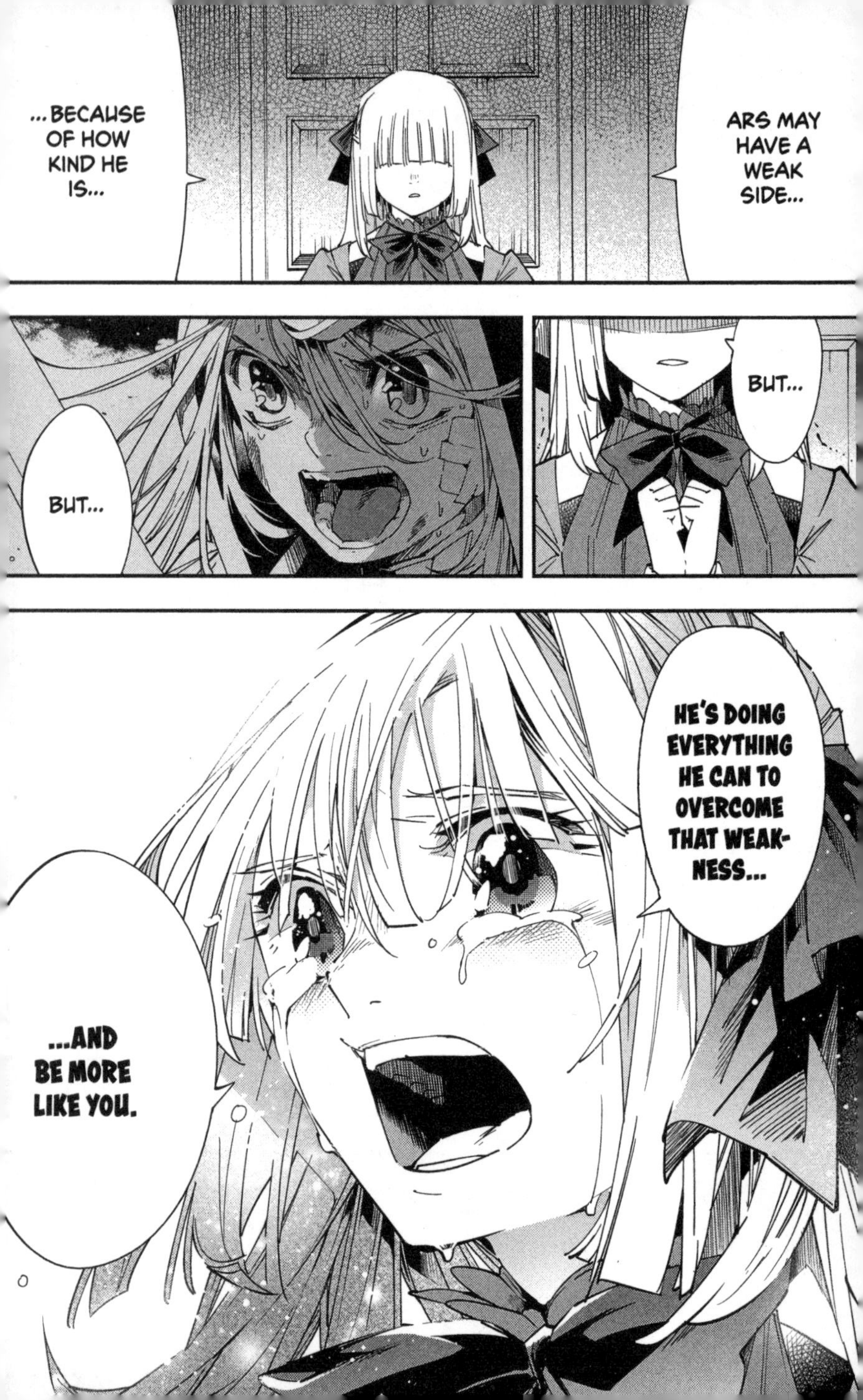
ARS MAY HAVE A WEAK SIDE...
...BECAUSE OF HOW KIND HE IS...
BUT...
BUT...
HE'S DOING EVERYTHING HE CAN TO OVERCOME THAT WEAK-NESS...
...AND BE MORE LIKE YOU.

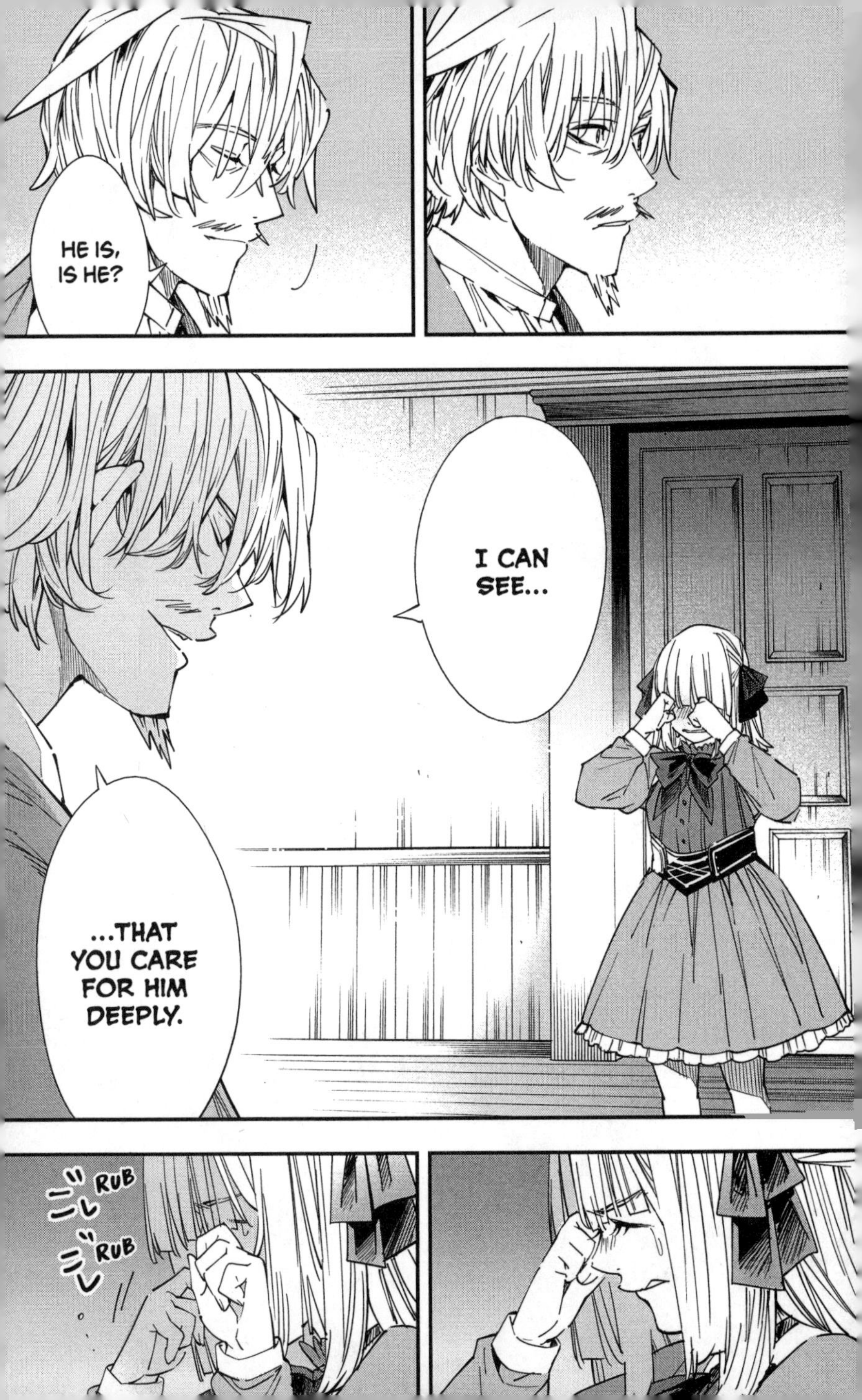
HE IS, IS HE?
I CAN SEE...
...THAT YOU CARE FOR HIM DEEPLY.
RUB
RUB

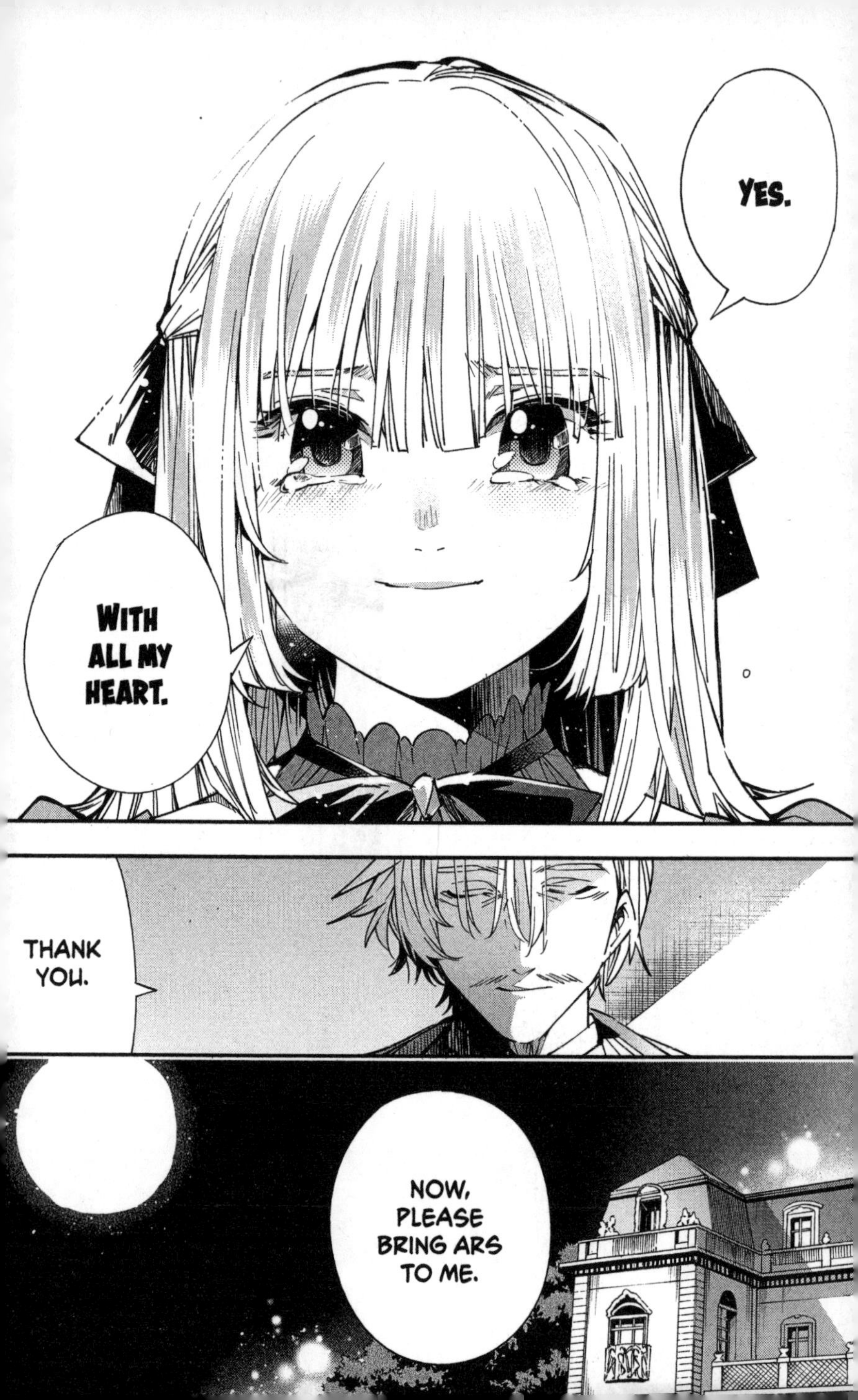
YES.
WITH ALL MY HEART.
THANK YOU.
NOW, PLEASE BRING ARS TO ME.

As a Reincarnated
ARISTOCRAT,
I'll Use My Appraisal Skill to
Rise in the World

As a Reincarnated ARISTOCRAT, I'll Use My Appraisal Skill to Rise in the World

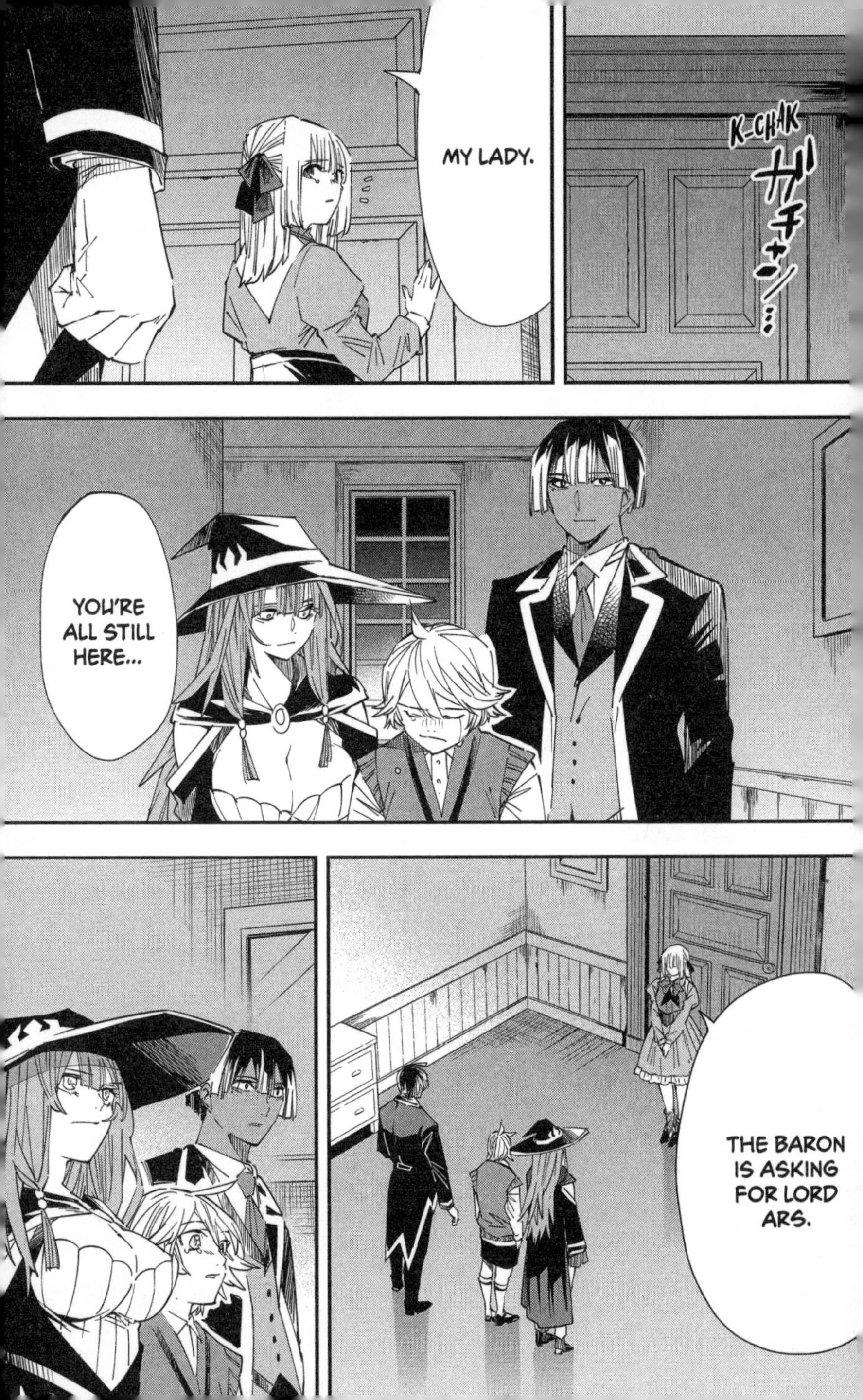
K-CHAK
ガチャン…
MY LADY.
YOU'RE ALL STILL HERE...
THE BARON IS ASKING FOR LORD ARS.

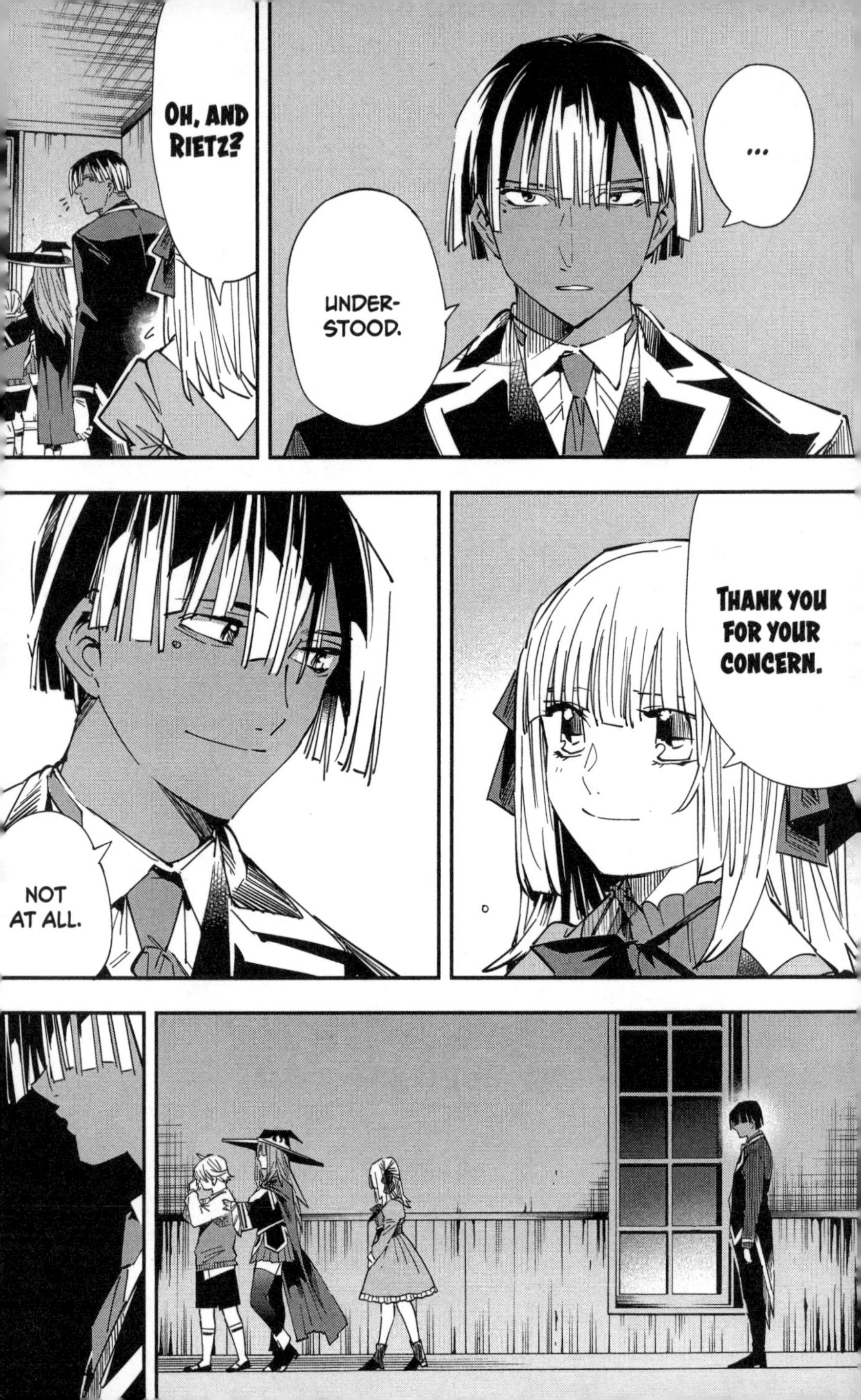
...
UNDER-STOOD.
OH, AND RIETZ?
THANK YOU FOR YOUR CONCERN.
NOT AT ALL.

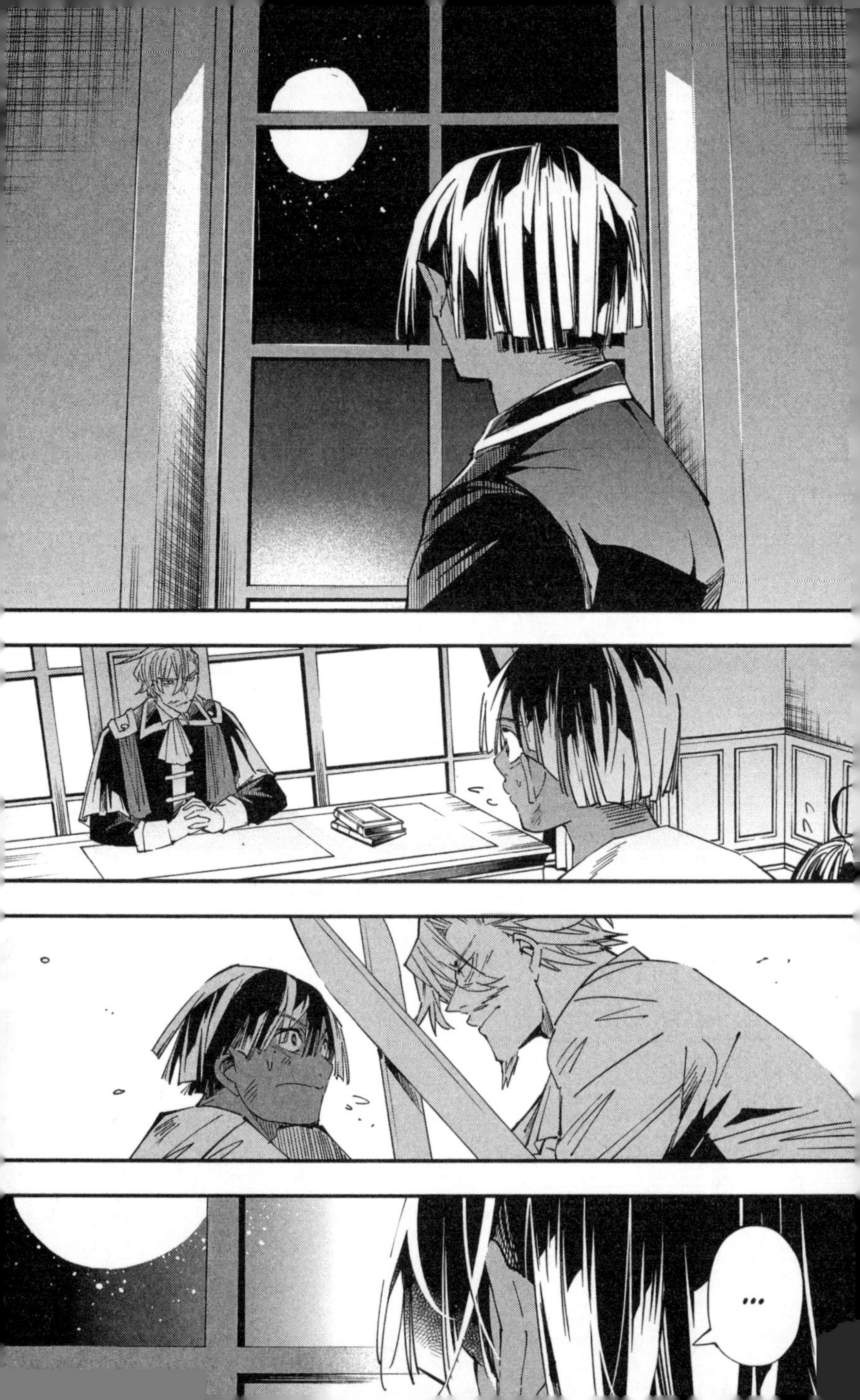
...

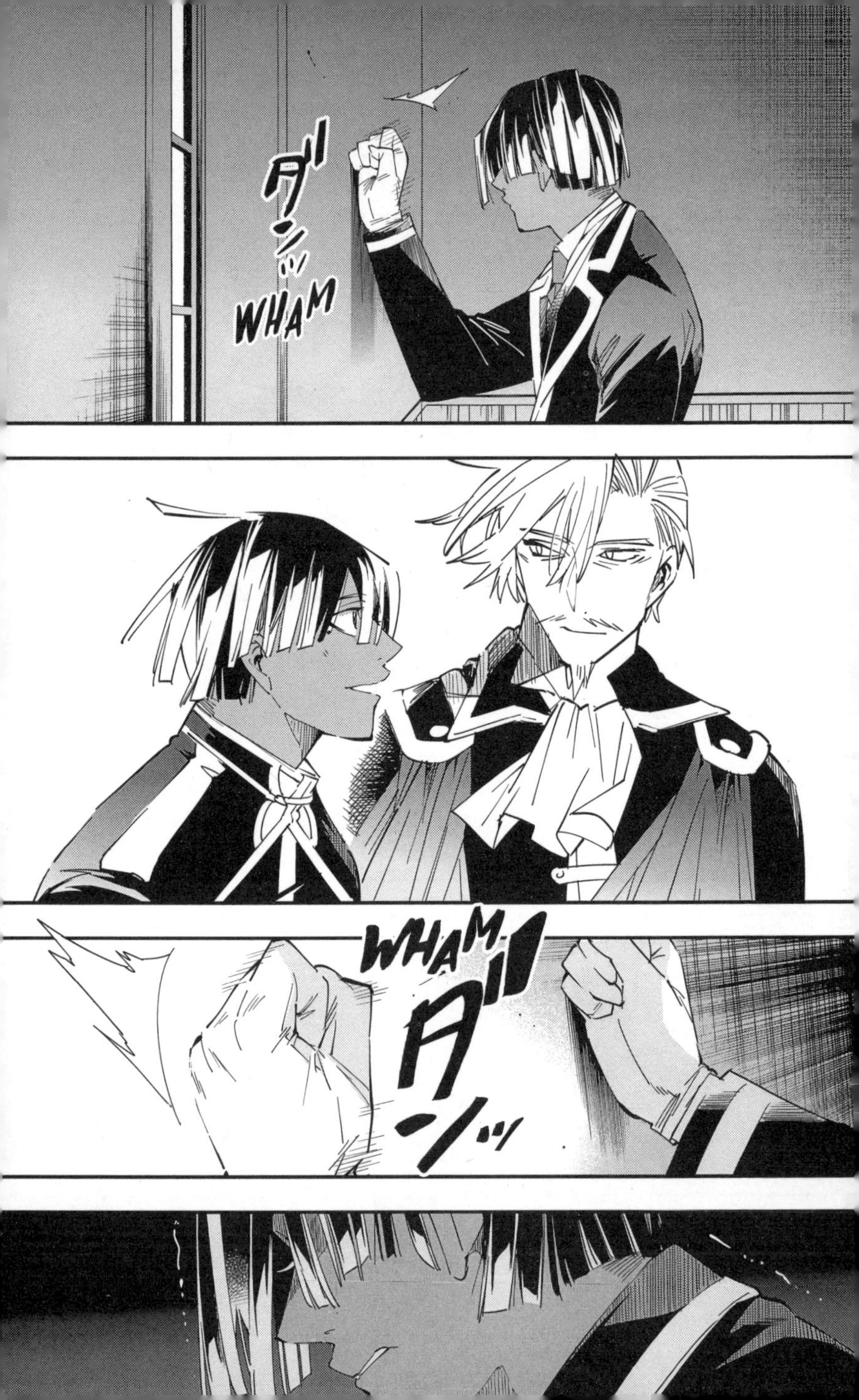
ダンッ
WHAM
WHAM
ダンッ

Chapter 30: One Last Talk

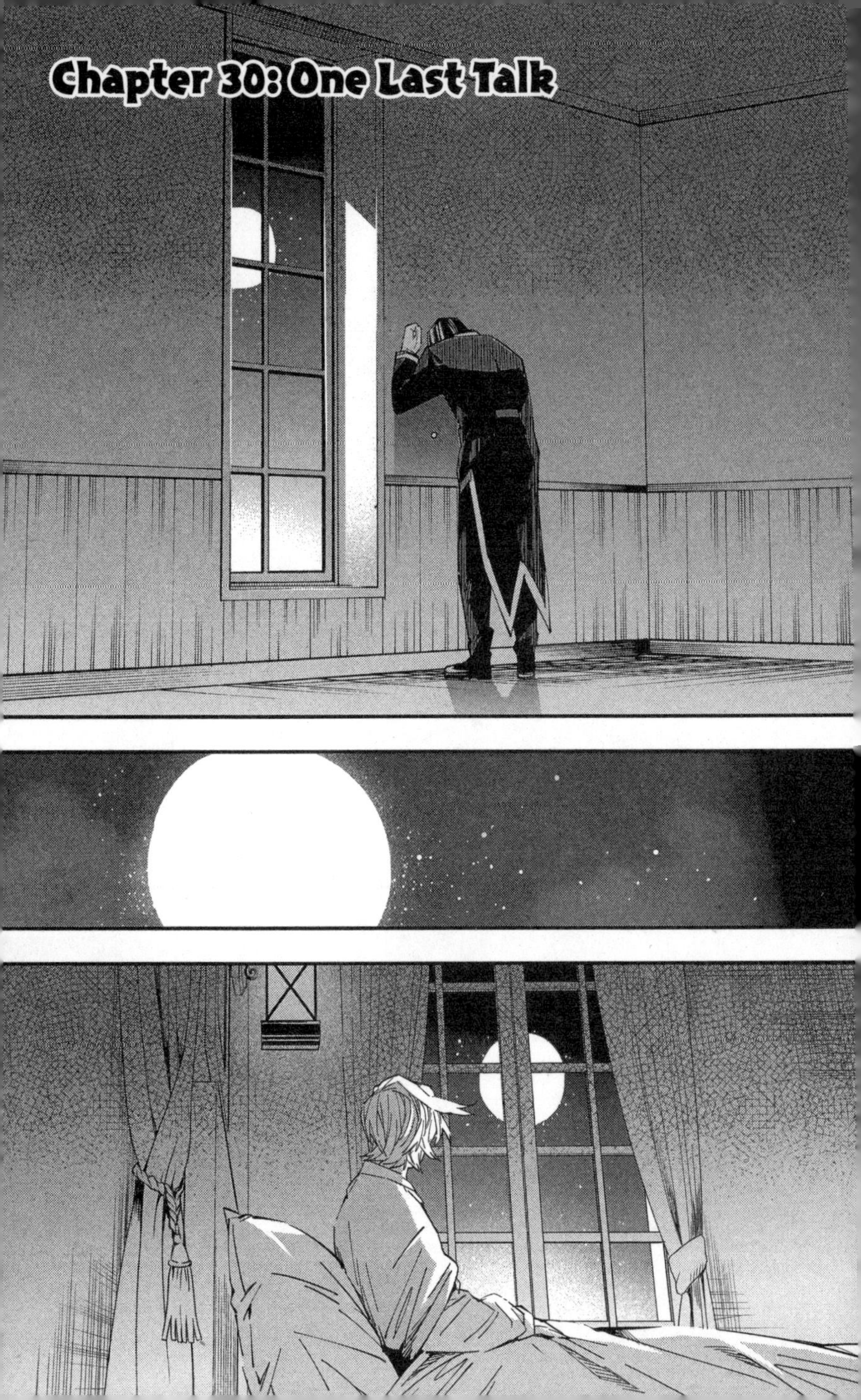

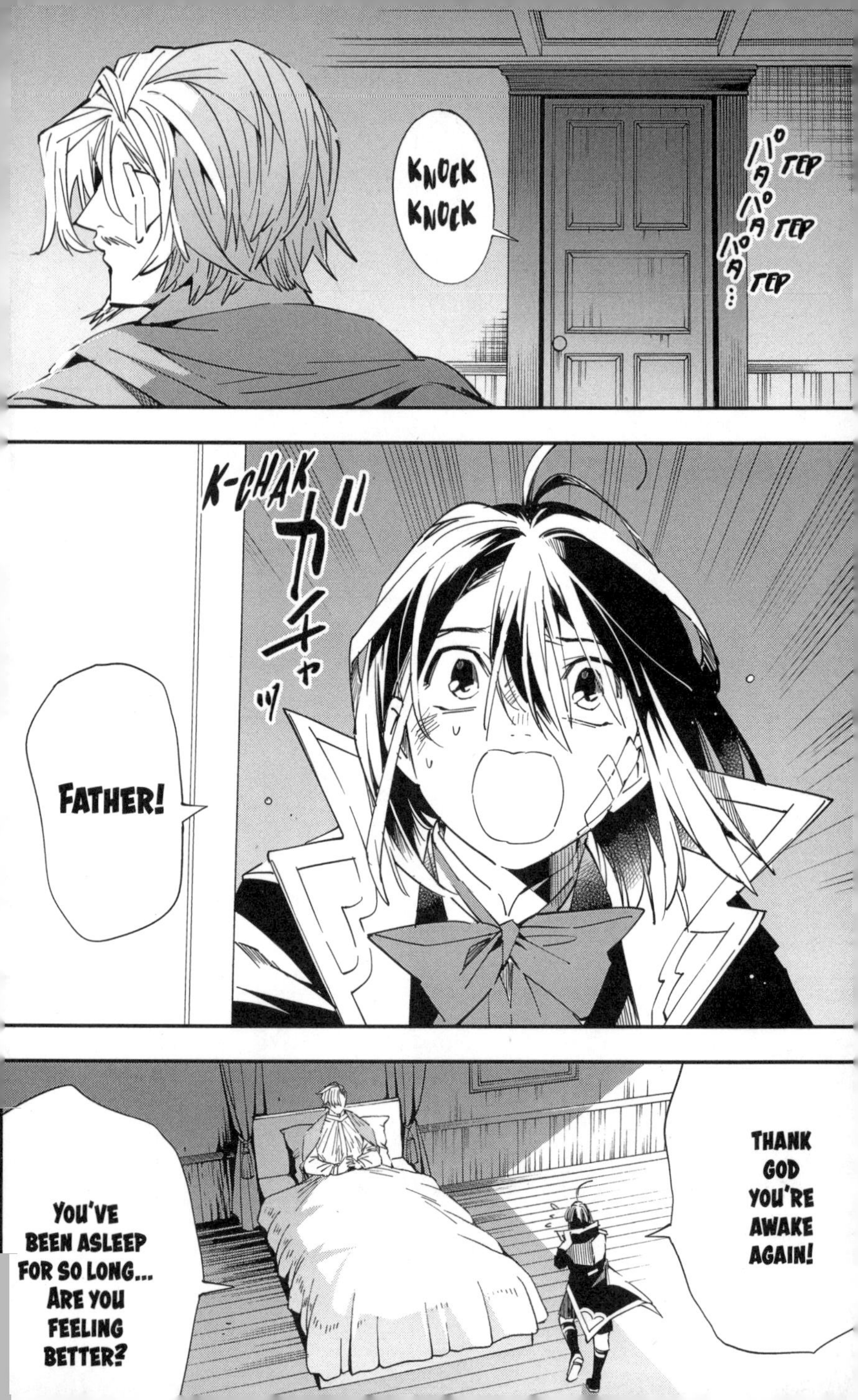

パタパタパタ…
TEP TEP TEP
KNOCK KNOCK
ガチャッ
K-CHAK
FATHER!
THANK GOD YOU'RE AWAKE AGAIN!
YOU'VE BEEN ASLEEP FOR SO LONG... ARE YOU FEELING BETTER?

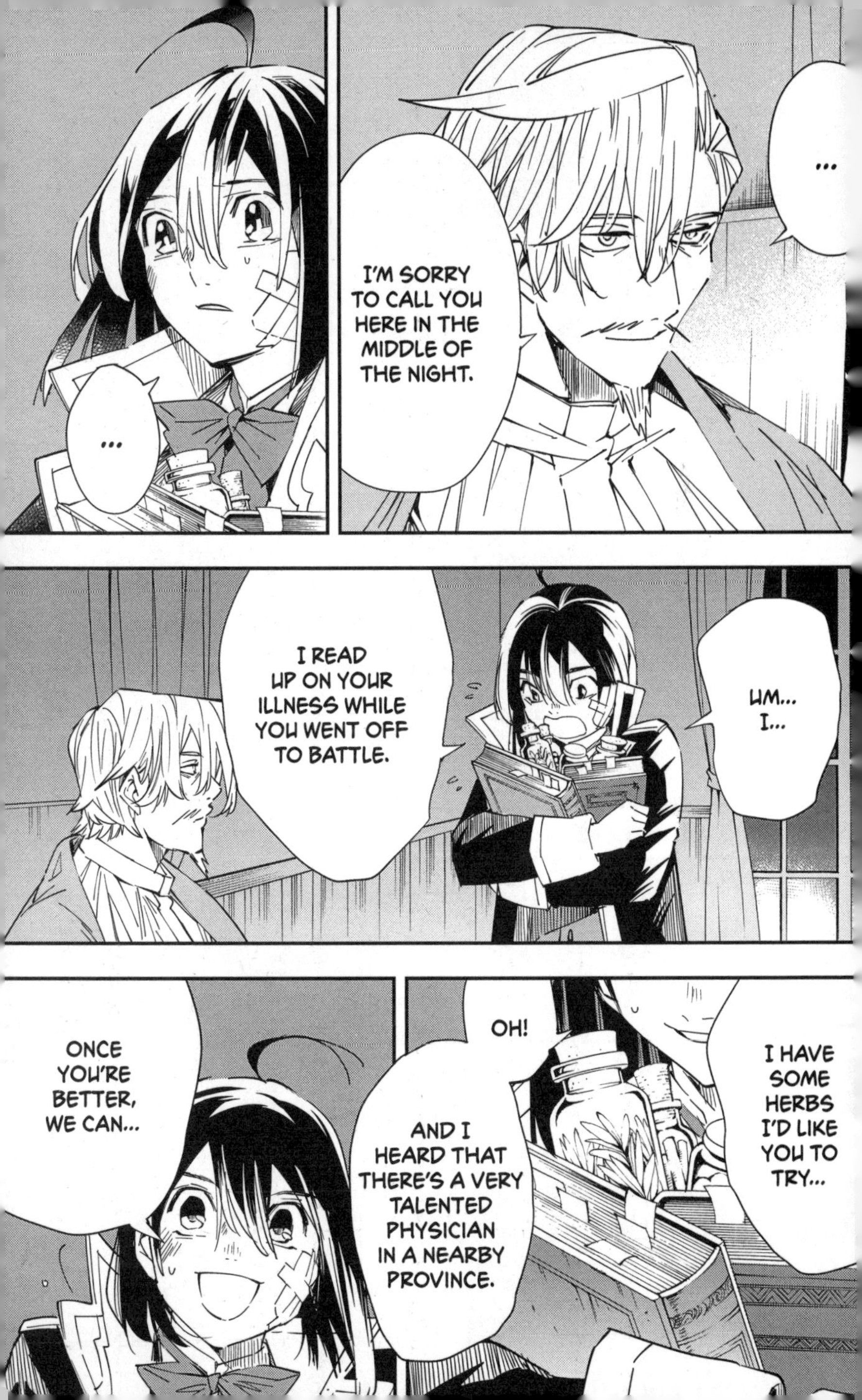
...
I'M SORRY TO CALL YOU HERE IN THE MIDDLE OF THE NIGHT.
...
UM... I...
I READ UP ON YOUR ILLNESS WHILE YOU WENT OFF TO BATTLE.
I HAVE SOME HERBS I'D LIKE YOU TO TRY...
OH!
AND I HEARD THAT THERE'S A VERY TALENTED PHYSICIAN IN A NEARBY PROVINCE.
ONCE YOU'RE BETTER, WE CAN...

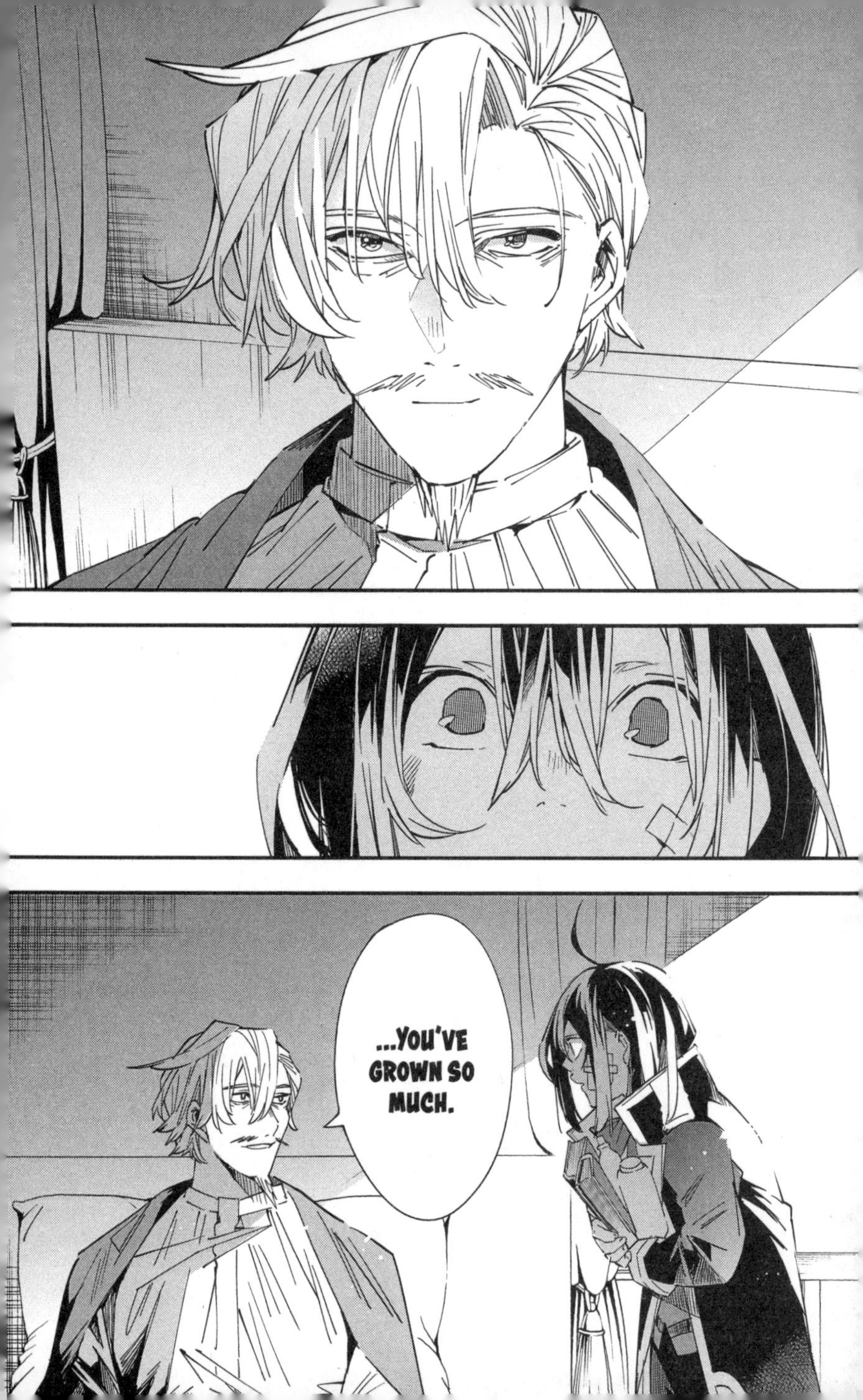
...YOU'VE GROWN SO MUCH.

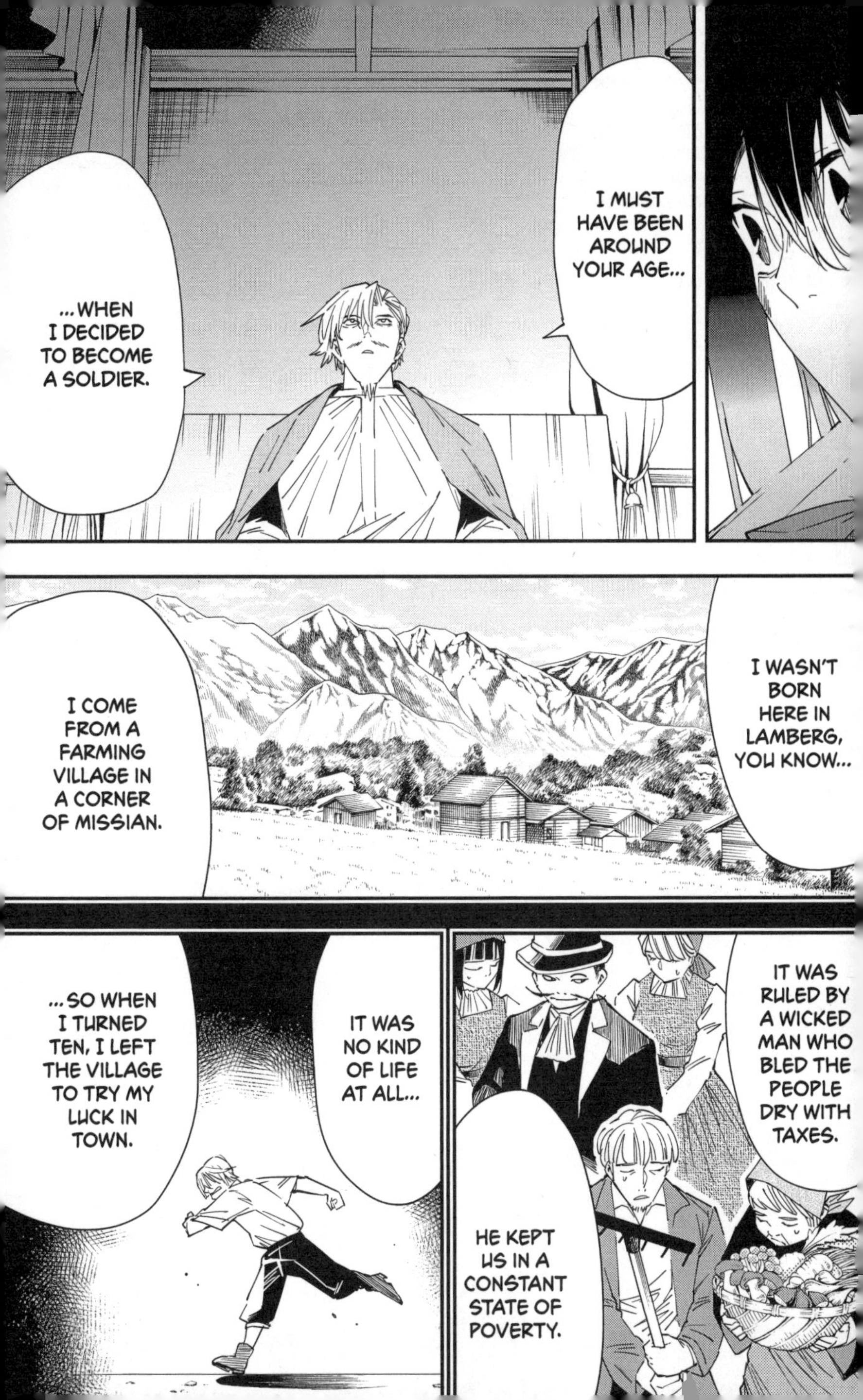
I MUST HAVE BEEN AROUND YOUR AGE...
...WHEN I DECIDED TO BECOME A SOLDIER.
I WASN'T BORN HERE IN LAMBERG, YOU KNOW...
I COME FROM A FARMING VILLAGE IN A CORNER OF MISSIAN.
IT WAS RULED BY A WICKED MAN WHO BLED THE PEOPLE DRY WITH TAXES.
HE KEPT US IN A CONSTANT STATE OF POVERTY.
IT WAS NO KIND OF LIFE AT ALL...
...SO WHEN I TURNED TEN, I LEFT THE VILLAGE TO TRY MY LUCK IN TOWN.

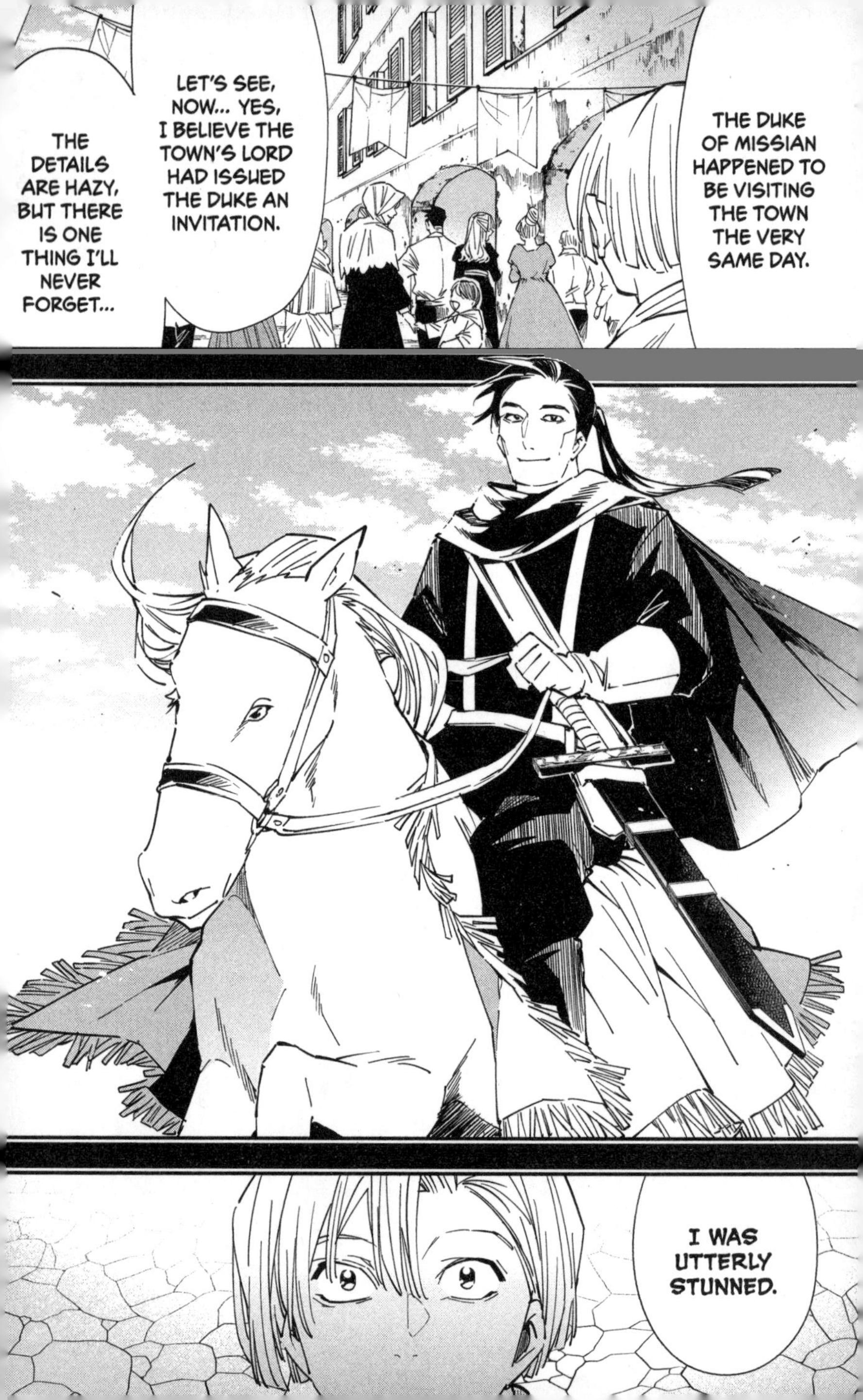
THE DUKE OF MISSIAN HAPPENED TO BE VISITING THE TOWN THE VERY SAME DAY.
LET'S SEE, NOW... YES, I BELIEVE THE TOWN'S LORD HAD ISSUED THE DUKE AN INVITATION.
THE DETAILS ARE HAZY, BUT THERE IS ONE THING I'LL NEVER FORGET...
I WAS UTTERLY STUNNED.

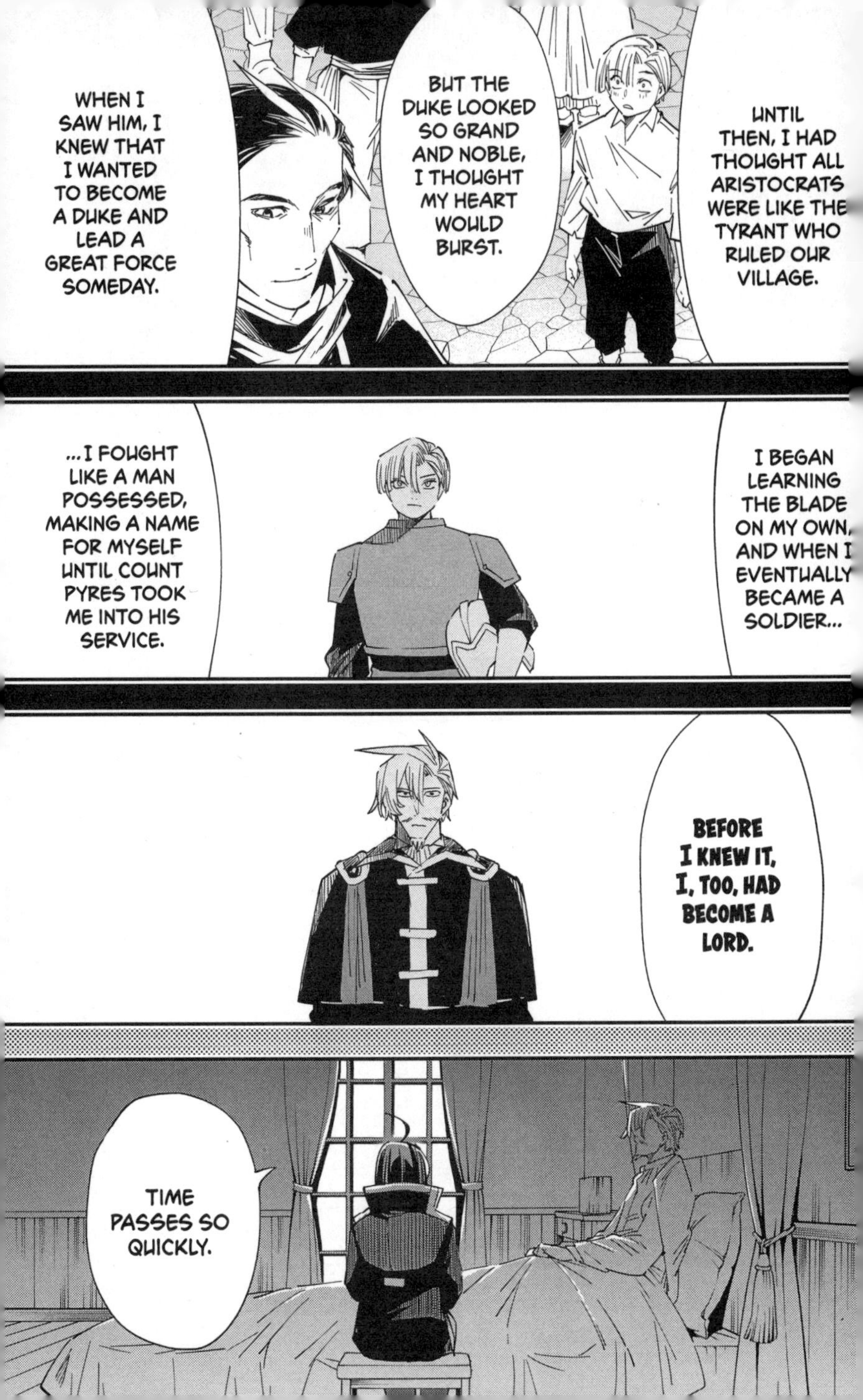
UNTIL THEN, I HAD THOUGHT ALL ARISTOCRATS WERE LIKE THE TYRANT WHO RULED OUR VILLAGE.
BUT THE DUKE LOOKED SO GRAND AND NOBLE, I THOUGHT MY HEART WOULD BURST.
WHEN I SAW HIM, I KNEW THAT I WANTED TO BECOME A DUKE AND LEAD A GREAT FORCE SOMEDAY.
I BEGAN LEARNING THE BLADE ON MY OWN, AND WHEN I EVENTUALLY BECAME A SOLDIER...
...I FOUGHT LIKE A MAN POSSESSED, MAKING A NAME FOR MYSELF UNTIL COUNT PYRES TOOK ME INTO HIS SERVICE.
BEFORE I KNEW IT, I, TOO, HAD BECOME A LORD.
TIME PASSES SO QUICKLY.

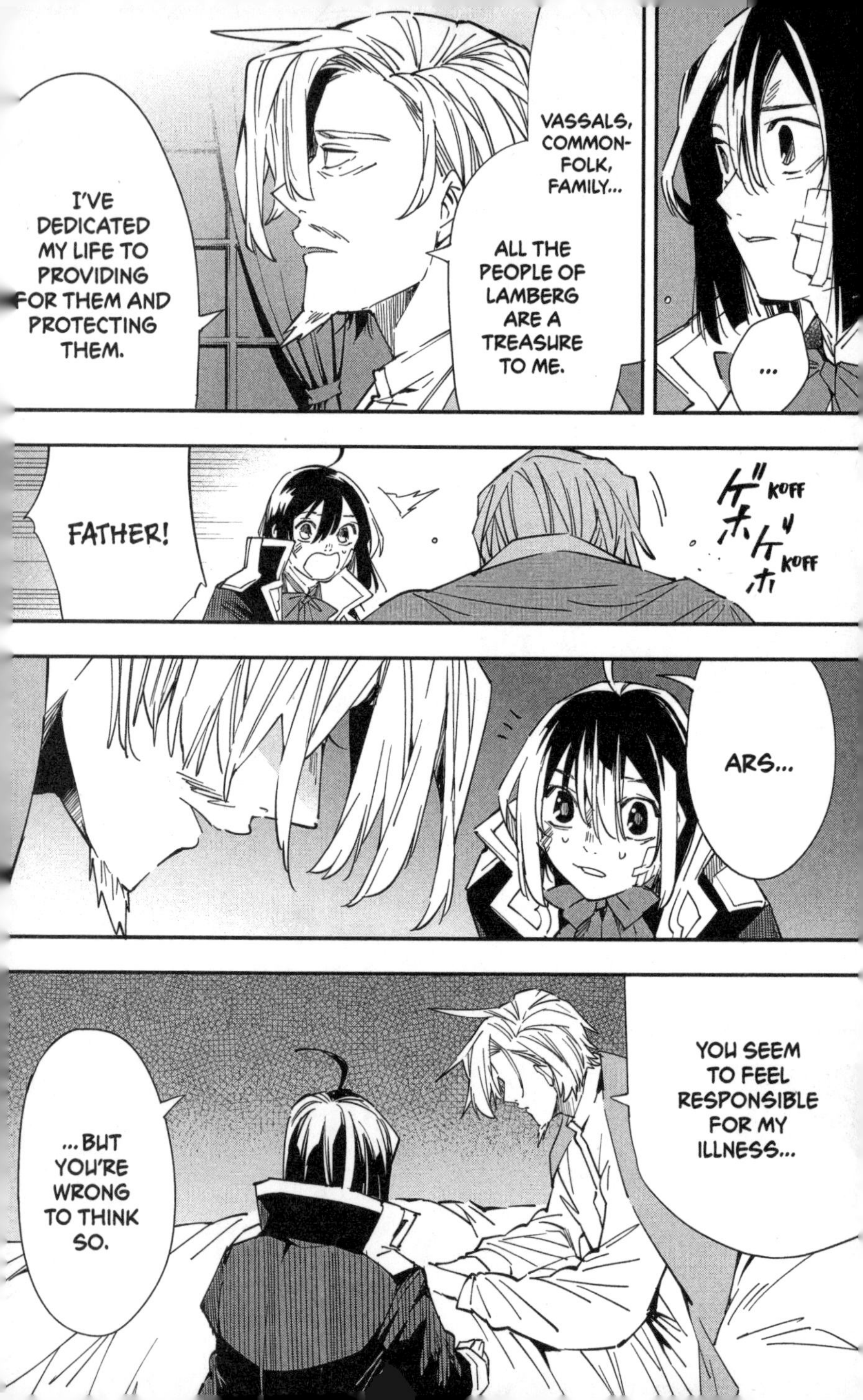
...
VASSALS, COMMON-FOLK, FAMILY...
ALL THE PEOPLE OF LAMBERG ARE A TREASURE TO ME.
I'VE DEDICATED MY LIFE TO PROVIDING FOR THEM AND PROTECTING THEM.
ゲホ KOFF
ゲホ KOFF
FATHER!
ARS...
YOU SEEM TO FEEL RESPONSIBLE FOR MY ILLNESS...
...BUT YOU'RE WRONG TO THINK SO.

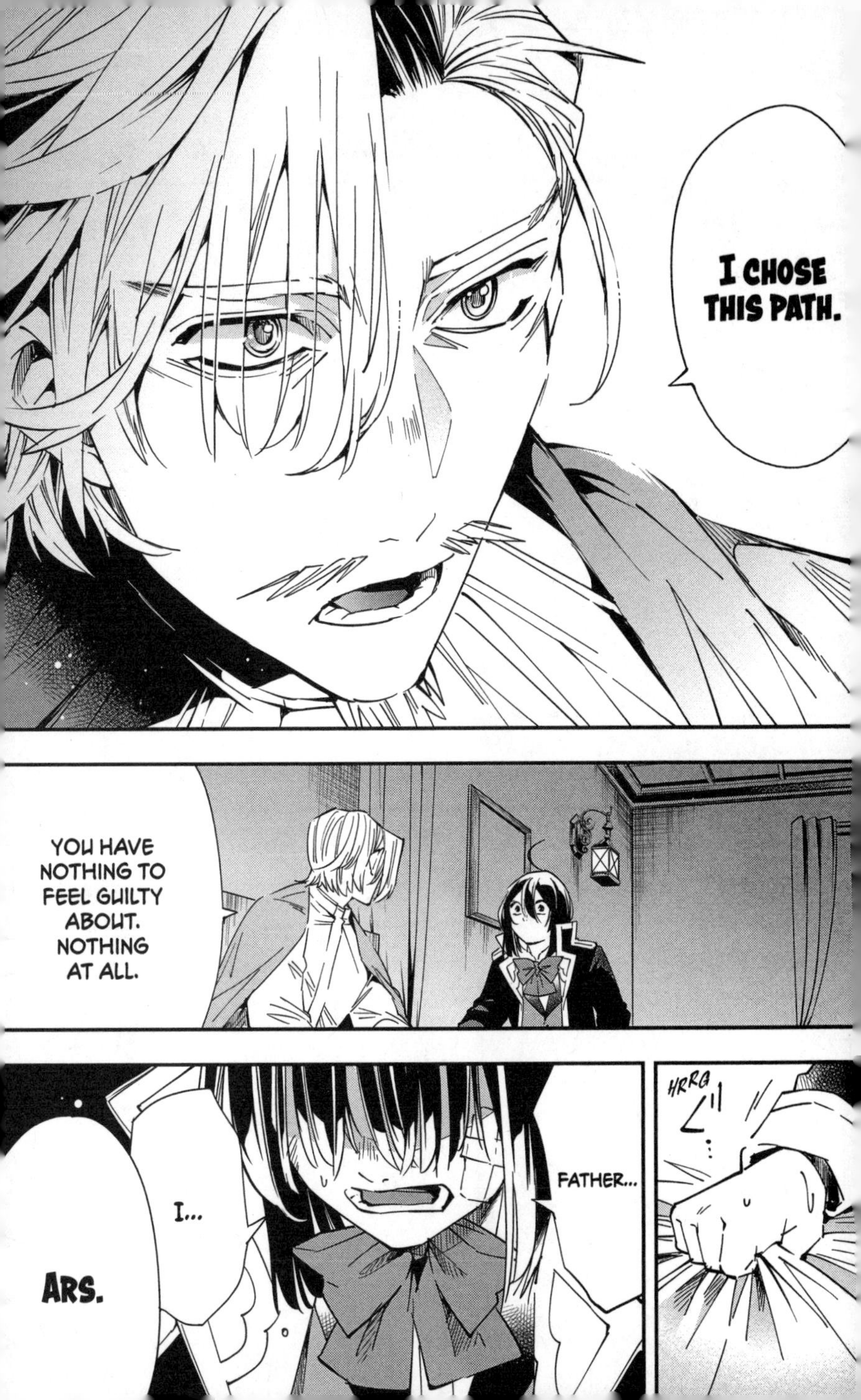
I CHOSE THIS PATH.
YOU HAVE NOTHING TO FEEL GUILTY ABOUT. NOTHING AT ALL.
HRRG
FATHER...
I...
ARS.

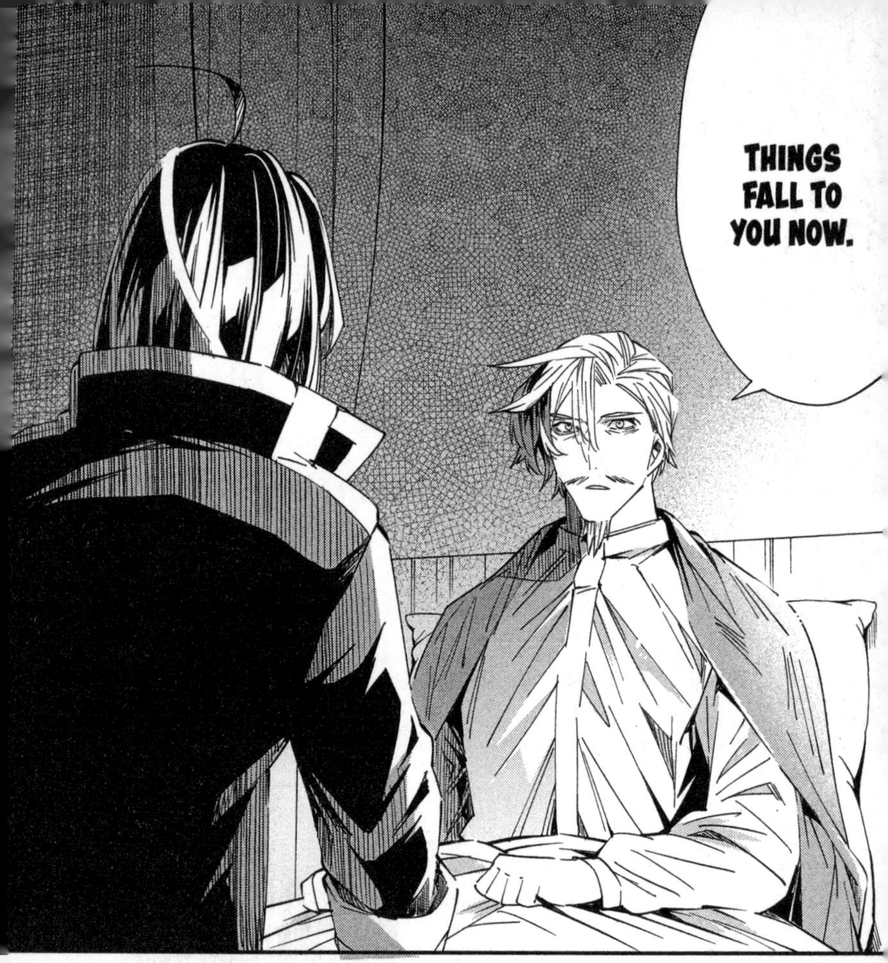
THINGS FALL TO YOU NOW.
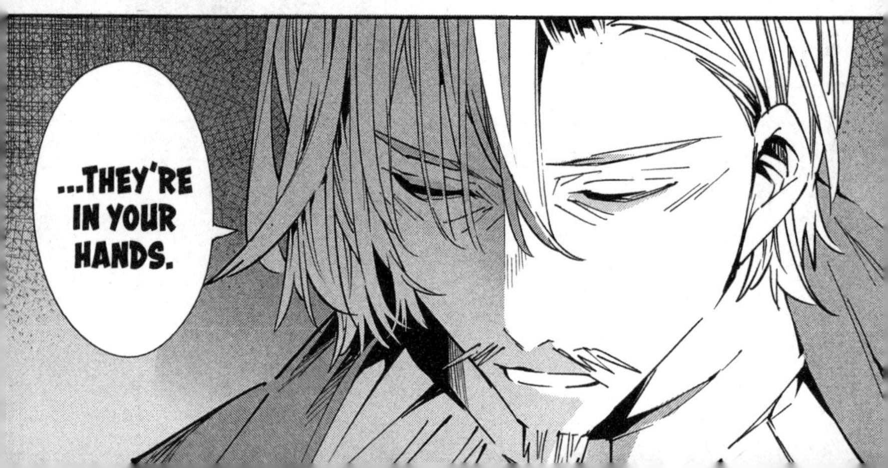
...THEY'RE IN YOUR HANDS.

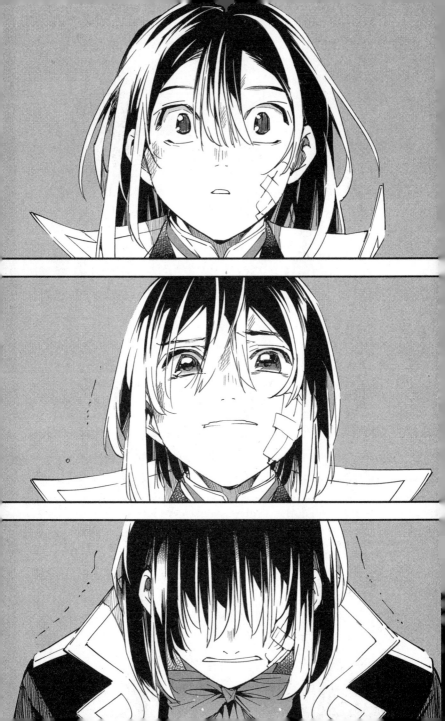

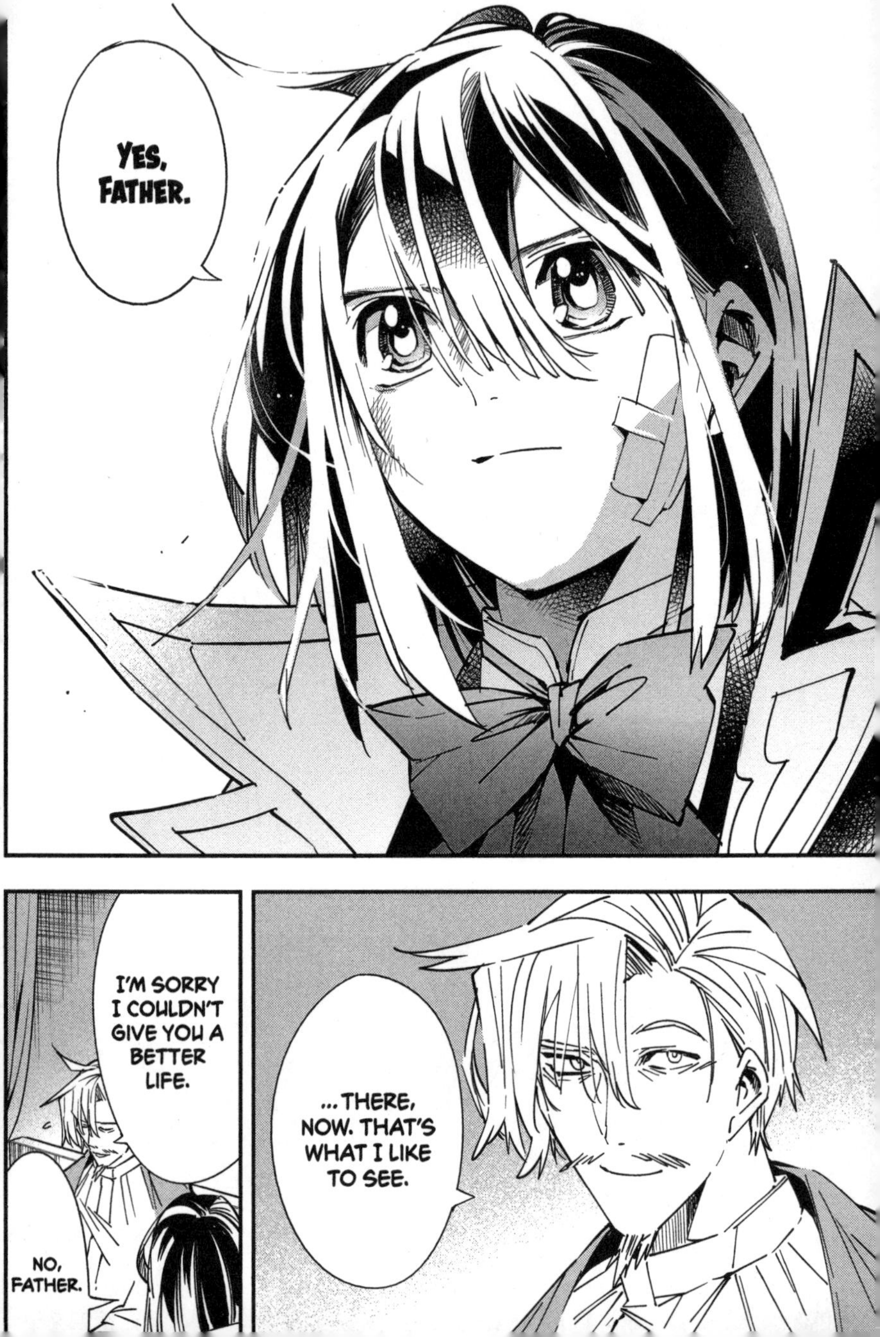
YES, FATHER.
...THERE, NOW. THAT'S WHAT I LIKE TO SEE.
I'M SORRY I COULDN'T GIVE YOU A BETTER LIFE.
NO, FATHER.

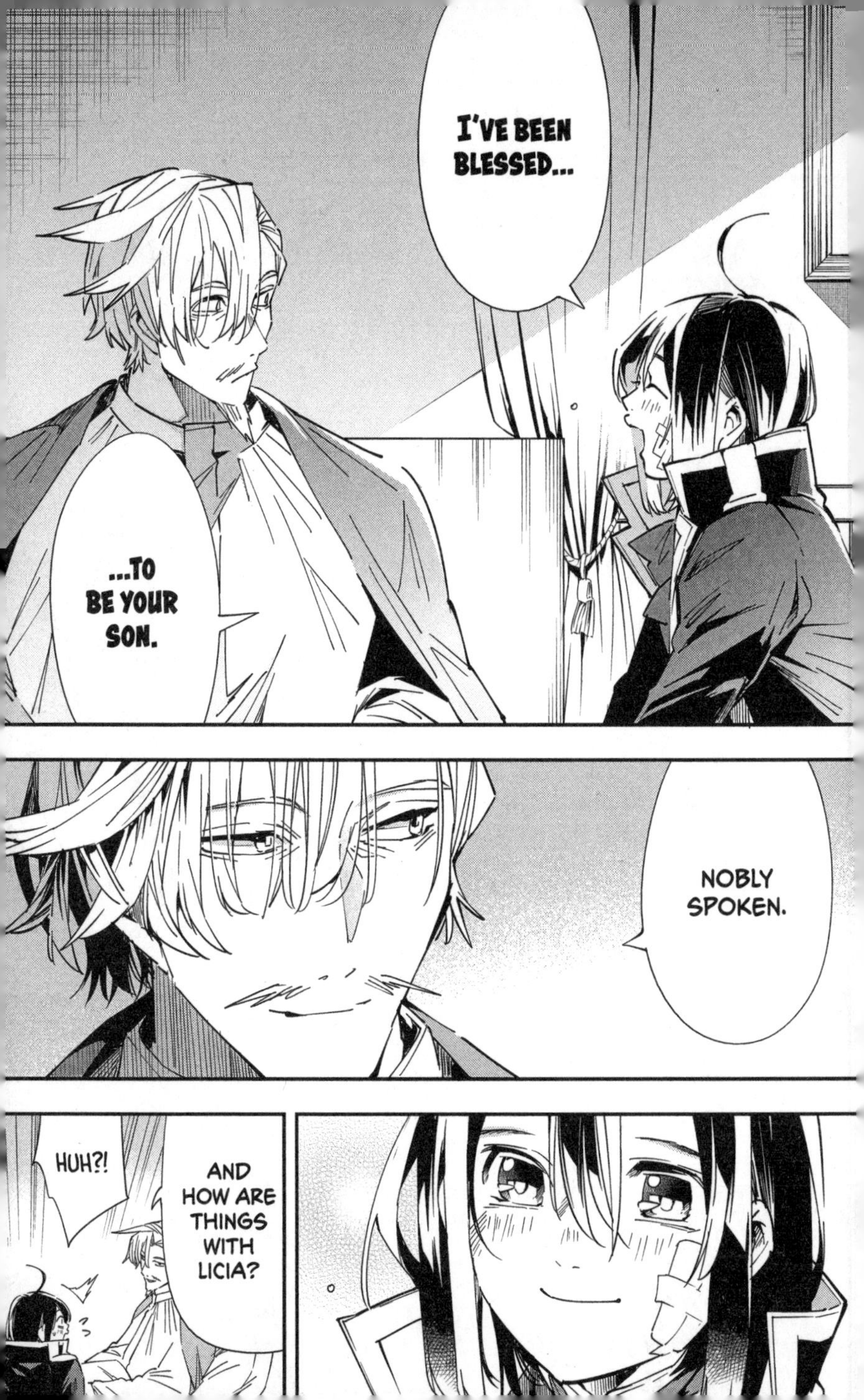
I'VE BEEN BLESSED...
...TO BE YOUR SON.
NOBLY SPOKEN.
AND HOW ARE THINGS WITH LICIA?
HUH?!

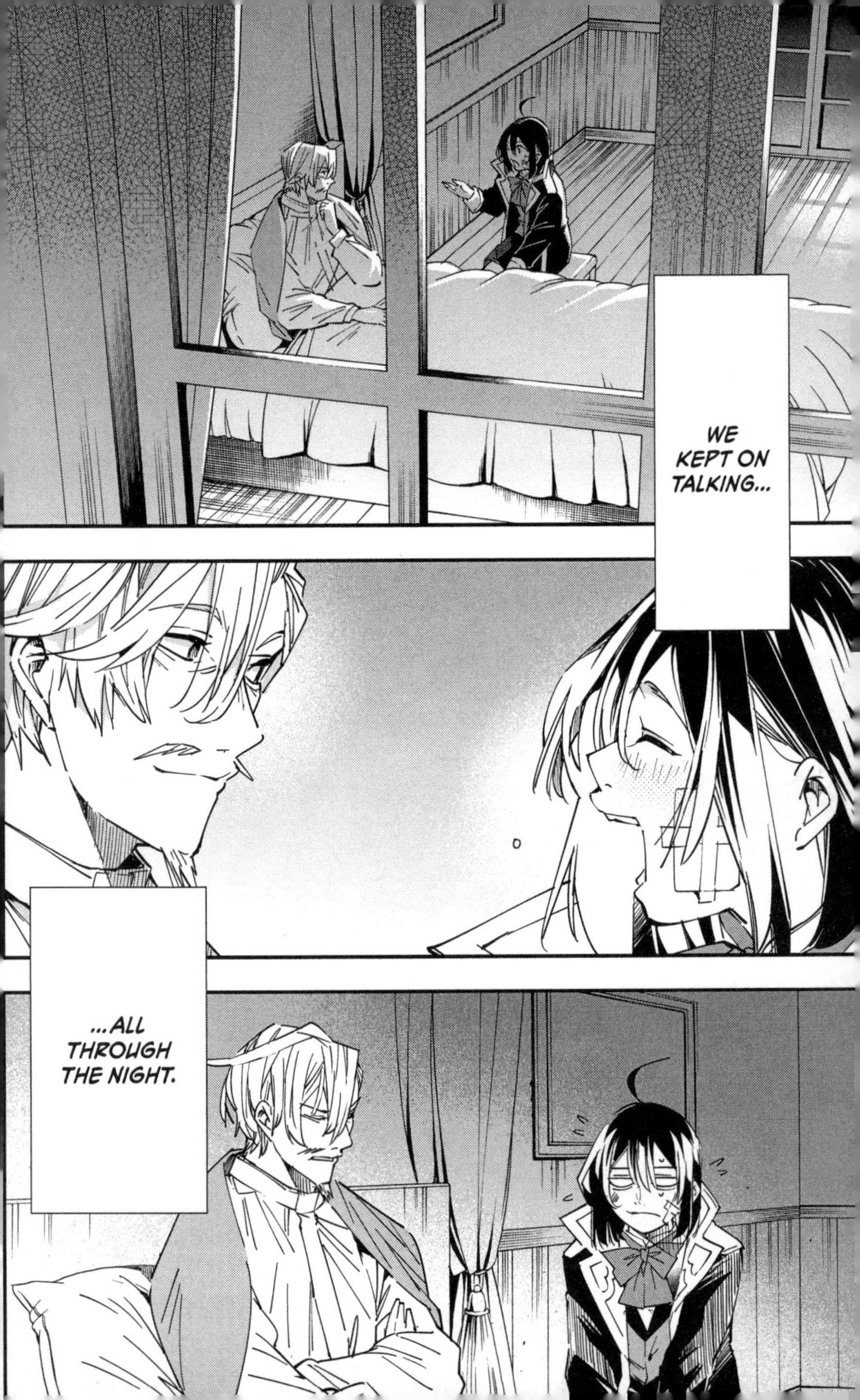
WE KEPT ON TALKING...
...ALL THROUGH THE NIGHT.

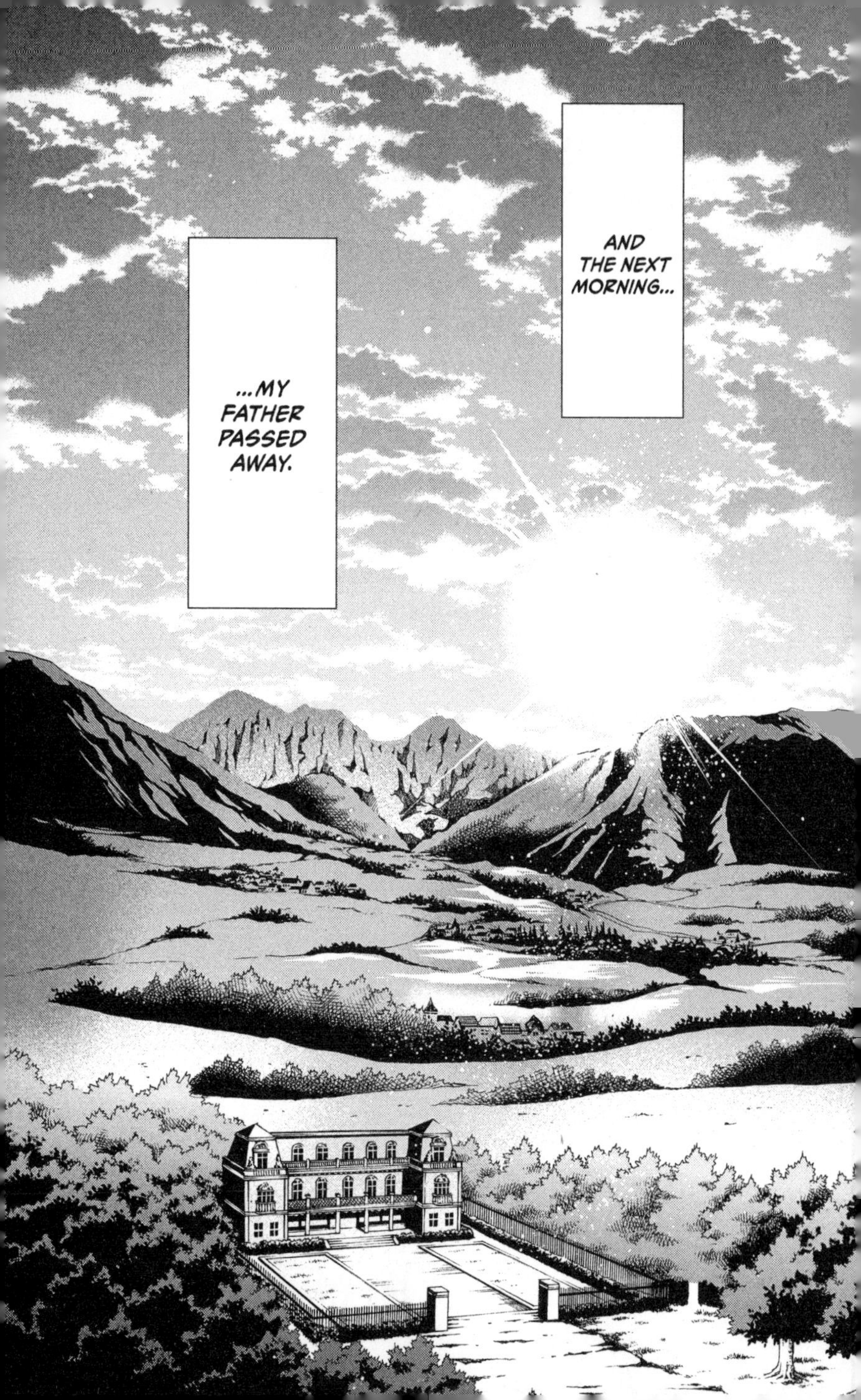
AND THE NEXT MORNING...
...MY FATHER PASSED AWAY.

As a Reincarnated
ARISTOCRAT,
I'll Use My Appraisal Skill to
Rise in the World

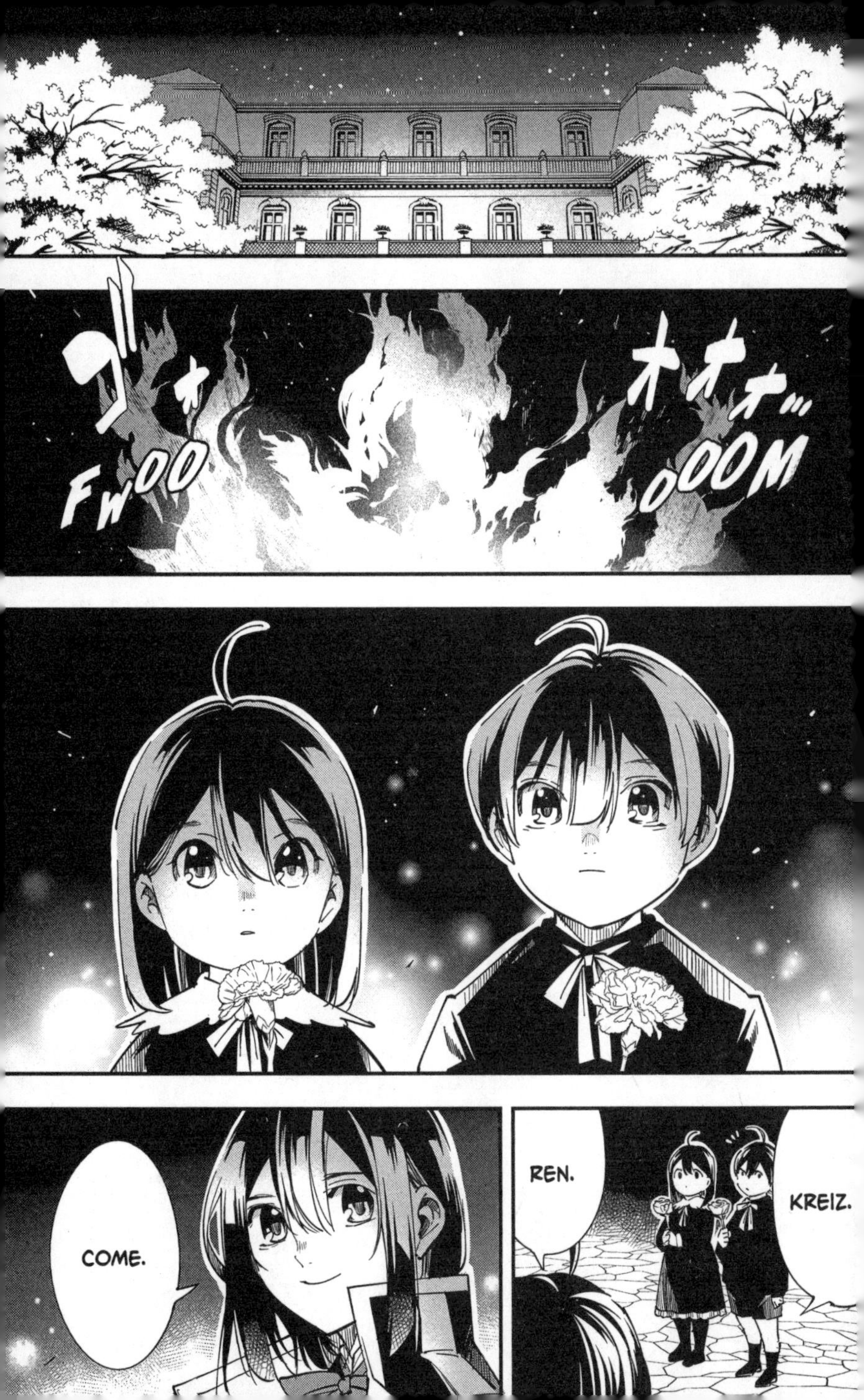
FWOO OOOM
KREIZ.
REN.
COME.

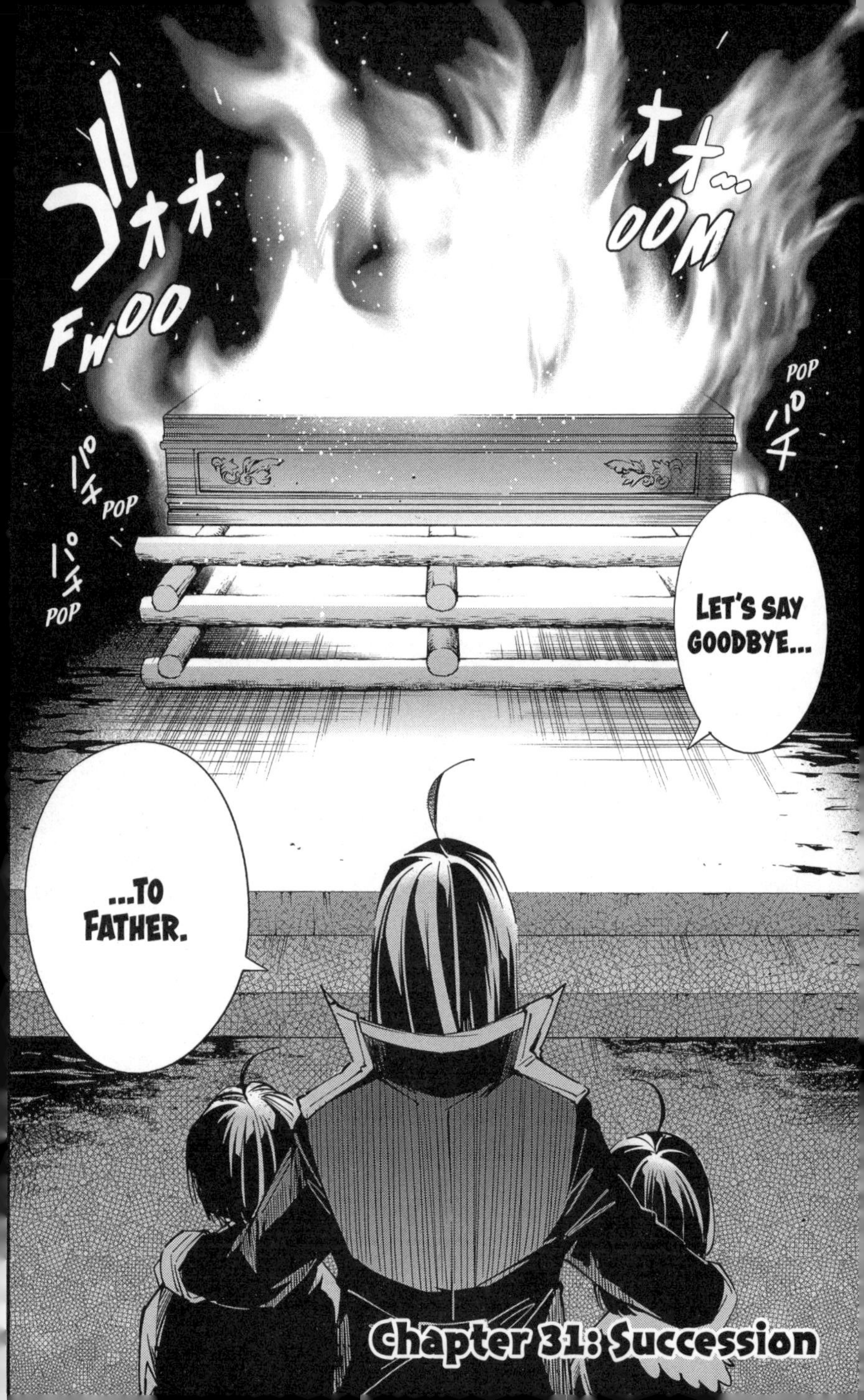
オオ…
OOM
パチ
POP
LET'S SAY GOODBYE...
ゴォォ
FWOO
パチ
POP
パチ
POP
...TO FATHER.
Chapter 31: Succession

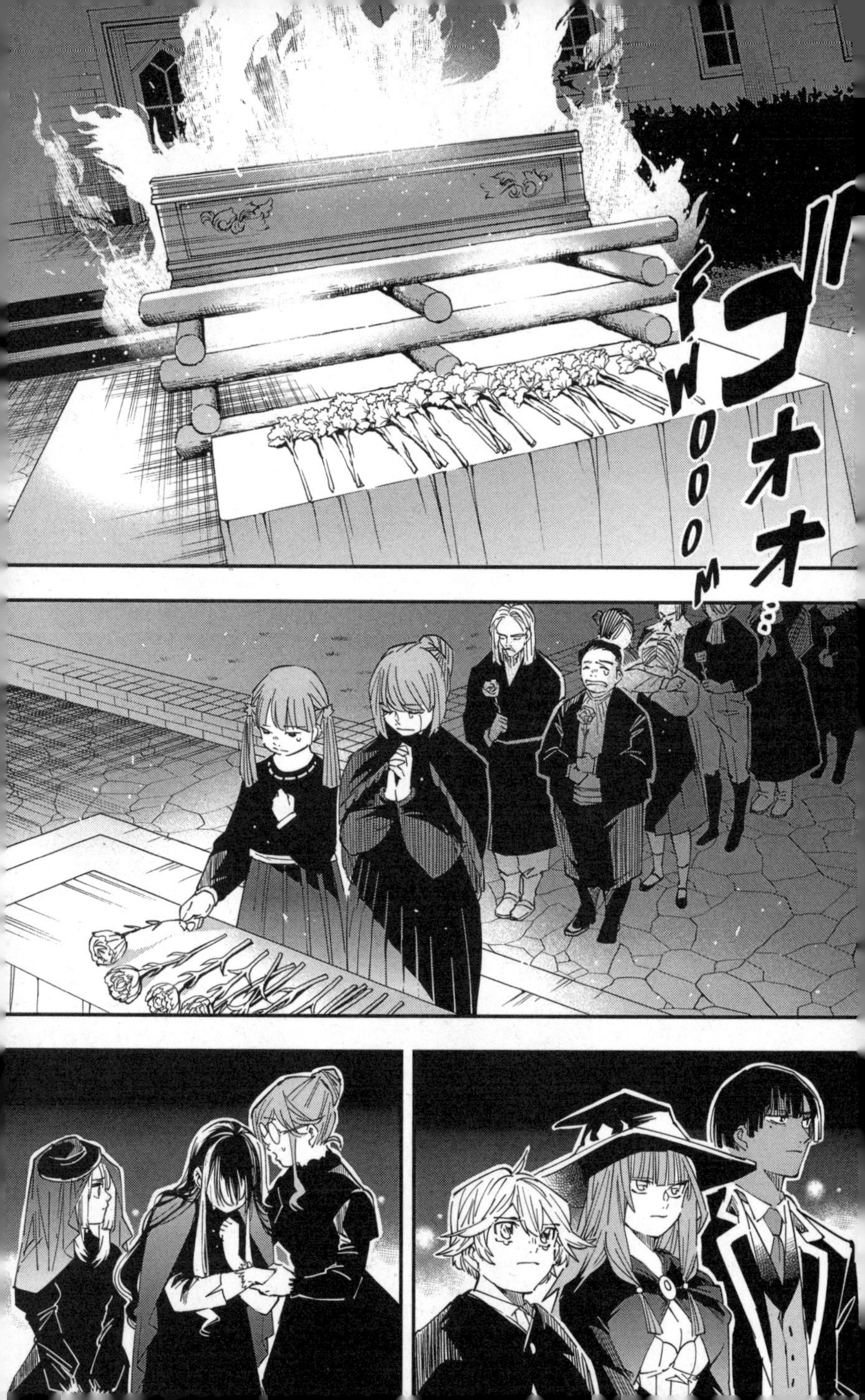
ゴオオ…
FWOOOOM

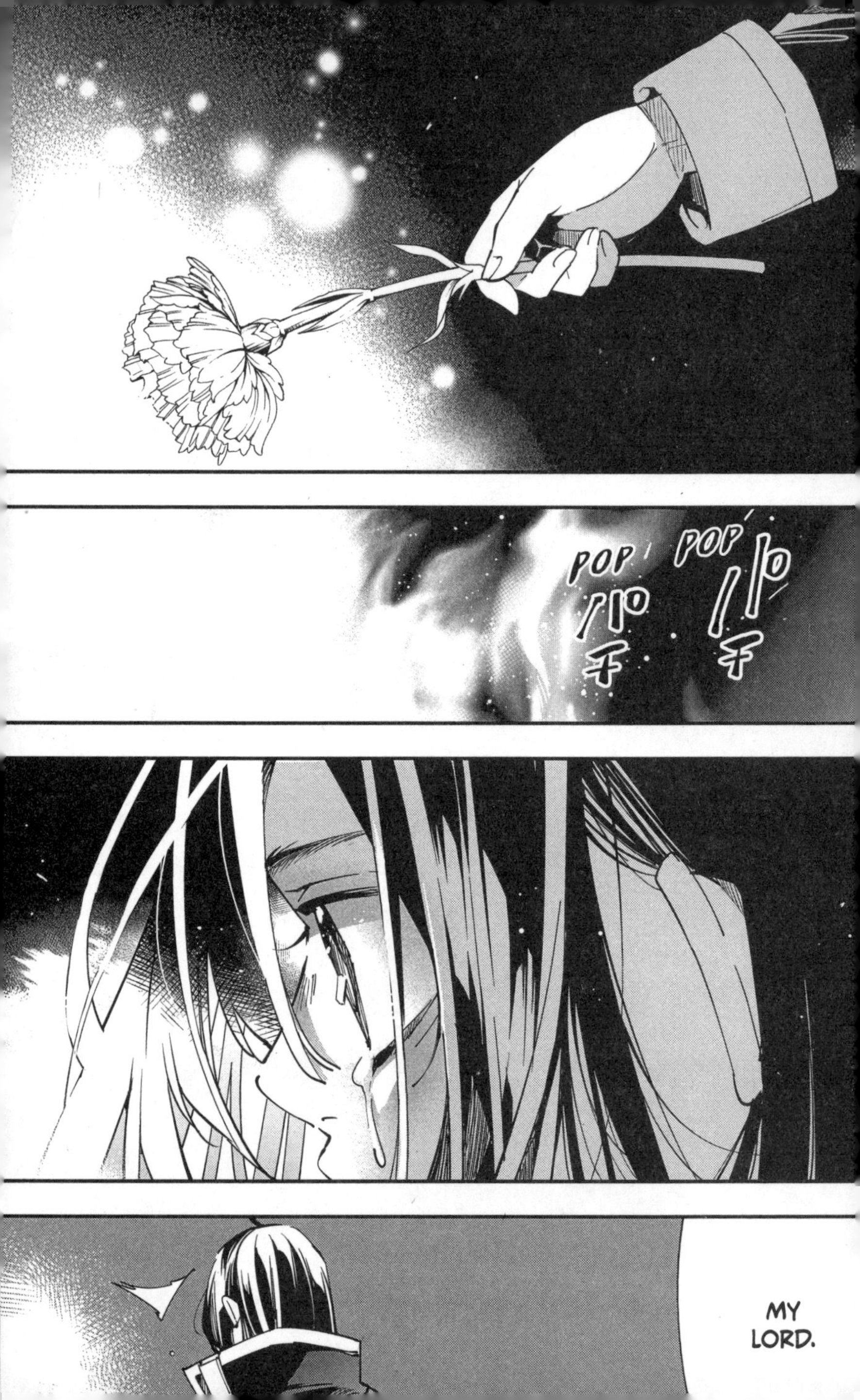
POP
パチ
POP
パチ
MY LORD.

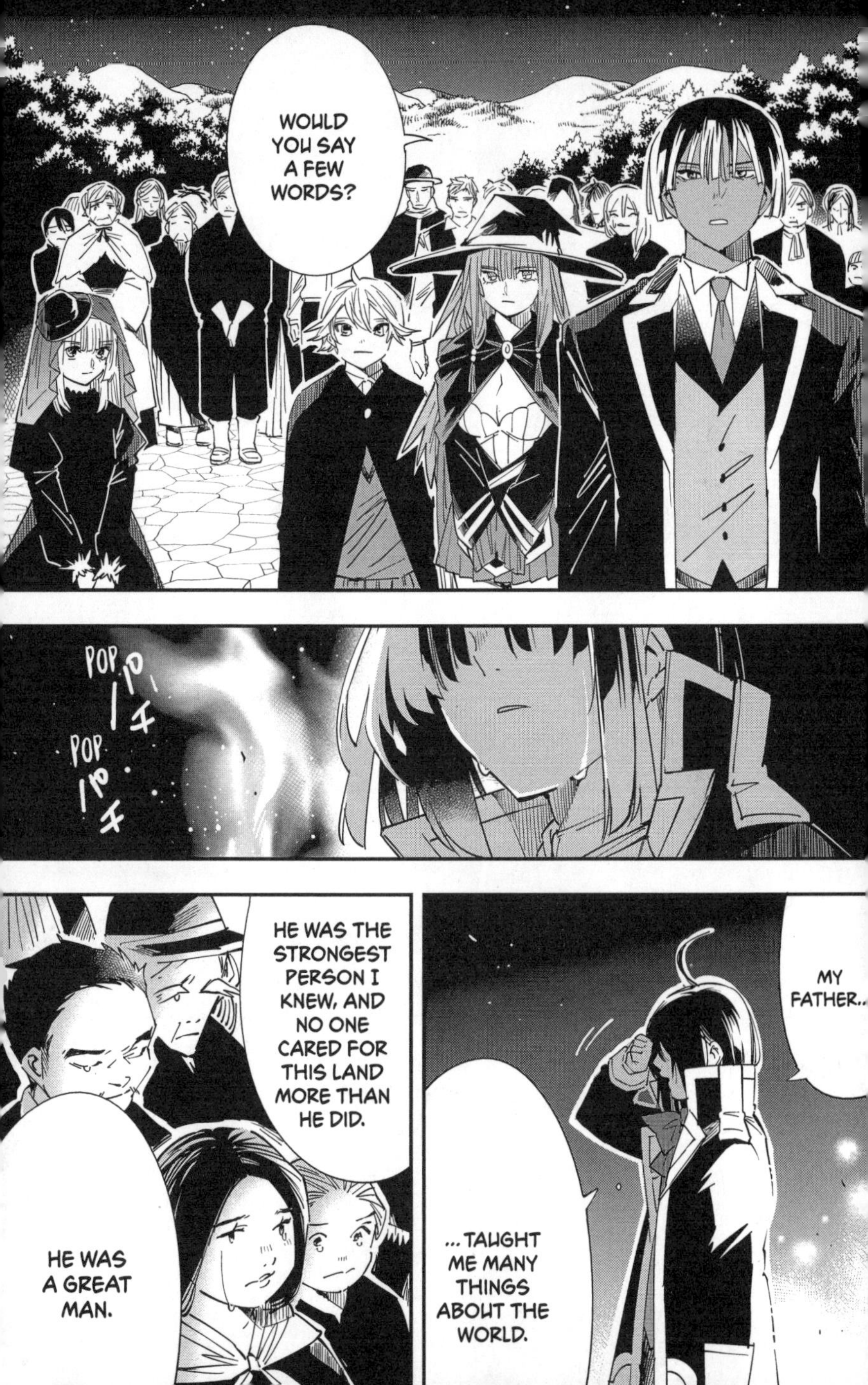

WOULD YOU SAY A FEW WORDS?
POP パチ
POP パチ
MY FATHER..
...TAUGHT ME MANY THINGS ABOUT THE WORLD.
HE WAS THE STRONGEST PERSON I KNEW, AND NO ONE CARED FOR THIS LAND MORE THAN HE DID.
HE WAS A GREAT MAN.

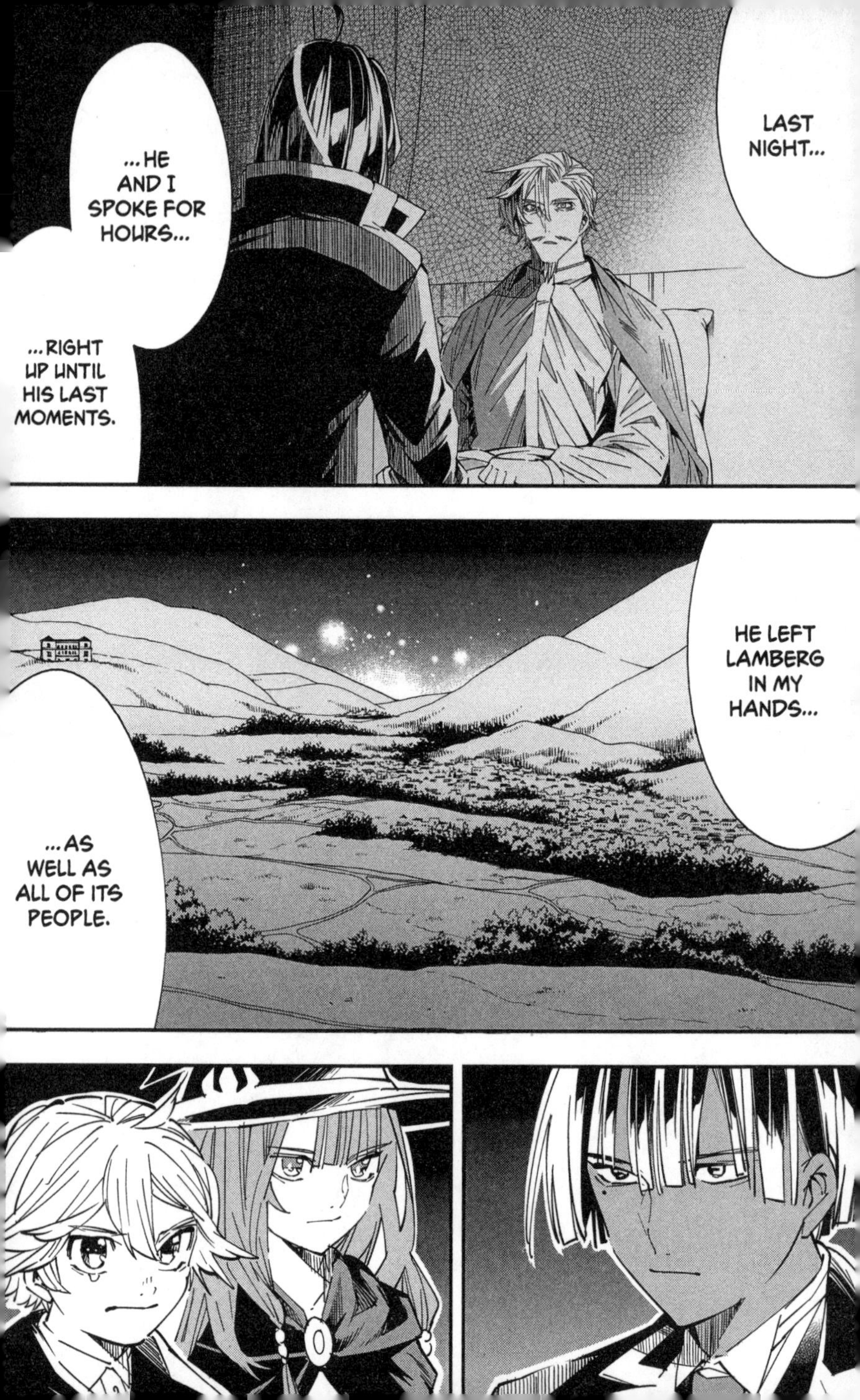
LAST NIGHT...
...HE AND I SPOKE FOR HOURS...
...RIGHT UP UNTIL HIS LAST MOMENTS.
HE LEFT LAMBERG IN MY HANDS...
...AS WELL AS ALL OF ITS PEOPLE.

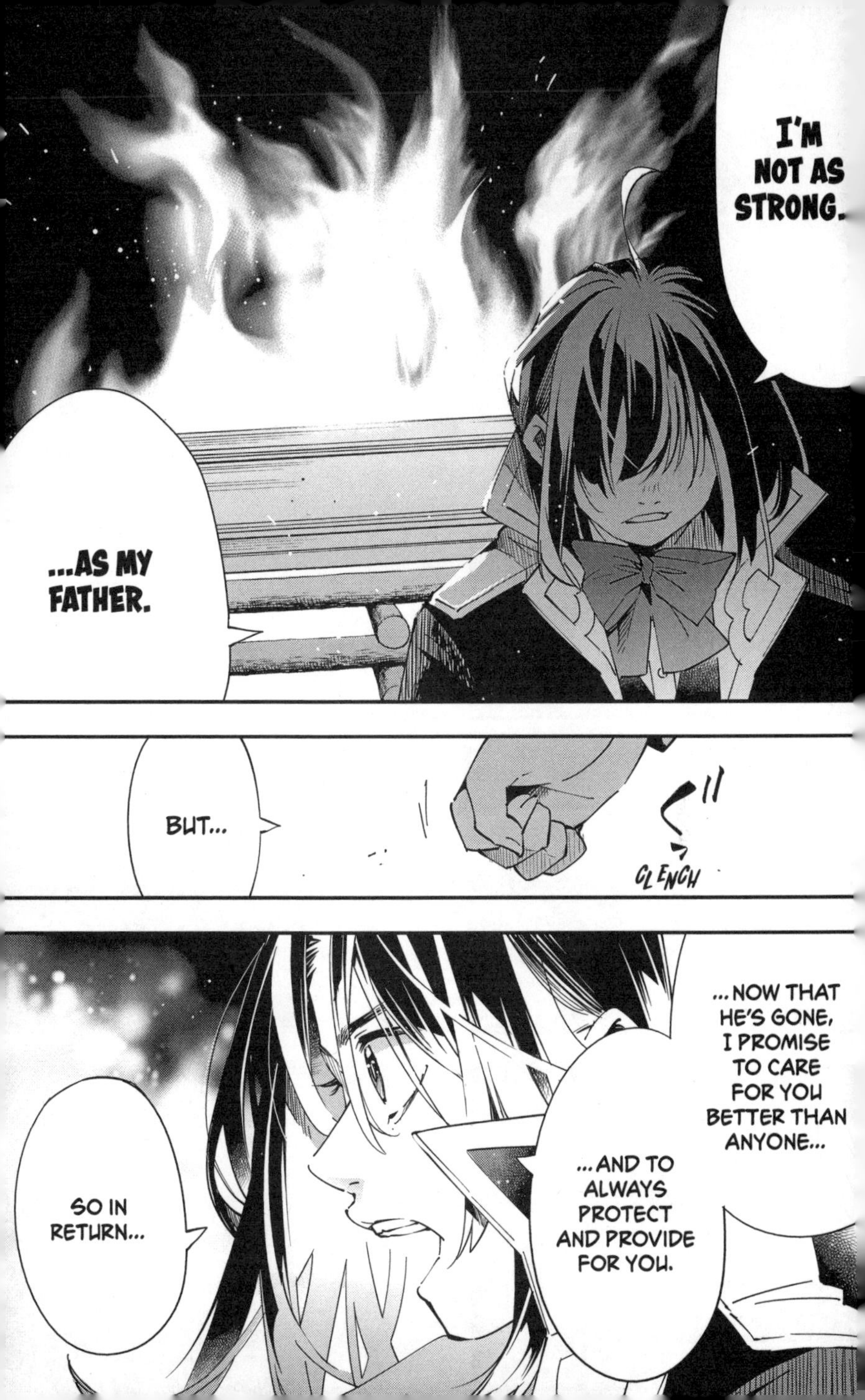
I'M NOT AS STRONG.
...AS MY FATHER.
CLENCH
BUT...
...NOW THAT HE'S GONE, I PROMISE TO CARE FOR YOU BETTER THAN ANYONE...
...AND TO ALWAYS PROTECT AND PROVIDE FOR YOU.
SO IN RETURN...

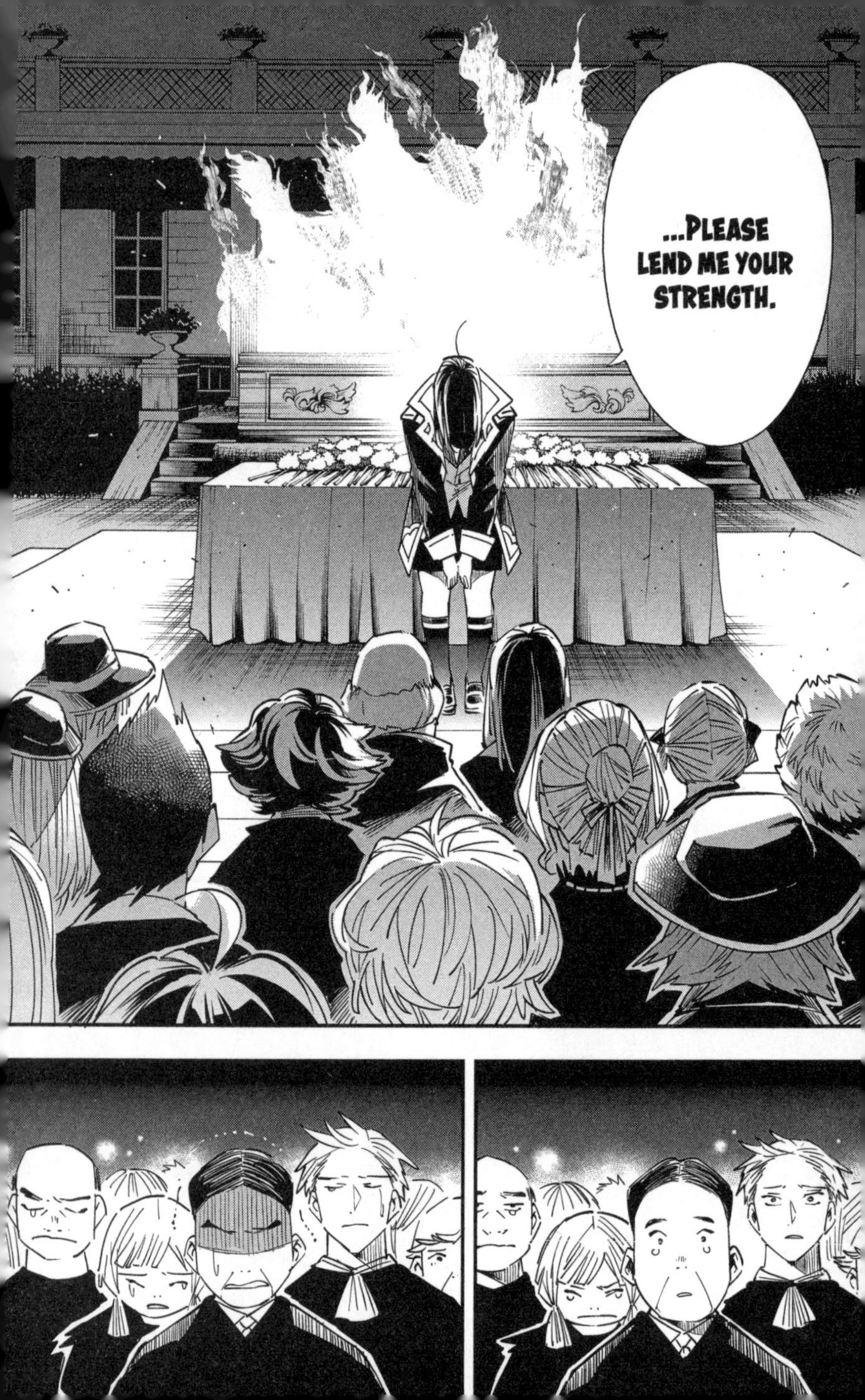
...PLEASE LEND ME YOUR STRENGTH.

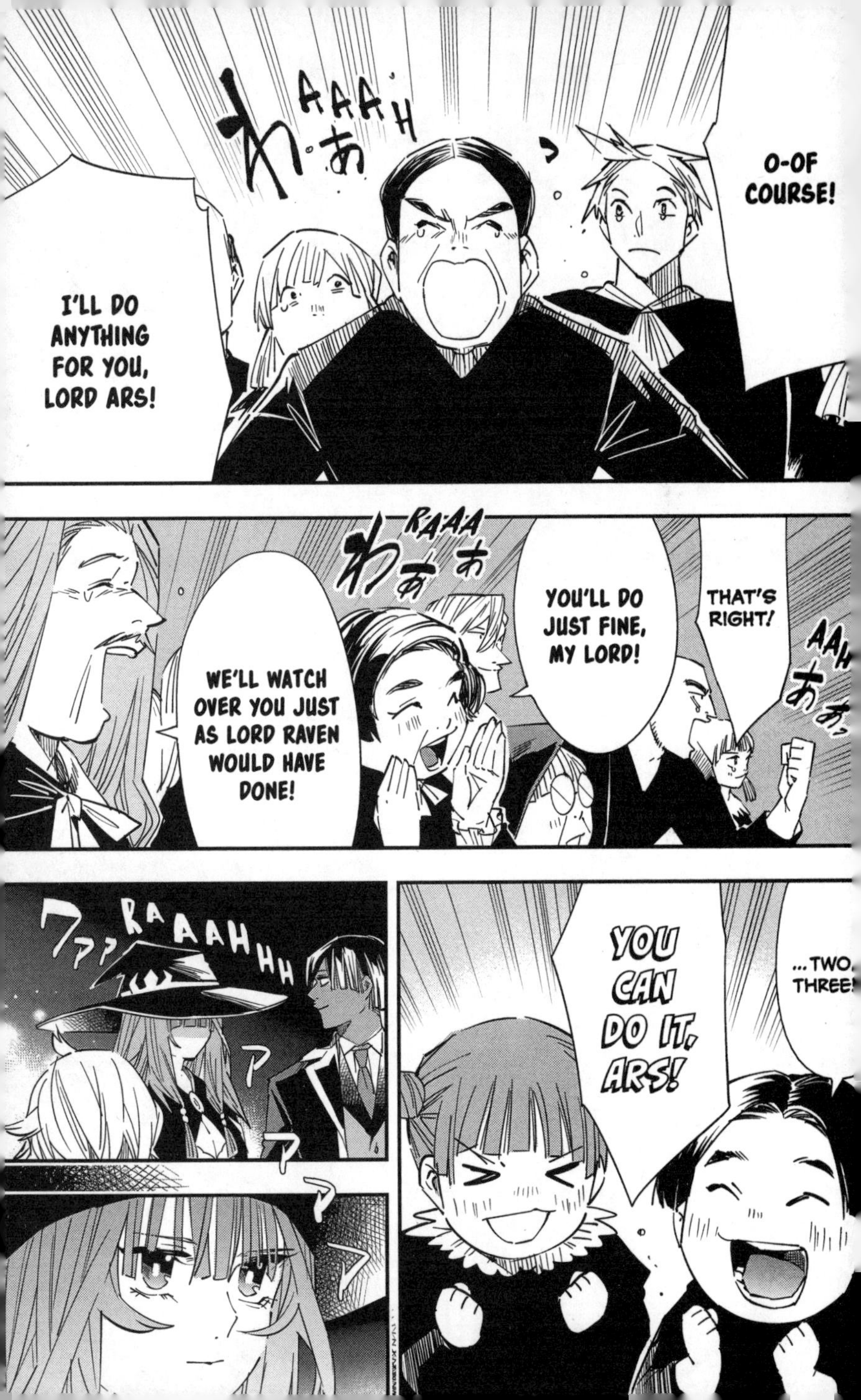
O-OF COURSE!
わあ AAAAH
I'LL DO ANYTHING FOR YOU, LORD ARS!
AAAH あああ
THAT'S RIGHT!
YOU'LL DO JUST FINE, MY LORD!
わあぁ RAAAA
WE'LL WATCH OVER YOU JUST AS LORD RAVEN WOULD HAVE DONE!
...TWO, THREE!
YOU CAN DO IT, ARS!
ワァァ RAAAHHH

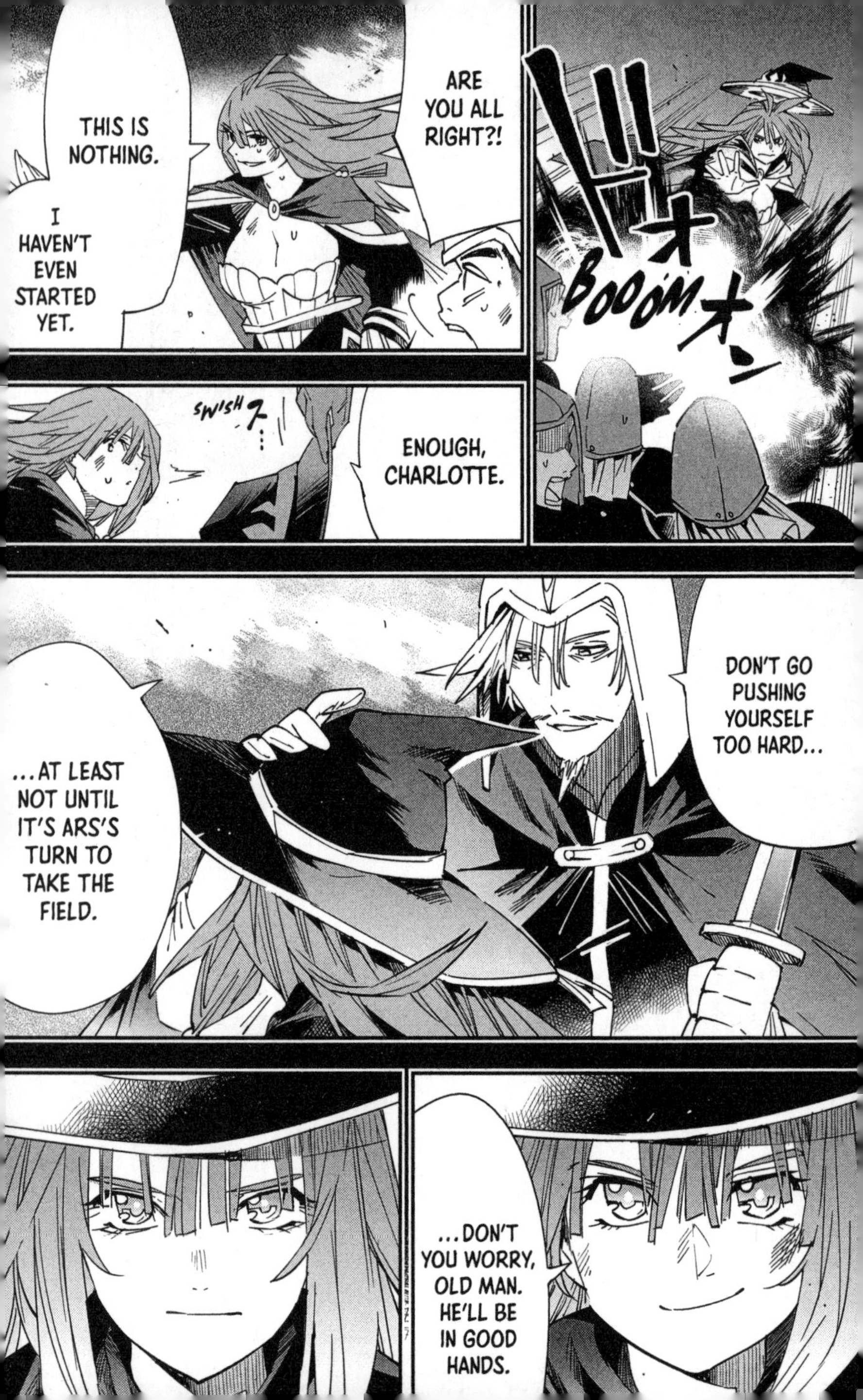
BOOOM
ARE YOU ALL RIGHT?!
THIS IS NOTHING.
I HAVEN'T EVEN STARTED YET.
SWISH
ENOUGH, CHARLOTTE.
DON'T GO PUSHING YOURSELF TOO HARD...
...AT LEAST NOT UNTIL IT'S ARS'S TURN TO TAKE THE FIELD.
...DON'T YOU WORRY, OLD MAN. HE'LL BE IN GOOD HANDS.

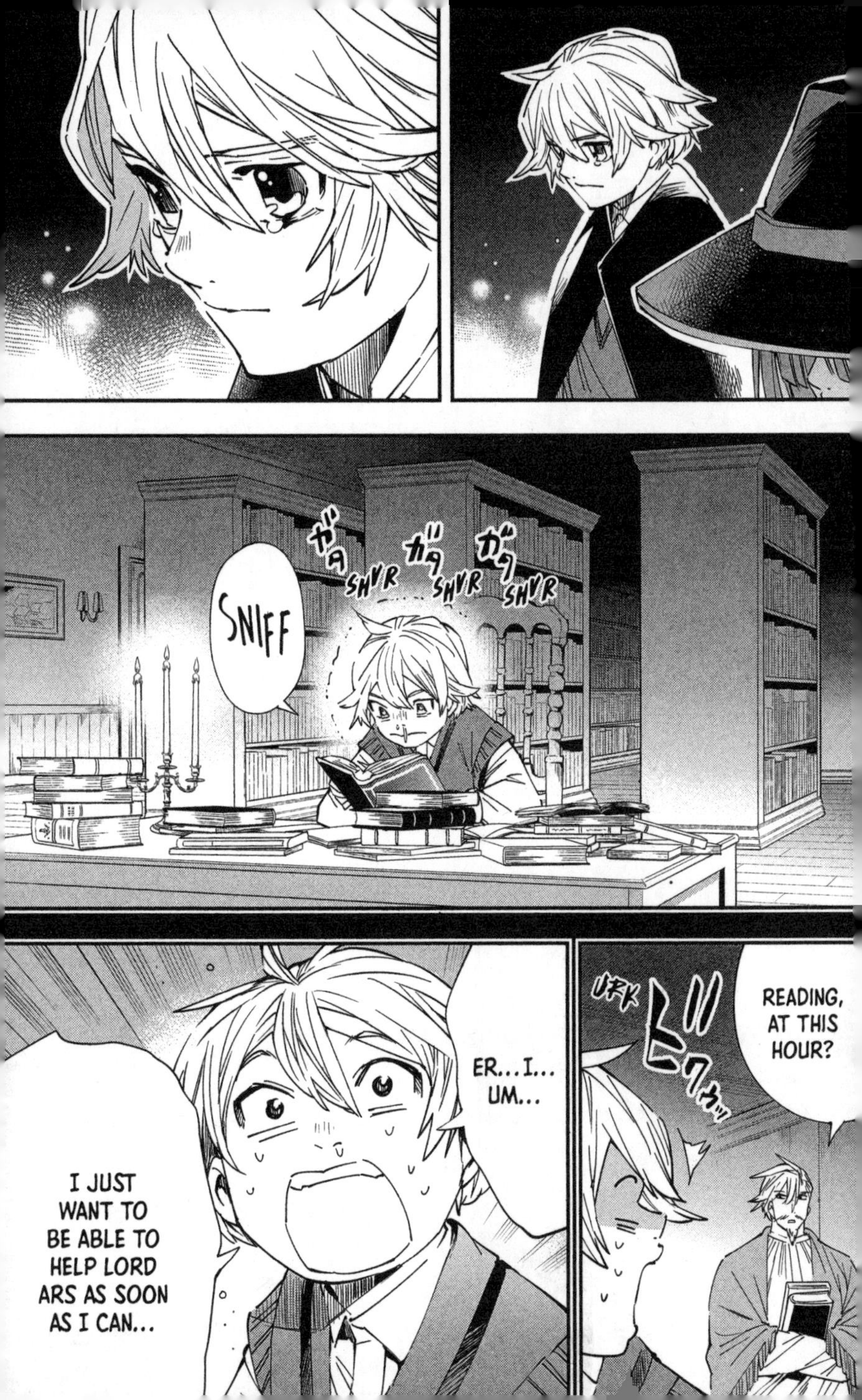

ガタ SHVR
ガタ SHVR
ガタ SHVR
SNIFF
READING, AT THIS HOUR?
ビクゥッ URK
ER...I... UM...
I JUST WANT TO BE ABLE TO HELP LORD ARS AS SOON AS I CAN...

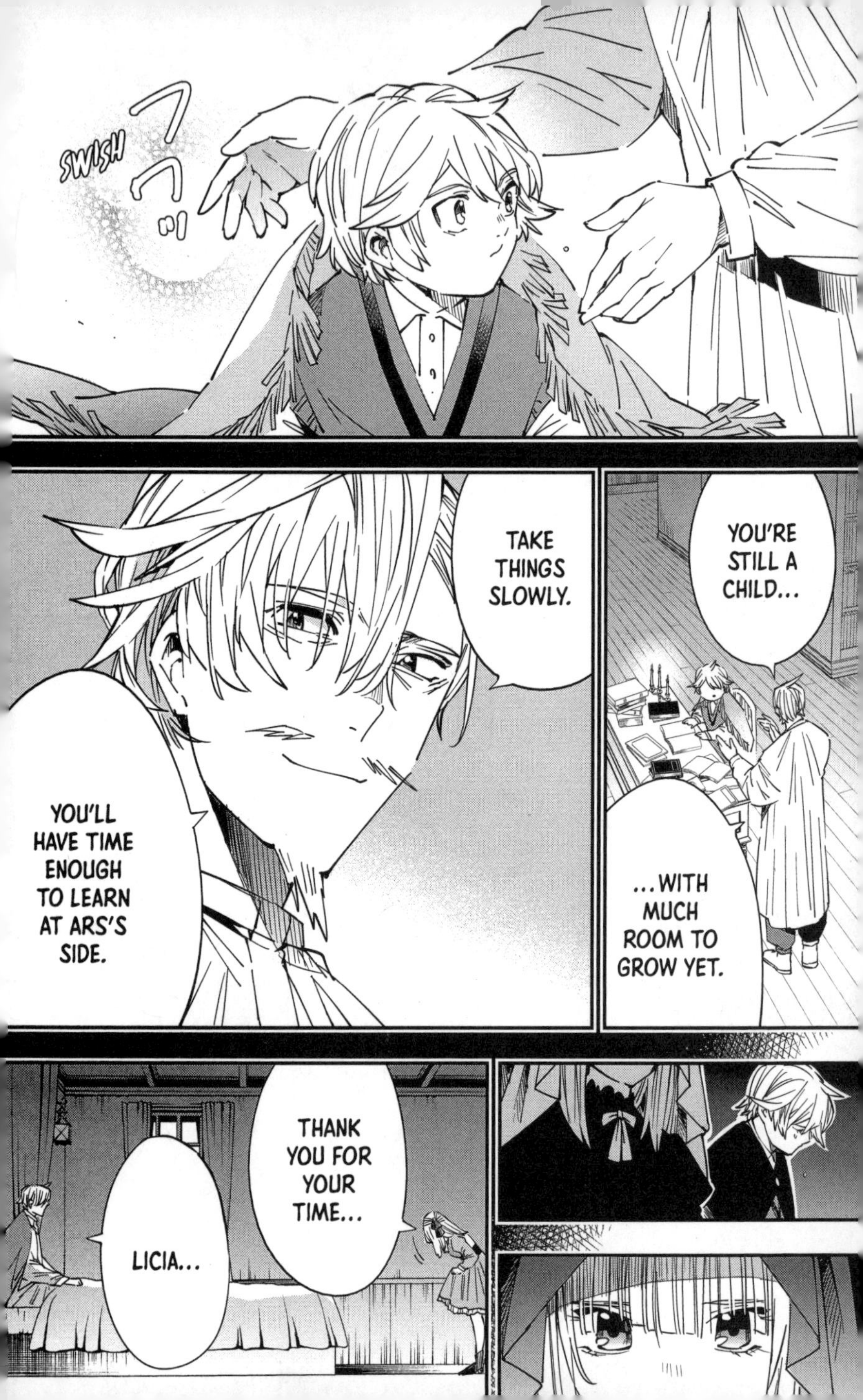
SWISH
YOU'RE STILL A CHILD...
...WITH MUCH ROOM TO GROW YET.
TAKE THINGS SLOWLY.
YOU'LL HAVE TIME ENOUGH TO LEARN AT ARS'S SIDE.
THANK YOU FOR YOUR TIME...
LICIA...

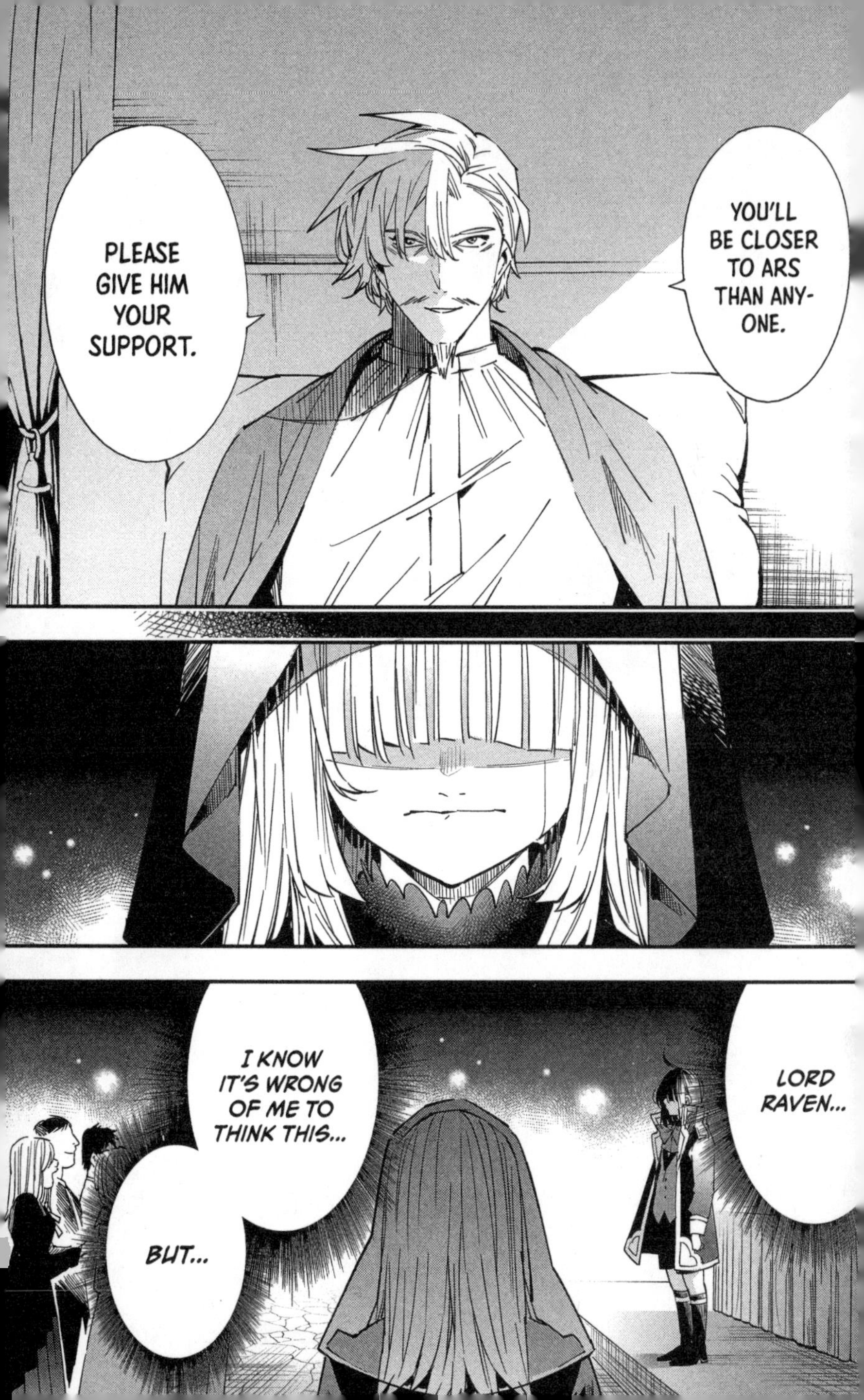
YOU'LL BE CLOSER TO ARS THAN ANY-ONE.
PLEASE GIVE HIM YOUR SUPPORT.
LORD RAVEN...
I KNOW IT'S WRONG OF ME TO THINK THIS...
BUT...

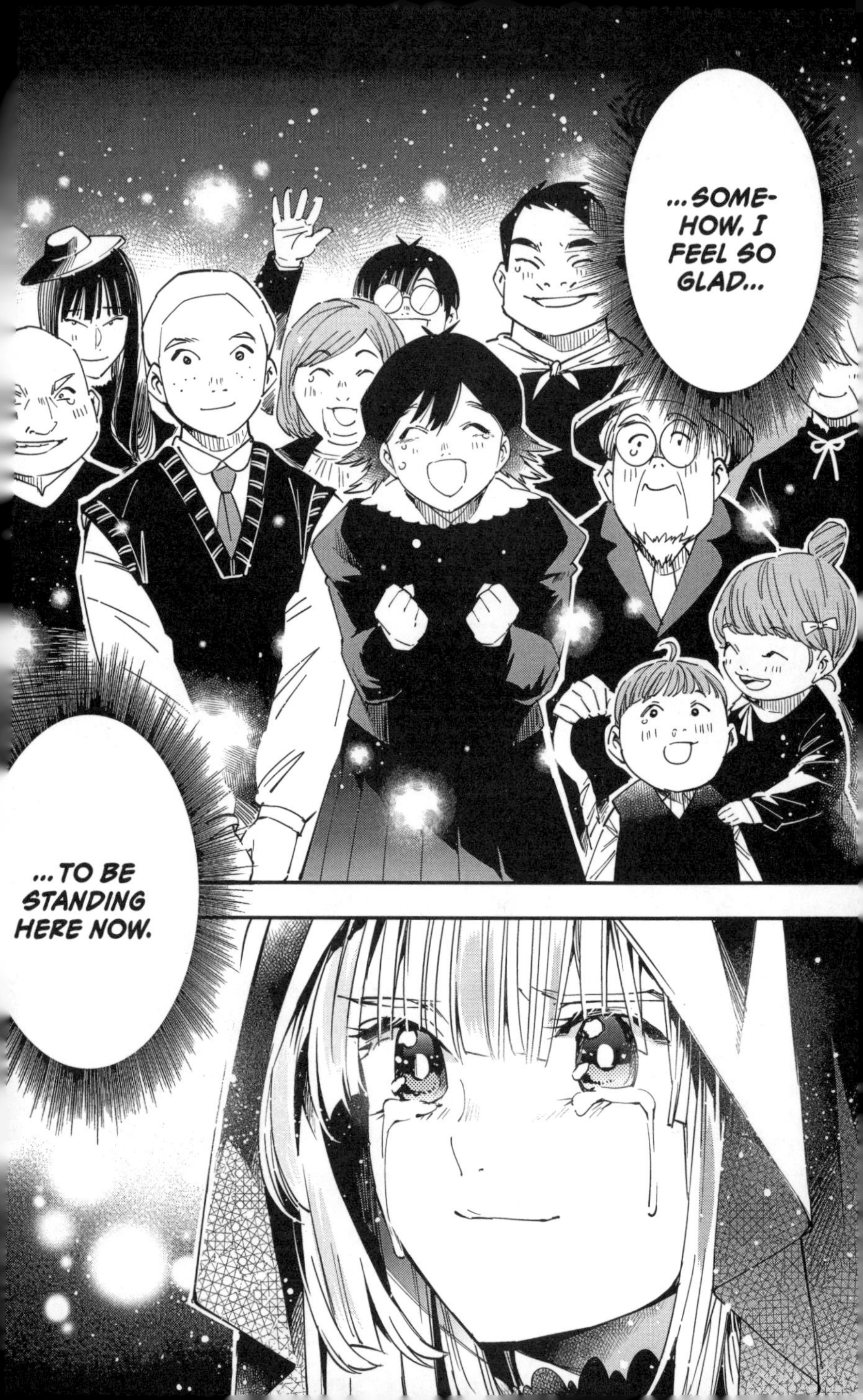
...SOME-HOW, I FEEL SO GLAD...
...TO BE STANDING HERE NOW.

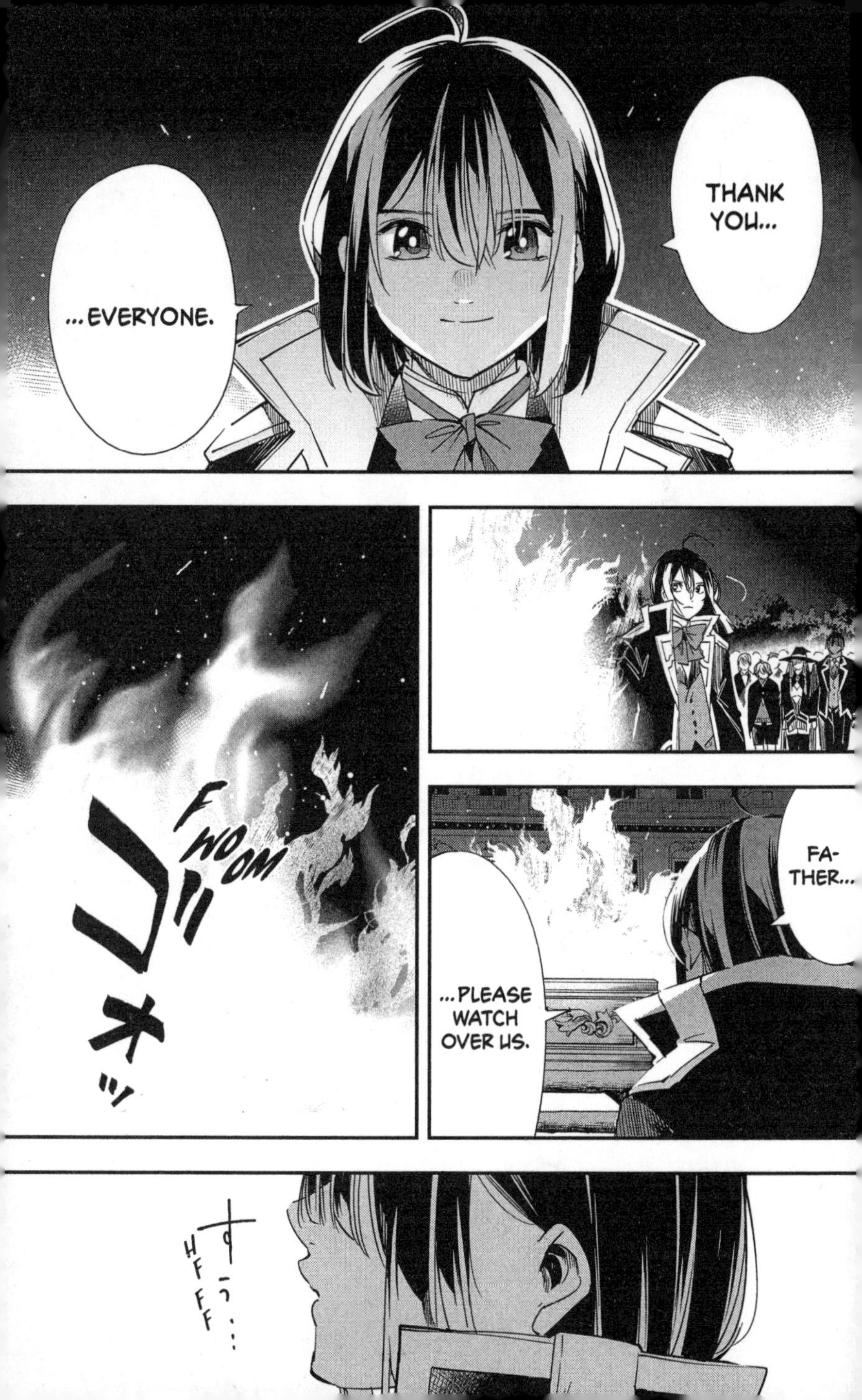
THANK YOU...
...EVERYONE.
FA-THER...
...PLEASE WATCH OVER US.
FWOOM
ゴォッ
すぅ…
HFFF

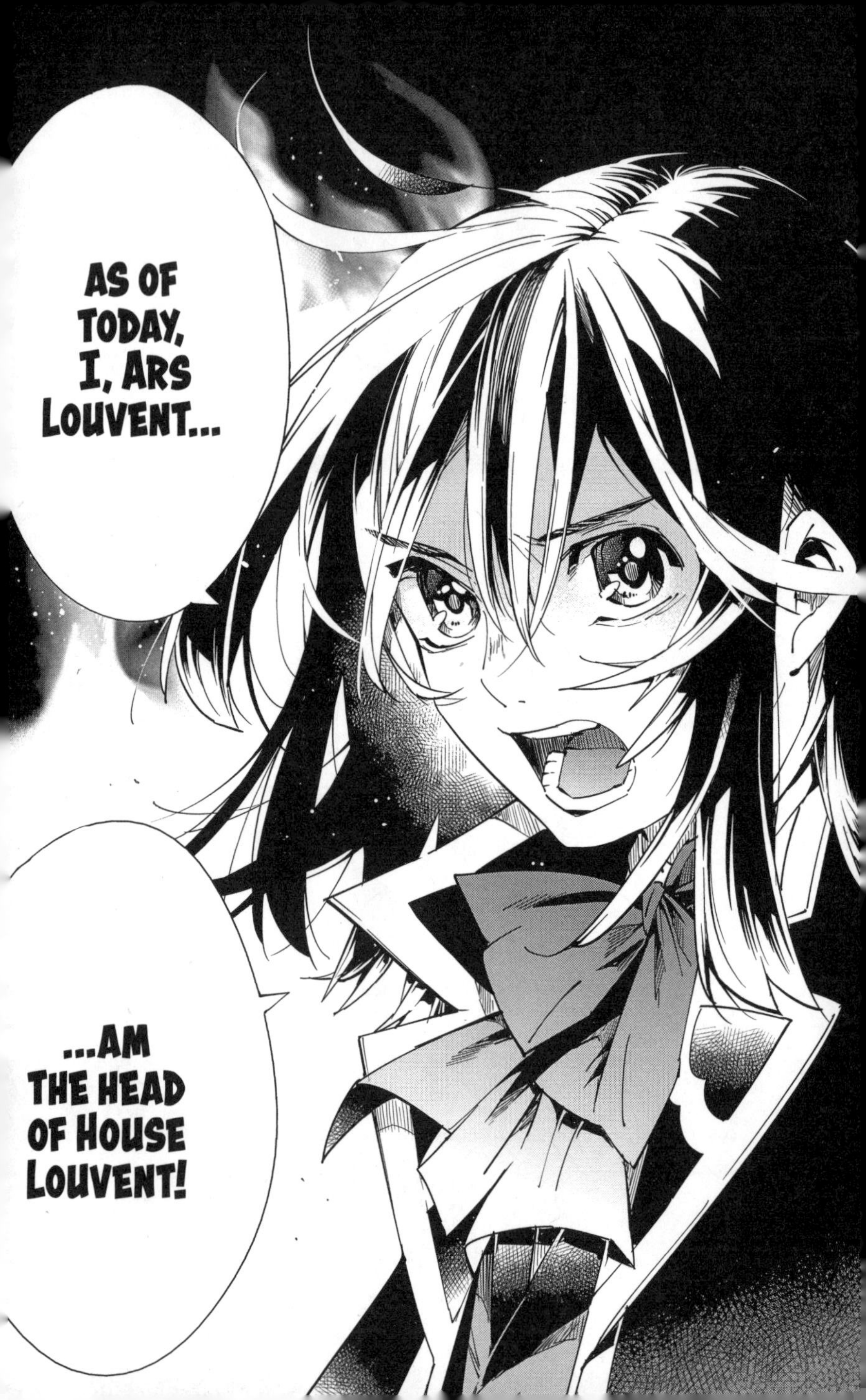
AS OF TODAY, I, ARS LOUVENT...
...AM THE HEAD OF HOUSE LOUVENT!

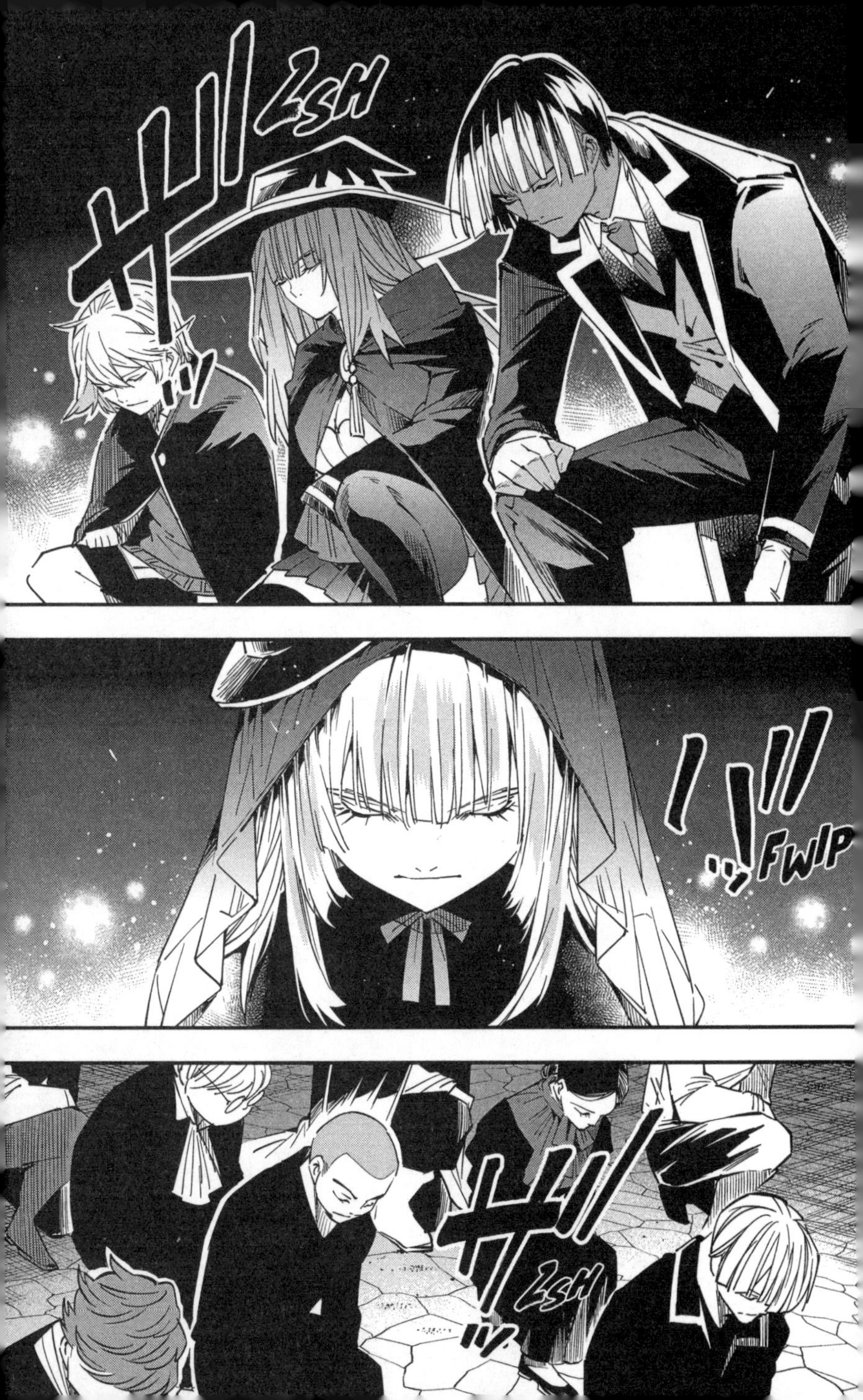
ZSH
FWIP
ZSH

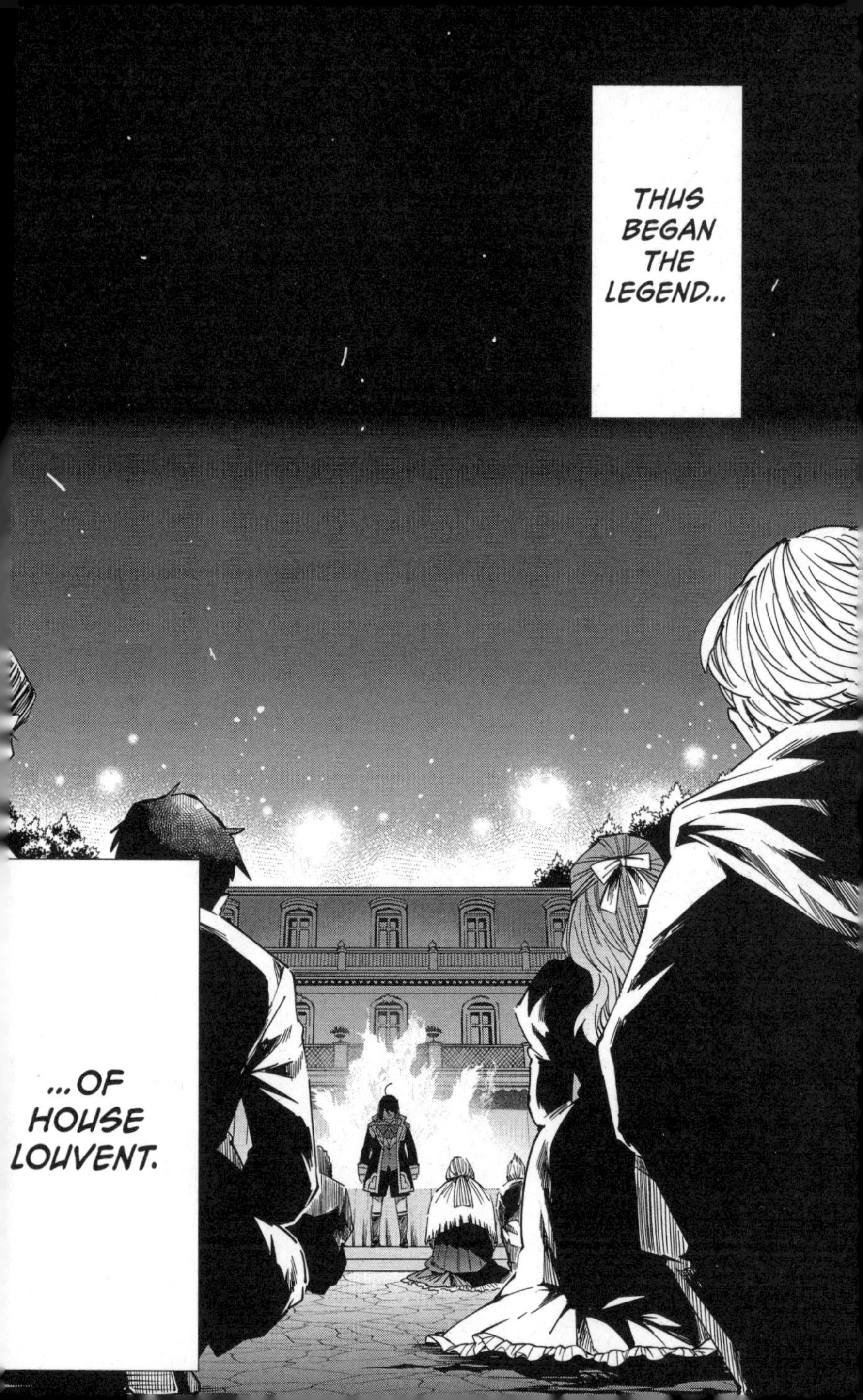
THUS BEGAN THE LEGEND...
...OF HOUSE LOUVENT.

As a Reincarnated
ARISTOCRAT,
I'll Use My Appraisal Skill to
Rise in the World

As a Reincarnated
ARISTOCRAT,
I'll Use My Appraisal Skill to
Rise in the World

Chapter 32: A New Era

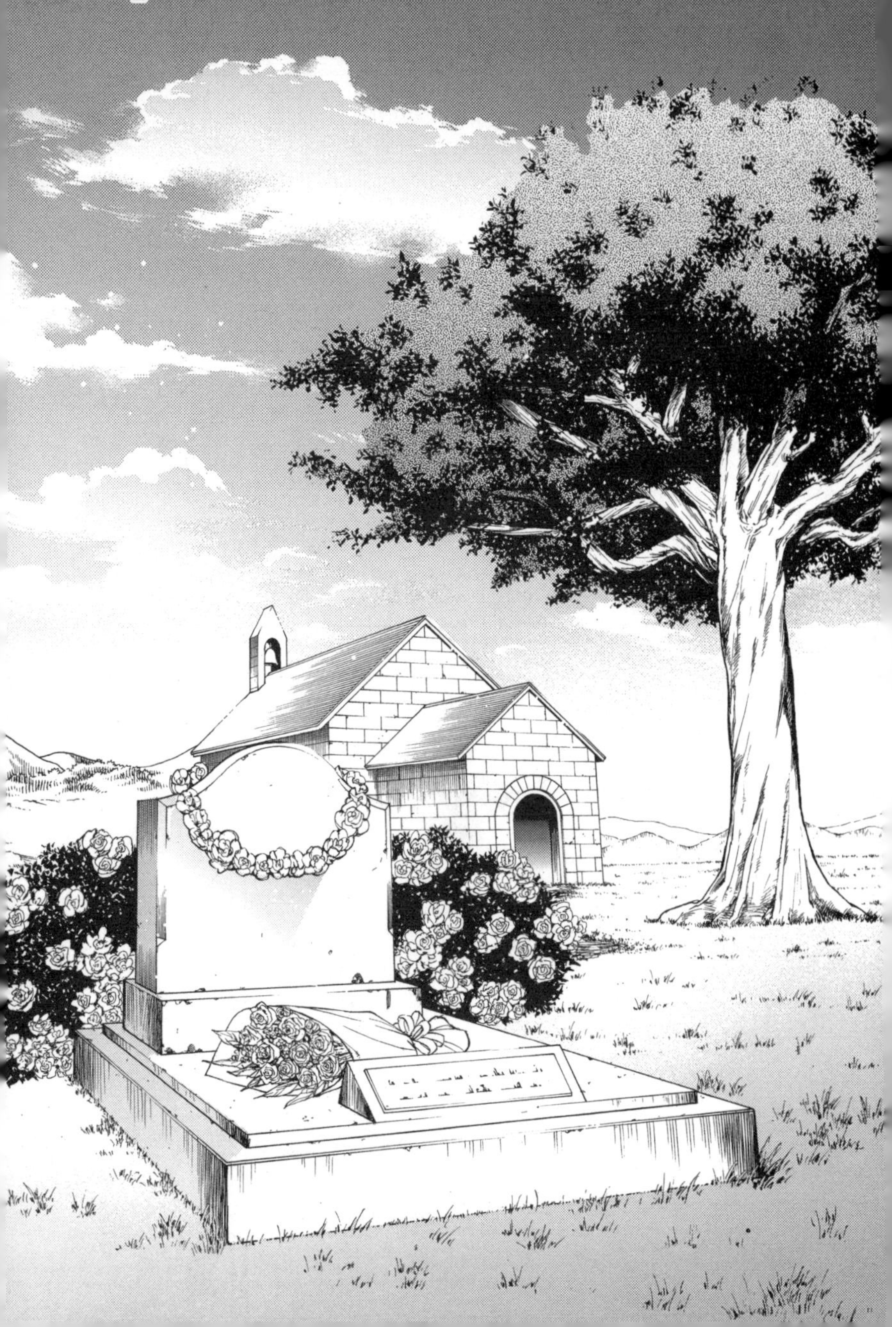

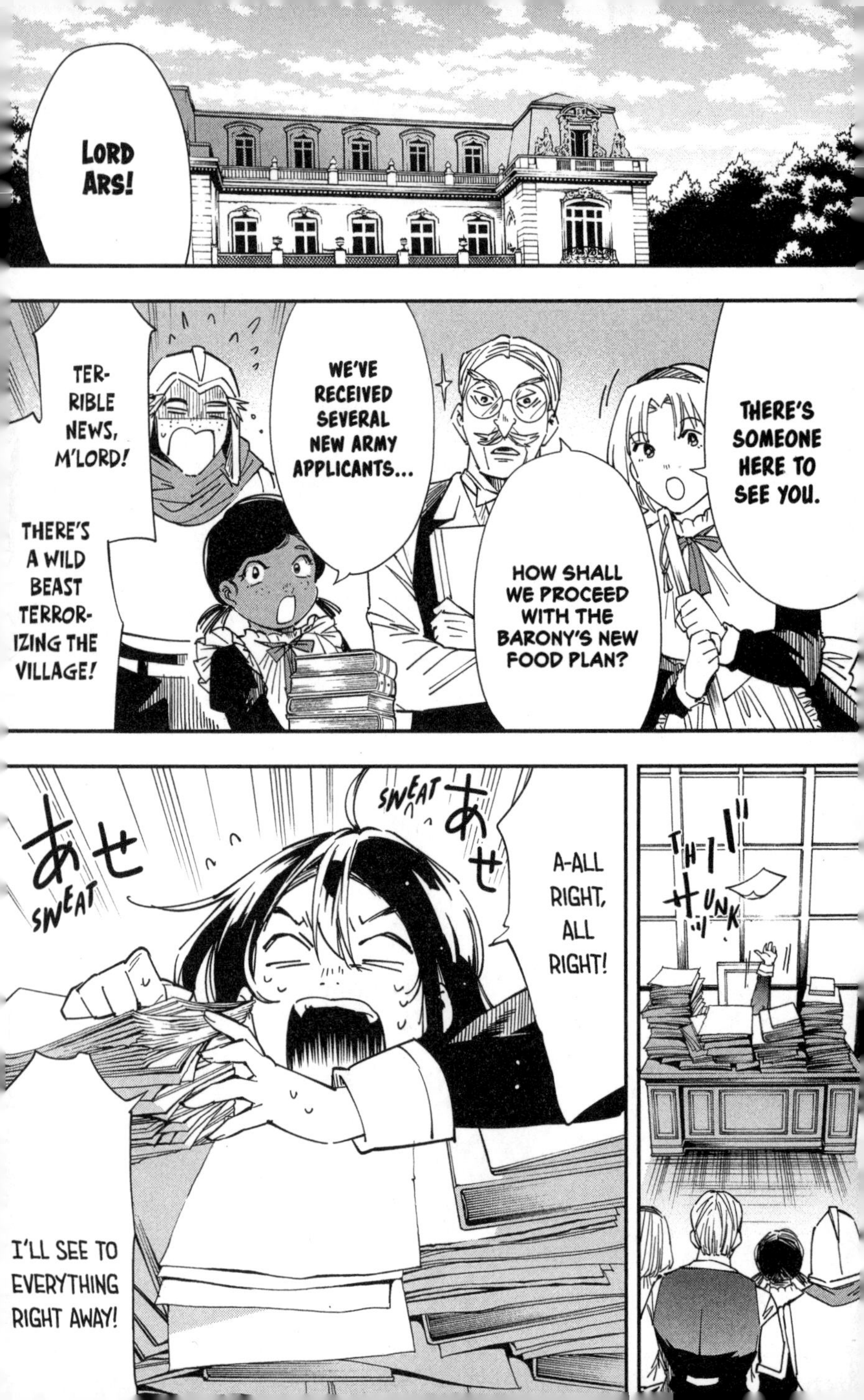
LORD ARS!
THERE'S SOMEONE HERE TO SEE YOU.
HOW SHALL WE PROCEED WITH THE BARONY'S NEW FOOD PLAN?
WE'VE RECEIVED SEVERAL NEW ARMY APPLICANTS...
TER-RIBLE NEWS, M'LORD!
THERE'S A WILD BEAST TERROR-IZING THE VILLAGE!
THUNK!
SWEAT
SWEAT
A-ALL RIGHT, ALL RIGHT!
I'LL SEE TO EVERYTHING RIGHT AWAY!

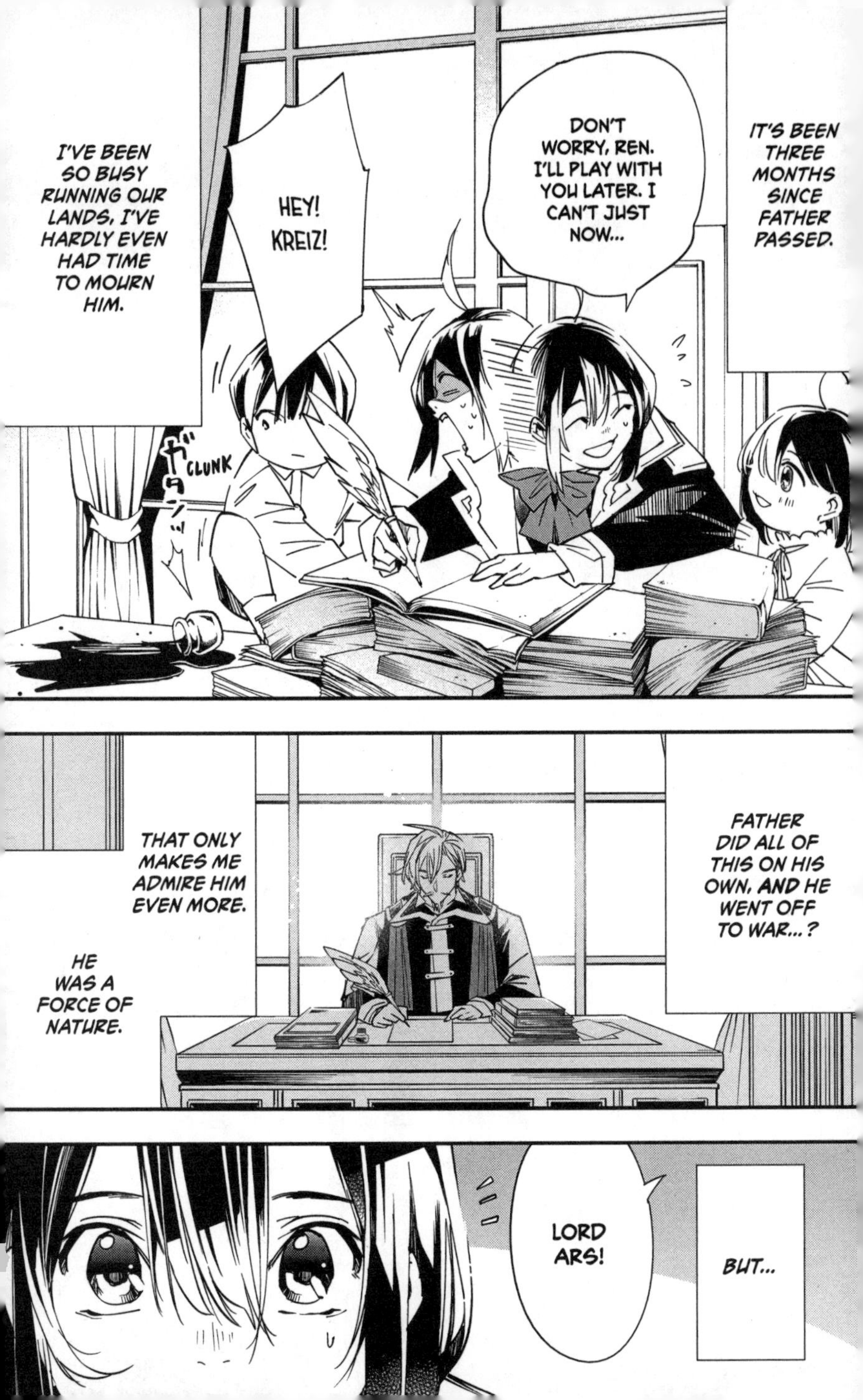
IT'S BEEN THREE MONTHS SINCE FATHER PASSED.
DON'T WORRY, REN. I'LL PLAY WITH YOU LATER. I CAN'T JUST NOW...
HEY! KREIZ!
I'VE BEEN SO BUSY RUNNING OUR LANDS, I'VE HARDLY EVEN HAD TIME TO MOURN HIM.
CLUNK
FATHER DID ALL OF THIS ON HIS OWN, AND HE WENT OFF TO WAR...?
THAT ONLY MAKES ME ADMIRE HIM EVEN MORE.
HE WAS A FORCE OF NATURE.
BUT...
LORD ARS!

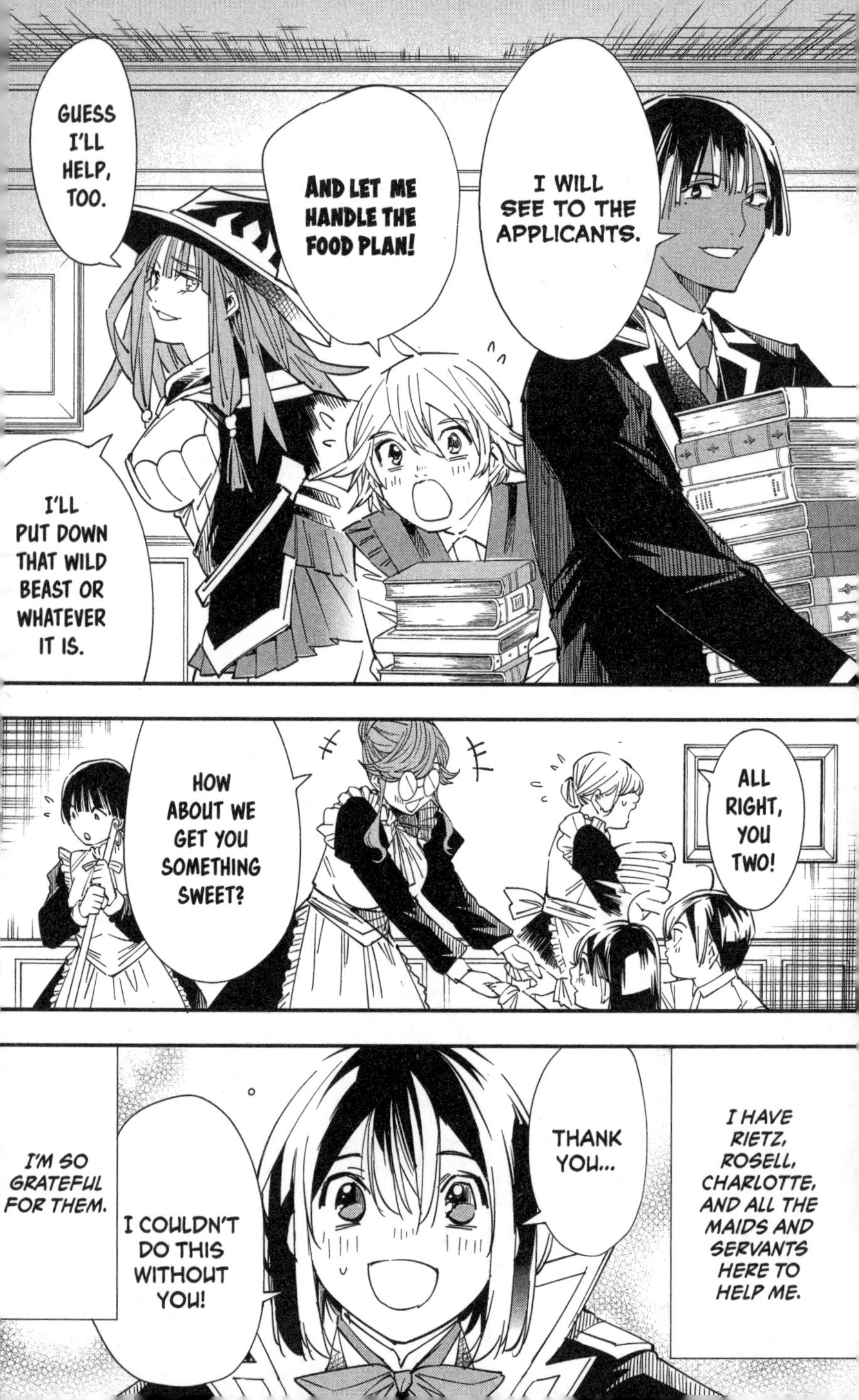
I WILL SEE TO THE APPLICANTS.
AND LET ME HANDLE THE FOOD PLAN!
GUESS I'LL HELP, TOO.
I'LL PUT DOWN THAT WILD BEAST OR WHATEVER IT IS.
ALL RIGHT, YOU TWO!
HOW ABOUT WE GET YOU SOMETHING SWEET?
I HAVE RIETZ, ROSELL, CHARLOTTE, AND ALL THE MAIDS AND SERVANTS HERE TO HELP ME.
THANK YOU...
I COULDN'T DO THIS WITHOUT YOU!
I'M SO GRATEFUL FOR THEM.

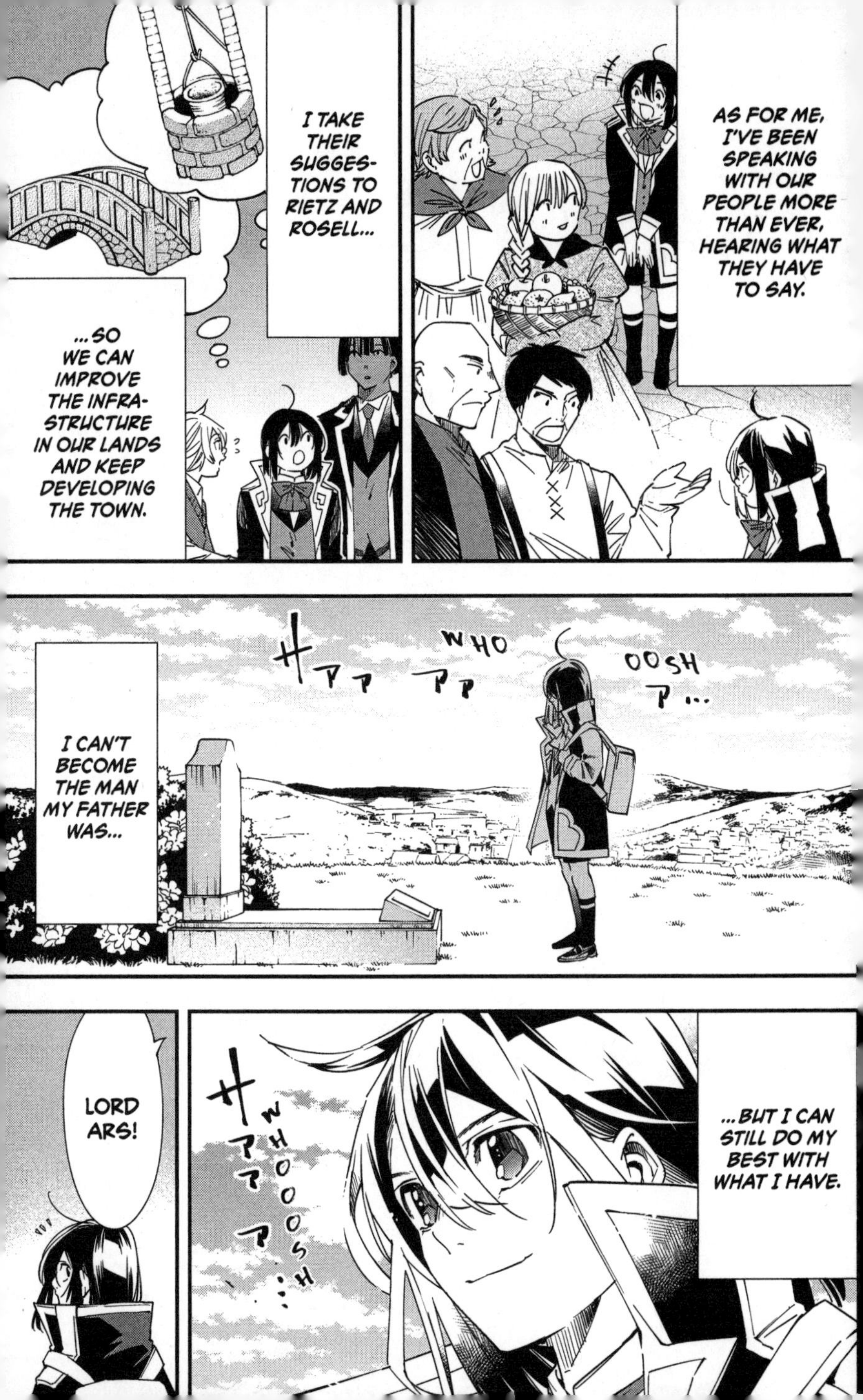
AS FOR ME, I'VE BEEN SPEAKING WITH OUR PEOPLE MORE THAN EVER, HEARING WHAT THEY HAVE TO SAY.
I TAKE THEIR SUGGES-TIONS TO RIETZ AND ROSELL...
...SO WE CAN IMPROVE THE INFRA-STRUCTURE IN OUR LANDS AND KEEP DEVELOPING THE TOWN.
WHO
OOSH...
I CAN'T BECOME THE MAN MY FATHER WAS...
...BUT I CAN STILL DO MY BEST WITH WHAT I HAVE.
WHOOOOSH...
LORD ARS!

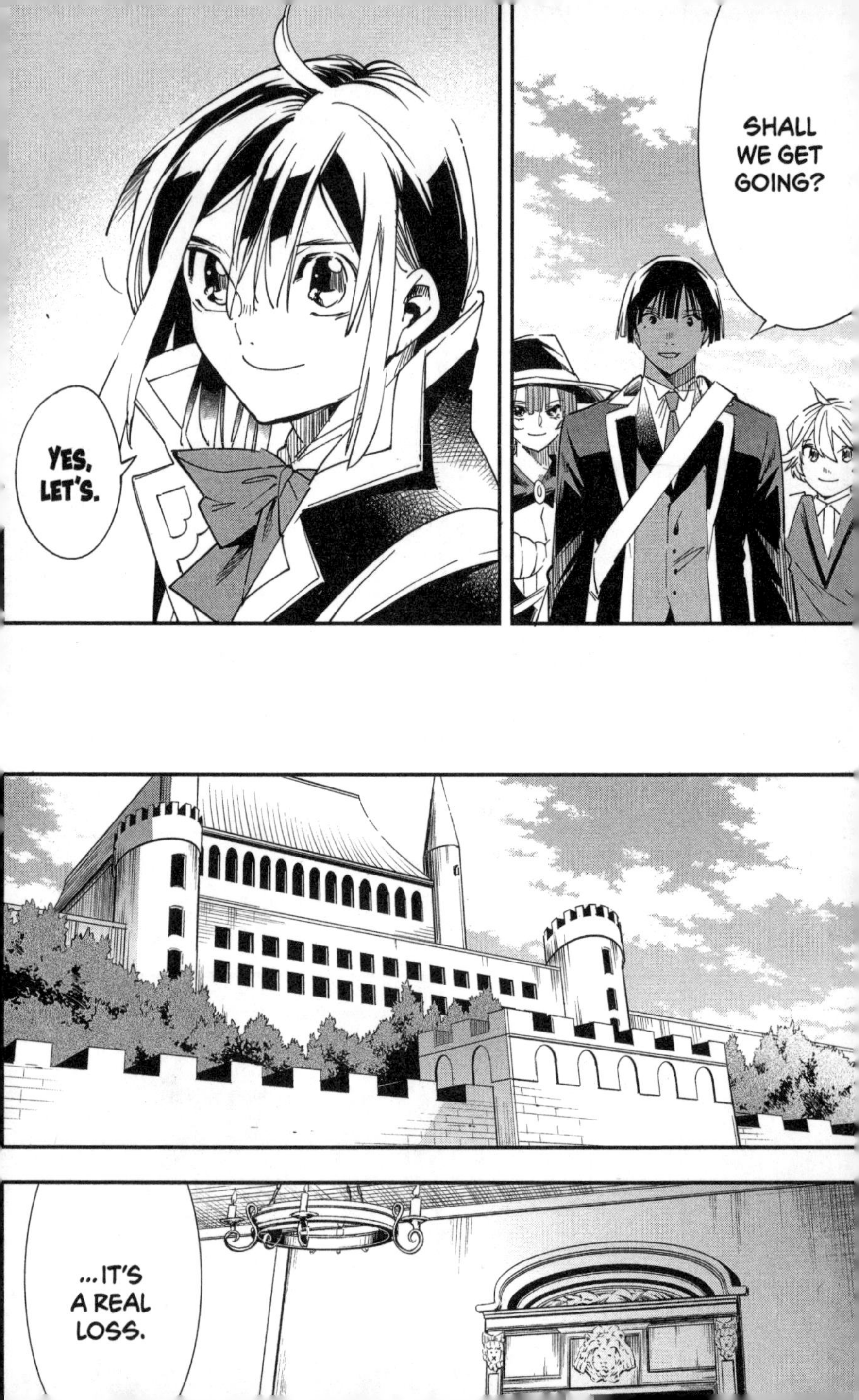
SHALL WE GET GOING?
YES, LET'S.
...IT'S A REAL LOSS.

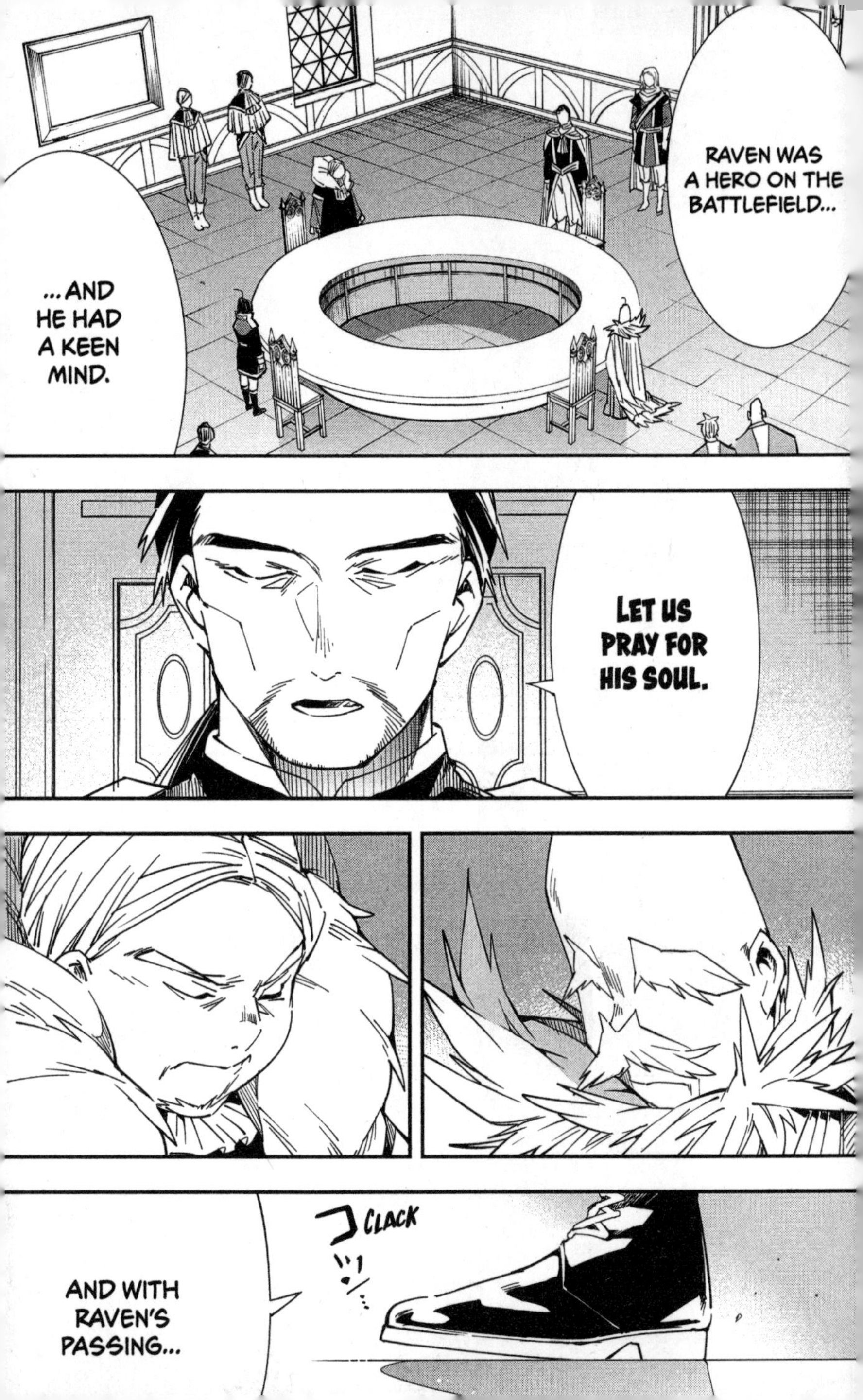
RAVEN WAS A HERO ON THE BATTLEFIELD...
...AND HE HAD A KEEN MIND.
LET US PRAY FOR HIS SOUL.
CLACK
AND WITH RAVEN'S PASSING...

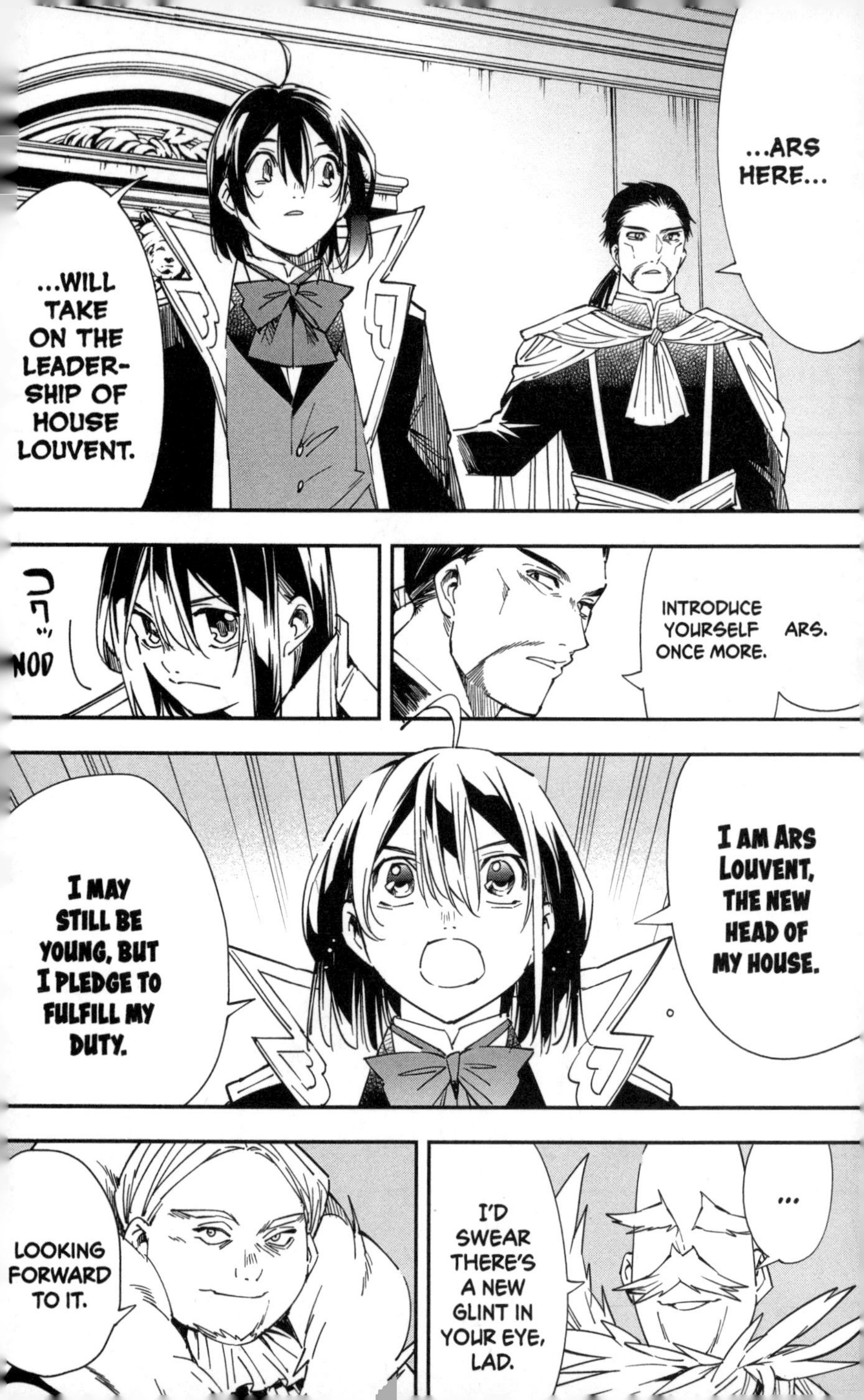
...ARS HERE...
...WILL TAKE ON THE LEADER-SHIP OF HOUSE LOUVENT.
INTRODUCE YOURSELF ONCE MORE. ARS.
コク
NOD
I AM ARS LOUVENT, THE NEW HEAD OF MY HOUSE.
I MAY STILL BE YOUNG, BUT I PLEDGE TO FULFILL MY DUTY.
...
I'D SWEAR THERE'S A NEW GLINT IN YOUR EYE, LAD.
LOOKING FORWARD TO IT.

YOU ARE OUR EQUAL HERE. WE EXPECT GREAT THINGS FROM YOU.

PAT

ARS...

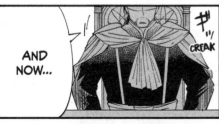

CLACK

CLACK

YES, MY LORD!

AND NOW...

CREAK

...TO BUSINESS.

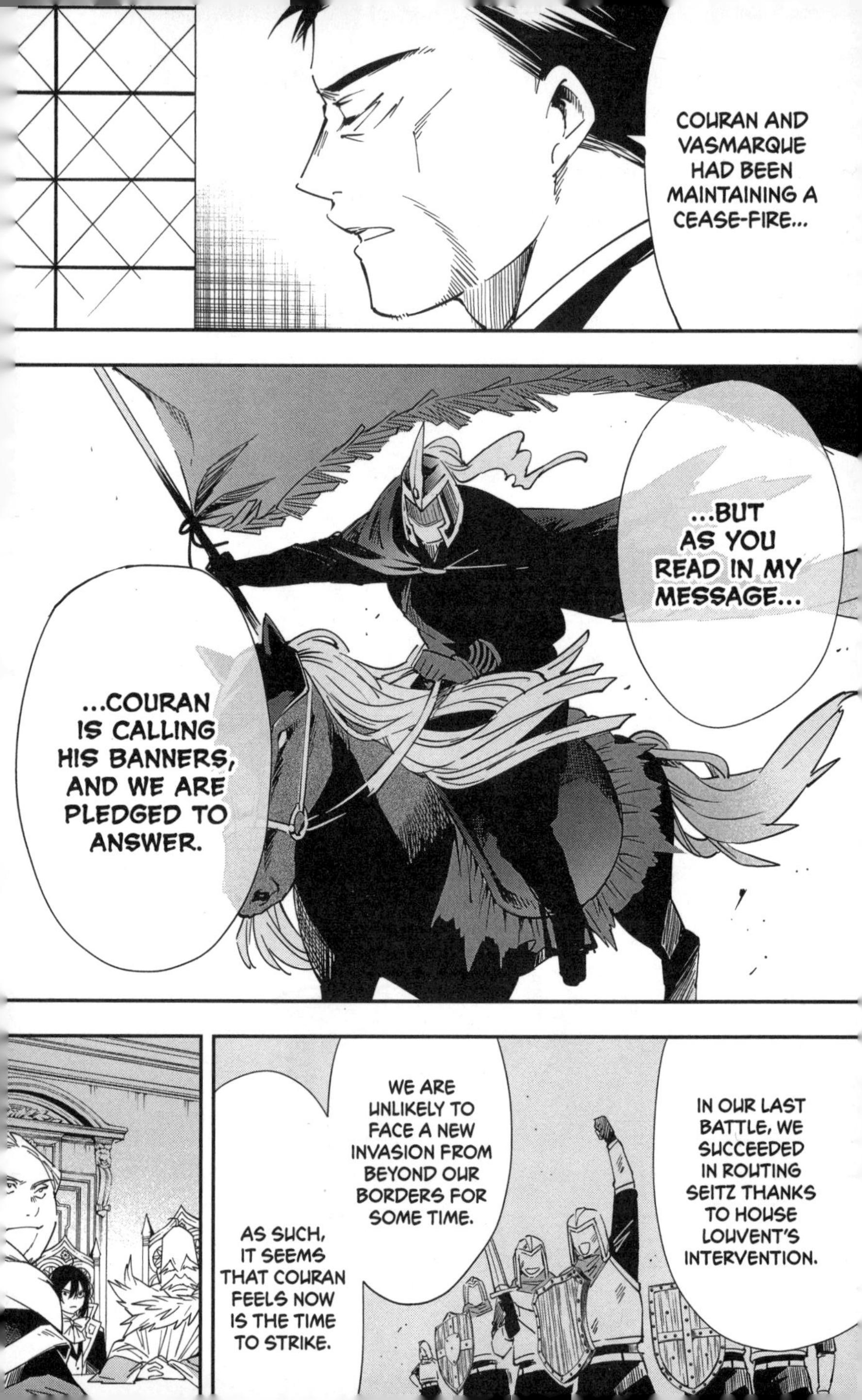
COURAN AND VASMARQUE HAD BEEN MAINTAINING A CEASE-FIRE...
...BUT AS YOU READ IN MY MESSAGE...
...COURAN IS CALLING HIS BANNERS, AND WE ARE PLEDGED TO ANSWER.
IN OUR LAST BATTLE, WE SUCCEEDED IN ROUTING SEITZ THANKS TO HOUSE LOUVENT'S INTERVENTION.
WE ARE UNLIKELY TO FACE A NEW INVASION FROM BEYOND OUR BORDERS FOR SOME TIME.
AS SUCH, IT SEEMS THAT COURAN FEELS NOW IS THE TIME TO STRIKE.

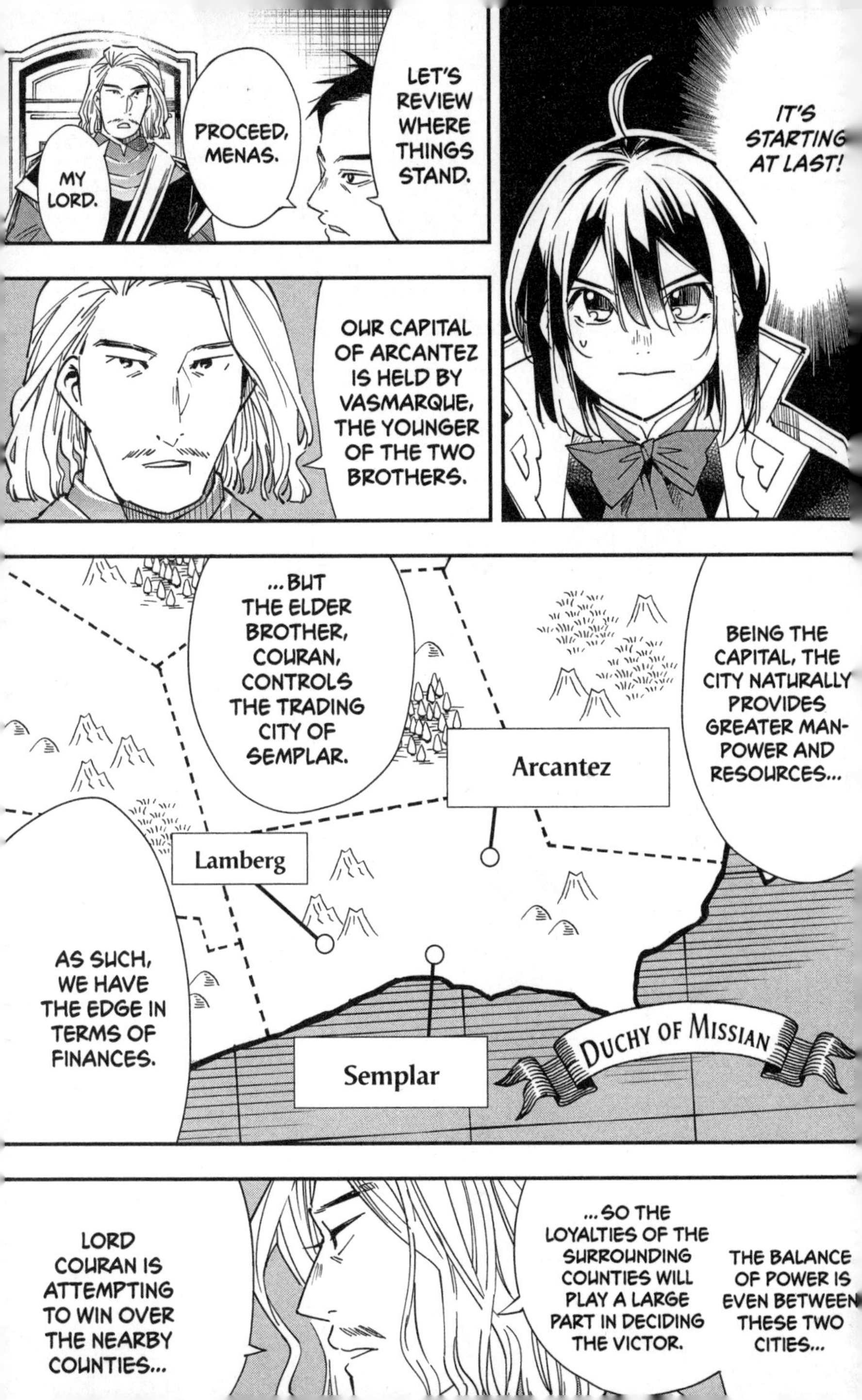
IT'S STARTING AT LAST!
LET'S REVIEW WHERE THINGS STAND.
PROCEED, MENAS.
MY LORD.
OUR CAPITAL OF ARCANTEZ IS HELD BY VASMARQUE, THE YOUNGER OF THE TWO BROTHERS.
BEING THE CAPITAL, THE CITY NATURALLY PROVIDES GREATER MAN-POWER AND RESOURCES...
...BUT THE ELDER BROTHER, COURAN, CONTROLS THE TRADING CITY OF SEMPLAR.
Arcantez
Lamberg
AS SUCH, WE HAVE THE EDGE IN TERMS OF FINANCES.
DUCHY OF MISSIAN
Semplar
THE BALANCE OF POWER IS EVEN BETWEEN THESE TWO CITIES...
...SO THE LOYALTIES OF THE SURROUNDING COUNTIES WILL PLAY A LARGE PART IN DECIDING THE VICTOR.
LORD COURAN IS ATTEMPTING TO WIN OVER THE NEARBY COUNTIES...

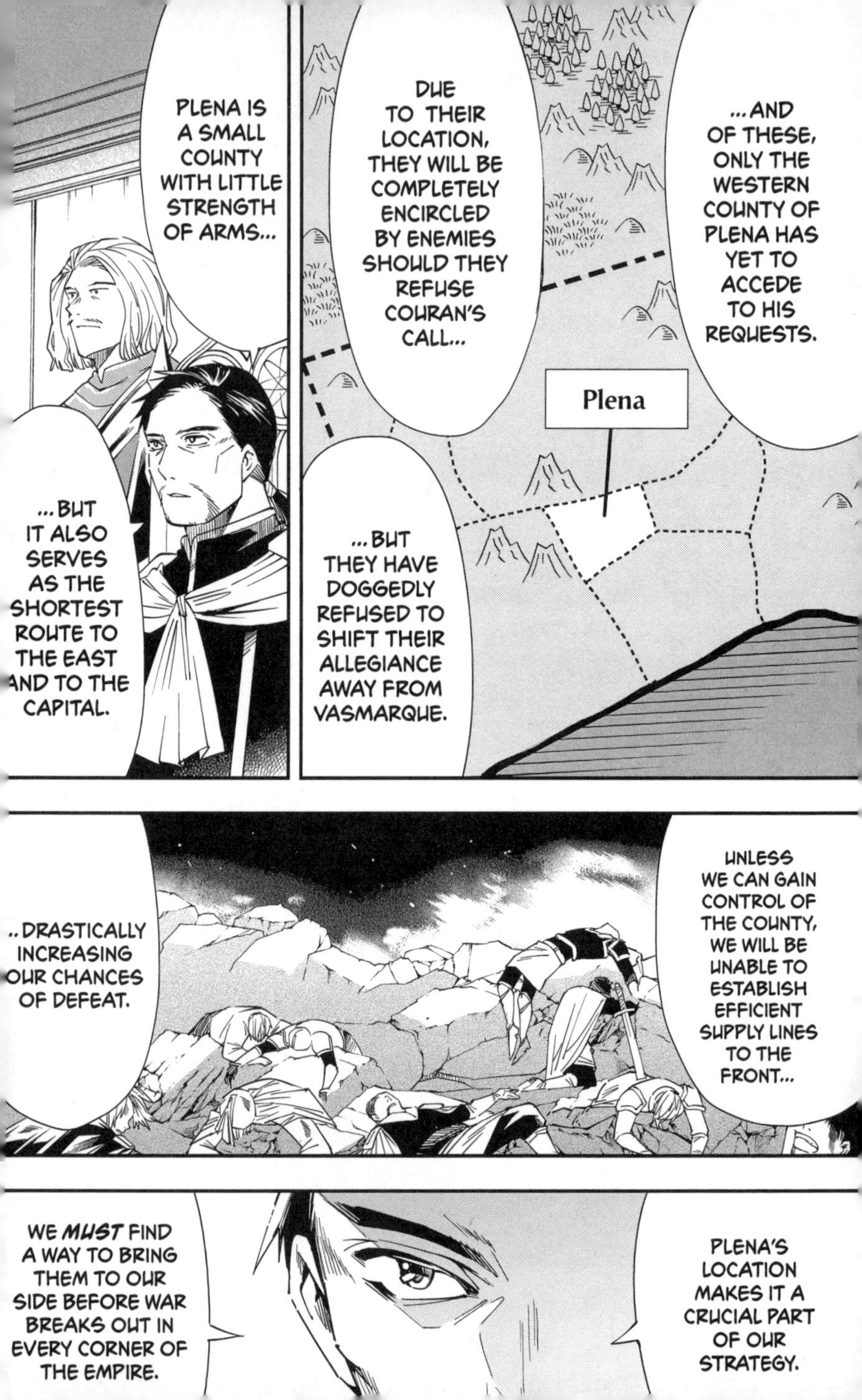
...AND OF THESE, ONLY THE WESTERN COUNTY OF PLENA HAS YET TO ACCEDE TO HIS REQUESTS.
DUE TO THEIR LOCATION, THEY WILL BE COMPLETELY ENCIRCLED BY ENEMIES SHOULD THEY REFUSE COURAN'S CALL...
Plena
...BUT THEY HAVE DOGGEDLY REFUSED TO SHIFT THEIR ALLEGIANCE AWAY FROM VASMARQUE.
PLENA IS A SMALL COUNTY WITH LITTLE STRENGTH OF ARMS...
...BUT IT ALSO SERVES AS THE SHORTEST ROUTE TO THE EAST AND TO THE CAPITAL.
UNLESS WE CAN GAIN CONTROL OF THE COUNTY, WE WILL BE UNABLE TO ESTABLISH EFFICIENT SUPPLY LINES TO THE FRONT...
..DRASTICALLY INCREASING OUR CHANCES OF DEFEAT.
PLENA'S LOCATION MAKES IT A CRUCIAL PART OF OUR STRATEGY.
WE *MUST* FIND A WAY TO BRING THEM TO OUR SIDE BEFORE WAR BREAKS OUT IN EVERY CORNER OF THE EMPIRE.

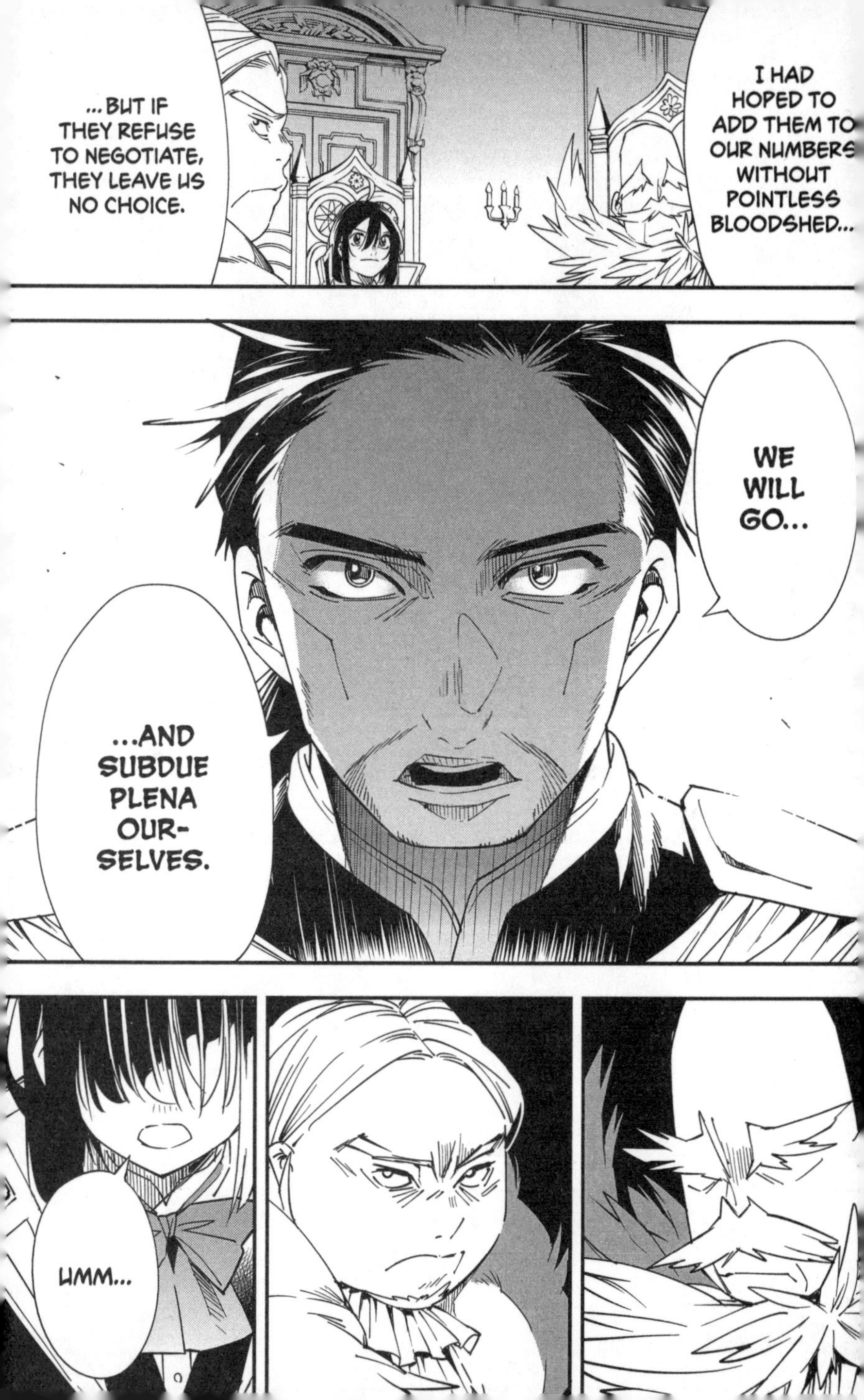
I HAD HOPED TO ADD THEM TO OUR NUMBERS WITHOUT POINTLESS BLOODSHED...
...BUT IF THEY REFUSE TO NEGOTIATE, THEY LEAVE US NO CHOICE.
WE WILL GO...
...AND SUBDUE PLENA OUR-SELVES.
UMM...

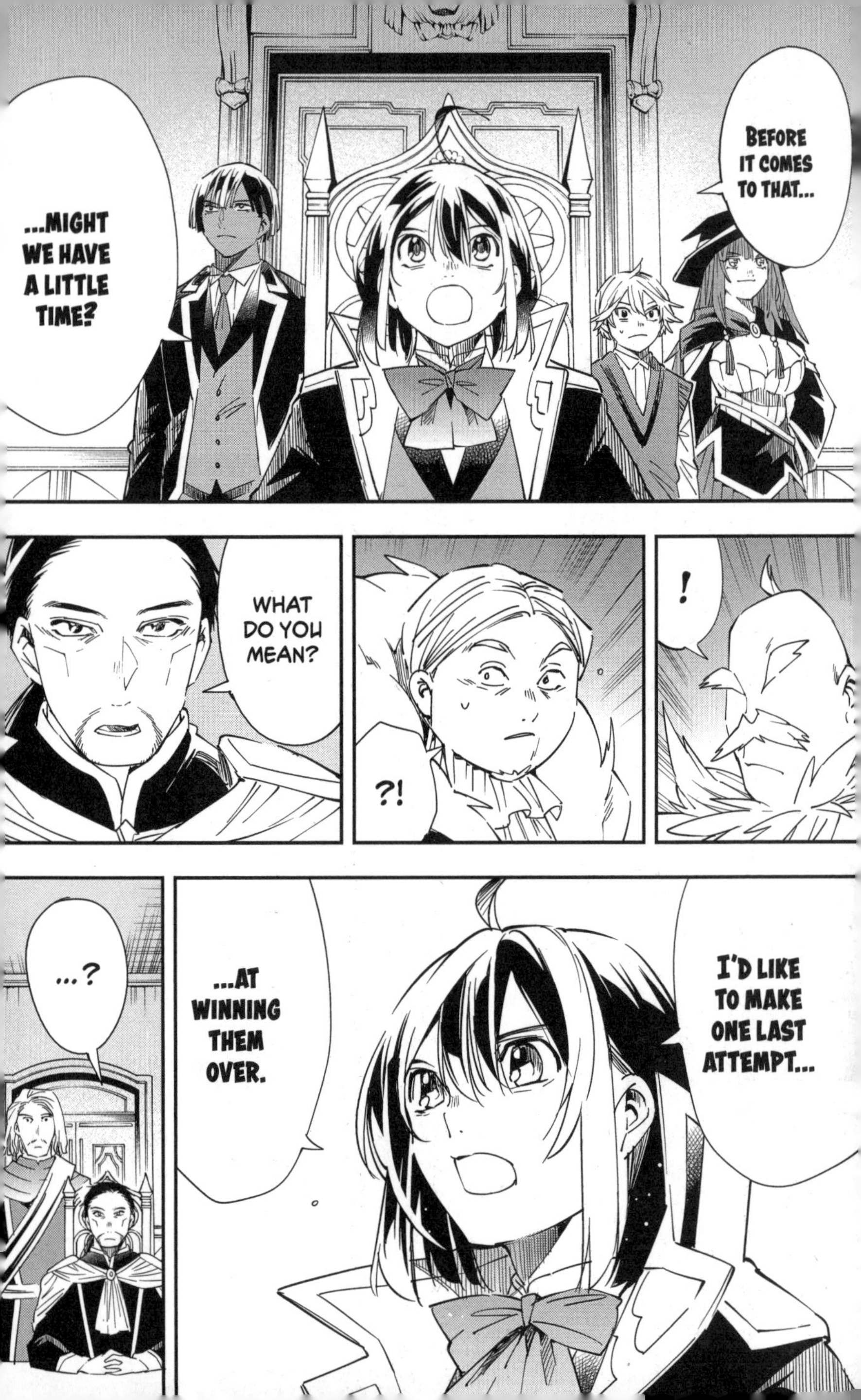
BEFORE IT COMES TO THAT...
...MIGHT WE HAVE A LITTLE TIME?
!
?!
WHAT DO YOU MEAN?
I'D LIKE TO MAKE ONE LAST ATTEMPT...
...AT WINNING THEM OVER.
...?

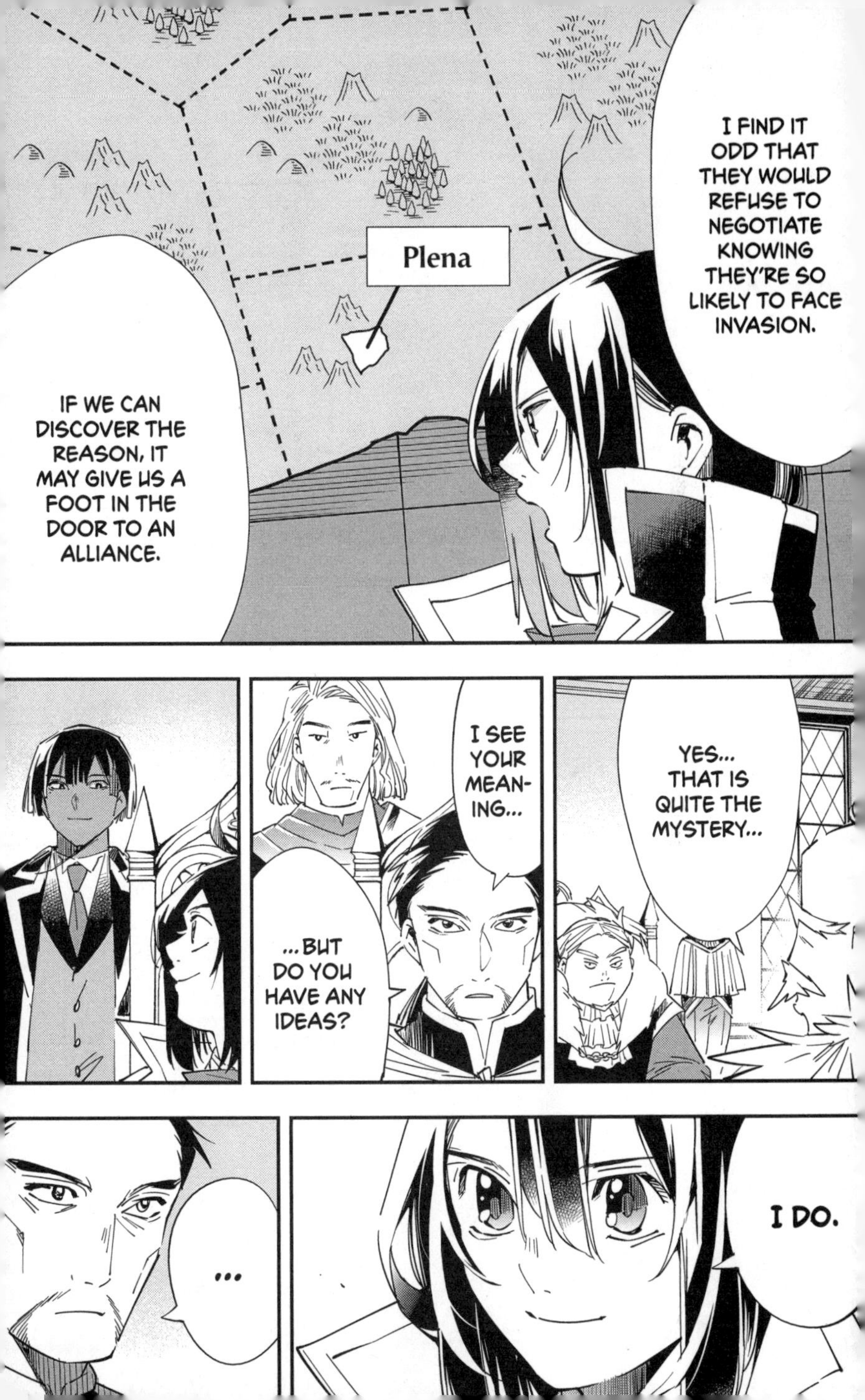
I FIND IT ODD THAT THEY WOULD REFUSE TO NEGOTIATE KNOWING THEY'RE SO LIKELY TO FACE INVASION.
Plena
IF WE CAN DISCOVER THE REASON, IT MAY GIVE US A FOOT IN THE DOOR TO AN ALLIANCE.
YES... THAT IS QUITE THE MYSTERY...
I SEE YOUR MEAN-ING...
...BUT DO YOU HAVE ANY IDEAS?
I DO.
...

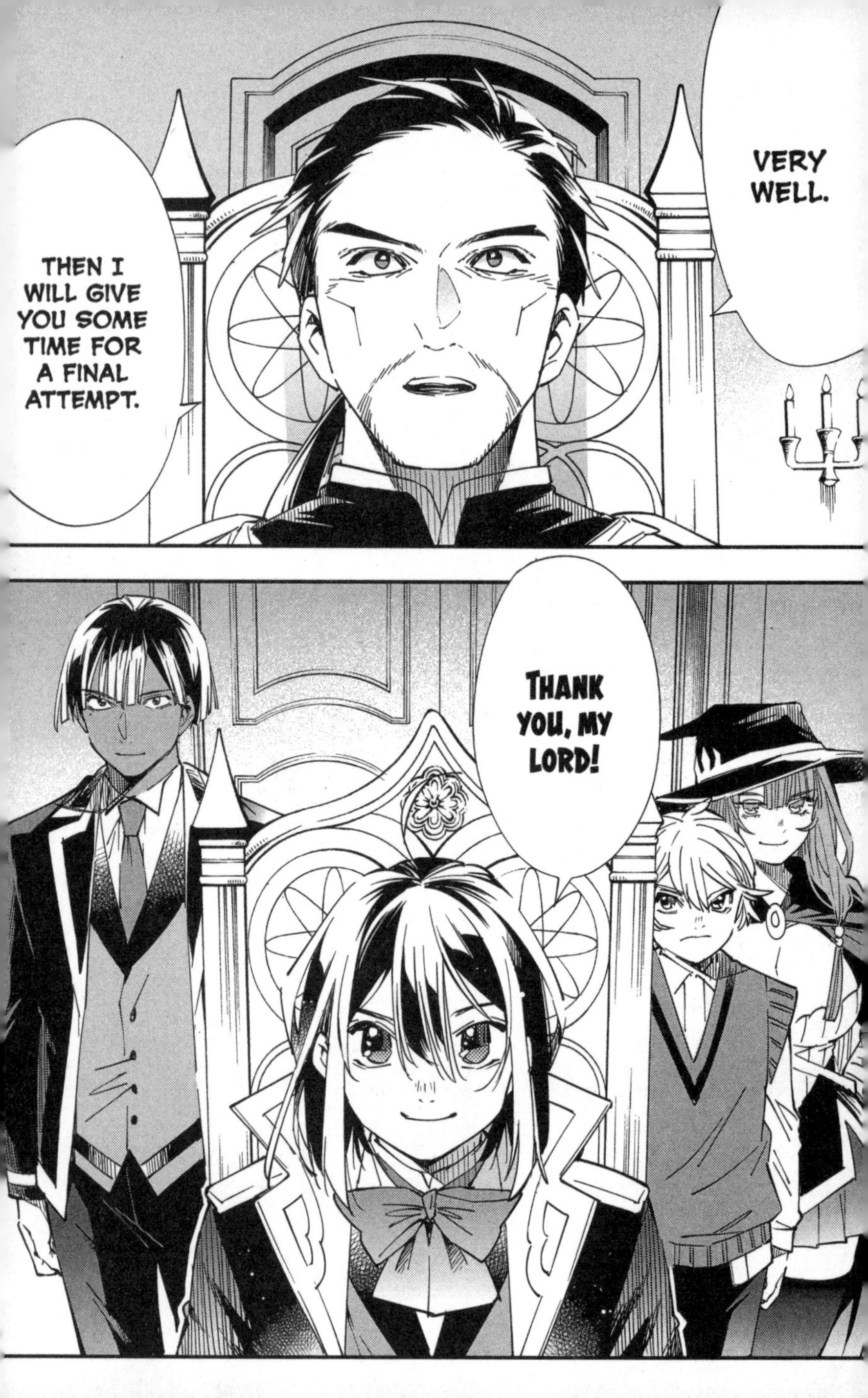
VERY WELL.
THEN I WILL GIVE YOU SOME TIME FOR A FINAL ATTEMPT.
THANK YOU, MY LORD!

As a Reincarnated
ARISTOCRAT,
I'll Use My Appraisal Skill to
Rise in the World

As a Reincarnated
ARISTOCRAT,
I'll Use My Appraisal Skill to
Rise in the World

Chapter 33: Reunion and Planning

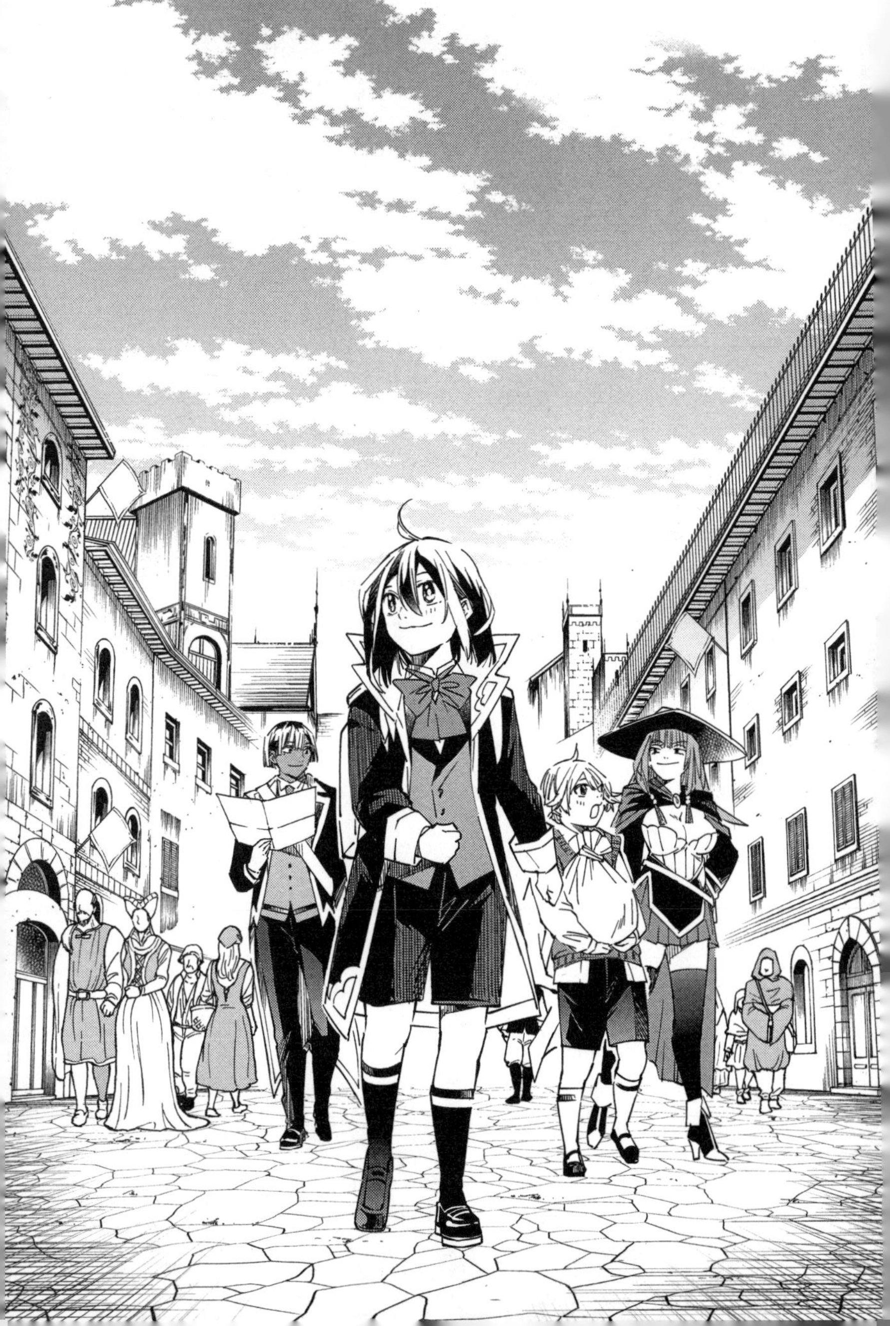

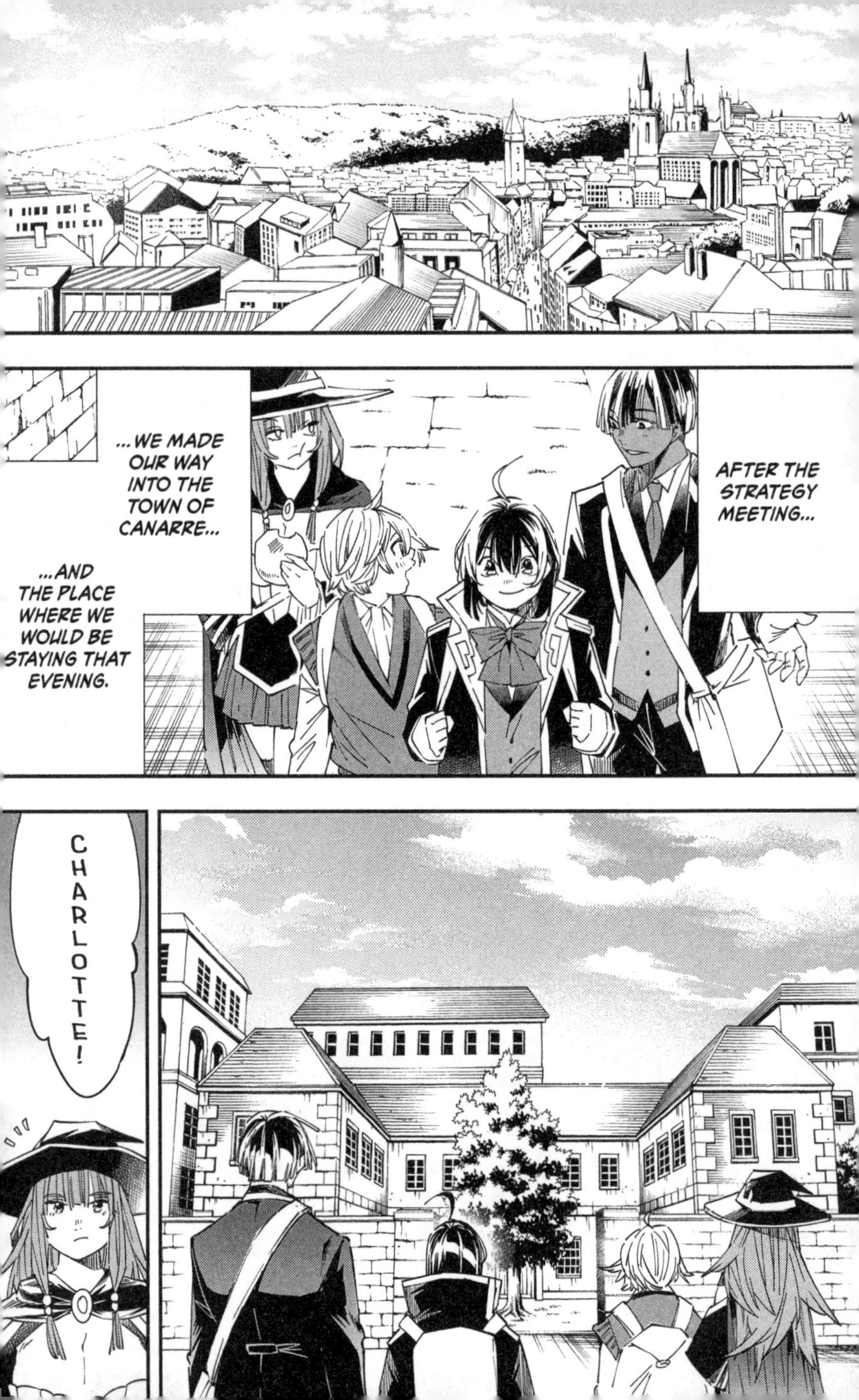
AFTER THE STRATEGY MEETING...
...WE MADE OUR WAY INTO THE TOWN OF CANARRE...
...AND THE PLACE WHERE WE WOULD BE STAYING THAT EVENING.
CHARLOTTE!

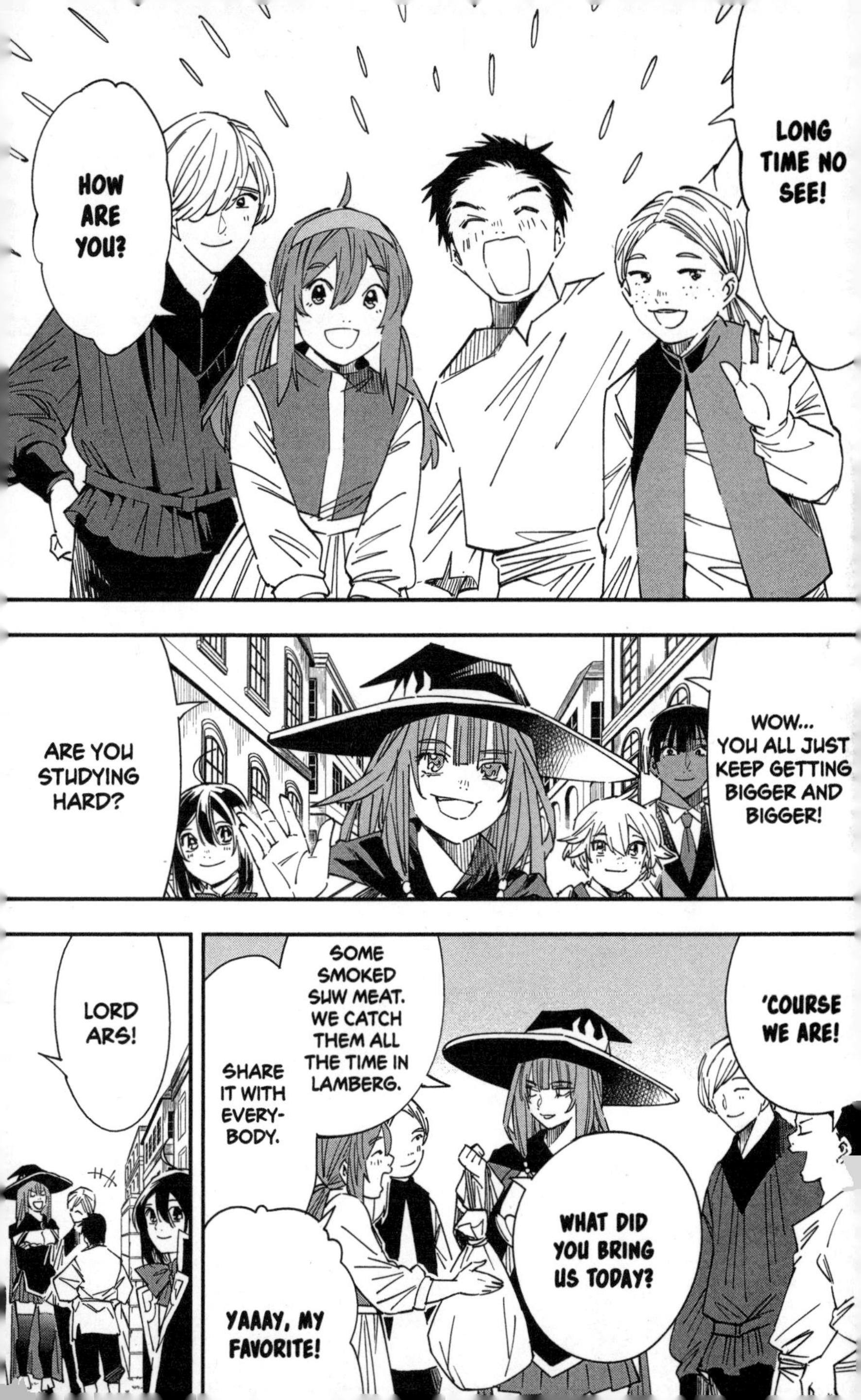
LONG TIME NO SEE!
HOW ARE YOU?
WOW... YOU ALL JUST KEEP GETTING BIGGER AND BIGGER!
ARE YOU STUDYING HARD?
'COURSE WE ARE!
WHAT DID YOU BRING US TODAY?
SOME SMOKED SUW MEAT. WE CATCH THEM ALL THE TIME IN LAMBERG.
SHARE IT WITH EVERY-BODY.
YAAAY, MY FAVORITE!
LORD ARS!

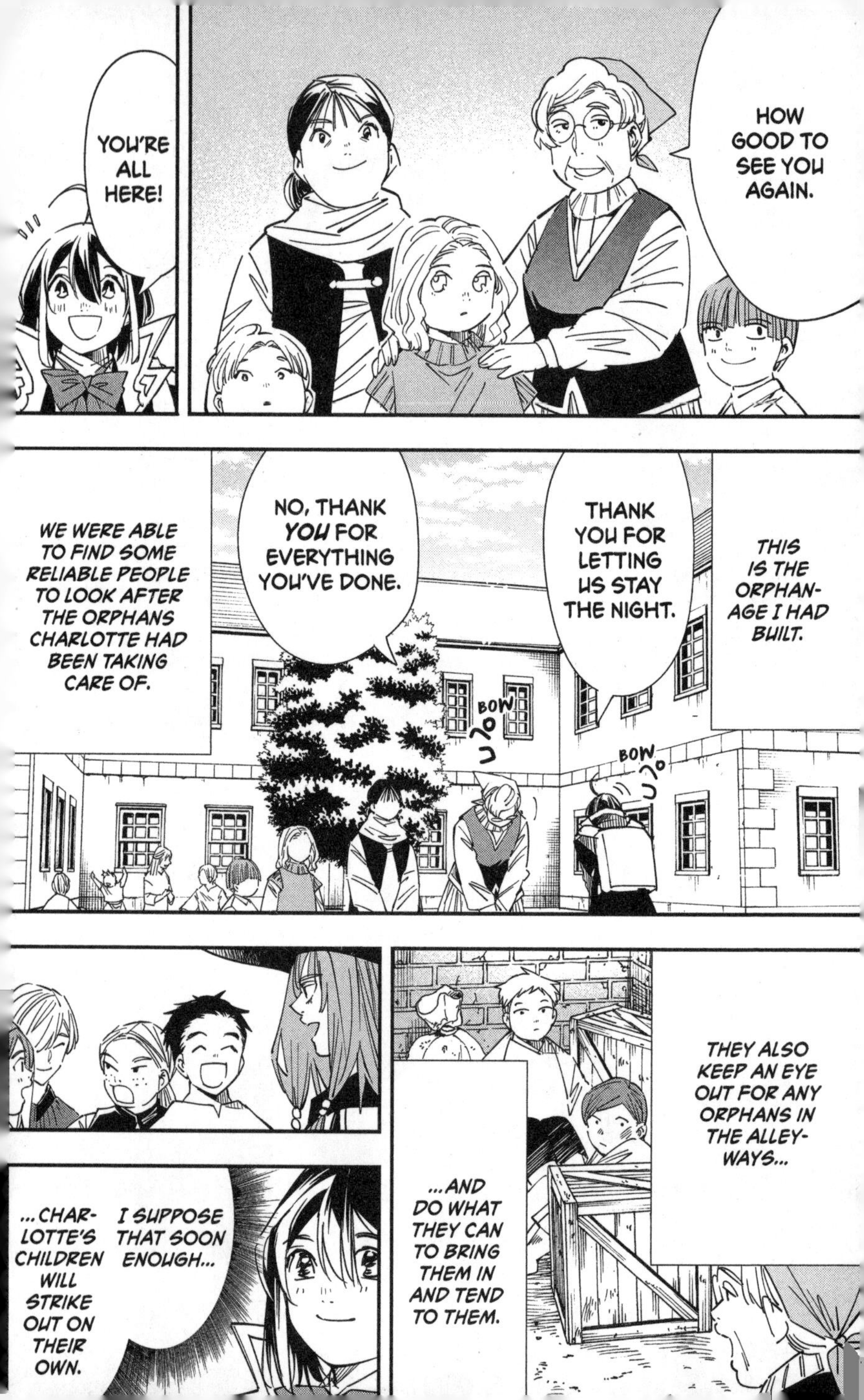
HOW GOOD TO SEE YOU AGAIN.
YOU'RE ALL HERE!
THIS IS THE ORPHANAGE I HAD BUILT.
THANK YOU FOR LETTING US STAY THE NIGHT.
NO, THANK *YOU* FOR EVERYTHING YOU'VE DONE.
WE WERE ABLE TO FIND SOME RELIABLE PEOPLE TO LOOK AFTER THE ORPHANS CHARLOTTE HAD BEEN TAKING CARE OF.
BOW
BOW
THEY ALSO KEEP AN EYE OUT FOR ANY ORPHANS IN THE ALLEYWAYS...
...AND DO WHAT THEY CAN TO BRING THEM IN AND TEND TO THEM.
I SUPPOSE THAT SOON ENOUGH...
...CHARLOTTE'S CHILDREN WILL STRIKE OUT ON THEIR OWN.

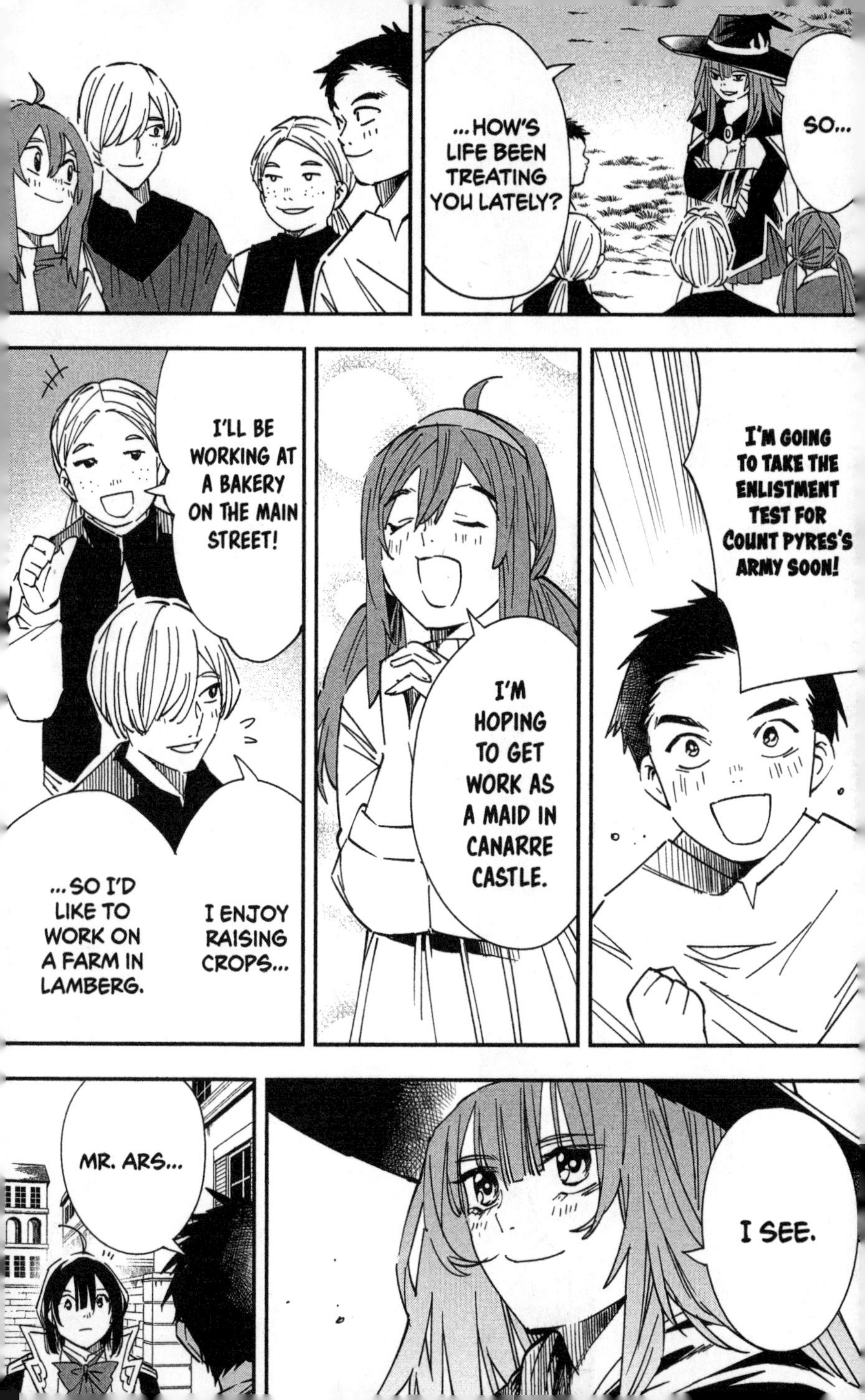
SO...
...HOW'S LIFE BEEN TREATING YOU LATELY?
I'M GOING TO TAKE THE ENLISTMENT TEST FOR COUNT PYRES'S ARMY SOON!
I'M HOPING TO GET WORK AS A MAID IN CANARRE CASTLE.
I'LL BE WORKING AT A BAKERY ON THE MAIN STREET!
I ENJOY RAISING CROPS...
...SO I'D LIKE TO WORK ON A FARM IN LAMBERG.
I SEE.
MR. ARS...

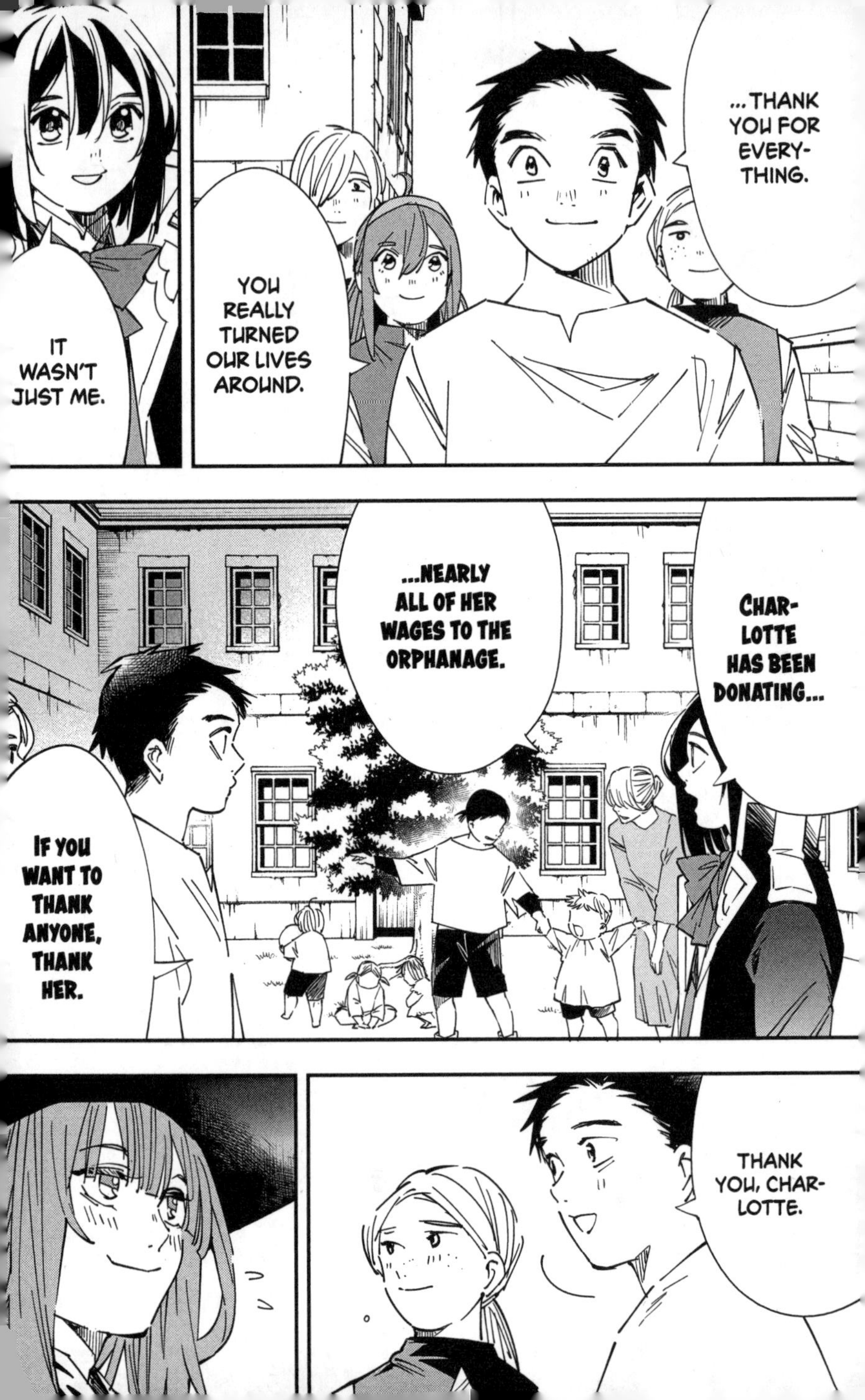
...THANK YOU FOR EVERY-THING.
YOU REALLY TURNED OUR LIVES AROUND.
IT WASN'T JUST ME.
CHAR-LOTTE HAS BEEN DONATING...
...NEARLY ALL OF HER WAGES TO THE ORPHANAGE.
IF YOU WANT TO THANK ANYONE, THANK HER.
THANK YOU, CHAR-LOTTE.

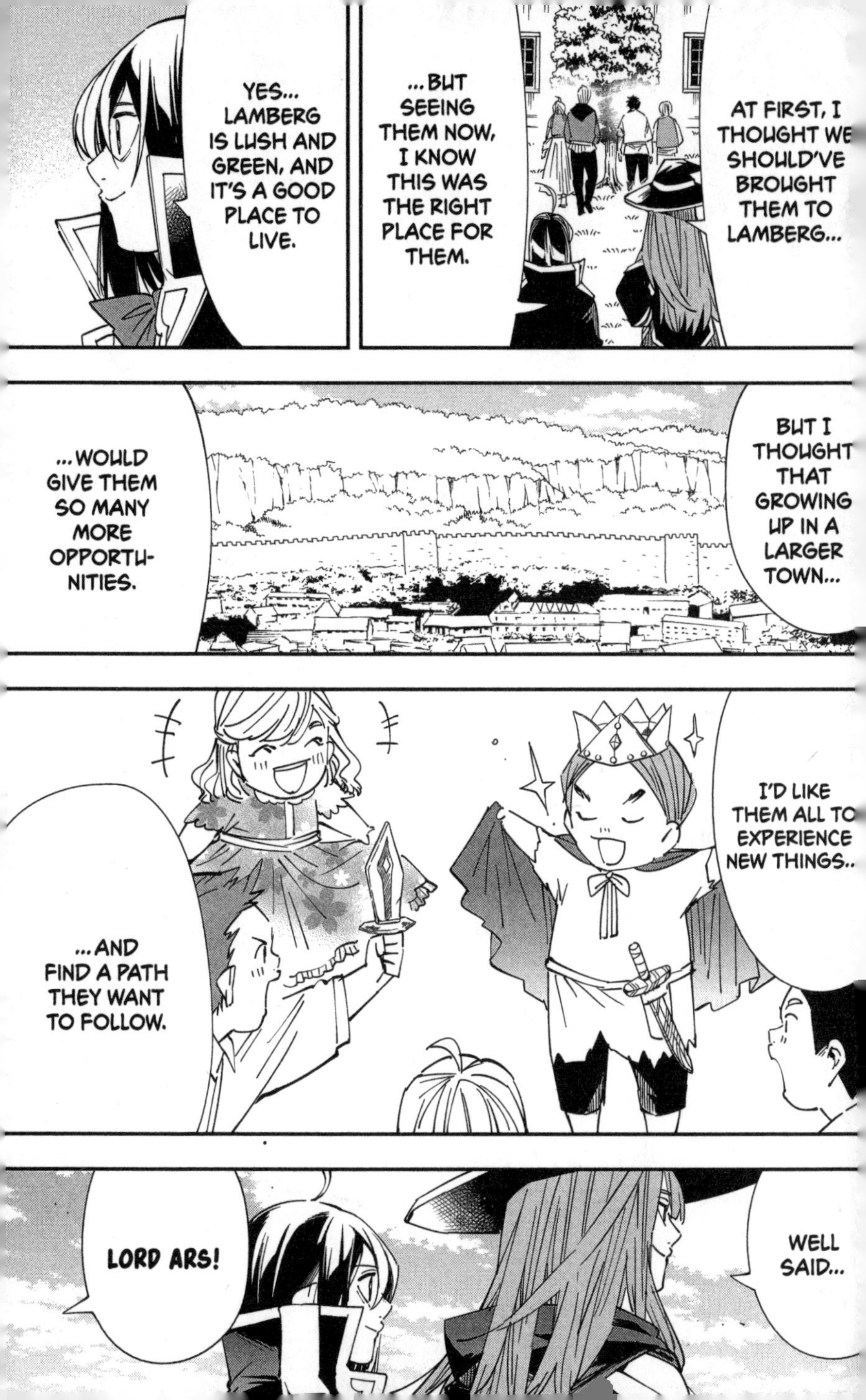
AT FIRST, I THOUGHT WE SHOULD'VE BROUGHT THEM TO LAMBERG...
...BUT SEEING THEM NOW, I KNOW THIS WAS THE RIGHT PLACE FOR THEM.
YES... LAMBERG IS LUSH AND GREEN, AND IT'S A GOOD PLACE TO LIVE.
BUT I THOUGHT THAT GROWING UP IN A LARGER TOWN...
...WOULD GIVE THEM SO MANY MORE OPPORTU-NITIES.
I'D LIKE THEM ALL TO EXPERIENCE NEW THINGS...
...AND FIND A PATH THEY WANT TO FOLLOW.
WELL SAID...
LORD ARS!

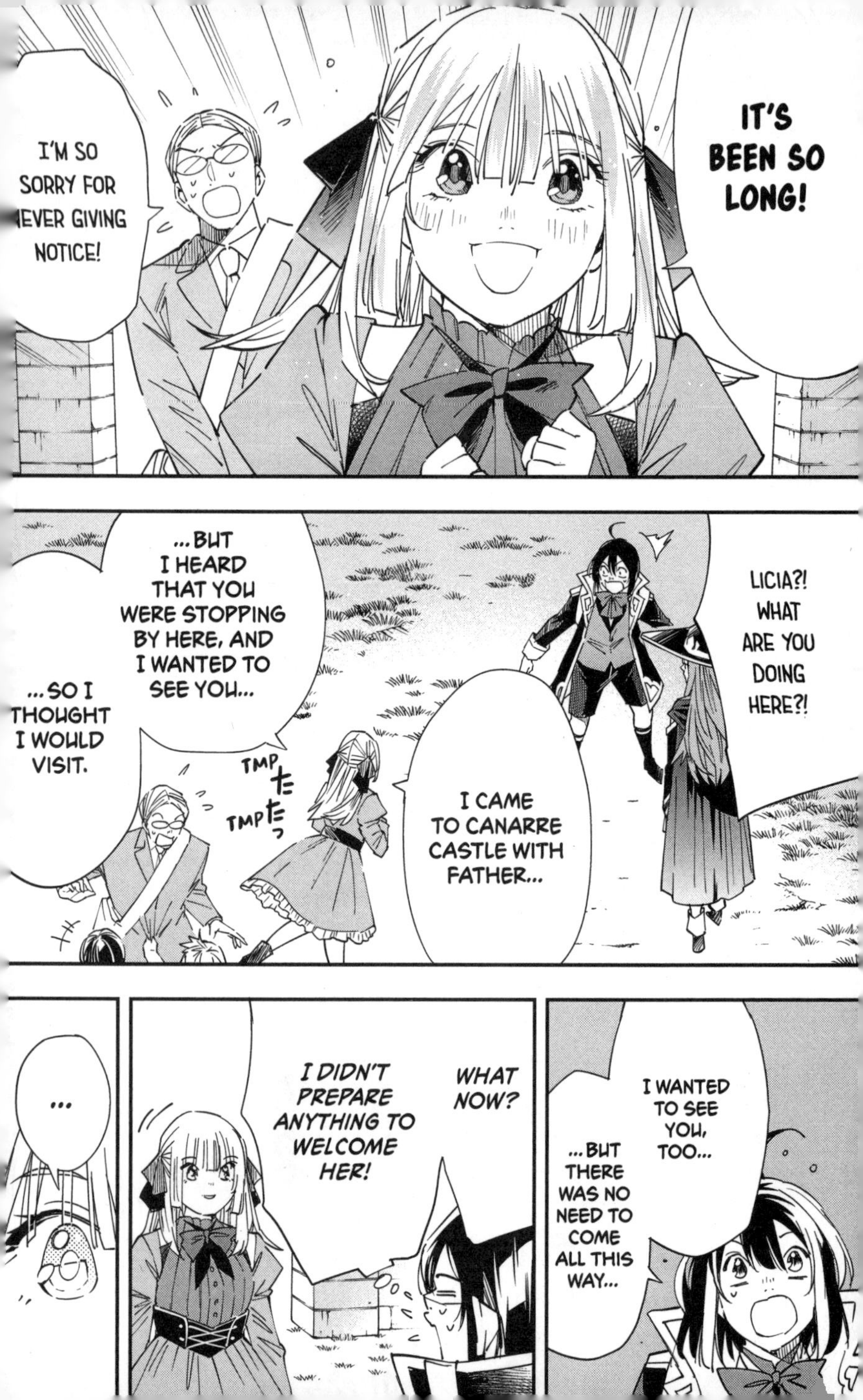
IT'S BEEN SO LONG!
I'M SO SORRY FOR NEVER GIVING NOTICE!
LICIA?! WHAT ARE YOU DOING HERE?!
I CAME TO CANARRE CASTLE WITH FATHER...
...BUT I HEARD THAT YOU WERE STOPPING BY HERE, AND I WANTED TO SEE YOU...
...SO I THOUGHT I WOULD VISIT.
TMP
TMP
I WANTED TO SEE YOU, TOO...
...BUT THERE WAS NO NEED TO COME ALL THIS WAY...
WHAT NOW?
I DIDN'T PREPARE ANYTHING TO WELCOME HER!
...

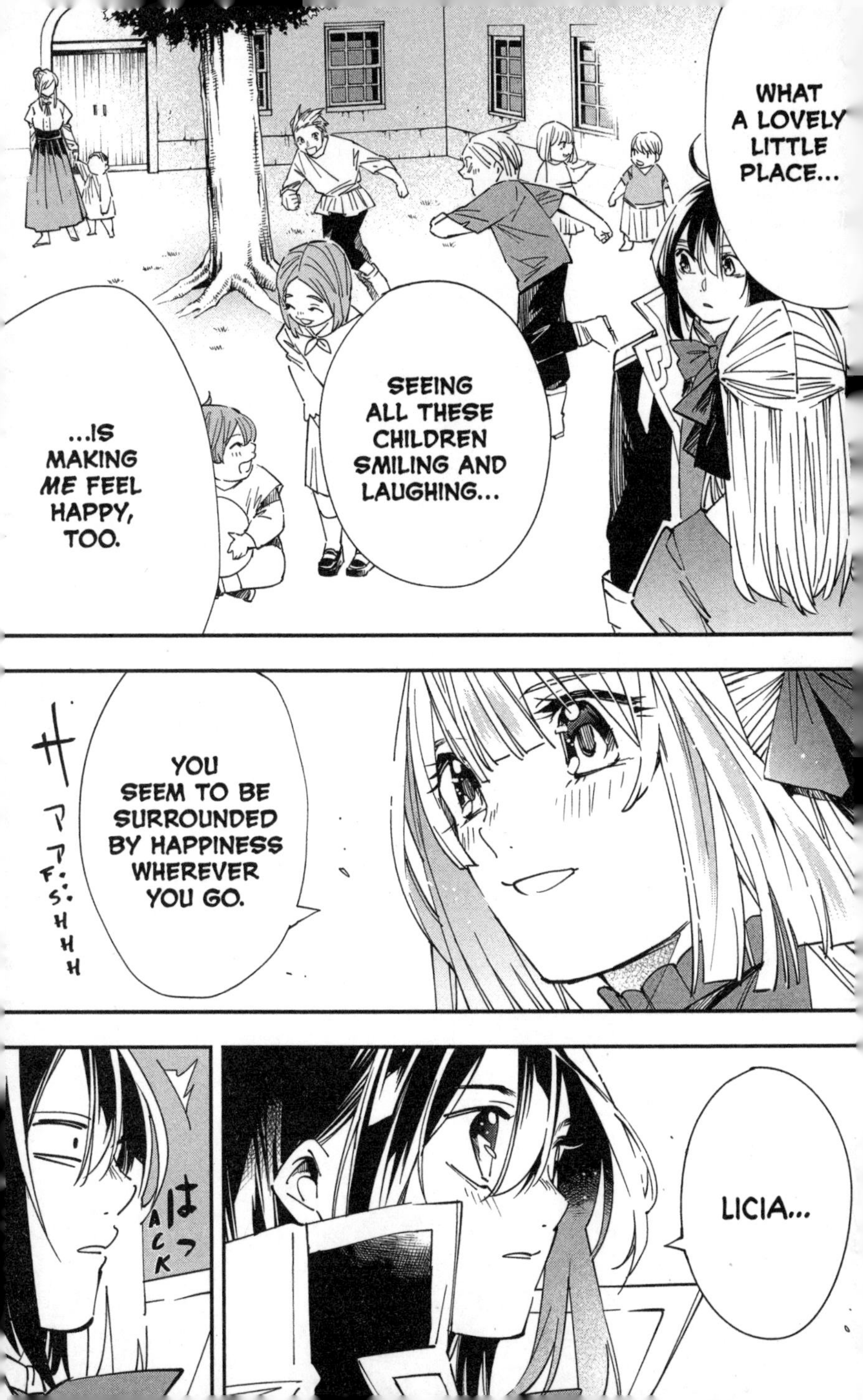

WHAT A LOVELY LITTLE PLACE...
SEEING ALL THESE CHILDREN SMILING AND LAUGHING...
...IS MAKING *ME* FEEL HAPPY, TOO.
YOU SEEM TO BE SURROUNDED BY HAPPINESS WHEREVER YOU GO.
サァァ
F-SHHH
LICIA...
はっ
ACK

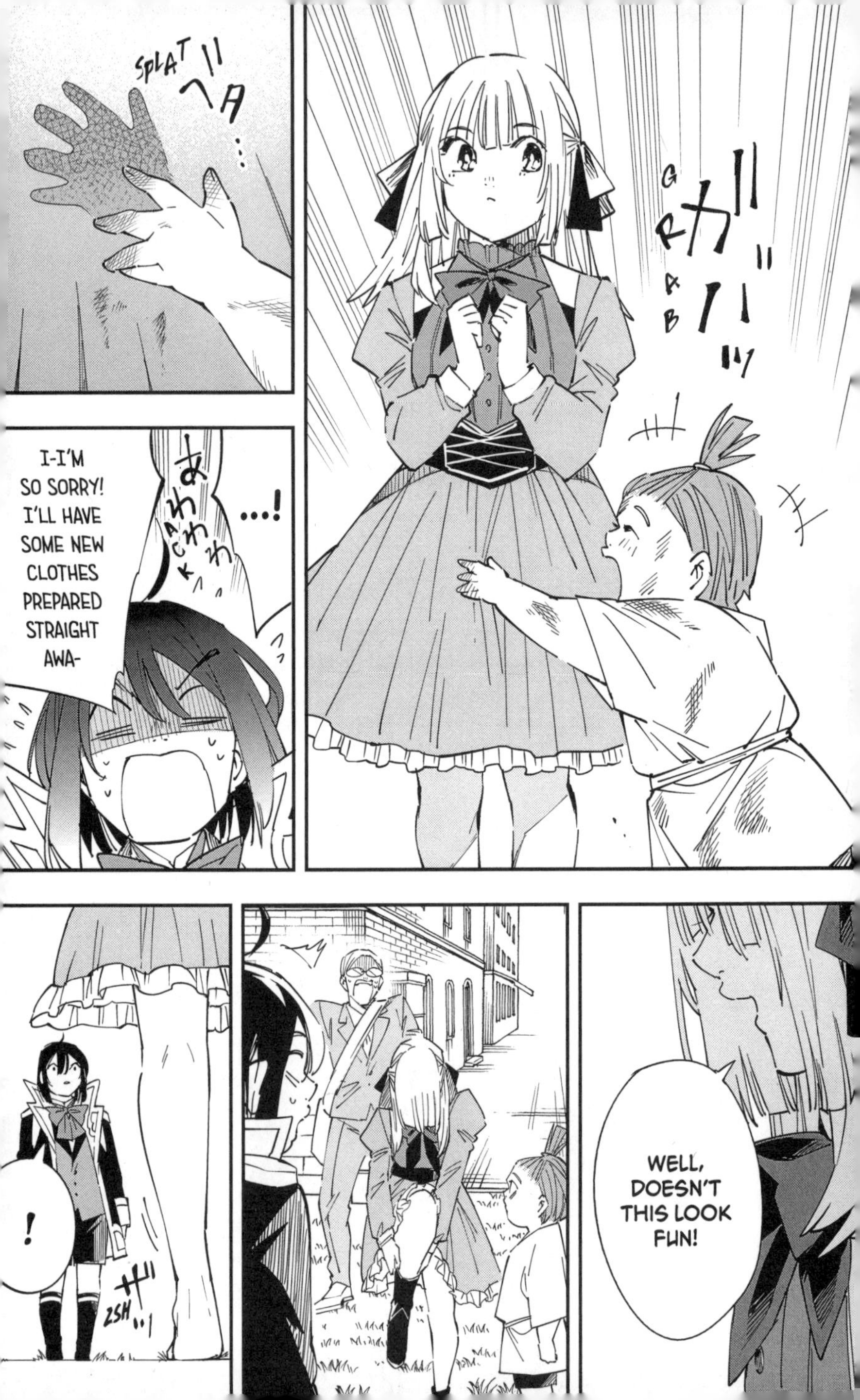
GRAB
SPLAT
I-I'M SO SORRY! I'LL HAVE SOME NEW CLOTHES PREPARED STRAIGHT AWA-
...!
ACK
WELL, DOESN'T THIS LOOK FUN!
!
ZSH

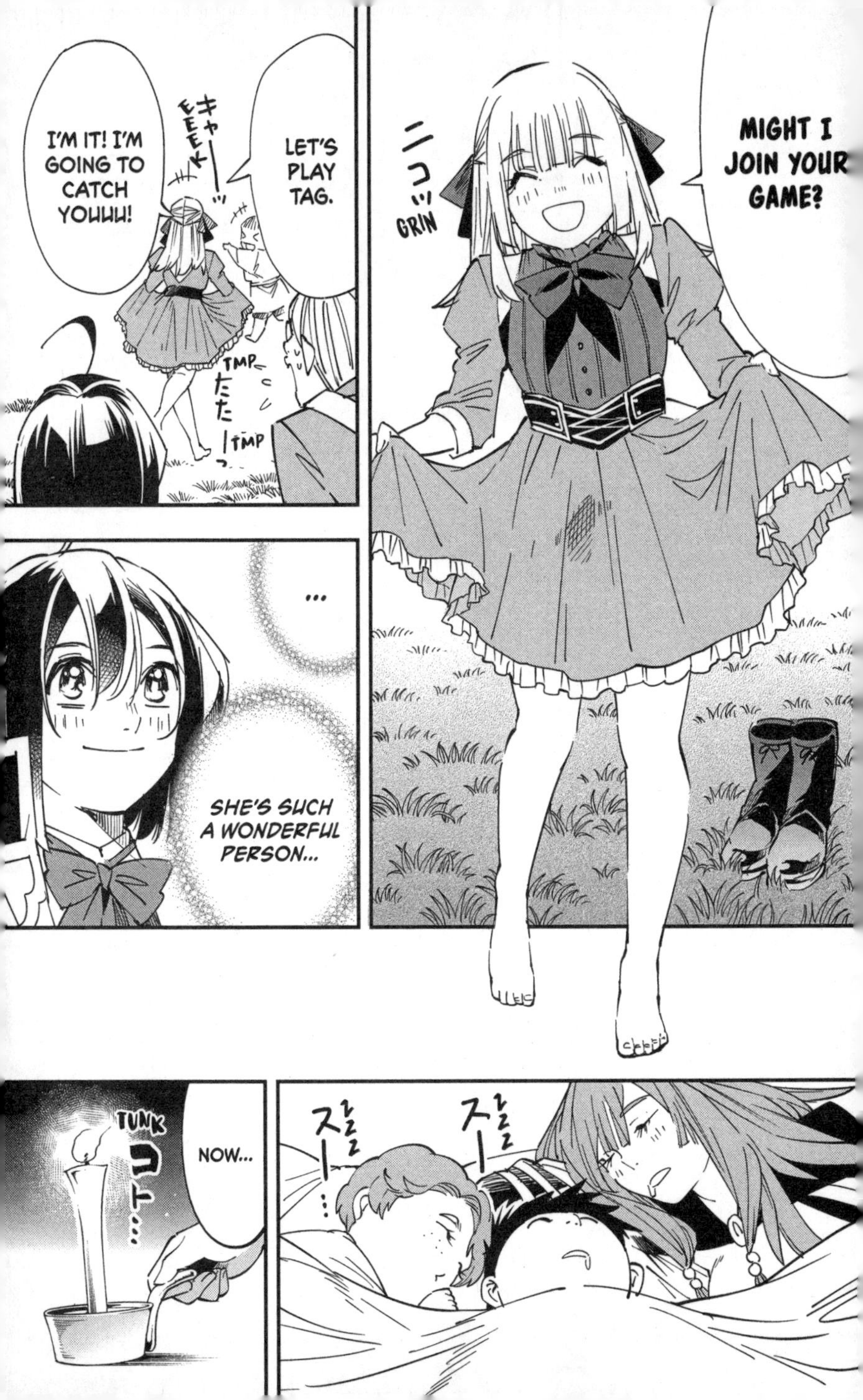
ニコッ
GRIN
MIGHT I JOIN YOUR GAME?
LET'S PLAY TAG.
キャーーッ
EEEK
I'M IT! I'M GOING TO CATCH YOUUU!
TMP
たたたっ
TMP
...
SHE'S SUCH A WONDERFUL PERSON...
スー…
zzz
スー…
zzz
NOW...
TUNK
コト…

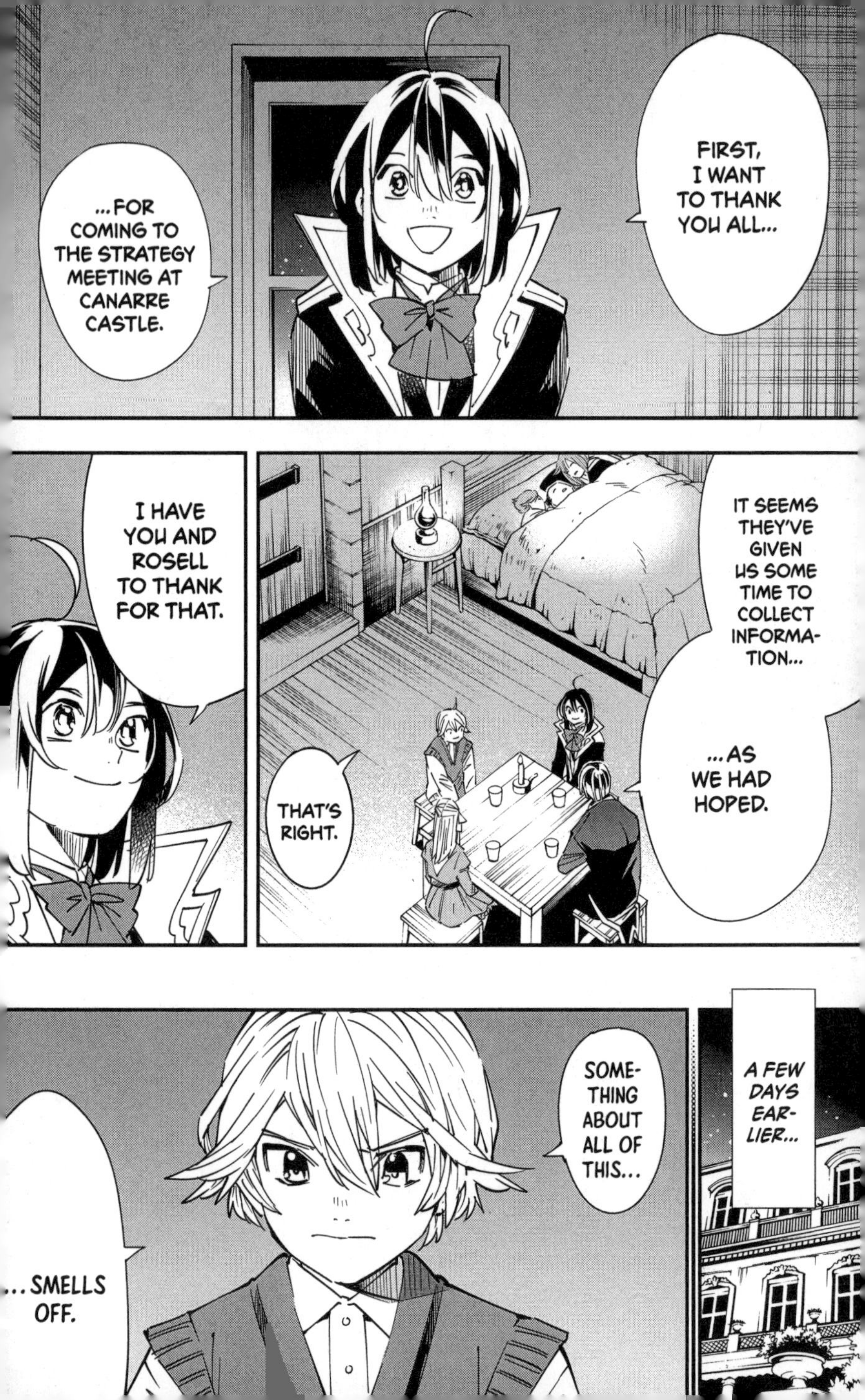
FIRST, I WANT TO THANK YOU ALL...
...FOR COMING TO THE STRATEGY MEETING AT CANARRE CASTLE.
IT SEEMS THEY'VE GIVEN US SOME TIME TO COLLECT INFORMATION...
...AS WE HAD HOPED.
THAT'S RIGHT.
I HAVE YOU AND ROSELL TO THANK FOR THAT.
A FEW DAYS EARLIER...
SOMETHING ABOUT ALL OF THIS...
...SMELLS OFF.

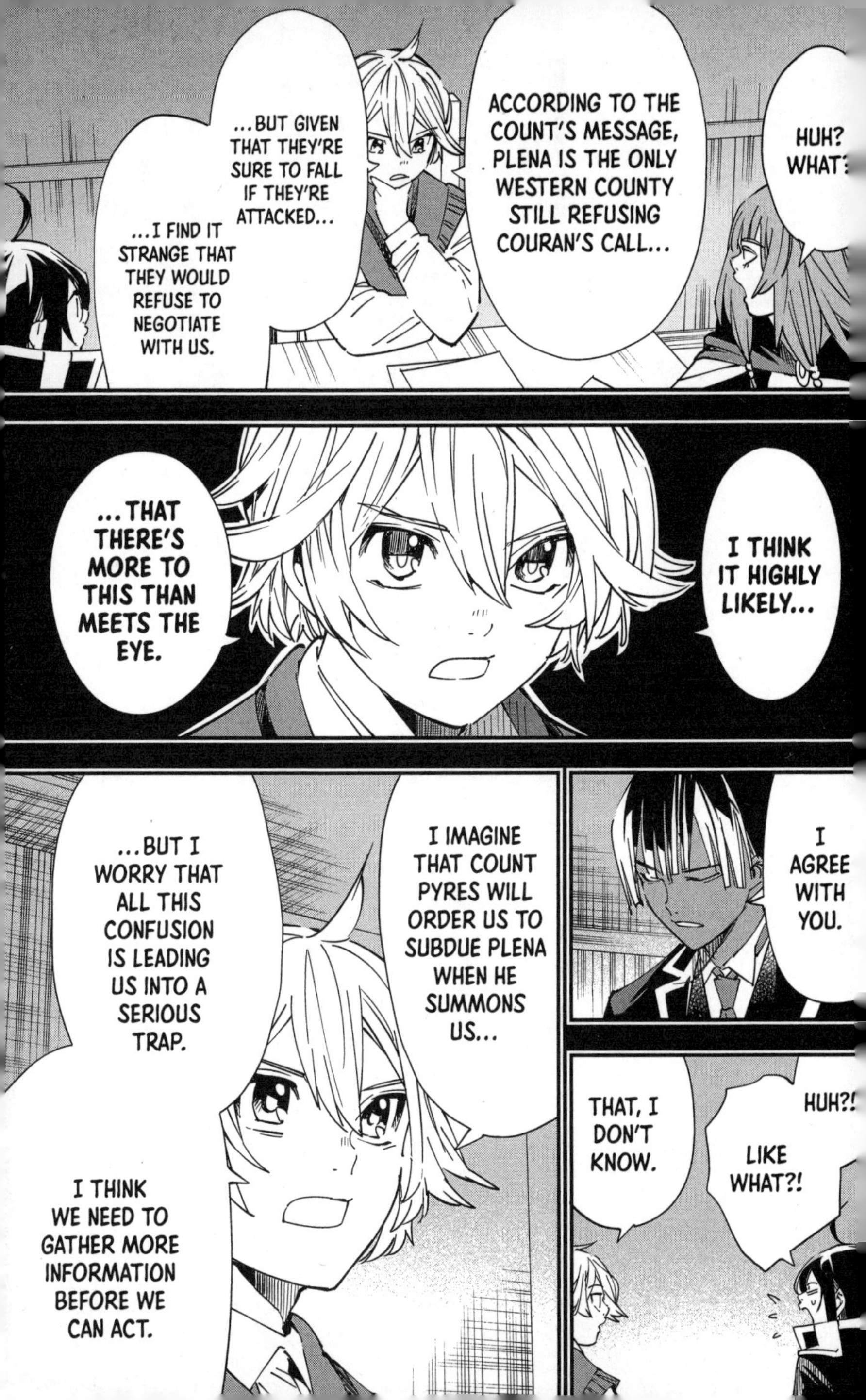
HUH? WHAT?
ACCORDING TO THE COUNT'S MESSAGE, PLENA IS THE ONLY WESTERN COUNTY STILL REFUSING COURAN'S CALL...
...BUT GIVEN THAT THEY'RE SURE TO FALL IF THEY'RE ATTACKED...
...I FIND IT STRANGE THAT THEY WOULD REFUSE TO NEGOTIATE WITH US.
I THINK IT HIGHLY LIKELY...
...THAT THERE'S MORE TO THIS THAN MEETS THE EYE.
I AGREE WITH YOU.
HUH?!
LIKE WHAT?!
THAT, I DON'T KNOW.
I IMAGINE THAT COUNT PYRES WILL ORDER US TO SUBDUE PLENA WHEN HE SUMMONS US...
...BUT I WORRY THAT ALL THIS CONFUSION IS LEADING US INTO A SERIOUS TRAP.
I THINK WE NEED TO GATHER MORE INFORMATION BEFORE WE CAN ACT.

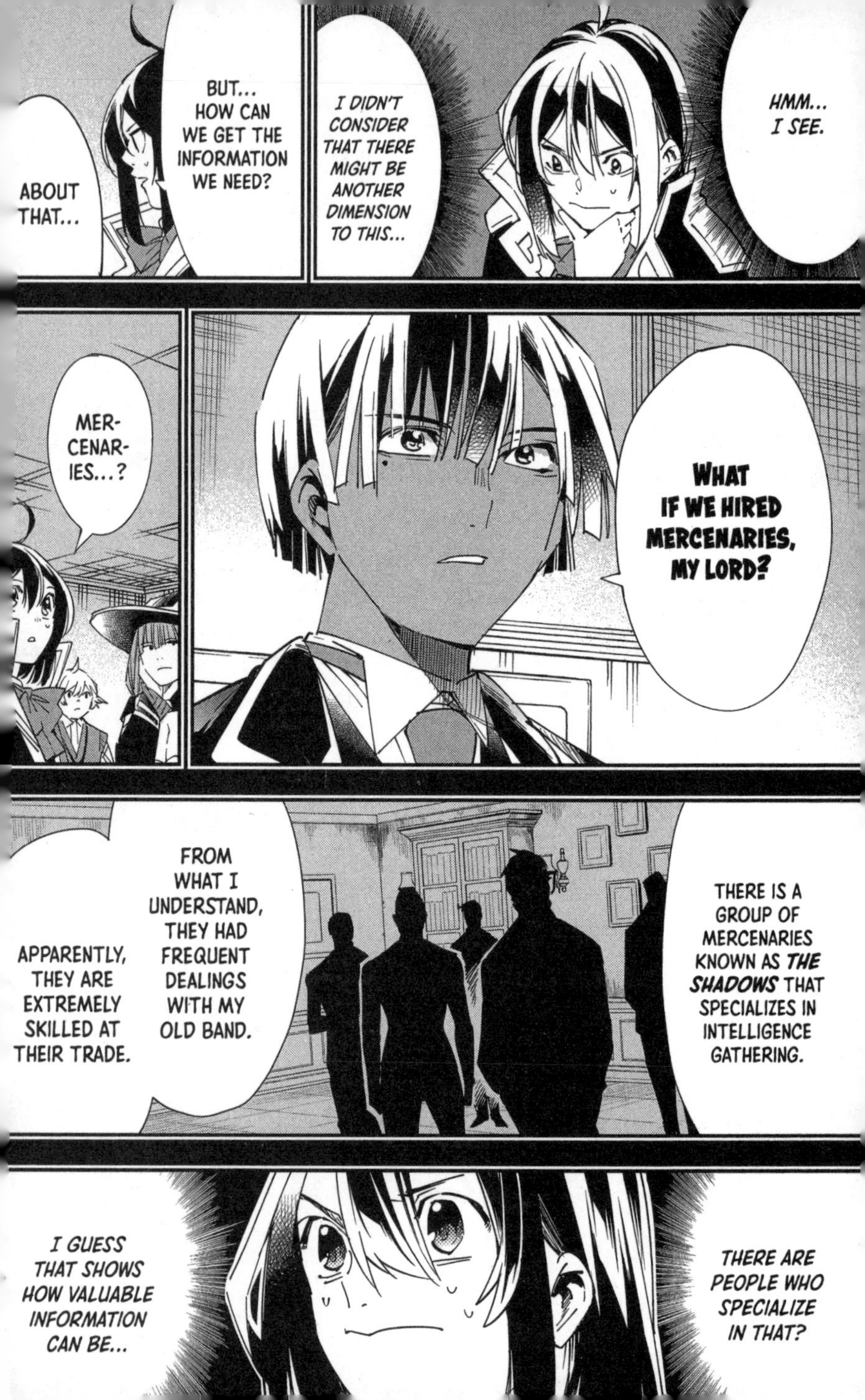
HMM... I SEE.
I DIDN'T CONSIDER THAT THERE MIGHT BE ANOTHER DIMENSION TO THIS...
BUT... HOW CAN WE GET THE INFORMATION WE NEED?
ABOUT THAT...
WHAT IF WE HIRED MERCENARIES, MY LORD?
MER-CENAR-IES...?
THERE IS A GROUP OF MERCENARIES KNOWN AS *THE SHADOWS* THAT SPECIALIZES IN INTELLIGENCE GATHERING.
FROM WHAT I UNDERSTAND, THEY HAD FREQUENT DEALINGS WITH MY OLD BAND.
APPARENTLY, THEY ARE EXTREMELY SKILLED AT THEIR TRADE.
THERE ARE PEOPLE WHO SPECIALIZE IN THAT?
I GUESS THAT SHOWS HOW VALUABLE INFORMATION CAN BE...

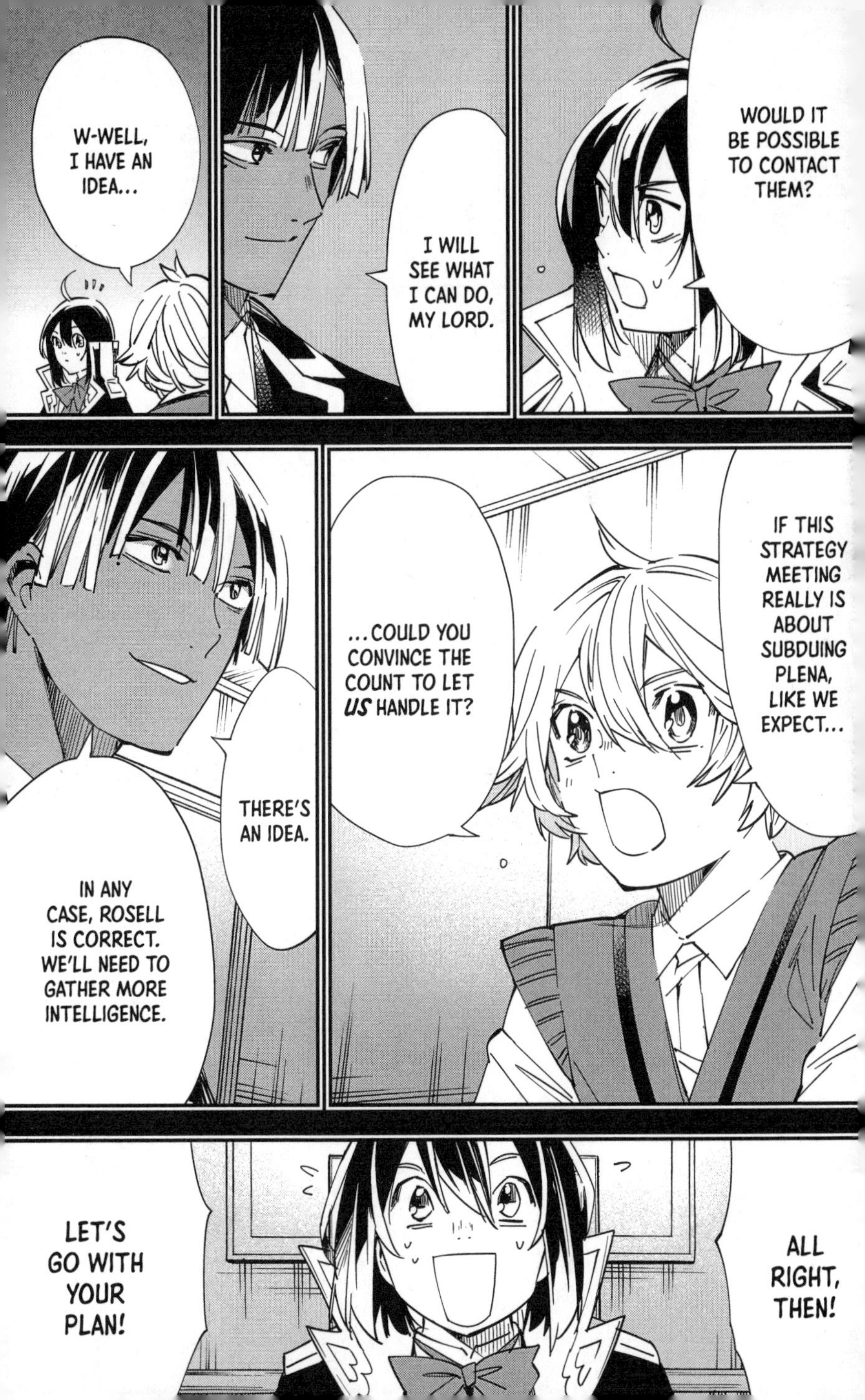
WOULD IT BE POSSIBLE TO CONTACT THEM?
I WILL SEE WHAT I CAN DO, MY LORD.
W-WELL, I HAVE AN IDEA...
IF THIS STRATEGY MEETING REALLY IS ABOUT SUBDUING PLENA, LIKE WE EXPECT...
...COULD YOU CONVINCE THE COUNT TO LET *US* HANDLE IT?
THERE'S AN IDEA.
IN ANY CASE, ROSELL IS CORRECT. WE'LL NEED TO GATHER MORE INTELLIGENCE.
ALL RIGHT, THEN!
LET'S GO WITH YOUR PLAN!

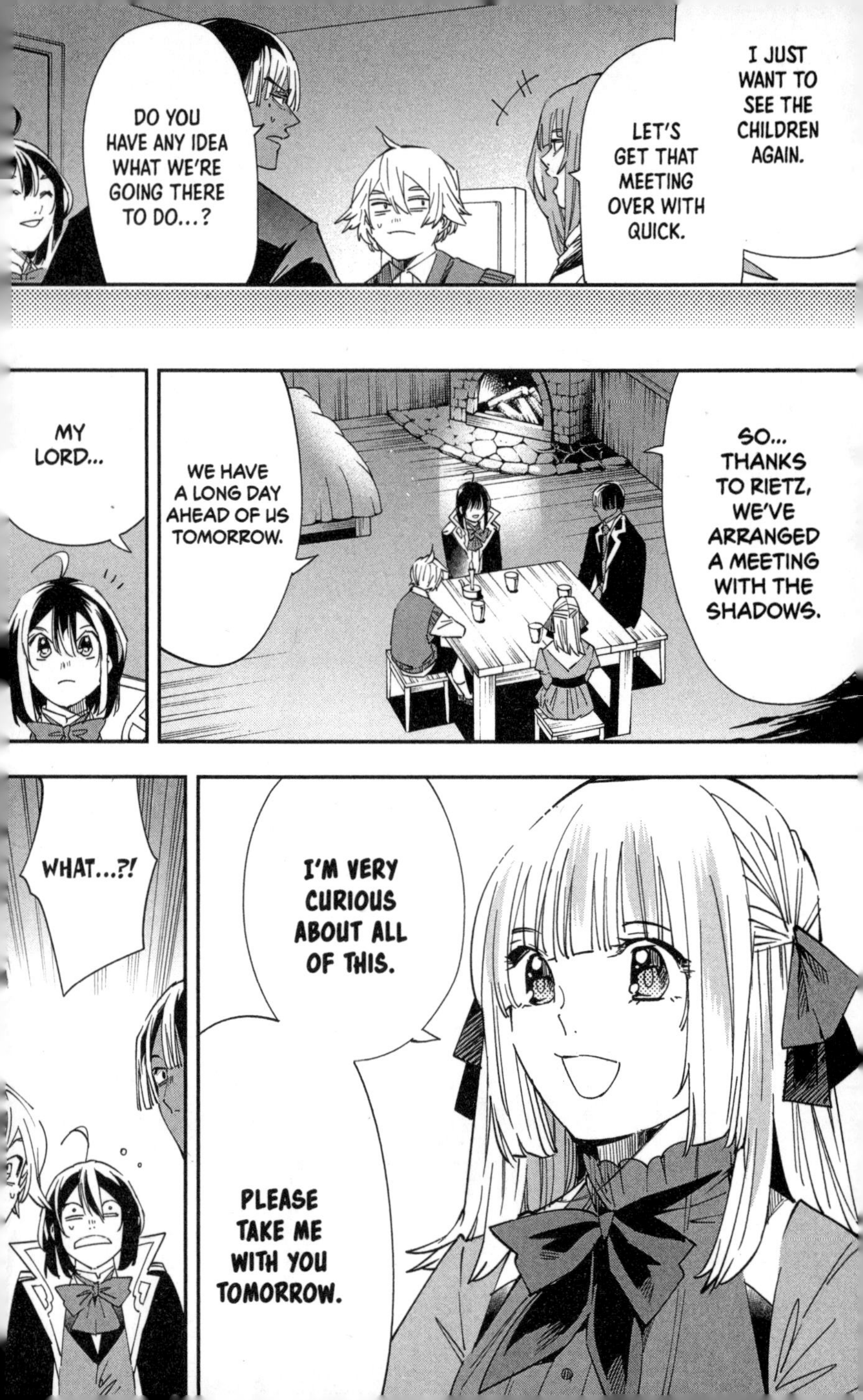
I JUST WANT TO SEE THE CHILDREN AGAIN.
LET'S GET THAT MEETING OVER WITH QUICK.
DO YOU HAVE ANY IDEA WHAT WE'RE GOING THERE TO DO...?
SO... THANKS TO RIETZ, WE'VE ARRANGED A MEETING WITH THE SHADOWS.
WE HAVE A LONG DAY AHEAD OF US TOMORROW.
MY LORD...
I'M VERY CURIOUS ABOUT ALL OF THIS.
PLEASE TAKE ME WITH YOU TOMORROW.
WHAT...?!

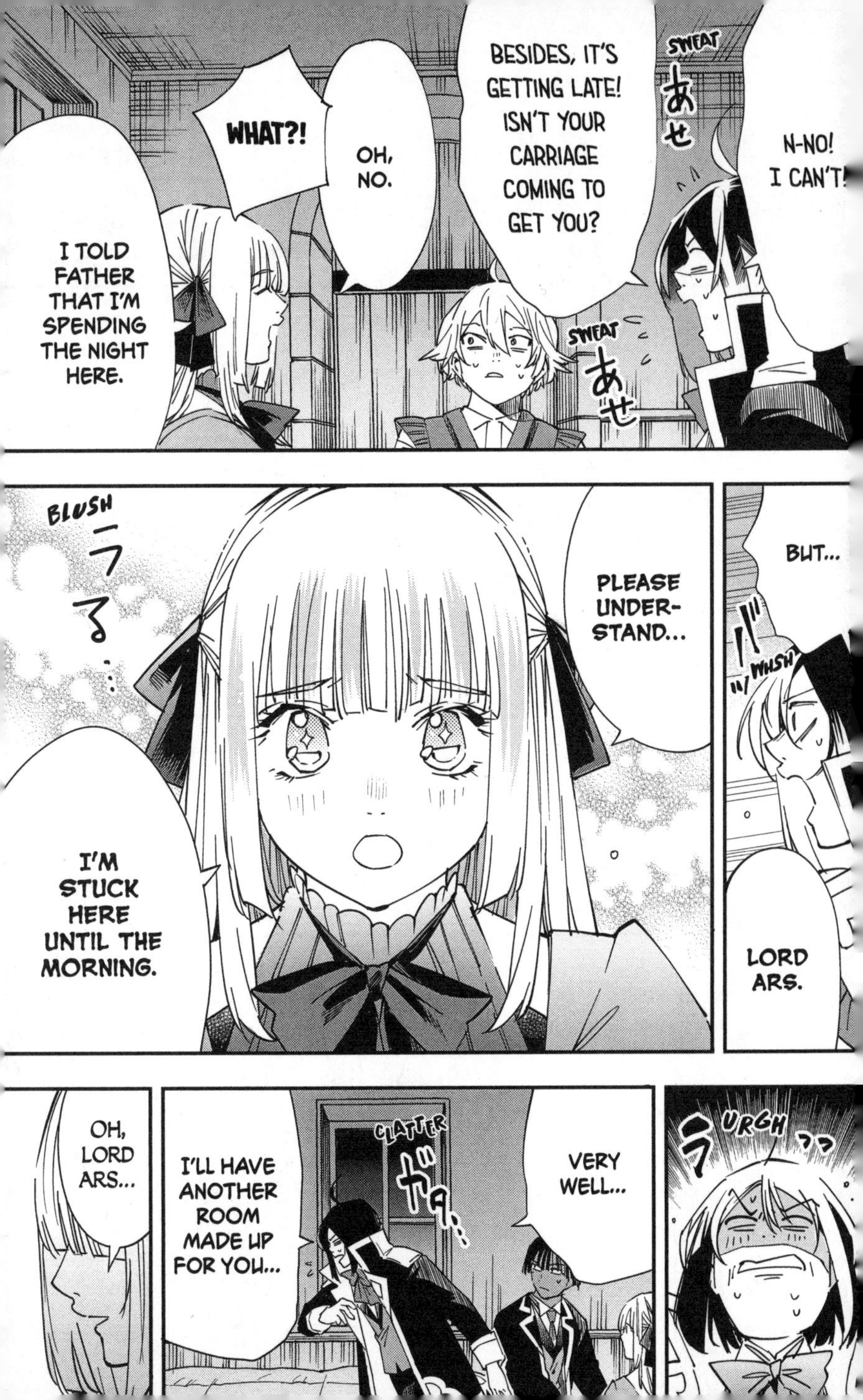

SWEAT
あせ
N-NO! I CAN'T!
BESIDES, IT'S GETTING LATE! ISN'T YOUR CARRIAGE COMING TO GET YOU?
OH, NO.
WHAT?!
SWEAT
あせ
I TOLD FATHER THAT I'M SPENDING THE NIGHT HERE.
BUT...
WHSH
LORD ARS.
PLEASE UNDER-STAND...
BLUSH
I'M STUCK HERE UNTIL THE MORNING.
URGH
VERY WELL...
CLATTER
I'LL HAVE ANOTHER ROOM MADE UP FOR YOU...
OH, LORD ARS...

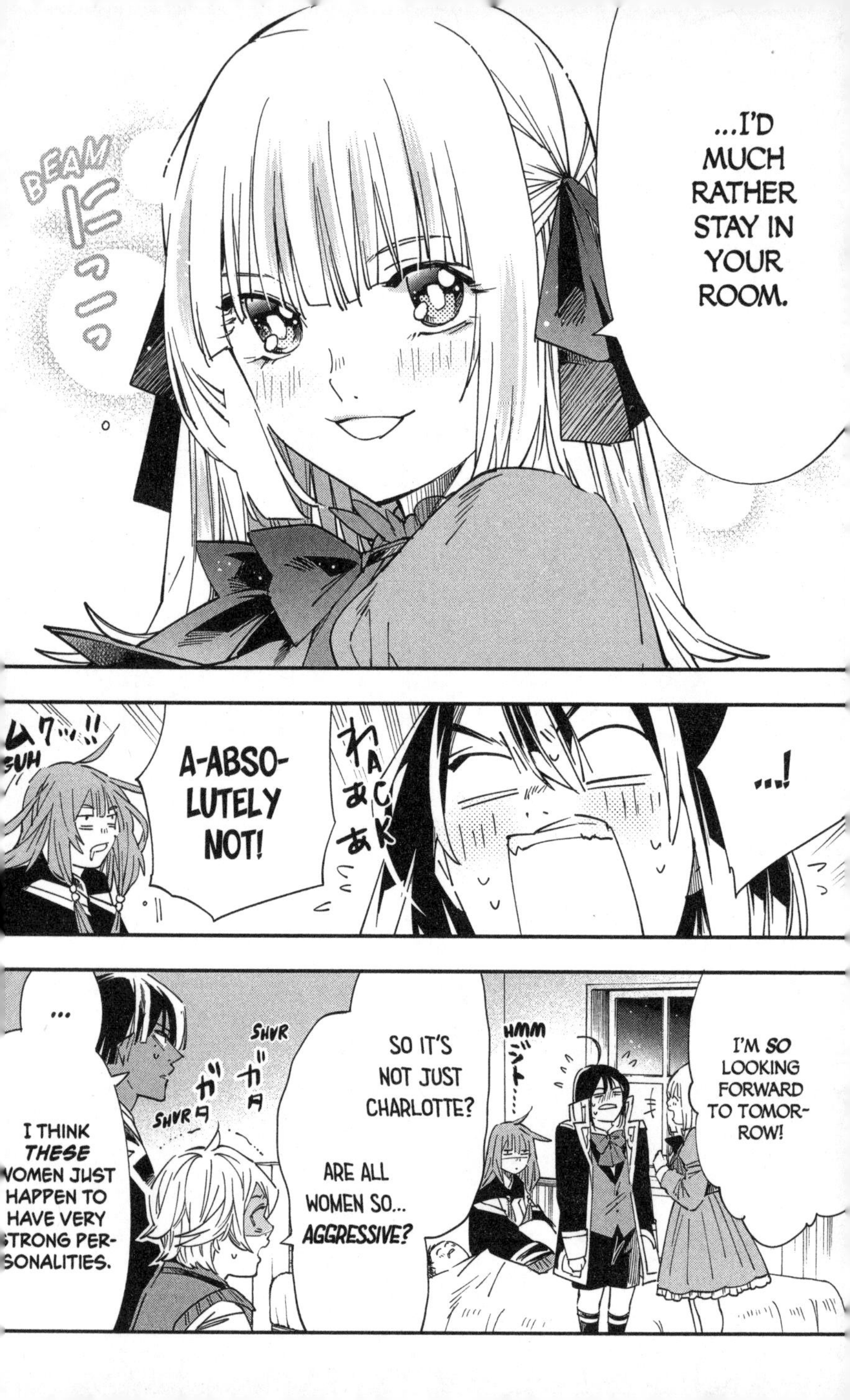
...I'D MUCH RATHER STAY IN YOUR ROOM.
BEAM にっこり
...!
わあああ
ACK
A-ABSOLUTELY NOT!
ムクッ!!
GUH
I'M SO LOOKING FORWARD TO TOMORROW!
HMM
ジト…
SO IT'S NOT JUST CHARLOTTE?
ARE ALL WOMEN SO... AGGRESSIVE?
SHVR
ガタ
SHVR
ガタ
...
I THINK THESE WOMEN JUST HAPPEN TO HAVE VERY STRONG PERSONALITIES.

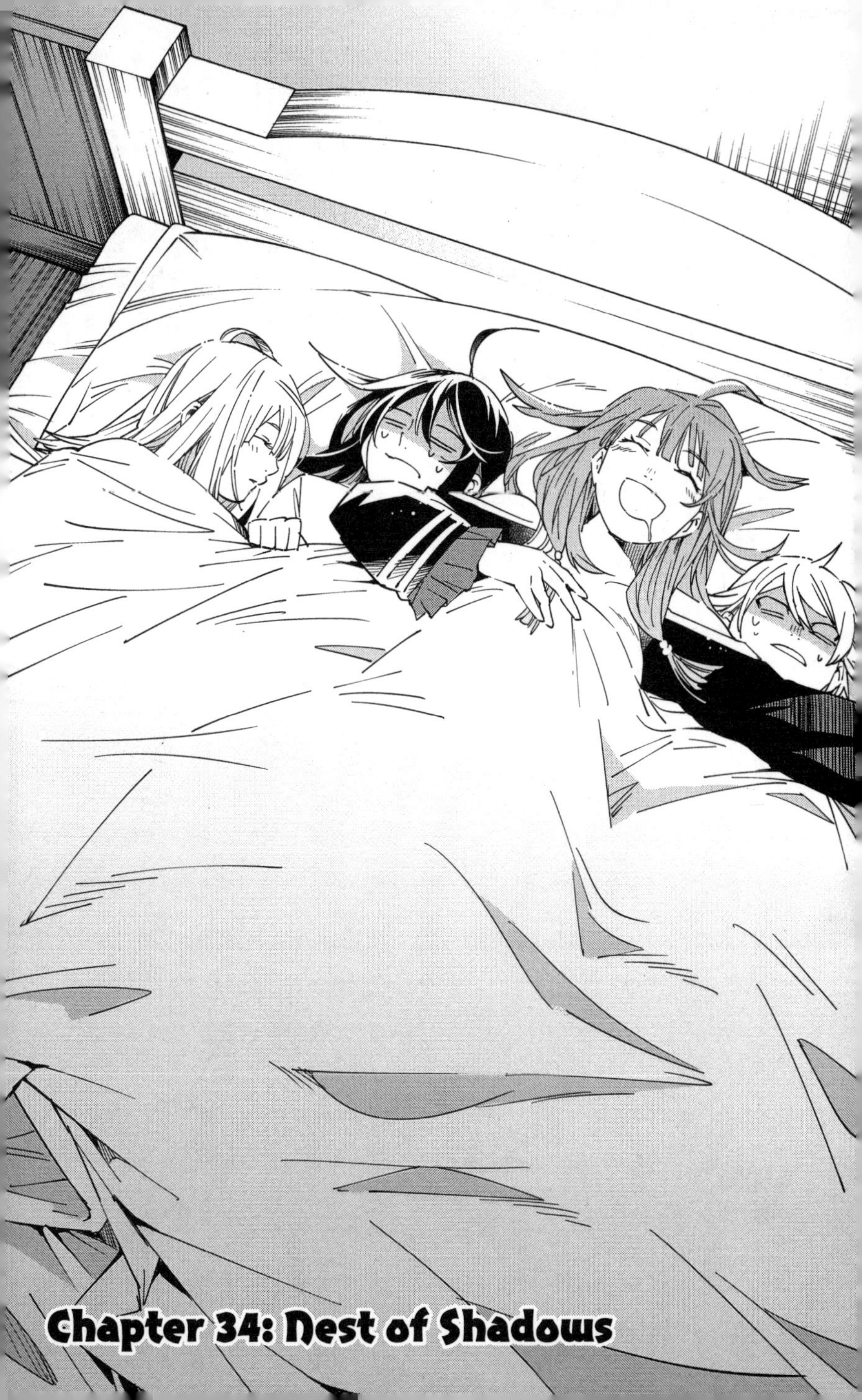

Chapter 34: Nest of Shadows

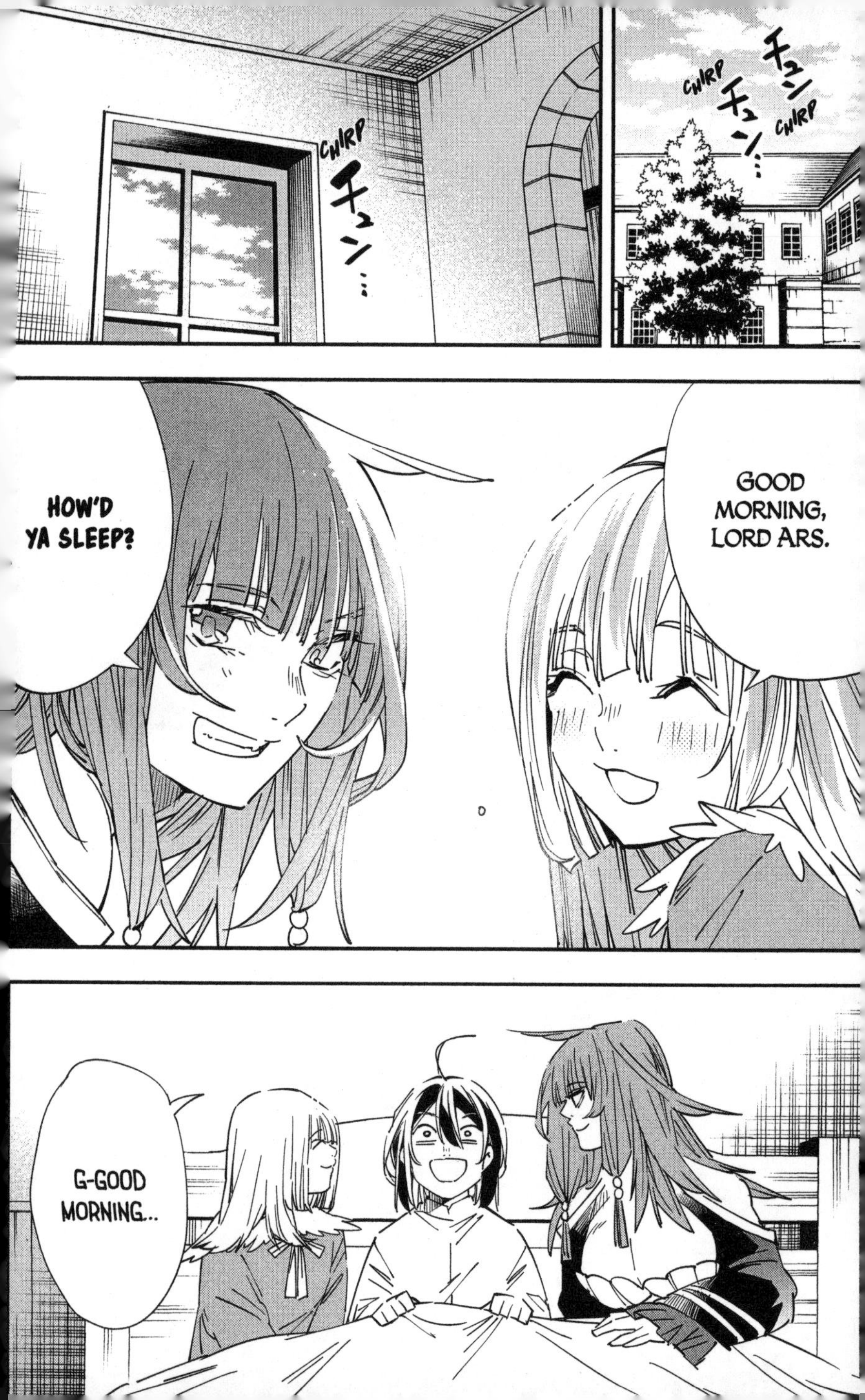
CHIRP
チュン
チュン…
CHIRP
CHIRP
チュン…
GOOD MORNING, LORD ARS.
HOW'D YA SLEEP?
G-GOOD MORNING...

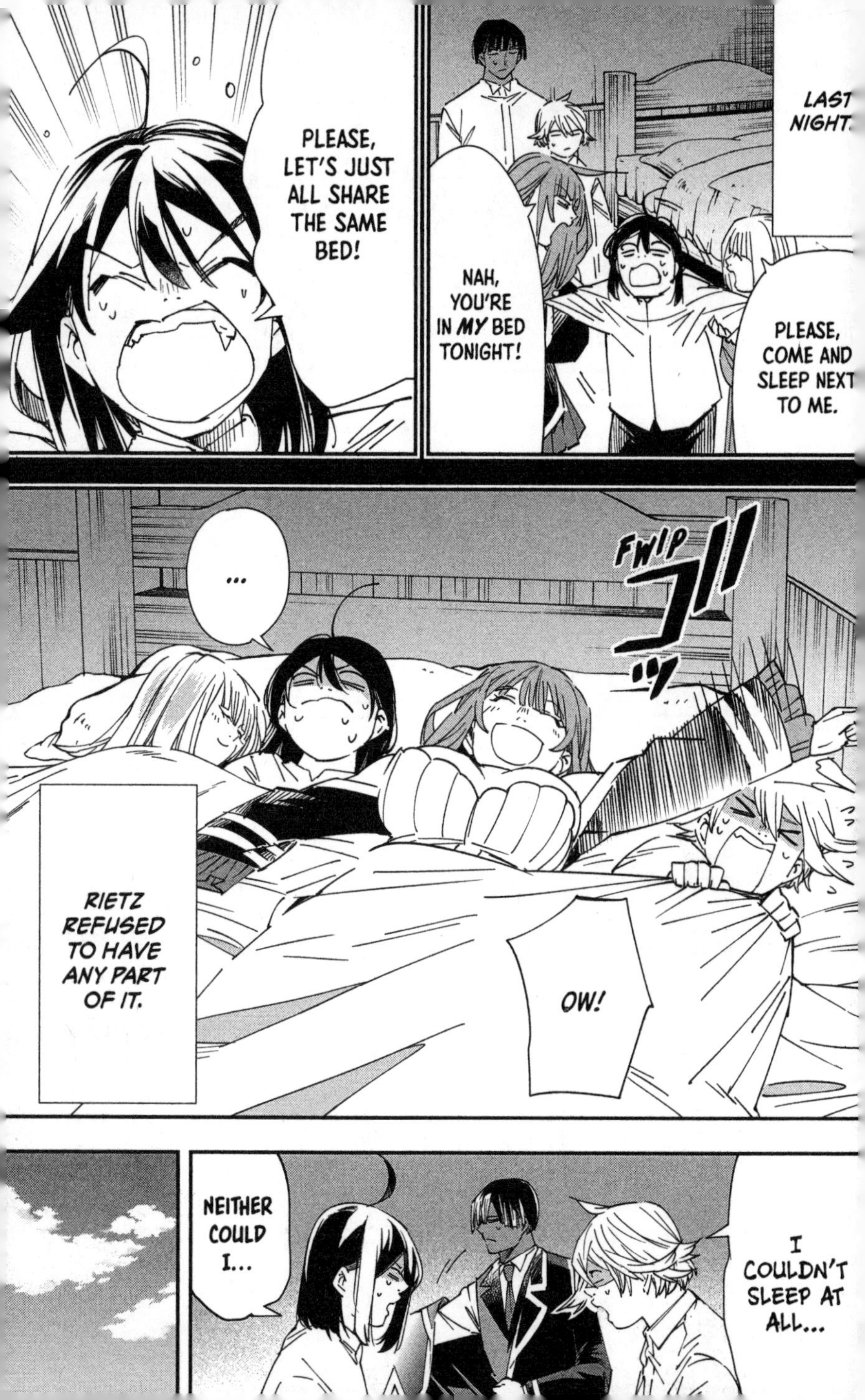
LAST NIGHT.
PLEASE, COME AND SLEEP NEXT TO ME.
NAH, YOU'RE IN MY BED TONIGHT!
PLEASE, LET'S JUST ALL SHARE THE SAME BED!
FWIP
...
OW!
RIETZ REFUSED TO HAVE ANY PART OF IT.
I COULDN'T SLEEP AT ALL...
NEITHER COULD I...

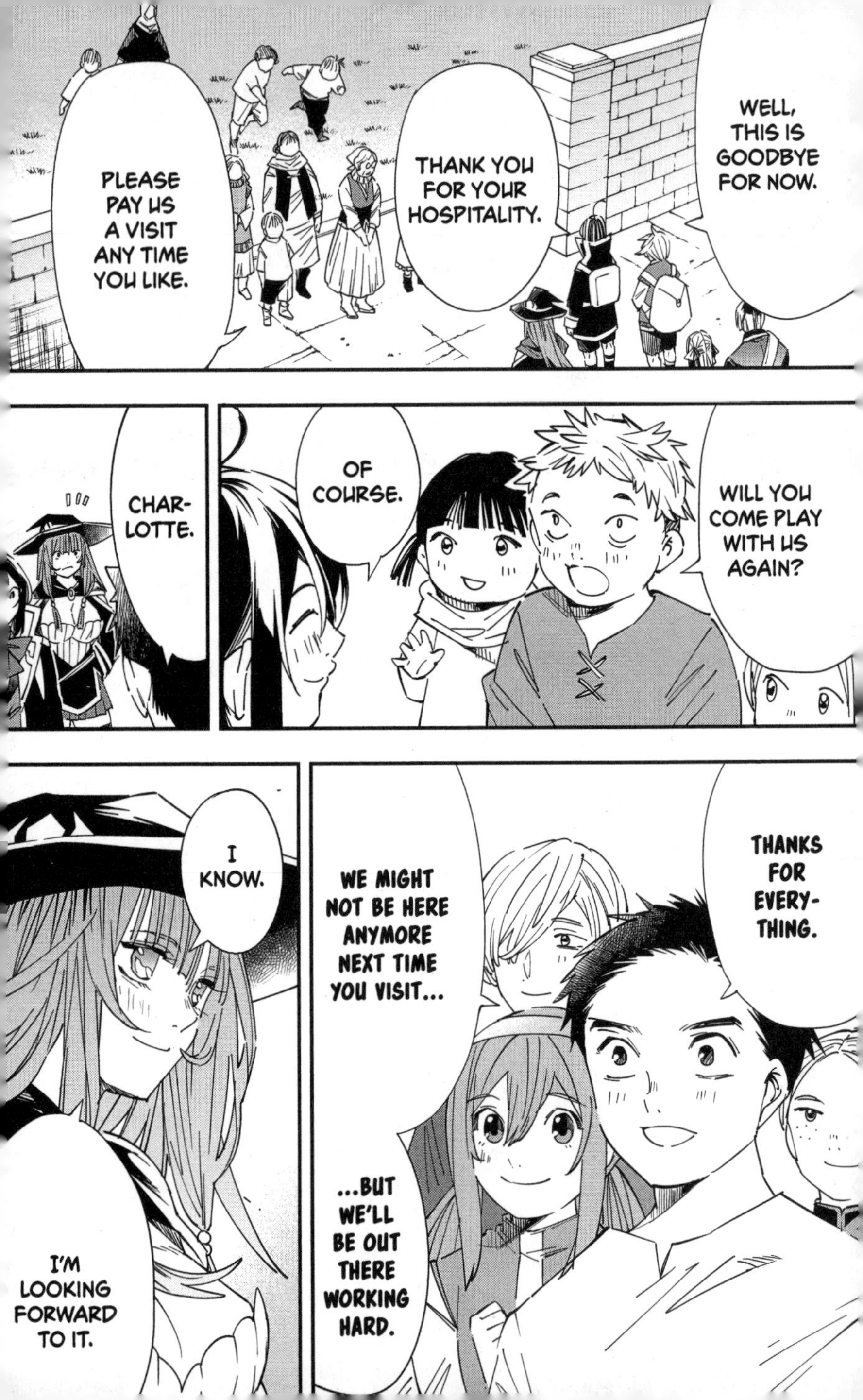
WELL, THIS IS GOODBYE FOR NOW.
THANK YOU FOR YOUR HOSPITALITY.
PLEASE PAY US A VISIT ANY TIME YOU LIKE.
WILL YOU COME PLAY WITH US AGAIN?
OF COURSE.
CHAR-LOTTE.
THANKS FOR EVERY-THING.
WE MIGHT NOT BE HERE ANYMORE NEXT TIME YOU VISIT...
...BUT WE'LL BE OUT THERE WORKING HARD.
I KNOW.
I'M LOOKING FORWARD TO IT.

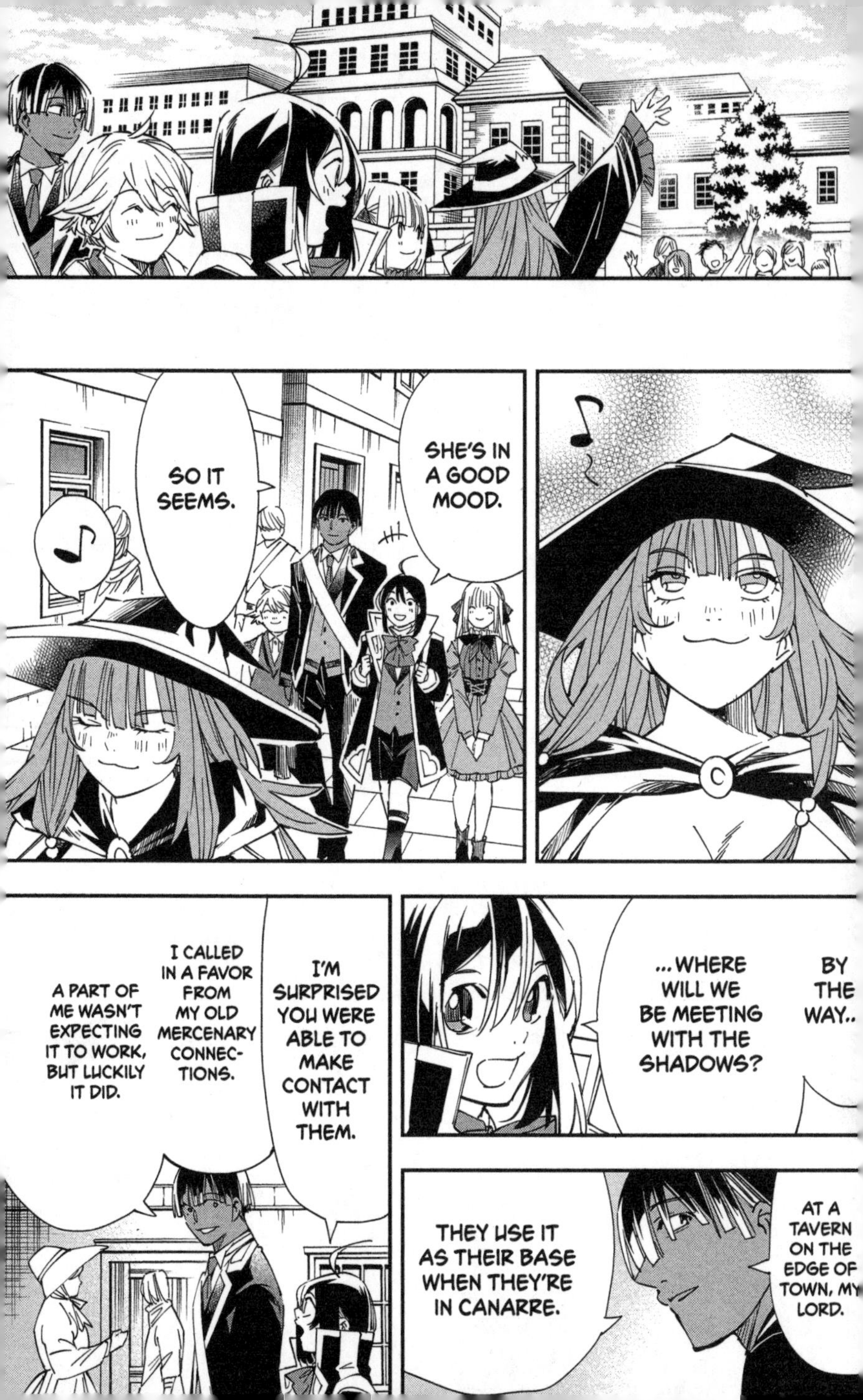
SHE'S IN A GOOD MOOD.
SO IT SEEMS.
BY THE WAY..
...WHERE WILL WE BE MEETING WITH THE SHADOWS?
AT A TAVERN ON THE EDGE OF TOWN, MY LORD.
THEY USE IT AS THEIR BASE WHEN THEY'RE IN CANARRE.
I'M SURPRISED YOU WERE ABLE TO MAKE CONTACT WITH THEM.
I CALLED IN A FAVOR FROM MY OLD MERCENARY CONNEC- TIONS.
A PART OF ME WASN'T EXPECTING IT TO WORK, BUT LUCKILY IT DID.

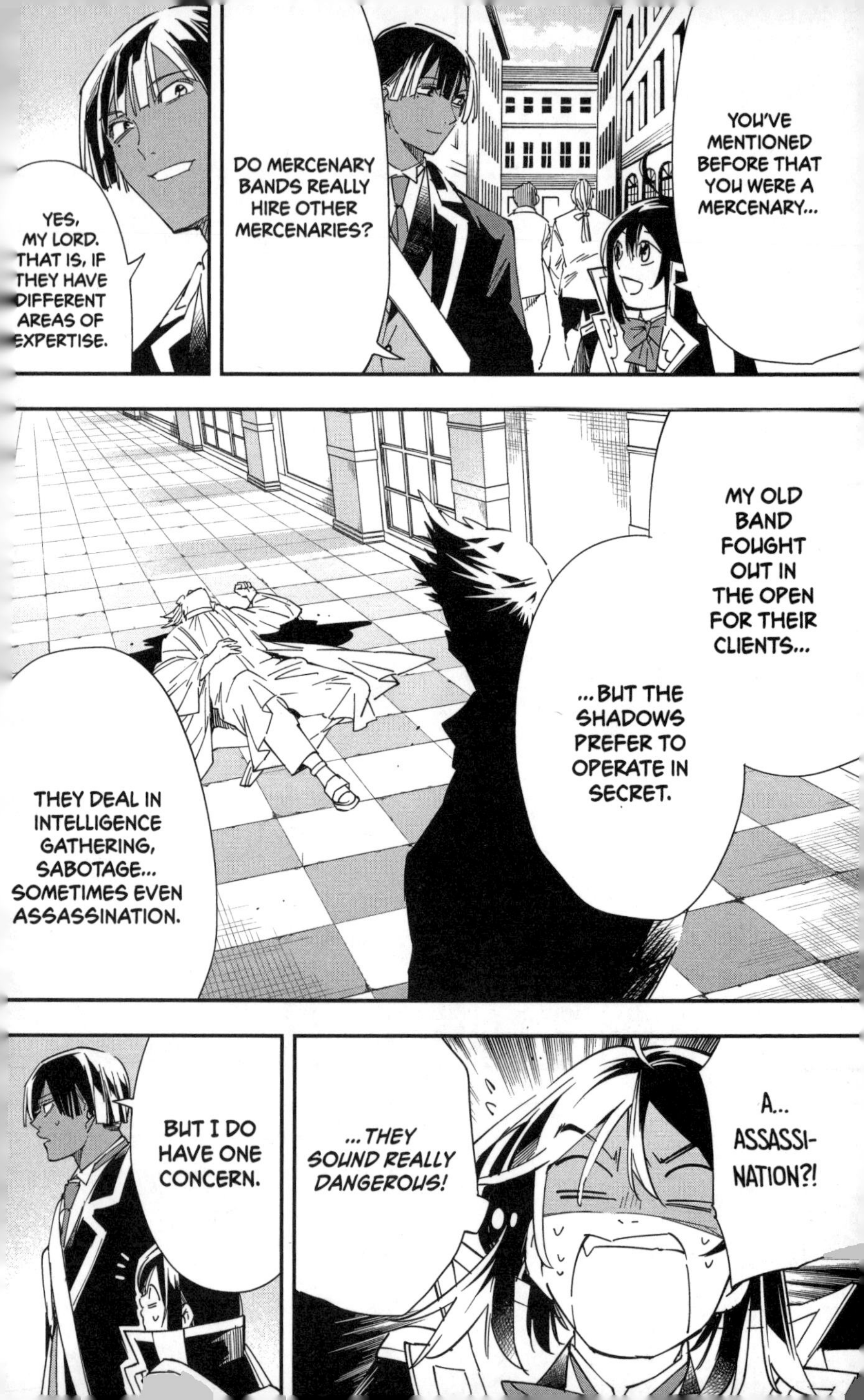
YOU'VE MENTIONED BEFORE THAT YOU WERE A MERCENARY...
DO MERCENARY BANDS REALLY HIRE OTHER MERCENARIES?
YES, MY LORD. THAT IS, IF THEY HAVE DIFFERENT AREAS OF EXPERTISE.
MY OLD BAND FOUGHT OUT IN THE OPEN FOR THEIR CLIENTS...
...BUT THE SHADOWS PREFER TO OPERATE IN SECRET.
THEY DEAL IN INTELLIGENCE GATHERING, SABOTAGE... SOMETIMES EVEN ASSASSINATION.
A... ASSASSI-NATION?!
...THEY SOUND REALLY DANGEROUS!
BUT I DO HAVE ONE CONCERN.

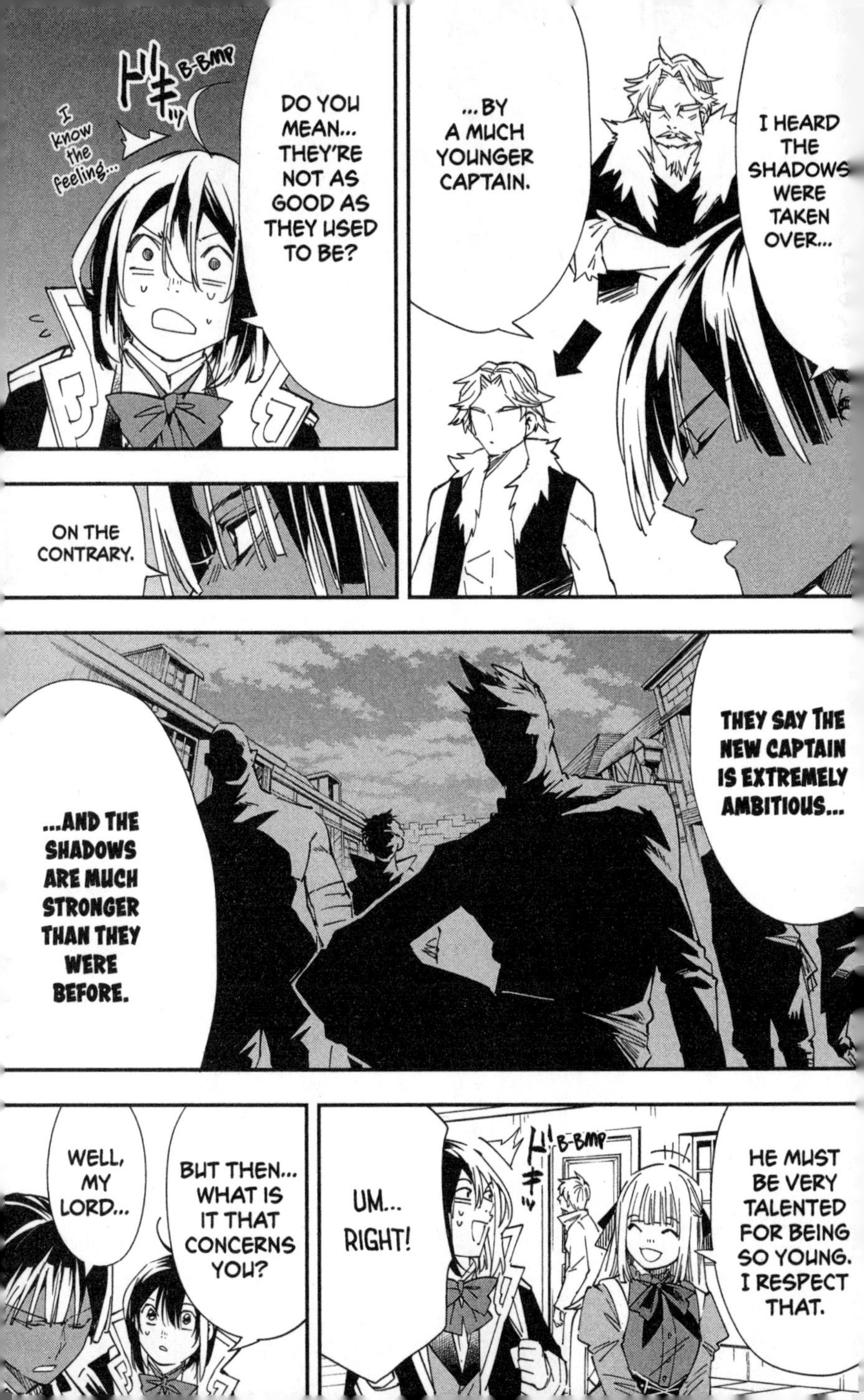
I HEARD THE SHADOWS WERE TAKEN OVER...
...BY A MUCH YOUNGER CAPTAIN.
B-BMP
I know the feeling...
DO YOU MEAN... THEY'RE NOT AS GOOD AS THEY USED TO BE?
ON THE CONTRARY.
THEY SAY THE NEW CAPTAIN IS EXTREMELY AMBITIOUS...
...AND THE SHADOWS ARE MUCH STRONGER THAN THEY WERE BEFORE.
HE MUST BE VERY TALENTED FOR BEING SO YOUNG. I RESPECT THAT.
B-BMP
UM... RIGHT!
BUT THEN... WHAT IS IT THAT CONCERNS YOU?
WELL, MY LORD...

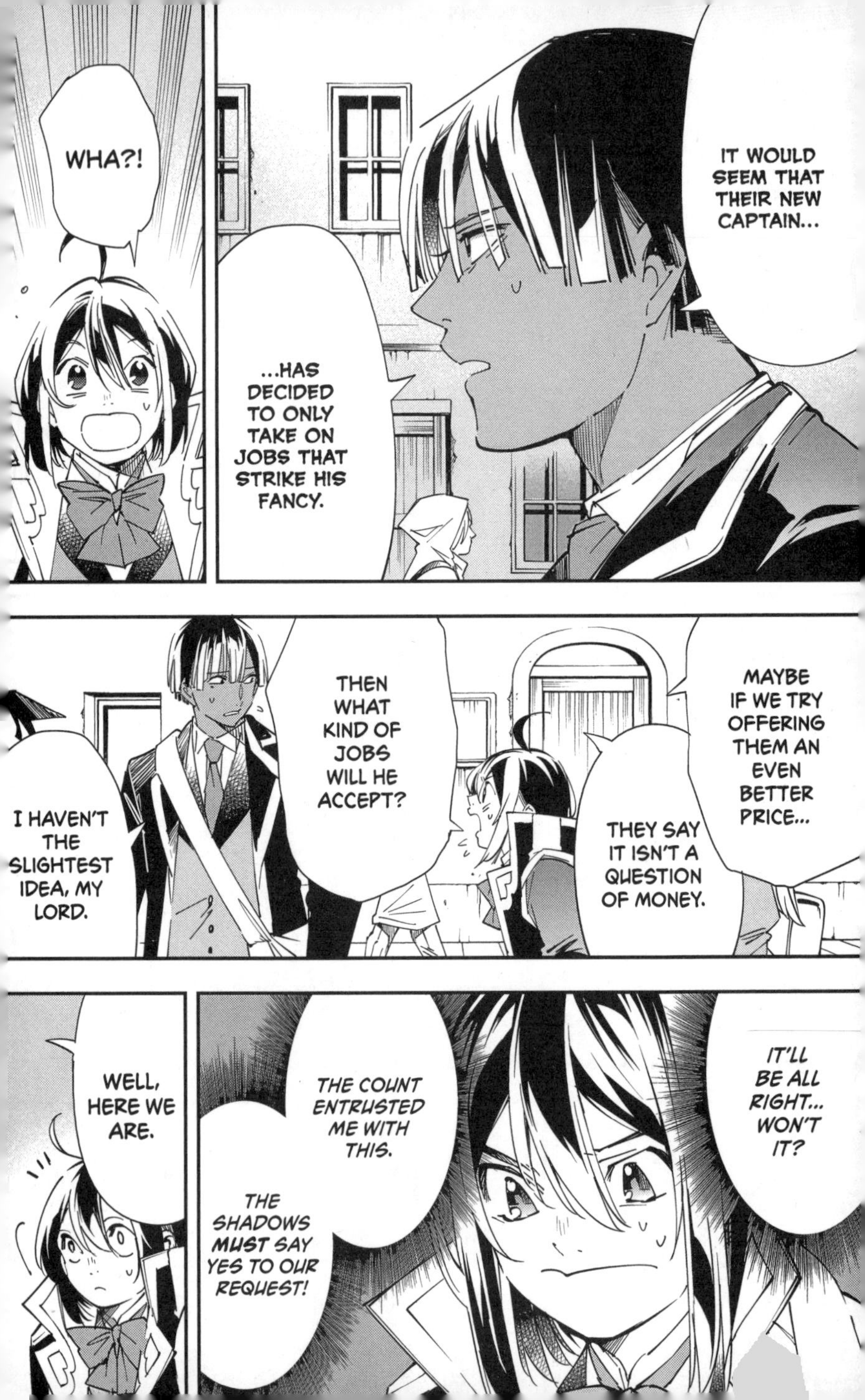
IT WOULD SEEM THAT THEIR NEW CAPTAIN...
...HAS DECIDED TO ONLY TAKE ON JOBS THAT STRIKE HIS FANCY.
WHA?!
MAYBE IF WE TRY OFFERING THEM AN EVEN BETTER PRICE...
THEY SAY IT ISN'T A QUESTION OF MONEY.
THEN WHAT KIND OF JOBS WILL HE ACCEPT?
I HAVEN'T THE SLIGHTEST IDEA, MY LORD.
IT'LL BE ALL RIGHT... WON'T IT?
THE COUNT ENTRUSTED ME WITH THIS.
THE SHADOWS *MUST* SAY YES TO OUR REQUEST!
WELL, HERE WE ARE.

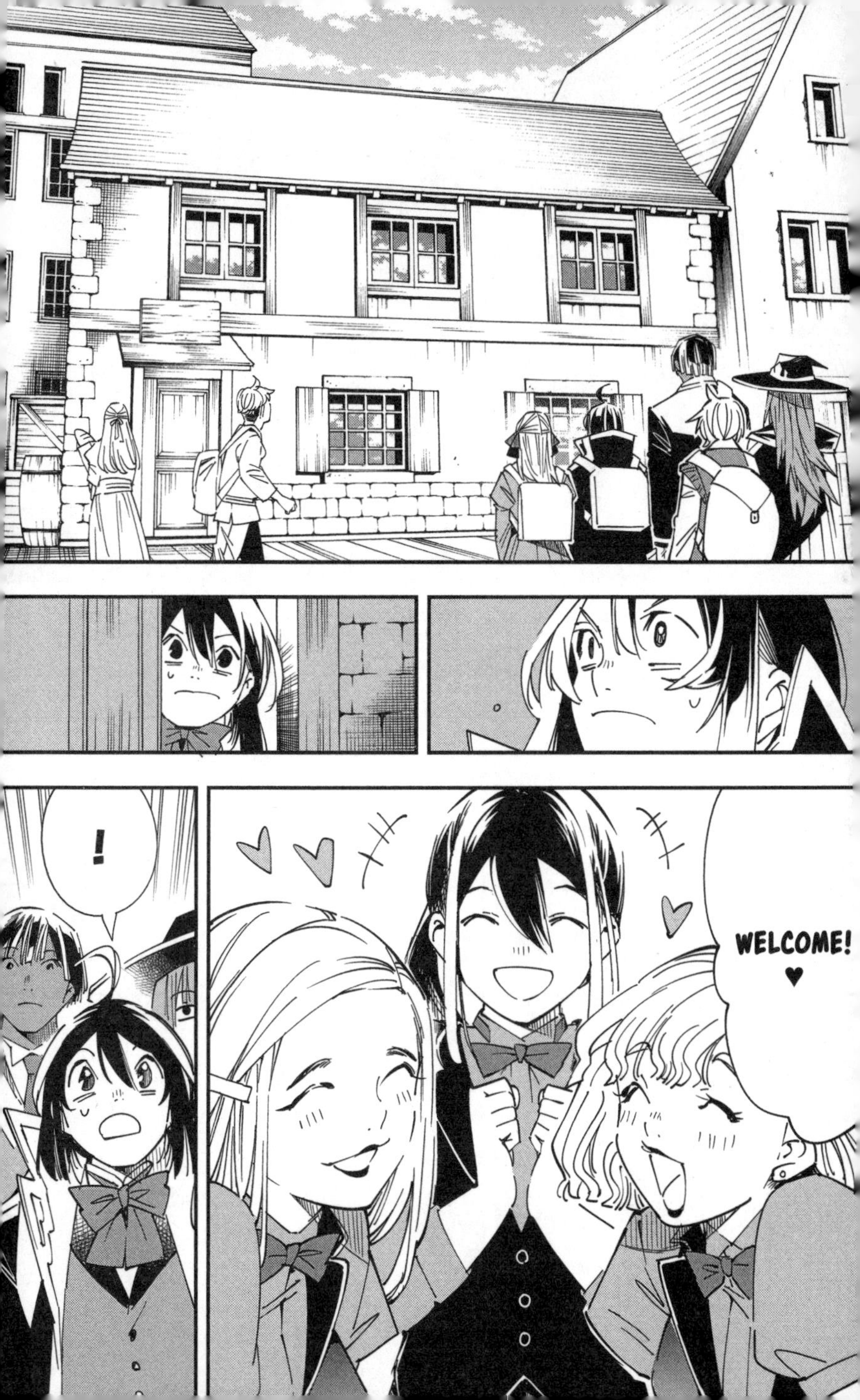
WELCOME! ♥
!

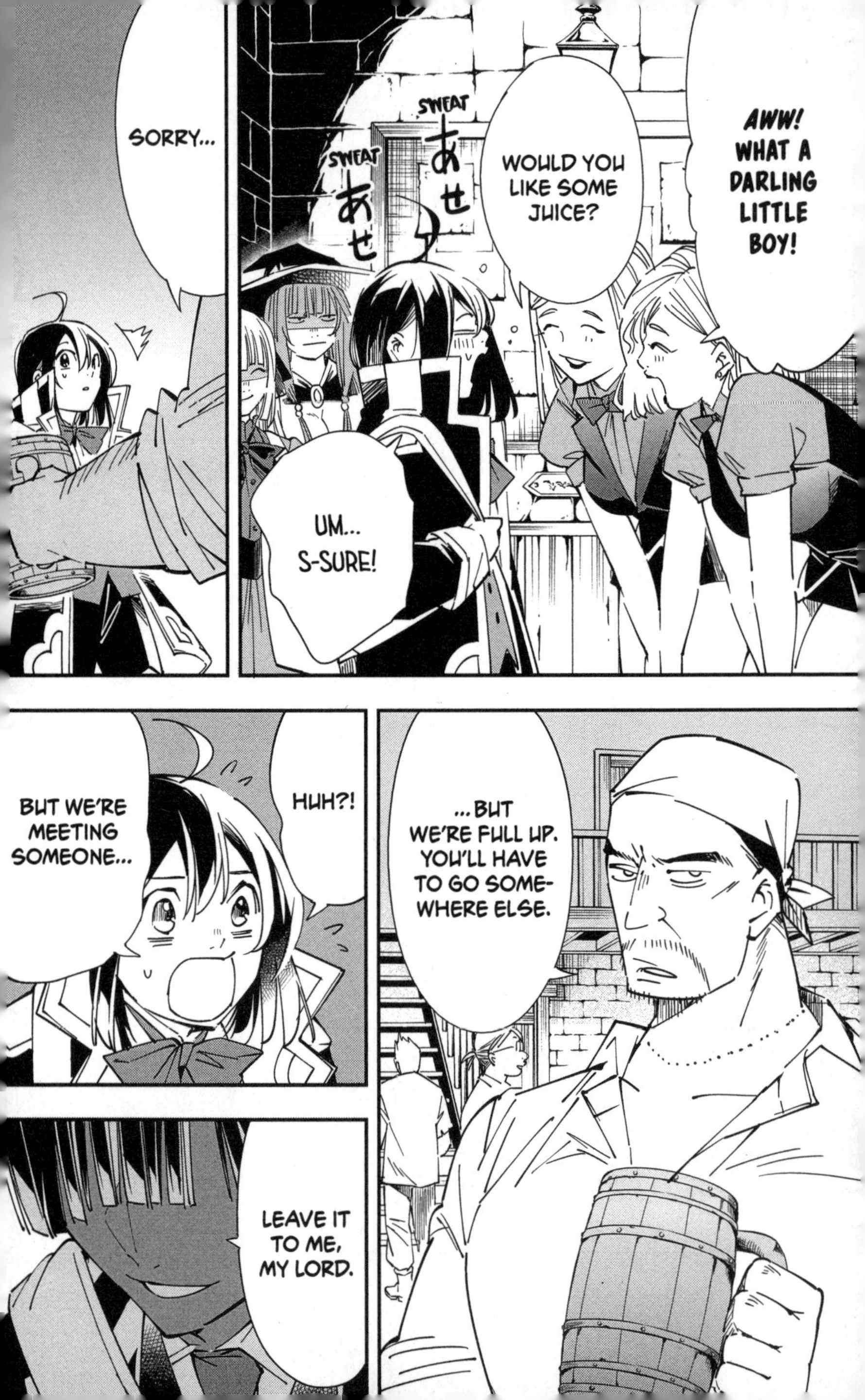
AWW! WHAT A DARLING LITTLE BOY!
WOULD YOU LIKE SOME JUICE?
SWEAT あせ
SWEAT あせ
UM... S-SURE!
SORRY...
...BUT WE'RE FULL UP. YOU'LL HAVE TO GO SOME-WHERE ELSE.
HUH?!
BUT WE'RE MEETING SOMEONE...
LEAVE IT TO ME, MY LORD.

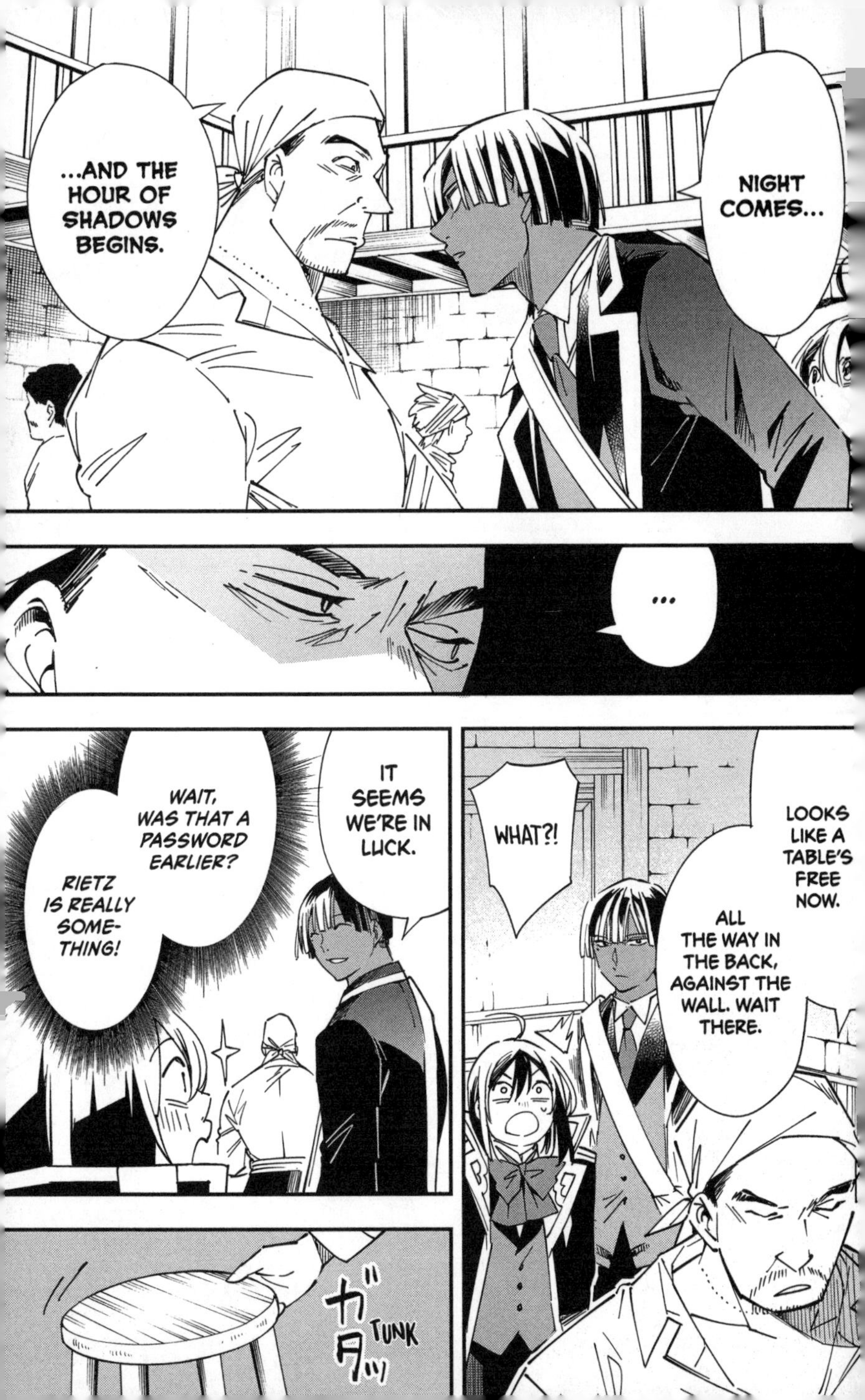
NIGHT COMES...
...AND THE HOUR OF SHADOWS BEGINS.
...
LOOKS LIKE A TABLE'S FREE NOW.
WHAT?!
ALL THE WAY IN THE BACK, AGAINST THE WALL. WAIT THERE.
IT SEEMS WE'RE IN LUCK.
WAIT, WAS THAT A PASSWORD EARLIER?
RIETZ IS REALLY SOME-THING!
ガタッ
TUNK

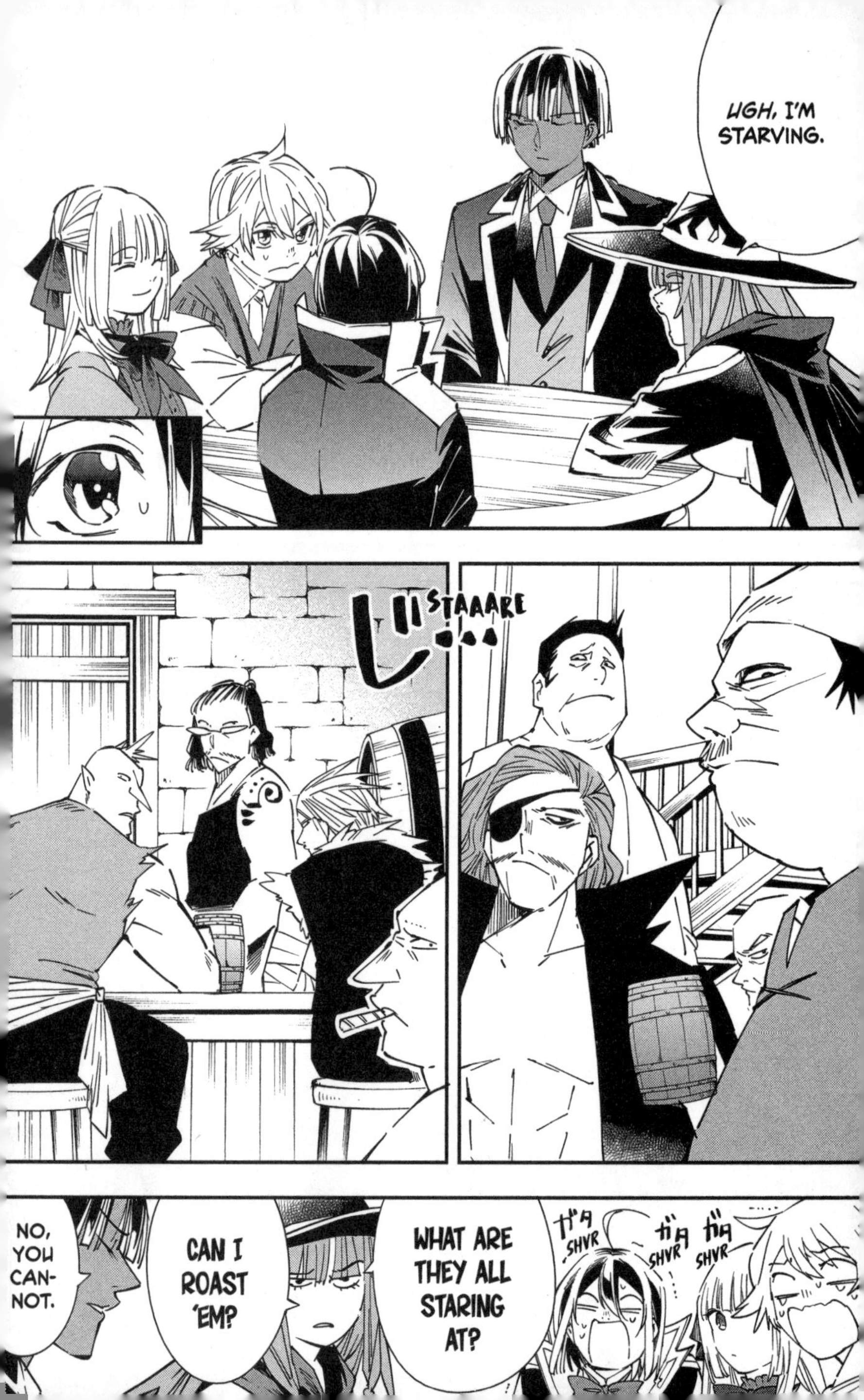

UGH, I'M STARVING.
じー STAAARE...
...
ガタ SHVR
ガタ SHVR
ガタ SHVR
WHAT ARE THEY ALL STARING AT?
CAN I ROAST 'EM?
NO, YOU CAN-NOT.

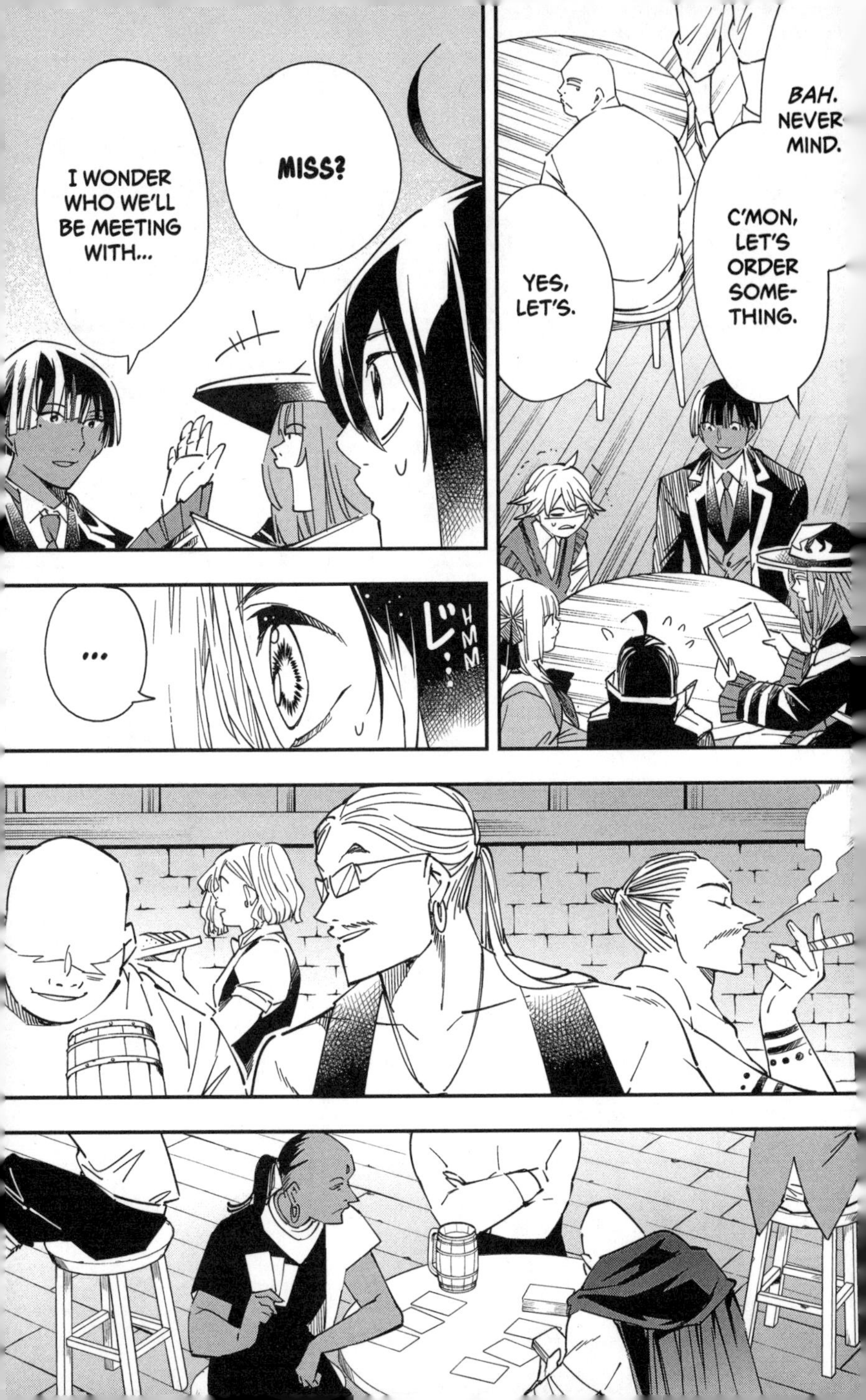
BAH. NEVER MIND.
C'MON, LET'S ORDER SOME-THING.
YES, LET'S.
MISS?
I WONDER WHO WE'LL BE MEETING WITH...
ジ HMM
...

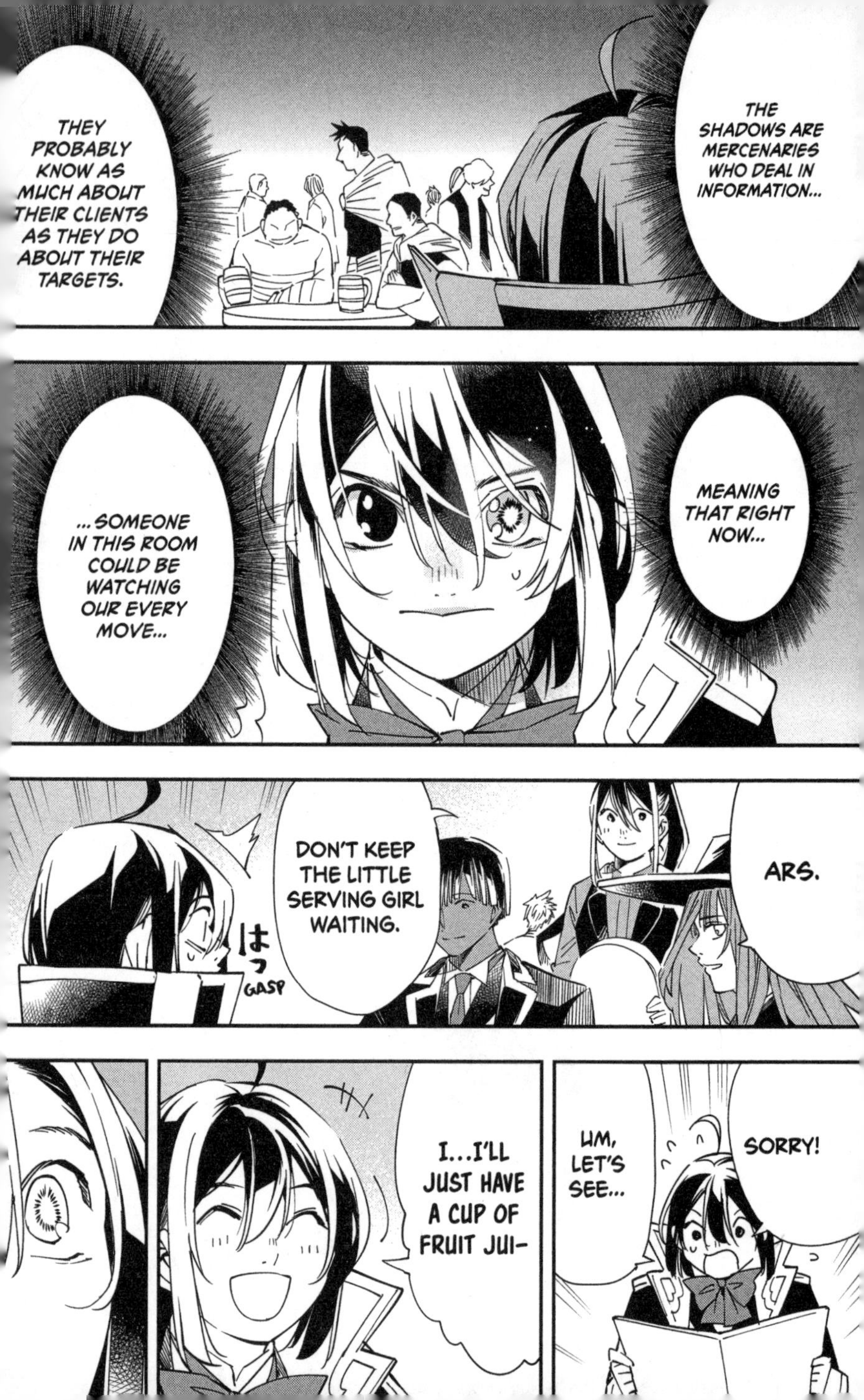
THE SHADOWS ARE MERCENARIES WHO DEAL IN INFORMATION...
THEY PROBABLY KNOW AS MUCH ABOUT THEIR CLIENTS AS THEY DO ABOUT THEIR TARGETS.
MEANING THAT RIGHT NOW...
...SOMEONE IN THIS ROOM COULD BE WATCHING OUR EVERY MOVE...
ARS.
DON'T KEEP THE LITTLE SERVING GIRL WAITING.
はっ
GASP
SORRY!
UM, LET'S SEE...
I...I'LL JUST HAVE A CUP OF FRUIT JUI-

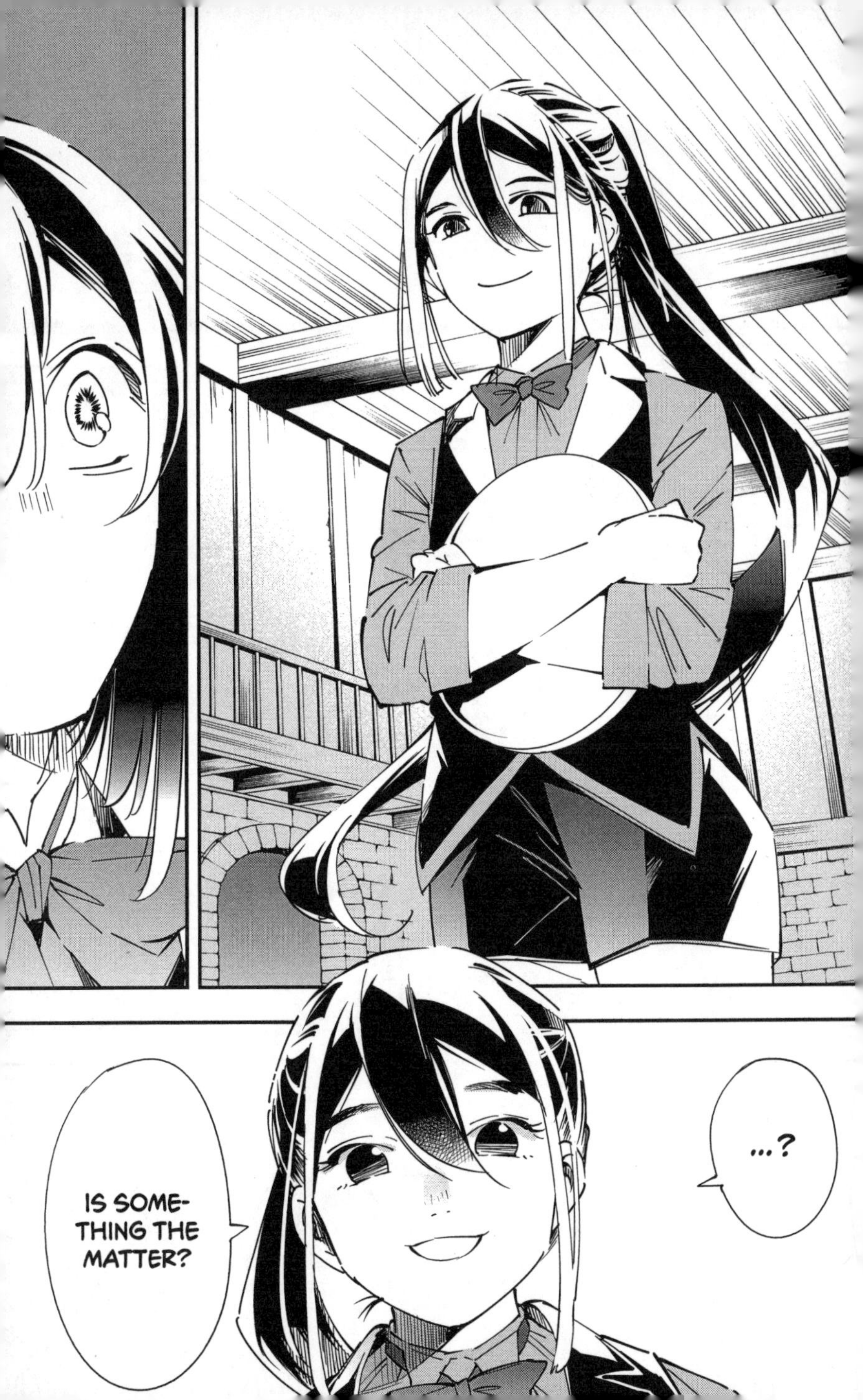
...?
IS SOME-THING THE MATTER?

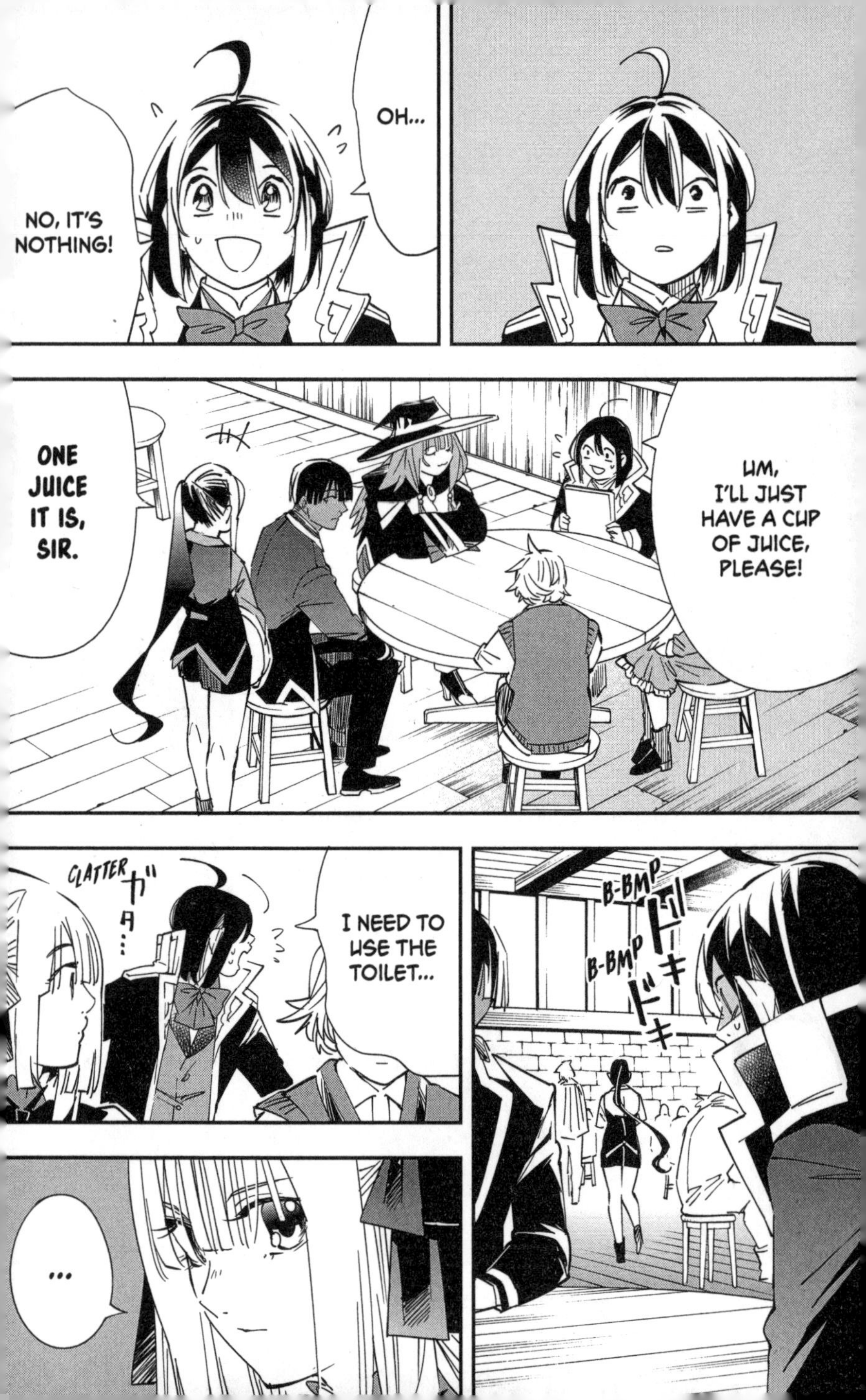
OH...
NO, IT'S NOTHING!
UM, I'LL JUST HAVE A CUP OF JUICE, PLEASE!
ONE JUICE IT IS, SIR.
B-BMP
ドキ
B-BMP
ドキ
I NEED TO USE THE TOILET...
CLATTER
ガタ...
...

WHAT DOES IT MEAN?

BUT...

NO, THAT CAN'T BE IT.

Rietz Muses · Age 23

Stats

	CURRENT	MAX
Command	96	99
Prowess	90	90
Intellect	96	99
Diplomacy	91	100
Ambition	21	

Aptitude

Fighter	A	Cavalier		Archer	A
Mage	C	Engineer	S	Armorer	A
Mariner	D	Pilot	C	Tactician	S

IS SOMETHING WRONG WITH MY APPRAISAL SKILL?

ちらっ
PEEK

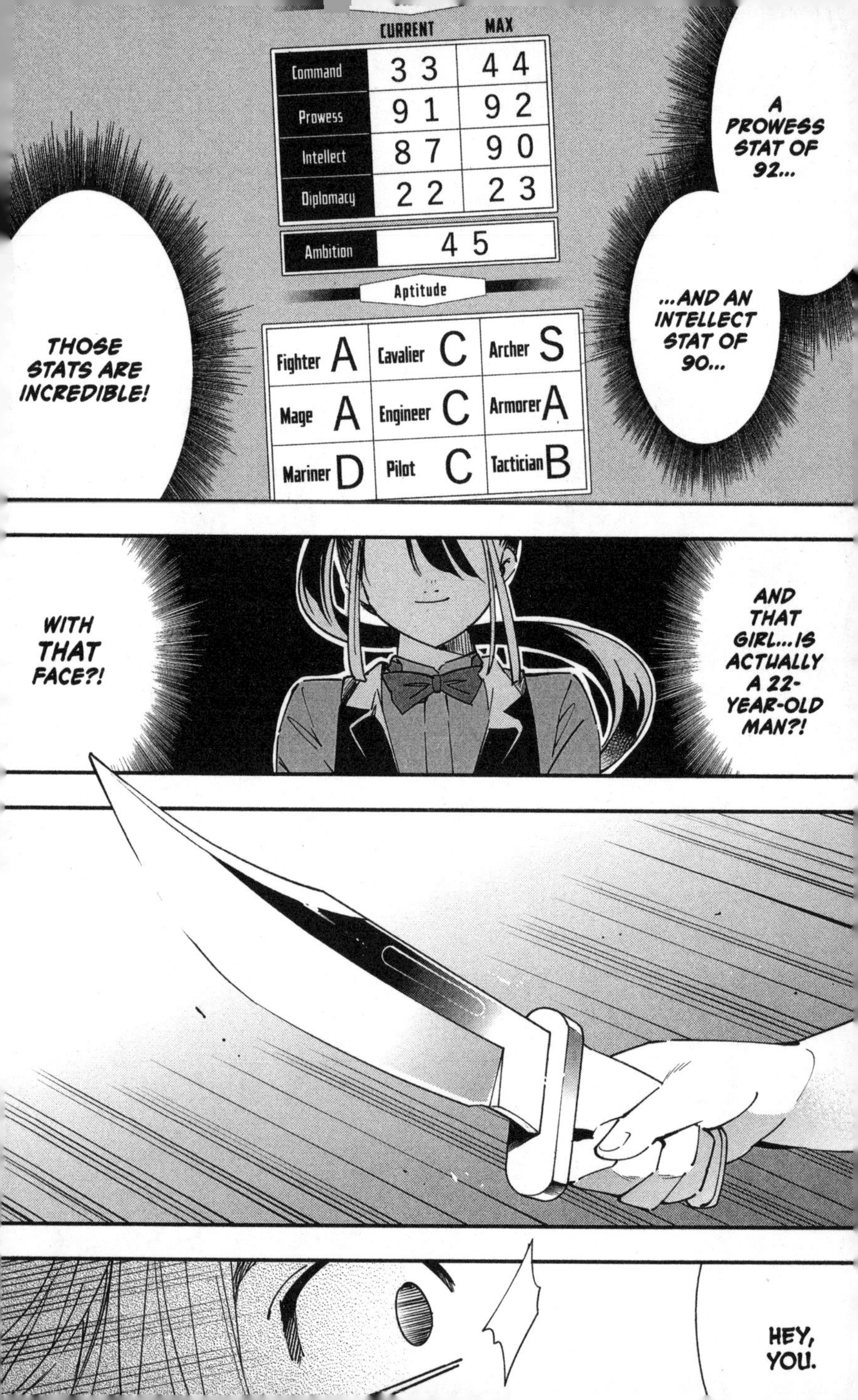
A PROWESS STAT OF 92...
...AND AN INTELLECT STAT OF 90...
CURRENT MAX
Command 33 44
Prowess 91 92
Intellect 87 90
Diplomacy 22 23
Ambition 45
Aptitude
Fighter A Cavalier C Archer S
Mage A Engineer C Armorer A
Mariner D Pilot C Tactician B
THOSE STATS ARE INCREDIBLE!
AND THAT GIRL...IS ACTUALLY A 22-YEAR-OLD MAN?!
WITH THAT FACE?!
HEY, YOU.

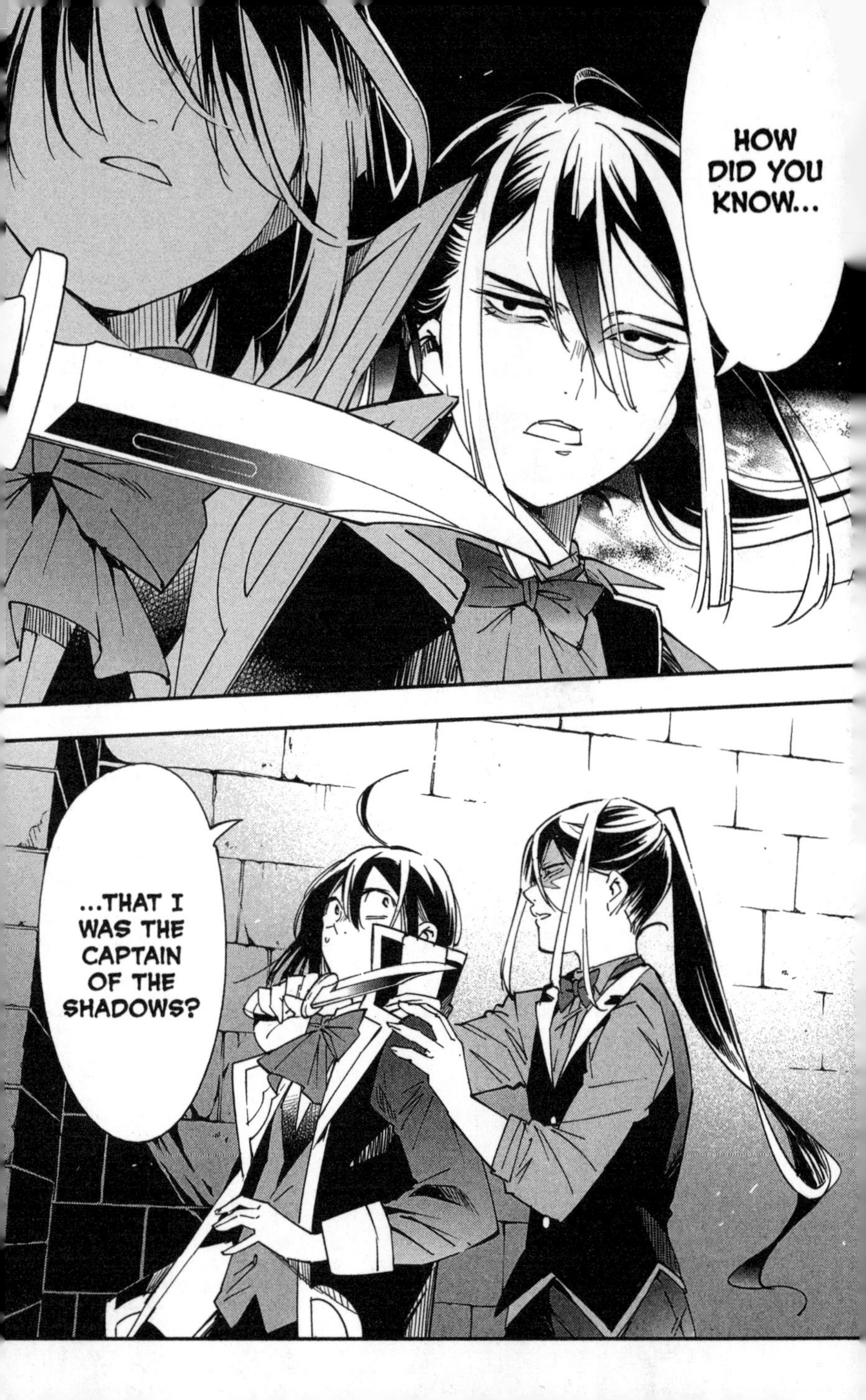
HOW DID YOU KNOW...
...THAT I WAS THE CAPTAIN OF THE SHADOWS?

As a Reincarnated
ARISTOCRAT,
I'll Use My Appraisal Skill to
Rise in the World

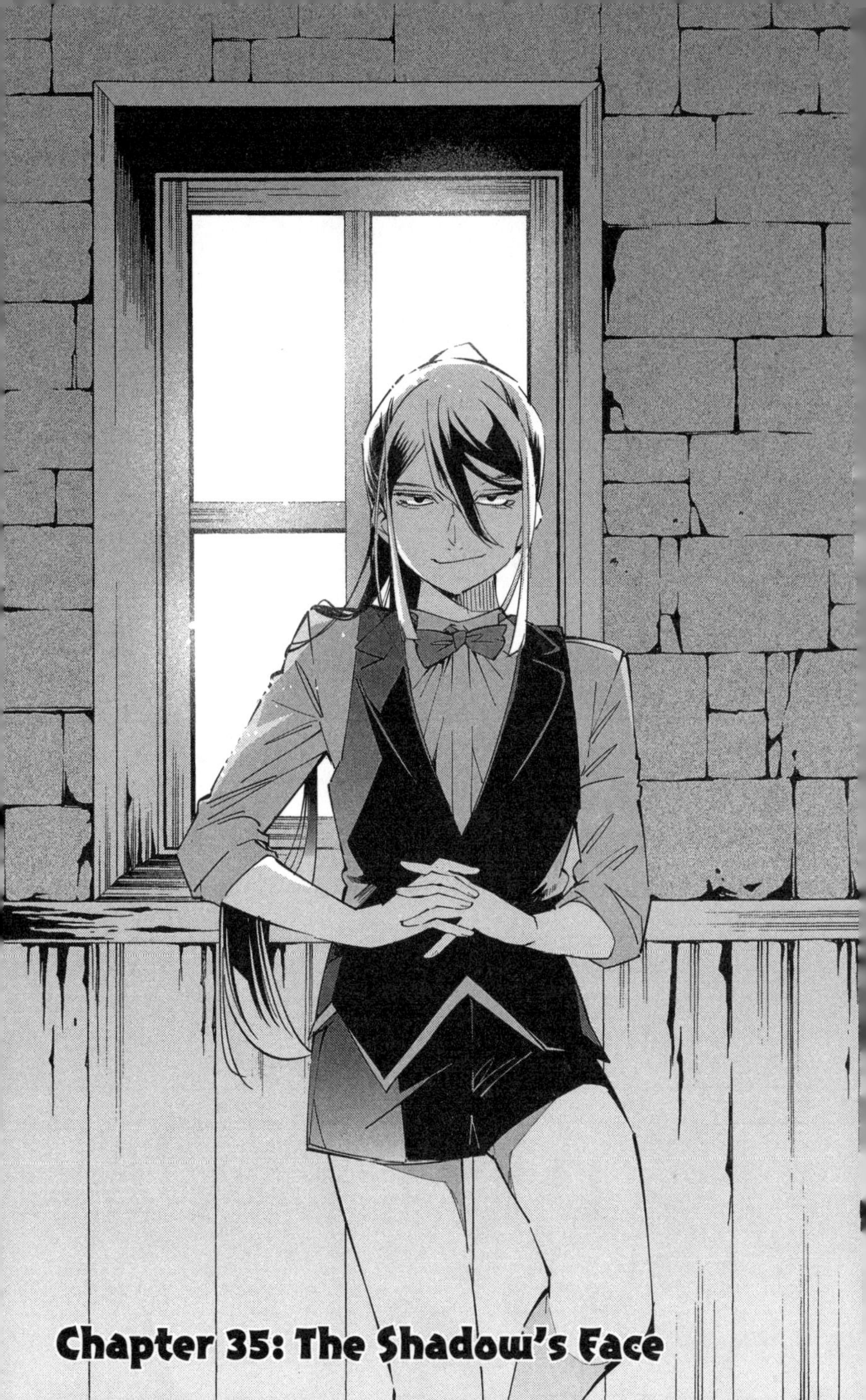

Chapter 35: The Shadow's Face

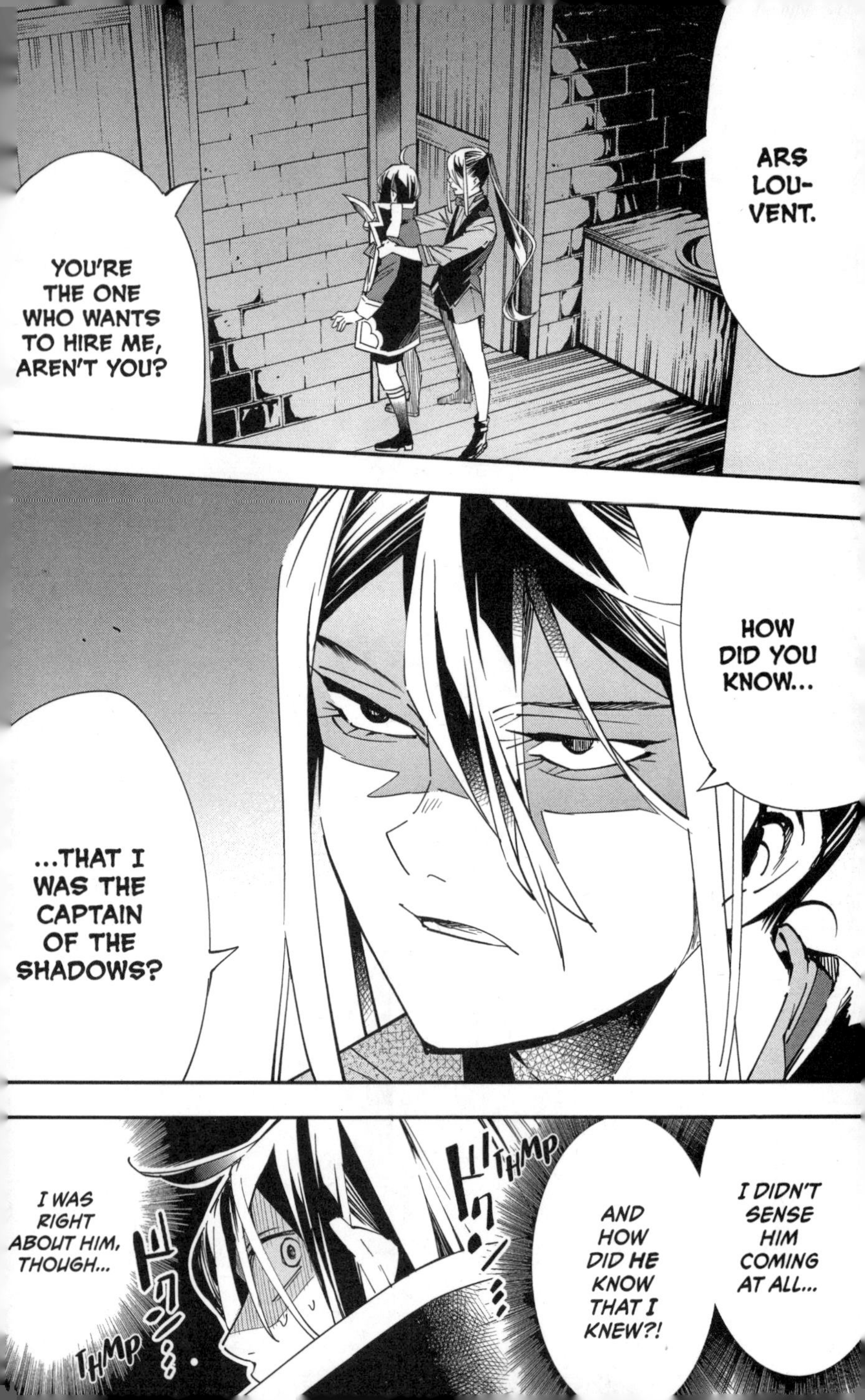
ARS LOU-VENT.
YOU'RE THE ONE WHO WANTS TO HIRE ME, AREN'T YOU?
HOW DID YOU KNOW...
...THAT I WAS THE CAPTAIN OF THE SHADOWS?
I DIDN'T SENSE HIM COMING AT ALL...
AND HOW DID HE KNOW THAT I KNEW?!
THMP
I WAS RIGHT ABOUT HIM, THOUGH...
THMP

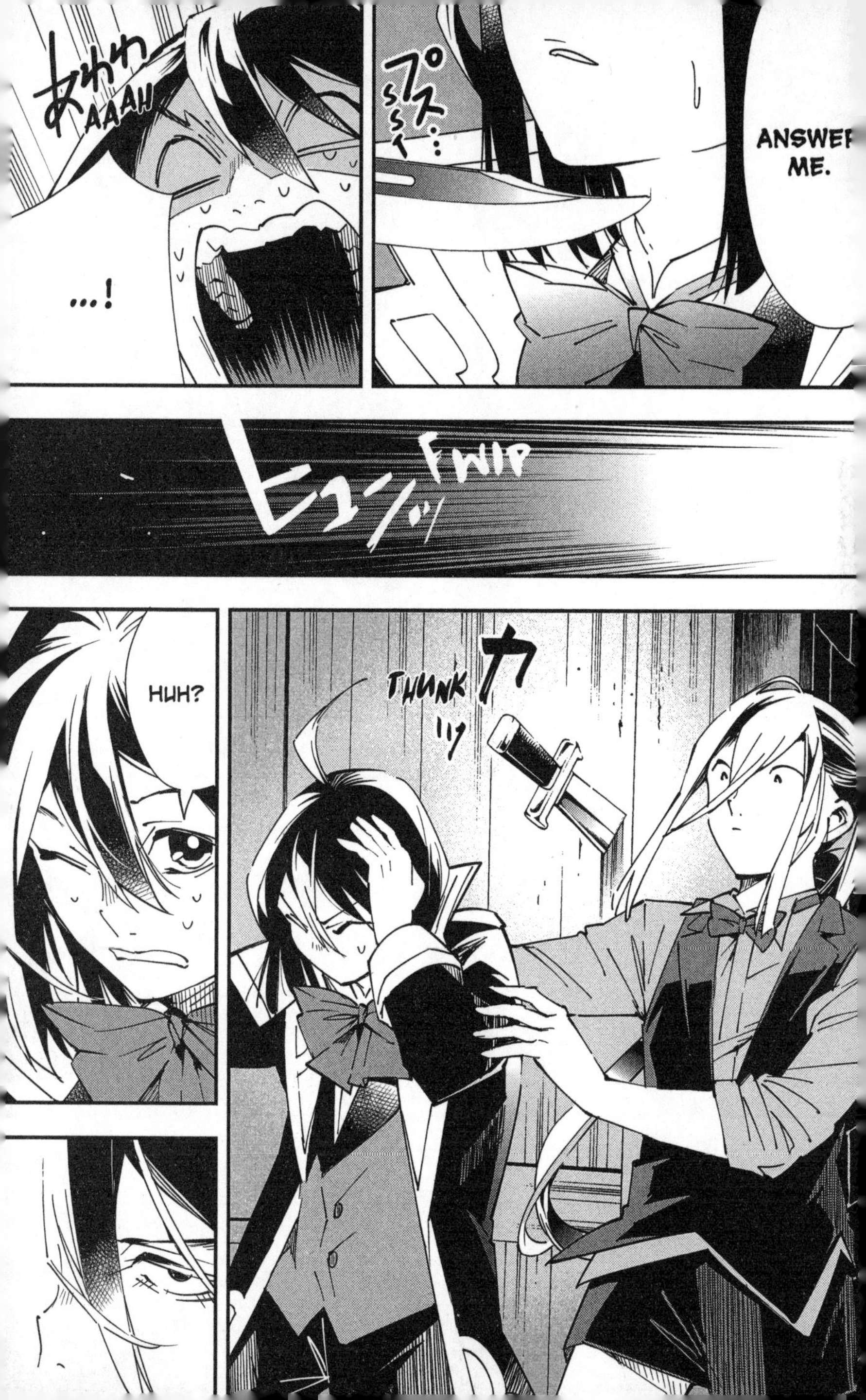
ANSWER ME.
プス…
あわわー
AAAH
...!
ヒュンッ
FWIP
カッ
THUNK
HUH?

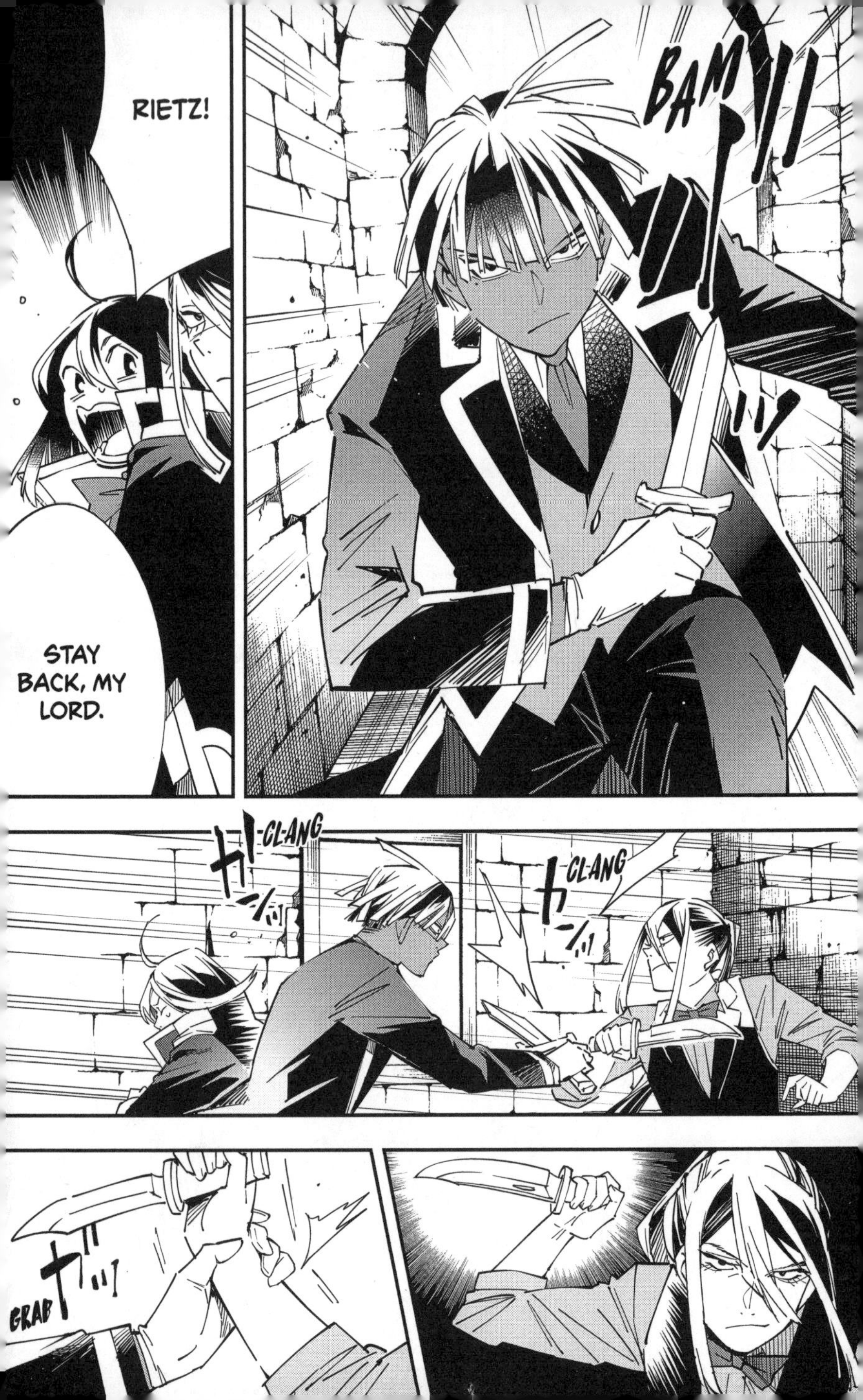
BAM!!
RIETZ!
STAY BACK, MY LORD.
CLANG
CLANG
GRAB

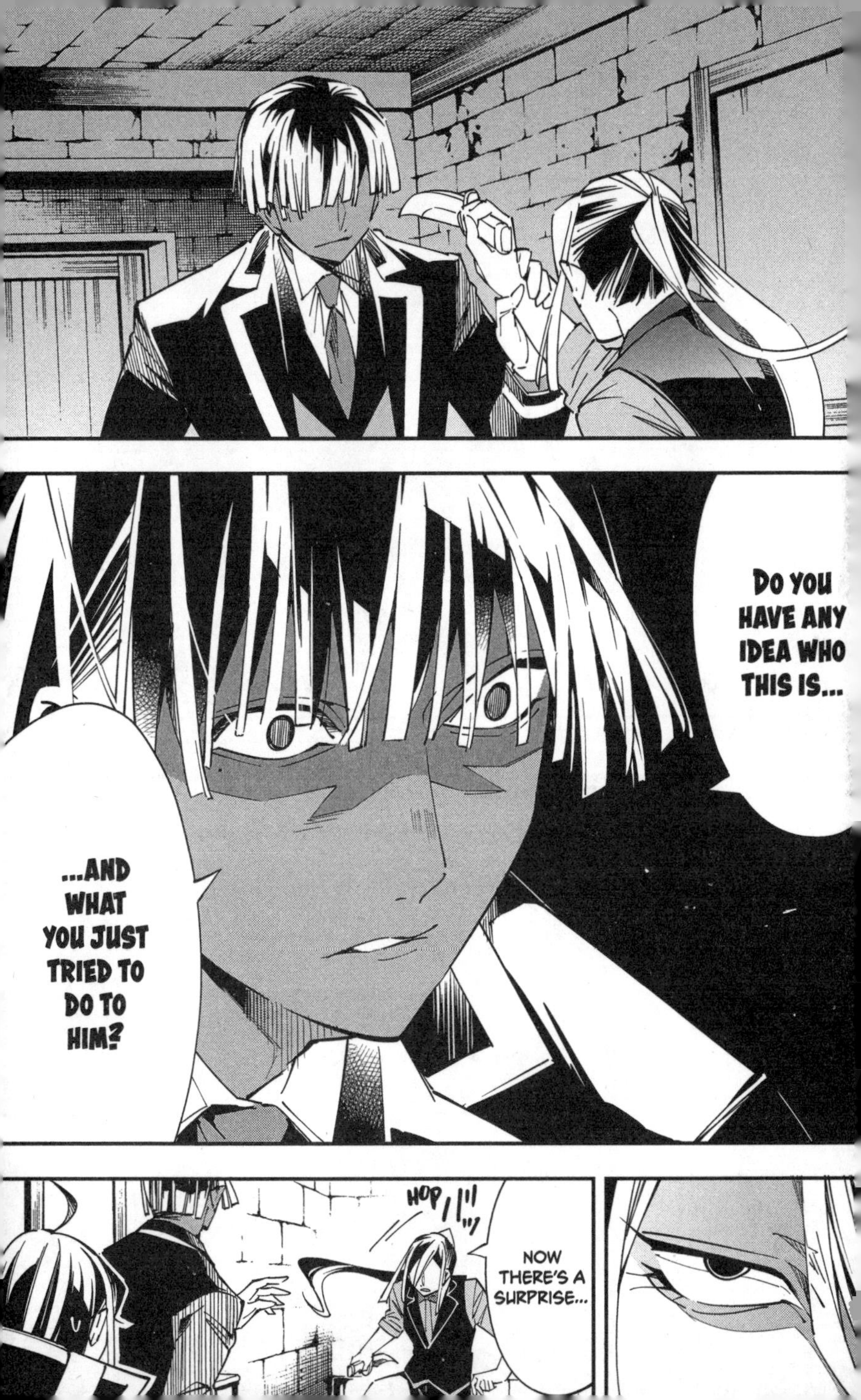
Do you have any idea who this is...
...AND WHAT YOU JUST TRIED TO DO TO HIM?
HOP
NOW THERE'S A SURPRISE...

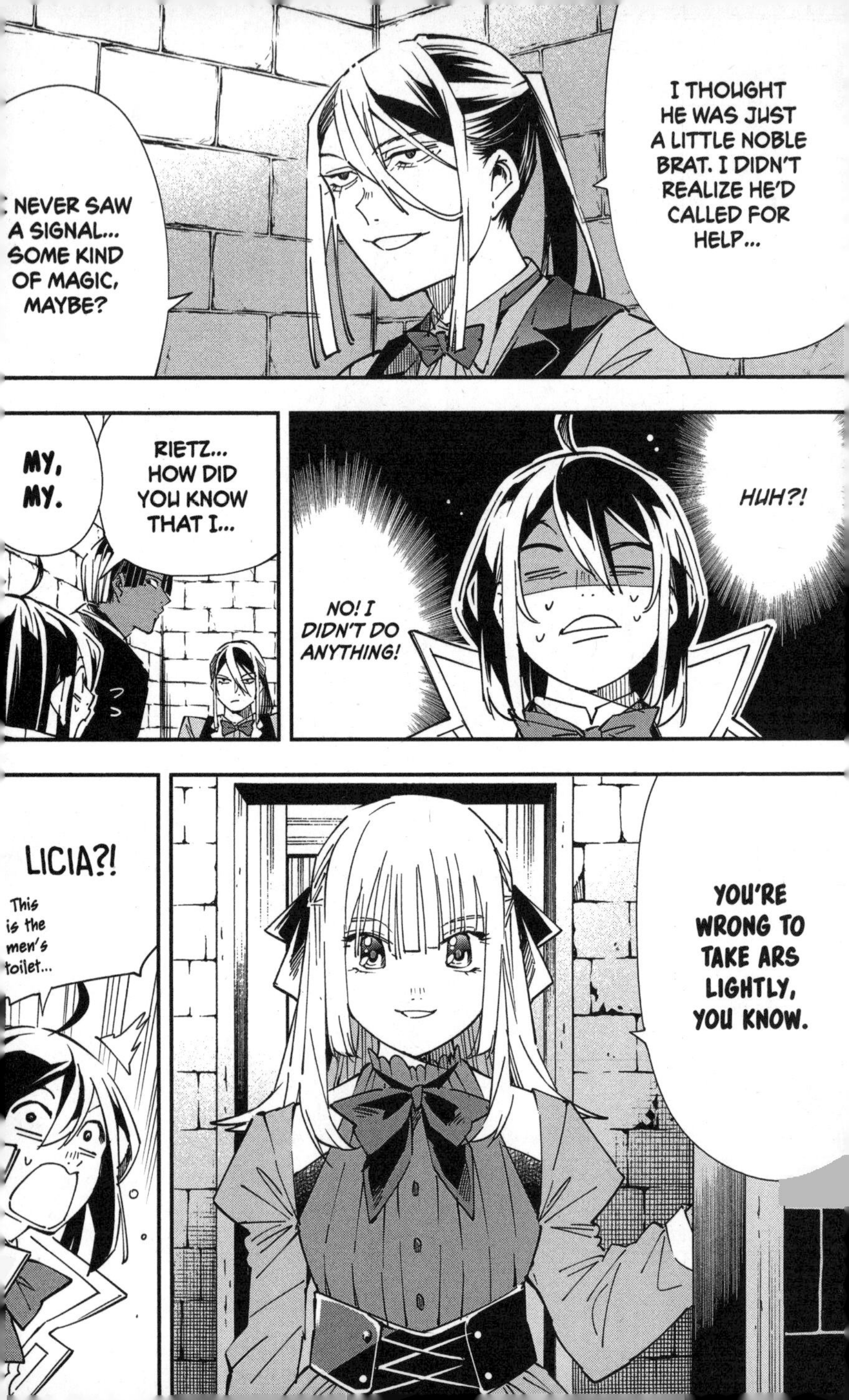
I THOUGHT HE WAS JUST A LITTLE NOBLE BRAT. I DIDN'T REALIZE HE'D CALLED FOR HELP...
NEVER SAW A SIGNAL... SOME KIND OF MAGIC, MAYBE?
HUH?!
NO! I DIDN'T DO ANYTHING!
RIETZ... HOW DID YOU KNOW THAT I...
MY, MY.
YOU'RE WRONG TO TAKE ARS LIGHTLY, YOU KNOW.
LICIA?!
This is the men's toilet...

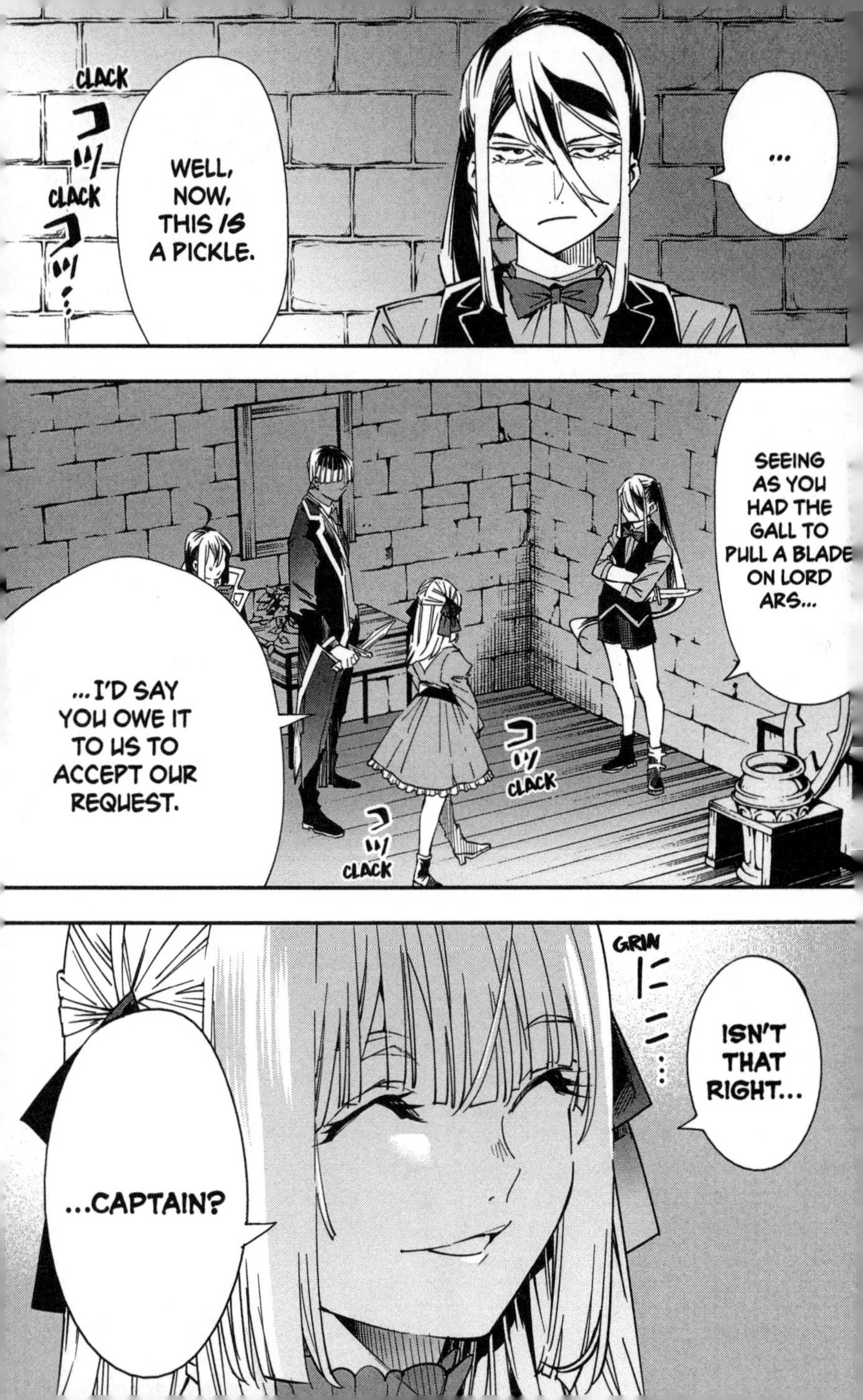
...
WELL, NOW, THIS IS A PICKLE.
CLACK
CLACK
SEEING AS YOU HAD THE GALL TO PULL A BLADE ON LORD ARS...
CLACK
CLACK
...I'D SAY YOU OWE IT TO US TO ACCEPT OUR REQUEST.
GRIN
ISN'T THAT RIGHT...
...CAPTAIN?

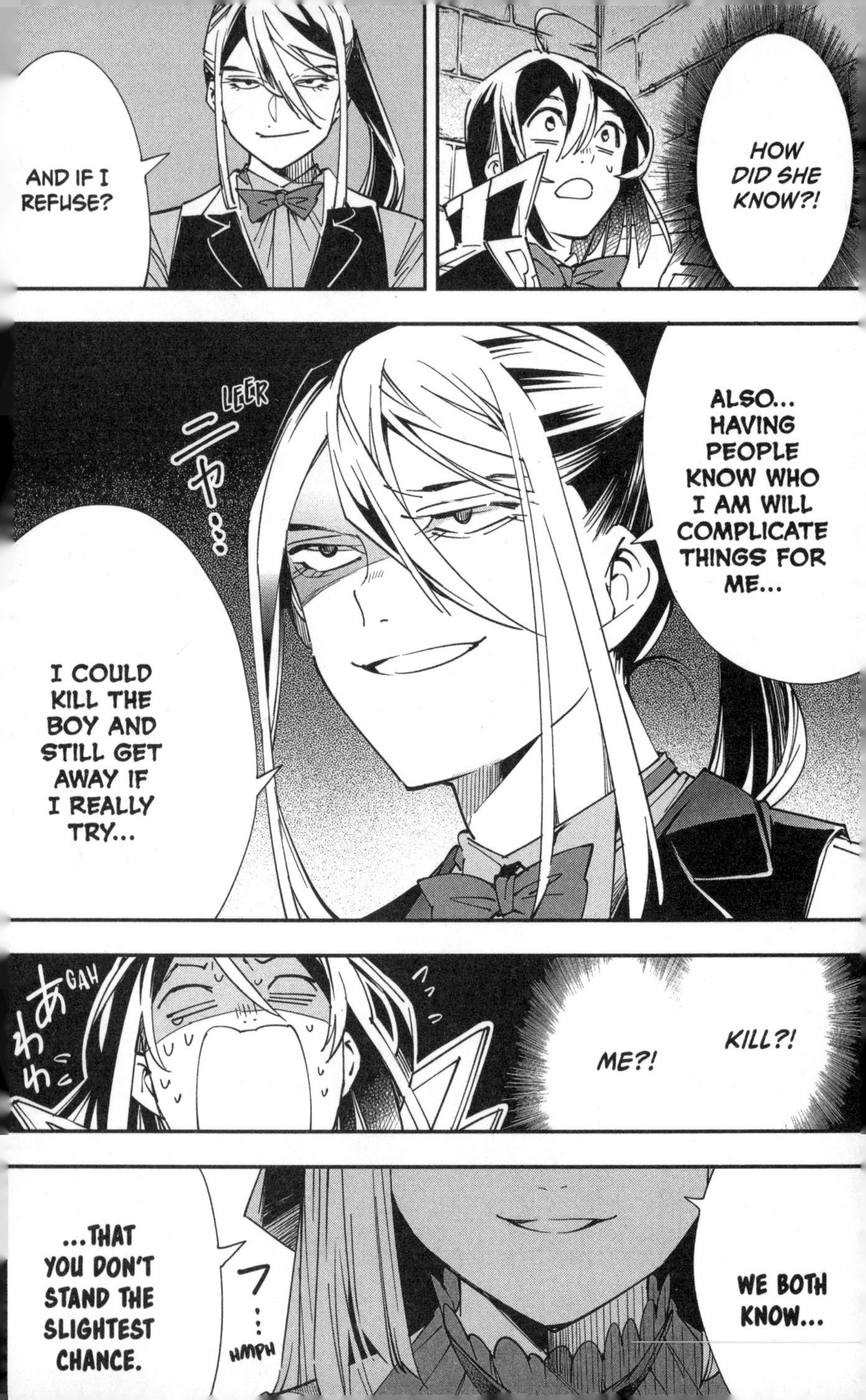
HOW DID SHE KNOW?!
AND IF I REFUSE?
ALSO... HAVING PEOPLE KNOW WHO I AM WILL COMPLICATE THINGS FOR ME...
LEER
ニヤ…
I COULD KILL THE BOY AND STILL GET AWAY IF I REALLY TRY...
KILL?!
ME?!
GAH
WE BOTH KNOW...
HMPH
...THAT YOU DON'T STAND THE SLIGHTEST CHANCE.

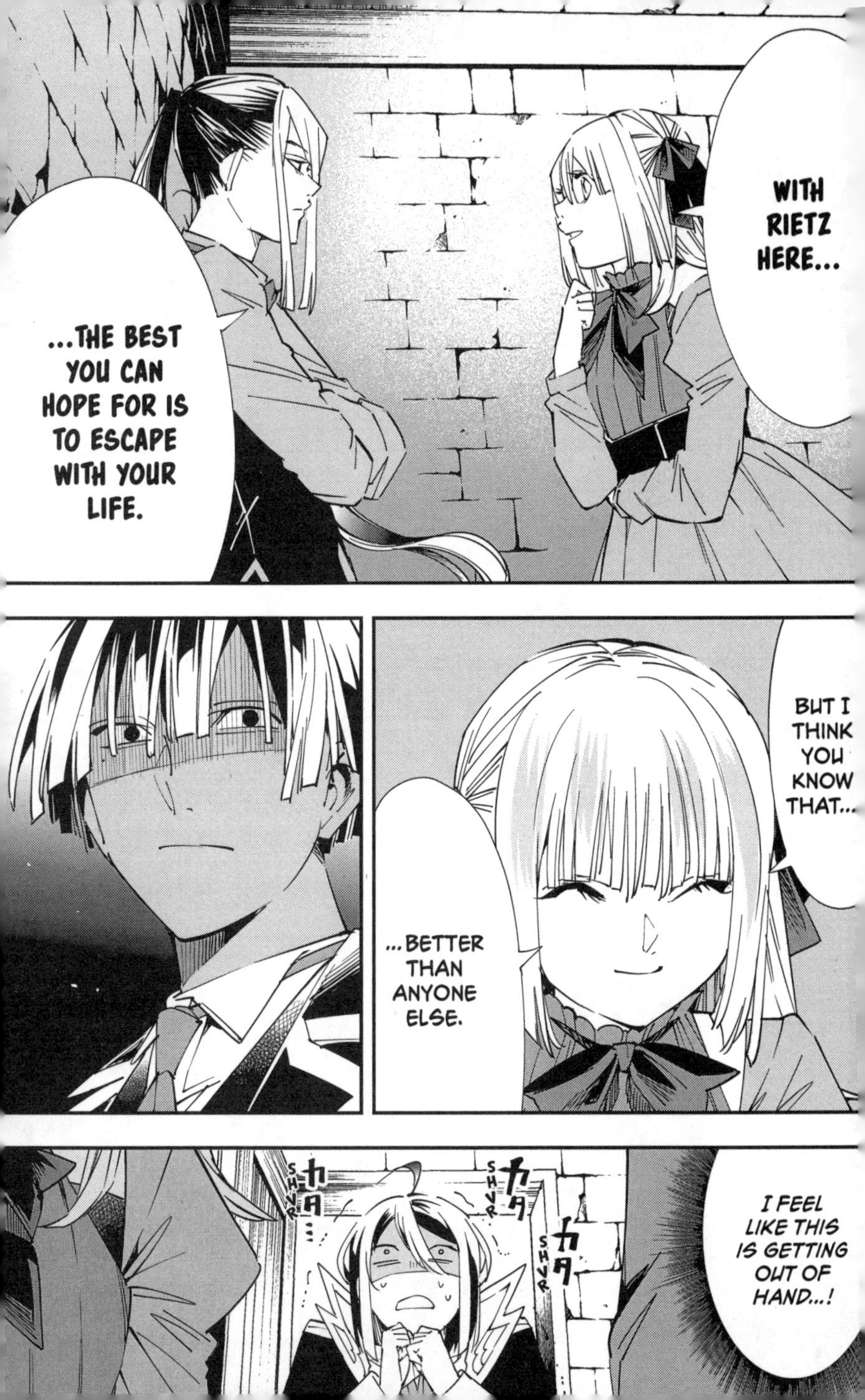
WITH RIETZ HERE...
...THE BEST YOU CAN HOPE FOR IS TO ESCAPE WITH YOUR LIFE.
BUT I THINK YOU KNOW THAT...
...BETTER THAN ANYONE ELSE.
I FEEL LIKE THIS IS GETTING OUT OF HAND...!
SHVR カタ
SHVR カタ
SHVR カタ

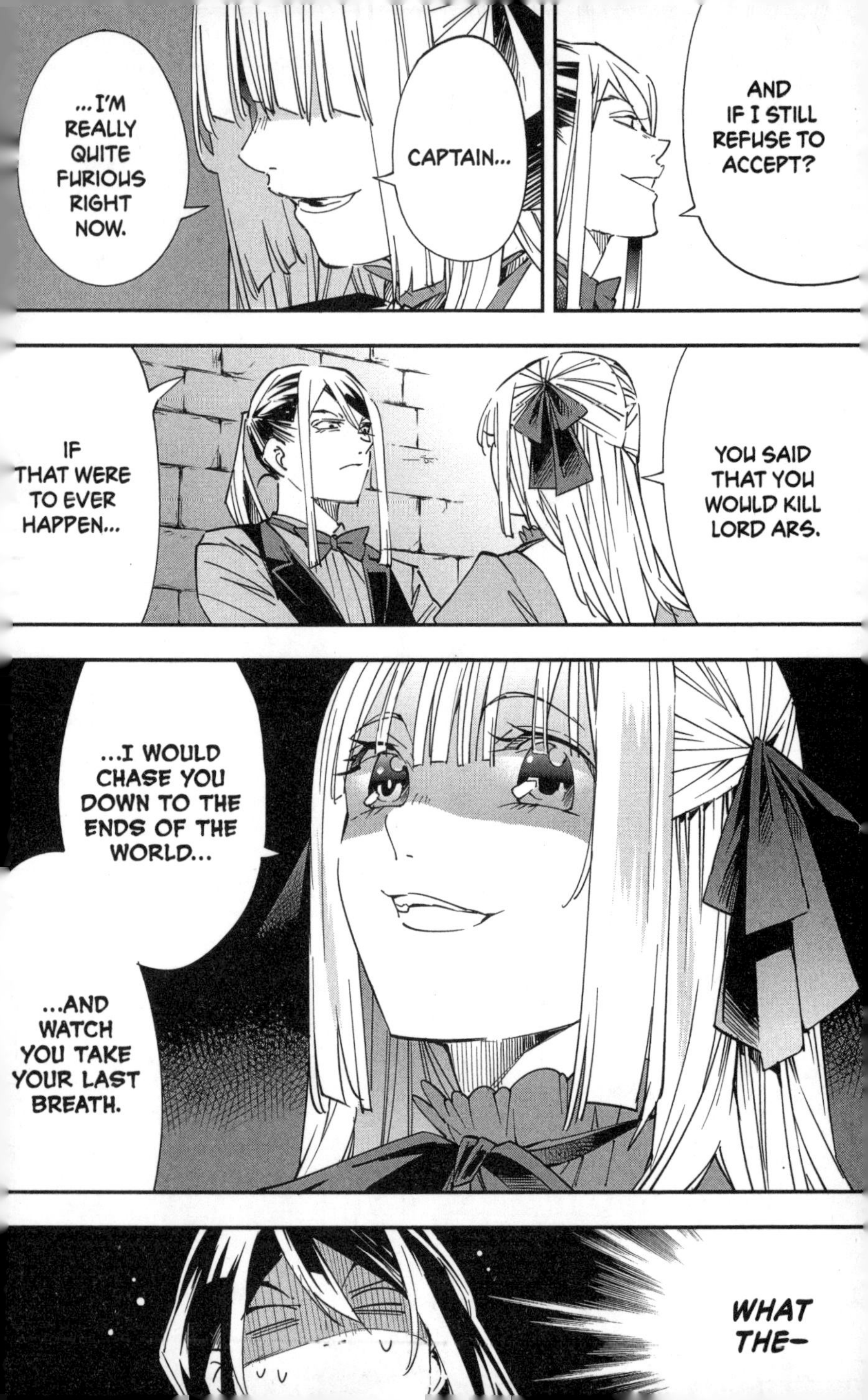
AND IF I STILL REFUSE TO ACCEPT?
CAPTAIN...
...I'M REALLY QUITE FURIOUS RIGHT NOW.
YOU SAID THAT YOU WOULD KILL LORD ARS.
IF THAT WERE TO EVER HAPPEN...
...I WOULD CHASE YOU DOWN TO THE ENDS OF THE WORLD...
...AND WATCH YOU TAKE YOUR LAST BREATH.
WHAT THE–

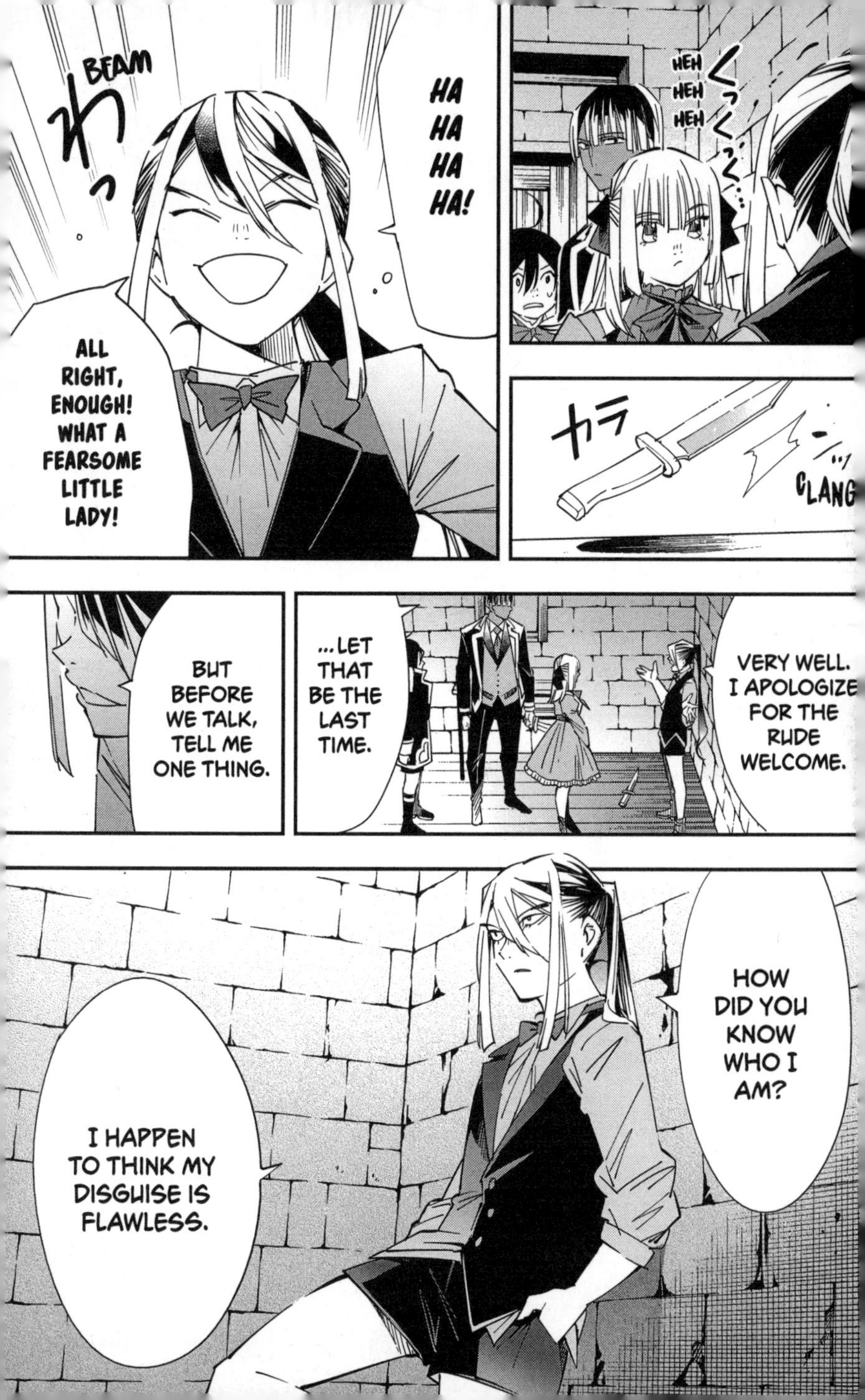
HEH HEH HEH
くっくっく…
カラ
CLANG
BEAM
わっ
HA HA HA HA!
ALL RIGHT, ENOUGH! WHAT A FEARSOME LITTLE LADY!
VERY WELL. I APOLOGIZE FOR THE RUDE WELCOME.
...LET THAT BE THE LAST TIME.
BUT BEFORE WE TALK, TELL ME ONE THING.
HOW DID YOU KNOW WHO I AM?
I HAPPEN TO THINK MY DISGUISE IS FLAWLESS.

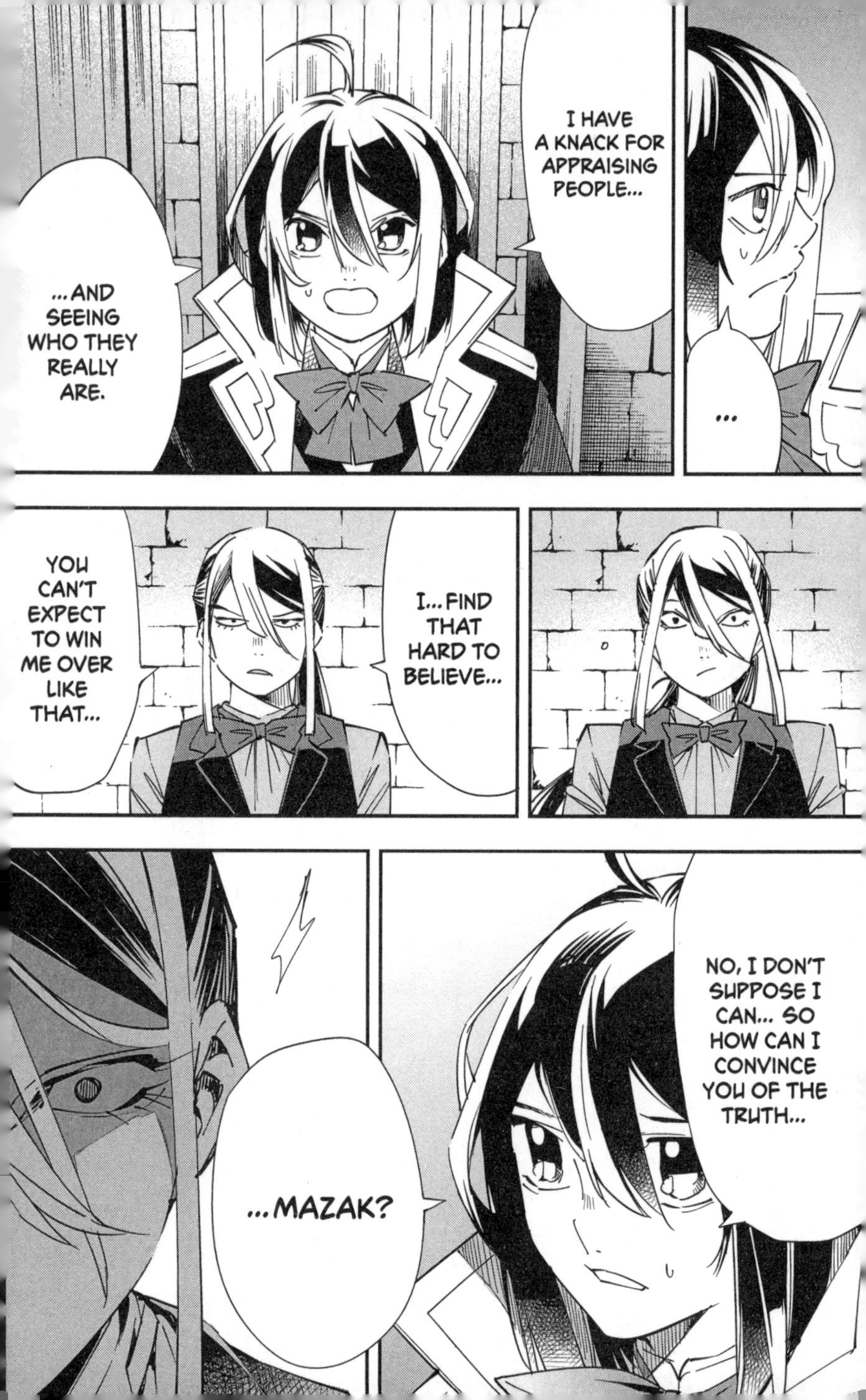
...
I HAVE A KNACK FOR APPRAISING PEOPLE...
...AND SEEING WHO THEY REALLY ARE.
I... FIND THAT HARD TO BELIEVE...
YOU CAN'T EXPECT TO WIN ME OVER LIKE THAT...
NO, I DON'T SUPPOSE I CAN... SO HOW CAN I CONVINCE YOU OF THE TRUTH...
...MAZAK?

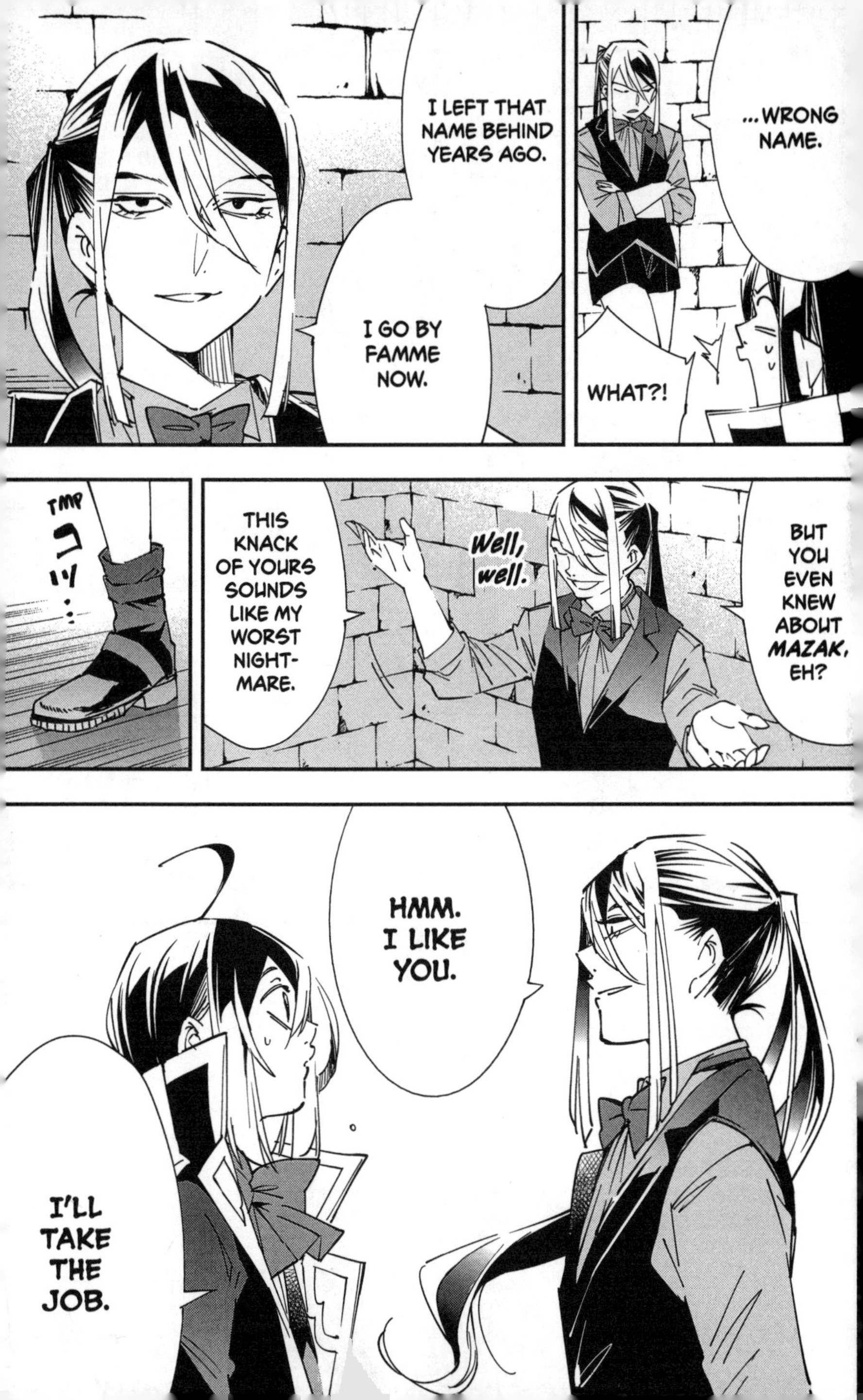
...WRONG NAME.
WHAT?!
I LEFT THAT NAME BEHIND YEARS AGO.
I GO BY FAMME NOW.
BUT YOU EVEN KNEW ABOUT *MAZAK*, EH?
Well, well.
THIS KNACK OF YOURS SOUNDS LIKE MY WORST NIGHT-MARE.
TMP
コツ…
HMM. I LIKE YOU.
I'LL TAKE THE JOB.

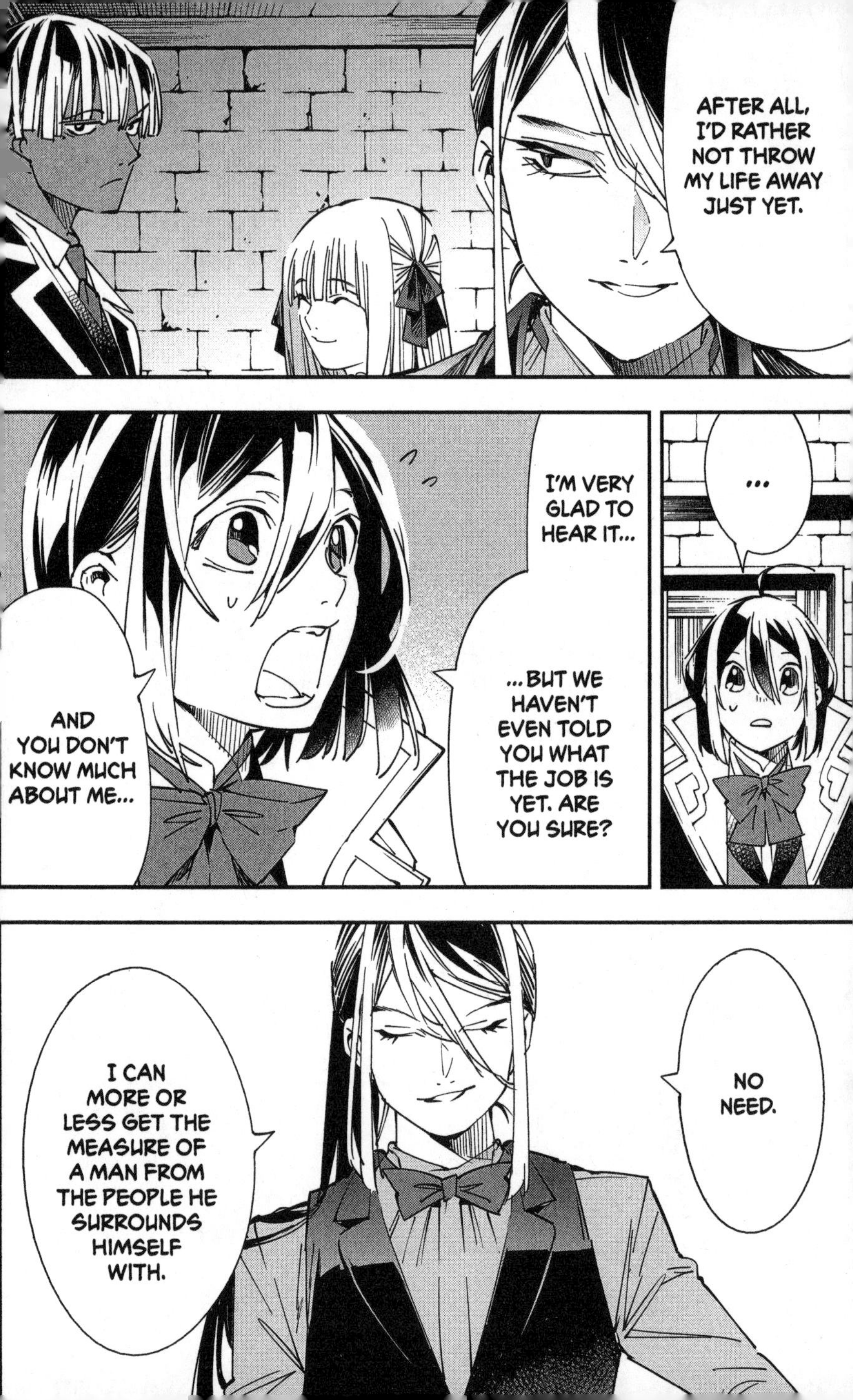
AFTER ALL, I'D RATHER NOT THROW MY LIFE AWAY JUST YET.
...
I'M VERY GLAD TO HEAR IT...
...BUT WE HAVEN'T EVEN TOLD YOU WHAT THE JOB IS YET. ARE YOU SURE?
AND YOU DON'T KNOW MUCH ABOUT ME...
NO NEED.
I CAN MORE OR LESS GET THE MEASURE OF A MAN FROM THE PEOPLE HE SURROUNDS HIMSELF WITH.

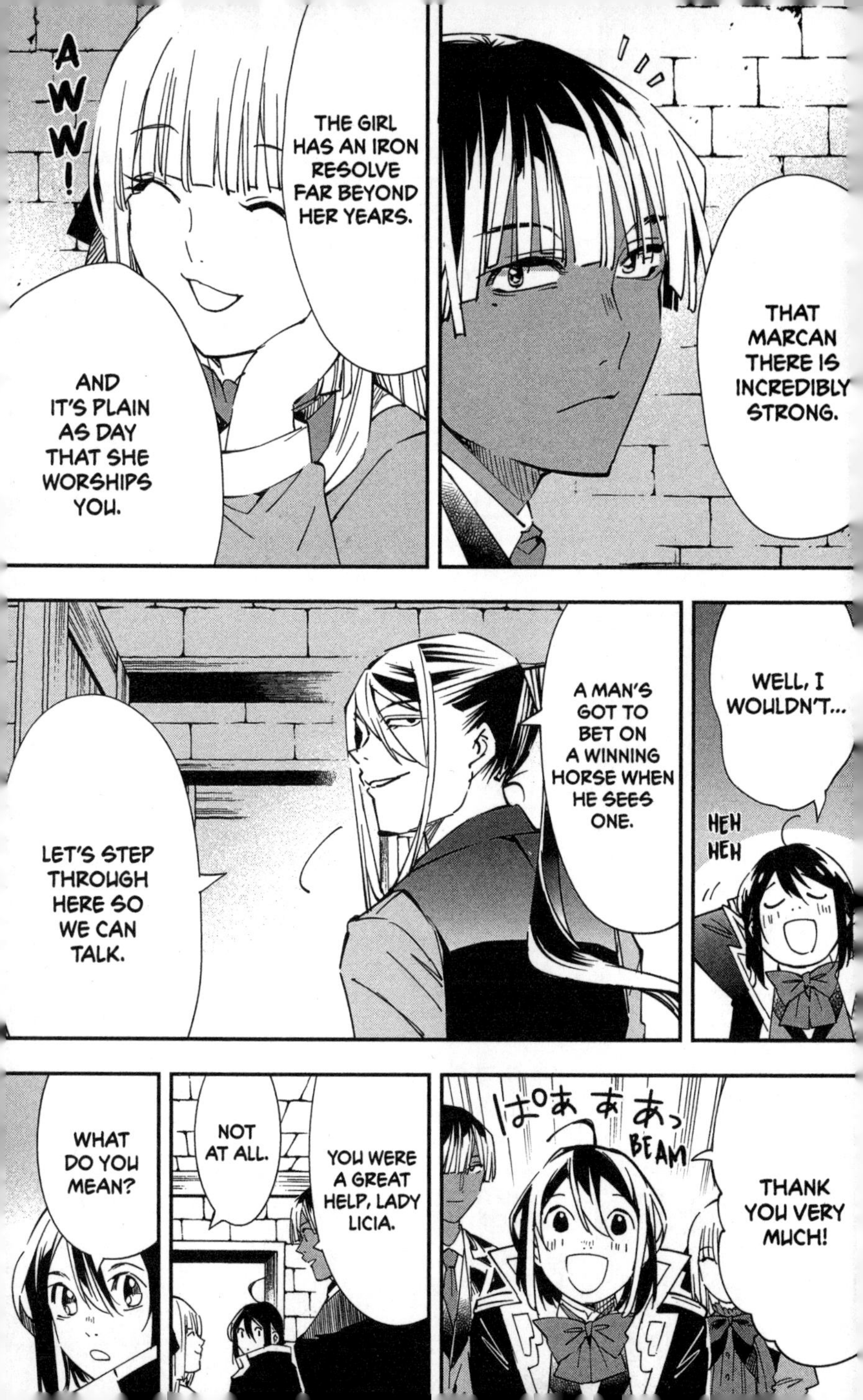
THAT MARCAN THERE IS INCREDIBLY STRONG.
THE GIRL HAS AN IRON RESOLVE FAR BEYOND HER YEARS.
AWWW!
AND IT'S PLAIN AS DAY THAT SHE WORSHIPS YOU.
WELL, I WOULDN'T...
HEH HEH
A MAN'S GOT TO BET ON A WINNING HORSE WHEN HE SEES ONE.
LET'S STEP THROUGH HERE SO WE CAN TALK.
THANK YOU VERY MUCH!
ぱあああっ
BEAM
YOU WERE A GREAT HELP, LADY LICIA.
NOT AT ALL.
WHAT DO YOU MEAN?

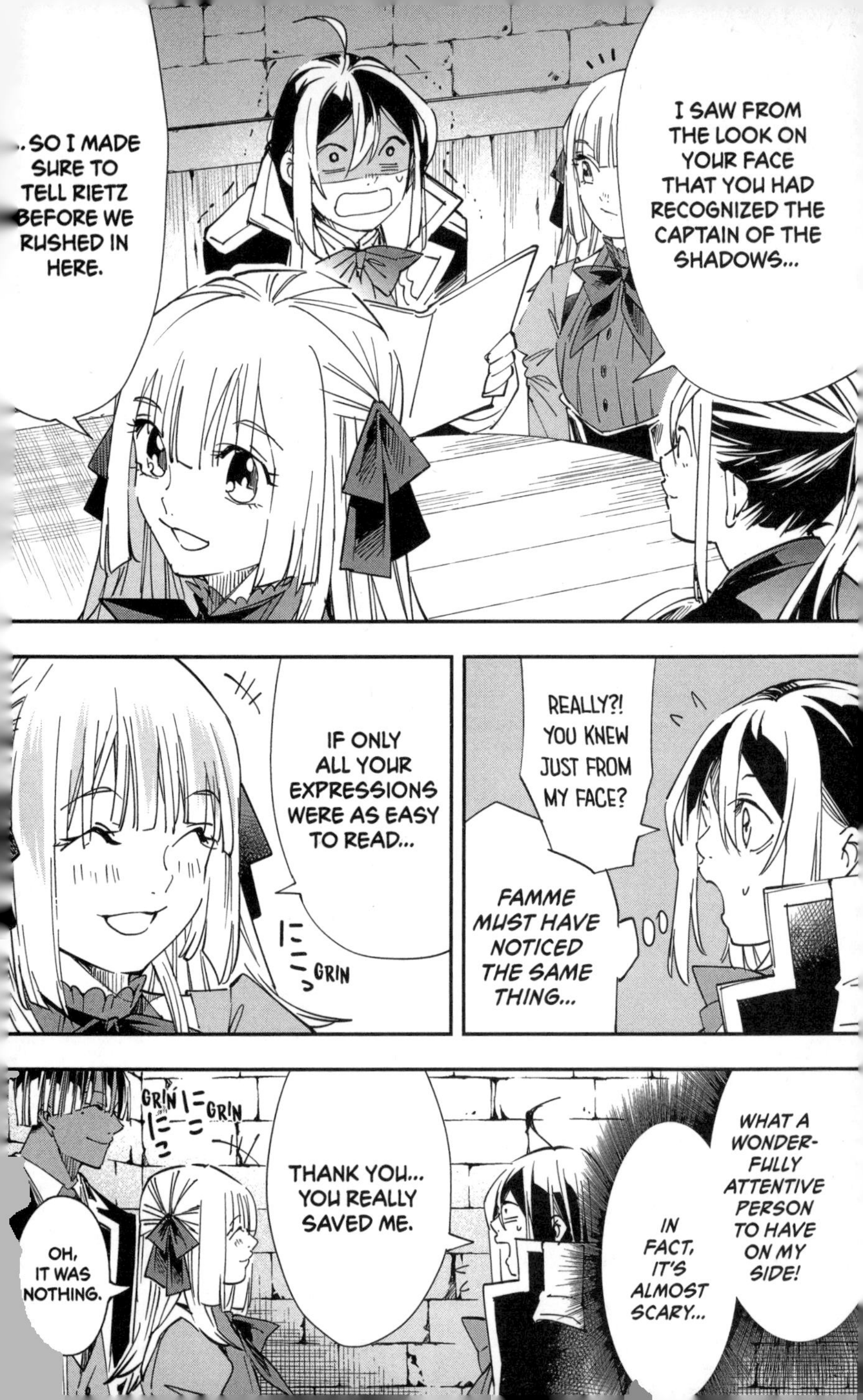
I SAW FROM THE LOOK ON YOUR FACE THAT YOU HAD RECOGNIZED THE CAPTAIN OF THE SHADOWS...
..SO I MADE SURE TO TELL RIETZ BEFORE WE RUSHED IN HERE.
REALLY?! YOU KNEW JUST FROM MY FACE?
FAMME MUST HAVE NOTICED THE SAME THING...
IF ONLY ALL YOUR EXPRESSIONS WERE AS EASY TO READ...
GRIN
WHAT A WONDER-FULLY ATTENTIVE PERSON TO HAVE ON MY SIDE!
IN FACT, IT'S ALMOST SCARY...
THANK YOU... YOU REALLY SAVED ME.
GRIN GRIN
OH, IT WAS NOTHING.

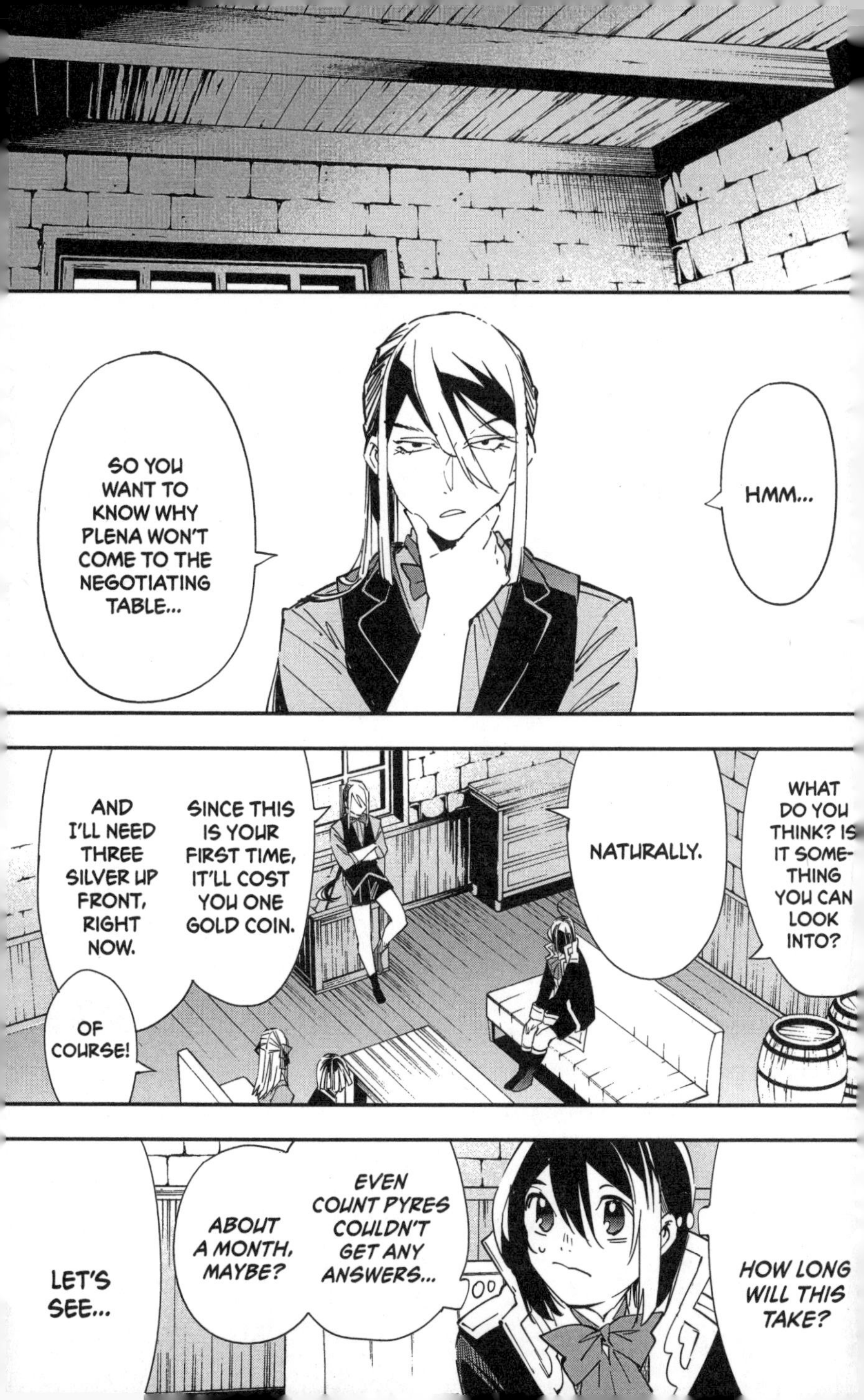
HMM...
SO YOU WANT TO KNOW WHY PLENA WON'T COME TO THE NEGOTIATING TABLE...
WHAT DO YOU THINK? IS IT SOMETHING YOU CAN LOOK INTO?
NATURALLY.
SINCE THIS IS YOUR FIRST TIME, IT'LL COST YOU ONE GOLD COIN.
AND I'LL NEED THREE SILVER UP FRONT, RIGHT NOW.
OF COURSE!
HOW LONG WILL THIS TAKE?
EVEN COUNT PYRES COULDN'T GET ANY ANSWERS...
ABOUT A MONTH, MAYBE?
LET'S SEE...

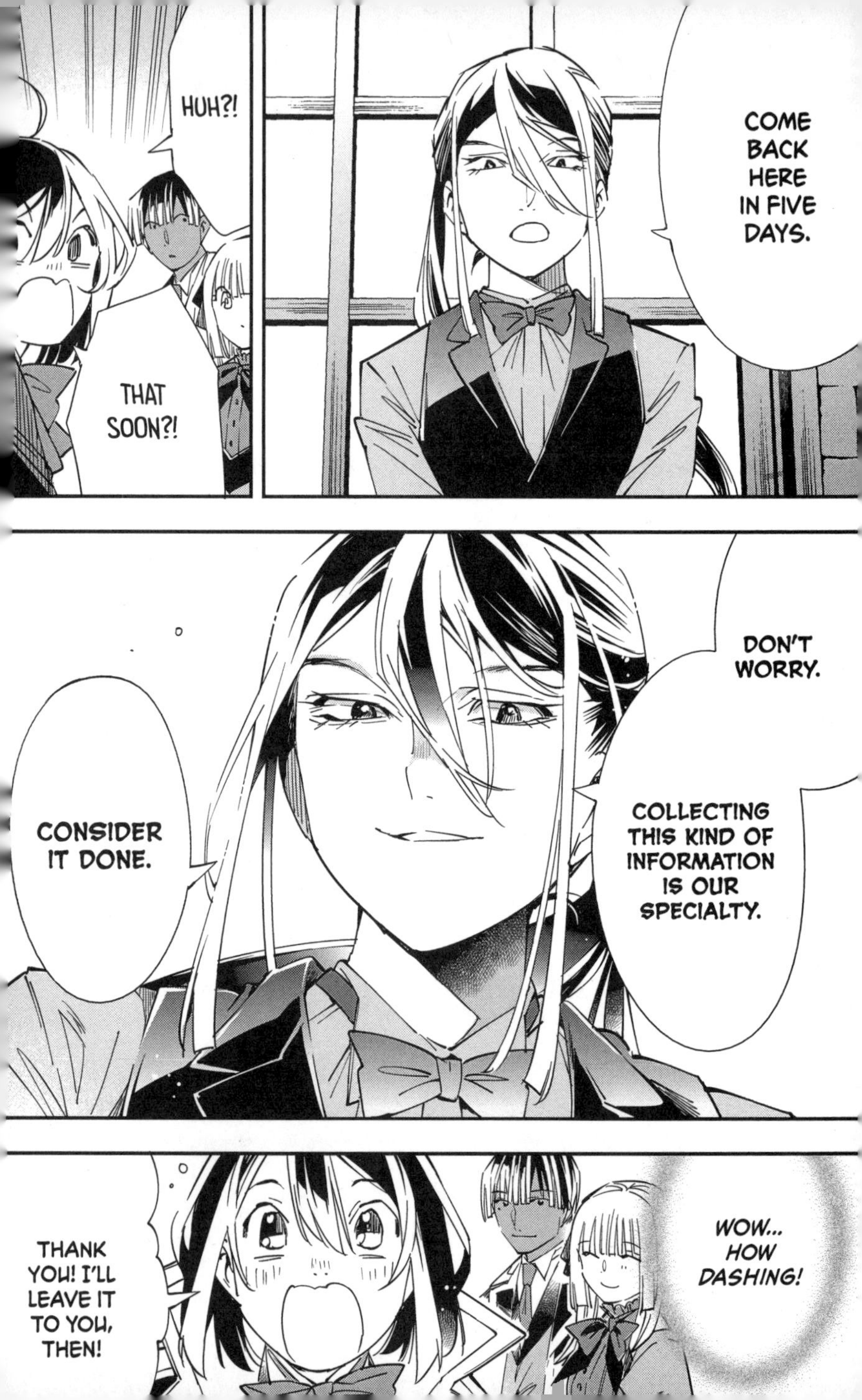
COME BACK HERE IN FIVE DAYS.
HUH?!
THAT SOON?!
DON'T WORRY.
COLLECTING THIS KIND OF INFORMATION IS OUR SPECIALTY.
CONSIDER IT DONE.
WOW... HOW DASHING!
THANK YOU! I'LL LEAVE IT TO YOU, THEN!

Bonus Story

by Miraijin A

Raven Louvent had entered into the service of Count Lumeire Pyres of Canarre. Within a few years, he achieved both great success in battle and a promotion to one of the count's primary vassals, making him an indispensible asset to the duchy.

The battle raged on. Seitz had launched an invasion of Canarre, but Canarre had pushed them back and forced them to withdraw. However, with Seitz's commander still alive and well, Seitz could have turned around and begun a fresh assault at any moment. Hoping to avert this possiblity, Raven had then sprung an ambush on the fleeing commander. While Lumeire chased down the main host astride his fine courser, Raven pursued the enemy commander and his guard. His horse was faster than any of theirs; he would soon be upon them.

The commander's men peeled off and rushed Raven in an attempt to protect their liege. But Raven was too strong, cutting them down with ease. He had been joined by several of Canarre's knights, all of them mighty warriors in their own right, so he now left them to handle the remaining soldiers while he made straight for the enemy commander. He was gaining on him by the second.

"Bastard! You want a fight, I'll give you one!" the commander growled as he turned to face his pursuer. Though he had fled the field knowing that his death or capture would mean disaster for the entire army, he was a powerfully built man who had risen through the ranks by dint of his strength. This was not someone who would be easily defeated.

Both wielding halberds, Raven and his foe began pressing each other fiercely astride their mounts. The enemy commander proved strong, even against an opponent such as Raven, yet he was clearly feeling the pressure. Raven's swings were so powerful that with every parry, the enemy's expression grew steadily more panicked.

"Hah!" cried Raven, swinging his halberd with all his strength. The enemy commander turned the swing aside, but the force of Raven's blow sent him flying out of the saddle. Having been dismounted, the commander fled for his life. Raven came charging up behind him on his horse and lopped off the man's head.

"Their commander is down!" he roared.

His men cheered.

＊ ＊ ＊

"Well fought, Raven! Another resounding success on the battlefield."

The victory banquet was in full swing at Canarre Castle, and Lumeire was heaping praise on his best knight.

"I don't deserve such praise, my lord," Raven murmured.

"Ha ha ha, don't be so modest. You took the enemy commander's head. If *that's* not worthy of praise, then nothing is!"

"But something about this battle struck me as odd," Raven remarked. "I believe the enemy had information about our strategy."

Lumeire's smile evaporated. "I felt much the same, so I decided to look into the matter. As it happens, we managed to extract some information from the prisoners we took. It would seem we have a traitor in Canarre."

"A traitor, you say?"

"Your valor won the day, but things could have gone very differently for us. We must find this traitor and bring them to justice." Lumeire's features contorted with rage as he said this. Treason was a coward's weapon, so his anger was hardly surprising.

"If there is a traitor in our midst," said Raven, "I will help you find them, my lord."

"Ha ha ha. You're not made for that sort of work. I would rather have you training the soldiers when you're not on the battlefield. Keep your focus there."

Raven may have been an excellent soldier, but he lacked the delicate touch required for rooting out a traitor. Even so, he was not a man to sulk at being told his skills would not be required. Instead, he took his lord's words to heart and turned his attention to drilling the troops.

Several months later, the identity of the traitor came to light: it was the baron of Lamberg. The news came as a shock—the baron was one of Lumeire's closest confidants—but a mountain of evidence soon put his crimes beyond any doubt. The baron was brought to Canarre to explain himself. Faced with such clear evidence against him, he admitted openly to his crime. Lumeire was furious, initially vowing to put the baron's entire family to death. But after his rage had cooled,

Lumeire reconsidered and announced that only the baron would be executed, with his children, wife, and co-conspirator vassals to merely be exiled from Missian.

Raven reflected on these events with the detached interest of an outside observer, wondering who would come to fill the baron's newly vacant seat. It was then that Lumeire summoned him to his chambers for a talk.

"Ah! There you are, Raven," Lumeire greeted him.

Raven had heard nothing as to the reason for the summons, so he waited uneasily for the count to continue. He didn't have long to wait.

"Raven Louvent," Lumeire said promptly, "I hereby name you baron of Lamberg!"

"Huh? What did you..." Raven began, thinking he must have misheard.

"No doubt you're aware that I had the former baron executed. I've thought on who should fill his seat, and given your success on the battlefield, I've decided it should go to you. I trust you'll accept."

Raven couldn't believe what he was hearing. It was true enough that he dreamed of someday becoming a nobleman, but he assumed that such an honor would come in the distant future, if at all. Despite his shock, he couldn't let such an opportunity pass him by.

"I accept," he declared.

"I knew that you would!" Lumeire said with a smile. "Here's to you, Baron!" And with that, Raven officially became the new baron of Lamberg.

Following his meeting with Raven, Lumeire

summoned the other county lords to announce the man's elevation to the rank of baron. Raven had achieved much since becoming a vassal, so no one contested the news. Even Raven's low birth did not count against him. With war threatening on the horizon, the lords understood that strength weighed more than birth. The county of Canarre was particularly susceptible to conflict, being on the border of the duchy. As such, men of Canarre tended to place greater stock in ability than did men in other counties. Raven's advancement now formally recognized by the other nobles, people converged on the castle to celebrate the new baron.

Coming up to congratulate him, Raven's friend Hammond cried, "I never thought you would be named a lord so quickly!"

"I'm as shocked as you are," Raven admitted. "Almost as shocked as when you became a lord after all your relatives died, one after another."

Hammond, too, had been granted the title of baron. Tradition among the nobles dictated that the firstborn son was always the one to inherit the title, leaving a fourthborn son like Hammond with little hope of inheriting. However, after illness and war lay waste to each of his brothers, Hammond became the only remaining heir.

"Do you remember what we promised before?" asked Hammond.

Raven stared back at him quizzically.

"That if both of us became lords," Hammond continued, "we would wed our children to each other."

"Ah," Raven said at last. "Yes, we did say that."

"I already have a fiancée. And you?"

"I…have nothing to report on that front. I've hardly given it any thought." For the past several years, all of Raven's attention had been focused on his work as a soldier, with marriage never even crossing his mind.

"Well," said Hammond, "our promise aside, you'll need an heir to carry on your line, so you should wed as soon as you can."

"When the time is right. And I do intend to keep my promise."

Hammond beamed. "I'm glad. I'm sure you'll have no shortage of options, so you shouldn't have any trouble wedding once you're ready!"

A few days after the celebration, Raven visited Lamberg Manor for the first time.

"So this is where I'll be living…" he murmured to himself. The place was far grander than any home he had known before. *This is how far I've come…* He was now that much closer to attaining what he had always dreamed of since he was a boy.

"And now the real work begins," he said. Becoming a lord in itself had never been the goal. What was more, governing his own barony would doubtless prove quite the challenge. With that thought in mind, Raven set his shoulders, pushed open the doors of the manor, and stepped inside.

The End

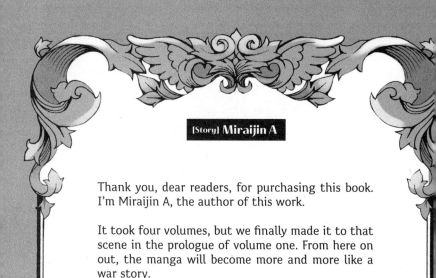

[Story] Miraijin A

Thank you, dear readers, for purchasing this book. I'm Miraijin A, the author of this work.

It took four volumes, but we finally made it to that scene in the prologue of volume one. From here on out, the manga will become more and more like a war story.

Manga is a visual medium, so I expect that the battle scenes will feel much more immediate and impactful than how I wrote them in the light novel. I'm really looking forward to seeing the end result.

Things will really pick up steam starting with volume five, so I hope that you'll stay on for the ride.

As a Reincarnated Aristocrat, I'll Use My Appraisal Skill to Rise in the World has made it through a whole year and four volumes, and it's all thanks to you. I look forward to your continued support.

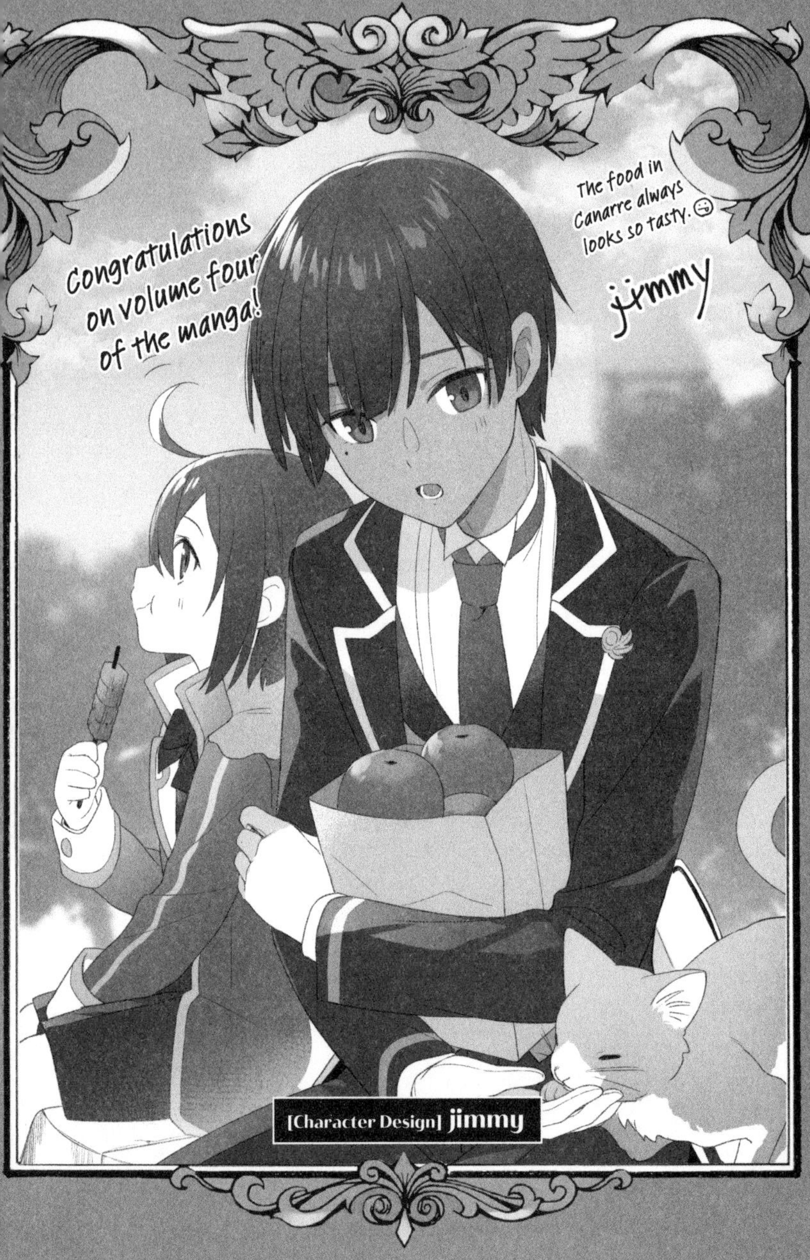
The food in
Canarre always
looks so tasty.
jimmy
Congratulations
on volume four
of the manga!
[Character Design] jimmy

Licia Pleide - Age 10

Stats

	CURRENT	MAX
Command	5	10
Prowess	5	10
Intellect	45	73
Diplomacy	77	100
Ambition	80	

Aptitude

Fighter	D	Cavalier	D	Archer	D
Mage	D	Engineer	D	Armorer	D
Mariner	D	Pilot	D	Tactician	B

A Kodansha Trade Paperback Original

As a Reincarnated Aristocrat, I'll Use My Appraisal Skill to Rise in the World 4 copyright © 2021 Miraijin A/Natsumi Inoue/jimmy
English translation copyright © 2023 Miraijin A/Natsumi Inoue/jimmy

Published in the United States by
Kodansha USA Publishing, LLC, New York.

Publication rights for this English edition arranged through
Kodansha Ltd., Tokyo.

First published in Japan in 2021 by Kodansha Ltd., Tokyo
as *Tensei kizoku, kantei sukiru de nariagaru*, volume 4.

ISBN 978-1-64651-515-8

Printed in the United States of America.

9 8 7 6 5 4 3 2 1

Translation: Stephen Paul
Lettering: Nicole Roderick
Editing: Andres Oliver
Kodansha USA Publishing edition cover design by Pekka Luhtala

Publisher: Kiichiro Sugawara

Director of Publishing Services: Ben Applegate
Director of Publishing Operations: Dave Barrett
Associate Director of Publishing Operations: Stephen Pakula
Publishing Services Managing Editors: Alanna Ruse, Madison Salters,
with Grace Chen
Production Manager: Jocelyn O'Dowd

KODANSHA.US

KODANSHA